MERCEDES IN PEACE AND WAR

Daimler Motorcarriage, 1886.

BERNARD P. BELLON

MERCEDES IN PEACE AND WAR

GERMAN AUTOMOBILE WORKERS, 1903–1945

COLUMBIA UNIVERSITY PRESS
NEW YORK

Photographs for chapters 1 and 2 are reproduced with the permission of Daimler-Benz A.G. Fotoarchiv. The photographs for chapter 7, except for the reproductions from the *Voelkischer Beobachter,* are courtesy of Dr. Helmuth Bauer, Stuttgart-Obertuerkheim.

COLUMBIA UNIVERSITY PRESS
NEW YORK   OXFORD
Copyright © 1990 Columbia University Press
All rights reserved

Library of Congress Cataloging-in-Publication Data

Bellon, Bernard P.
    Mercedes in peace and war : German automobile workers, 1903–1945
  / Bernard P. Bellon.
      p.   cm.
    Includes bibliographical references.
    ISBN 0-231-06856-5 (alk. paper)
    1. Automobile industry workers—Germany—History.   2. Automobile
  industry and trade—Germany—History.   3. Daimler-Benz
  Aktiengesellschaft—History.   I. Title.
    HD8039.A82G33   1990
    331.7'6292'09430941—dc20   89-23946
                                                      CIP

29.50

Casebound editions of Columbia University Press books are Smyth-sewn and printed on permanent and durable acid-free paper.

⊗

Printed in the United States of America
c 10 9 8 7 6 5 4 3 2 1

for my father,
and to the memory
of my dear mother

CONTENTS

TABLES

PREFACE

I N writing this book, I received the kind assistance of many organizations and individuals. In gratitude, I wish to acknowledge this help publicly. Columbia University's Travelling Fellowship, and generous awards from the Friedrich-Ebert-Stiftung and the Institut fuer Europaeische Geschichte in Mainz made possible trips to West Germany in 1981 and 1984–87, during which this work was researched and written. The College of Sciences and Liberal Studies at the Georgia Institute of Technology provided support for undertaking the revision of the manuscript.

I am also grateful to the Daimler-Benz A.G. for allowing me to visit its corporate archive and to undertake extensive research there. No limitations were placed on my research into the period prior to 1933, a credit to the able historian Otto Nuebel, who was archivist during my work with the company's papers for the first six chapters.

Unfortunately, this exemplary archival policy did not apply for the later, more difficult period of the firm's history. The company withheld access to its corporate papers from the Nazi period from me and other independent historians until the end of 1986. At the same time, to coincide with the coming one hundredth anniversary of the first Daimler and Benz autos, the firm called in the Gesellschaft fuer Unternehmensgeschichte (Society for Business History), a group supervised by, among others, Daimler-Benz's chairman at the time (Werner Breitschwerdt), to prepare a work on the company's history during Nazism. In accordance with this commission, archive officials renewed a ban on research using the firm's documents from the Nazi era, just as the Gesellschaft informed company officials in an initial assessment of the document collections that they potentially contained a "negative picture" of the company's history in Nazi Germany. In a private memo to company officials, the business historians of the Gesellschaft, led by Hans Pohl, promised a history which would show that "Daimler-Benz supported the National Socialist regime only to an unavoidable extent for a company of its importance." Furthermore, they explicitly supported a continuation of the company's closure of its post-1933 archival collections.

This ban directly affected my project, despite the assurance of a top executive of the company that I would be able to utilize Daimler-Benz's archival collections to write a last chapter on the Nazi period. When I sought to begin the research into the post-1933 period, archive officials announced that this would no longer be possible, for the collections would remain closed until Pohl's quasi-official history appeared at the end of 1986. Although I had made a limited request for materials about wages, working conditions, and labor organizations, Daimler-Benz had decided that there would be no research on the Nazi years during the West German mass media's celebrations of its automotive jubilee during 1986.

For forty-one years after the end of World War II, Daimler-Benz—the largest industrial corporation in West Germany—refused to open its collections to allow a single independent historian to examine this difficult part of its past, and, through the efforts of sympathetic business historians, had tried to construct a serviceable history for itself. Finally, in late November 1986, after several historians, including Eberhard Jaeckel, interceded on my behalf, Daimler-Benz relented and informed me that it would allow me to study its records from the National Socialist period. Without the aid of a catalogue or *Findbuch,* I worked with its closed archival materials in December 1986 and in January and February 1987.

While waiting for the opportunity to use Daimler-Benz's Nazi collections, I worked around the company's archival policy by using papers from numerous public archives in Germany, Britain, and the United States. The most important of these are the Imperial War Museum, the National Archives, the Washington National Records Center, the Bundesarchiv in Koblenz, the Berlin Document Center, the Wiener Library, and the Institut fuer Zeitgeschichte. I visited most of these during 1986. I also worked at the invaluable Zentrale Stelle der Landesjustizverwaltungen in Ludwigsburg, where records from numerous war crimes trials and investigations are located. I was also the beneficiary of important assistance from several historians and researchers, among them Fritz Stern, Otto Nuebel, and Helmuth Bauer. Without their kind help and generosity, the concluding study of the Nazi era could not have been written, and it is dedicated to them. No one other than myself, however, can be held responsible for any of its conclusions.

Along the way, my work has profited from two seminars: the Columbia University Seminar in Modern European Social History, to which an early draft of chapter six was given, and Eberhard Jaeckel's seminar on National Socialism at the University of Stuttgart. Fritz Stern's patient guidance, through scores of conversations and correspondences, contributed enormously to this project; his sense of the historian's responsibility has provided an especially important personal lesson for me. I must also publicly acknowledge my debt to two excellent historians and teachers, Robert Moeller and David Crew, for their inspiration, concern, and advice. Under their supervision, I first ventured onto the terrain of social history. In addition, my work has benefitted enormously from Robert O. Paxton's timely criticism. Many others provided a measure of assistance, among them Friedrich-Wilhelm Witt, Karl Otmar von Aretin, Claus Scharf, Ulrich Wengenroth, Martin Vogt, Ralph Melville, Edzard Reuter, Joerg Mettke, Steven Welch, Roland Mueller, Guenther Cordes, Alexandra Wiessler, Birgit Zenner, Raimonds Leimanis, Piotr Madajczyk, Laura Lee Downs, Charles Sullivan, Pierre Lanfranchi, Isabel Warner, Rainer Karnowski, Fr. Buetner, Fr. Franke-Neu, Angelika Ebbinghaus, Robert McMath, Kim Dawson, Karl Heinz Roth, William McNeil, Harvey Goldman, William Lazonick, Ron Fresne, Wolfgang Natter, and Jeff Luck. Kathryn Enniss ably compiled the index. Kate Wittenberg and Leslie Bialler guided this project through the Columbia University Press. In short, I have been the beneficiary of plenty of help and good advice.

MERCEDES IN PEACE AND WAR

INTRODUCTION

THIS is the first study about work, workers, and labor movement in a factory in the German automobile industry. It is intended as a contribution to German social history and to the history of the German working class. As such, it breaks with conventions which earlier marked these fields.[1]

First of all, this is a study of the work force of the automobile and motor factory complex of the Daimler-Motoren-Gesellschaft and Daimler-Benz Aktien-Gesellschaft in Stuttgart-Untertuerkheim from its opening in 1903 until 1945. It is not primarily a taxonomy of the work force, but rather emphasizes the social-political aspects of its theme. The work processes and labor movement at Daimler, not primarily the national organizations of the working class, occupy the center stage in this account. Although it is a "history from below," it neither eschews rational categories in some misguided effort to let the forgotten masses speak for themselves nor disregards the central concern of history for politics.

This book probes the junction of social history with "higher politics" on the field of German history. There are important sections on the history of the development of the firm's production and the company's relations with governmental authorities, for, as Gerald Feldman notes, "Businessmen are major actors and initiators" of many critical events in the history of the labor movement.[2] In the end, whatever success it attains is the result of the degree to which it is analytical and political history and the extent to which

1

it casts light on the workings of a large German factory over forty pivotal years, and on the political processes of the world war, revolution, stabilization and Nazi terror.

In Germany as elsewhere, the workplace was the source of a major part of workers' shared experience which trade union or political associations shaped into politics. Even today, the world of work is one of the most important aspects of a person's life: what one does for a living, and under which conditions he or she works, helps to shape personal identity and political perspectives. It is, arguably, the most important experience for many, although it is only one factor. For understanding the politics of the German labor movement, it is an element which cannot be overlooked. Indeed, the scarcity of factory and other local studies, which is now being redressed, could only have limited our understanding of the German labor movement and the political upheavals of this century.

One must not, however, necessarily attach primary explanatory power to factors internal to a workplace or, for that matter, to any community. Beyond the factory gates, there are many agents and institutions which affect the situation of workers, managers, and owners. The state is the most imposing of these. In addition, institutions and organizations to which workers belonged or which interacted with the firm or work force existed at local, regional, national, and even international levels, and they play an important role here.

Organizations which represented the working population were center stage in shaping modern German history. Trade unions, political parties and movements, and factory workers' committees struggled against a variety of political opponents which they deemed to represent the interests of a ruling class tied intrinsically to the capitalist order. At times, as during the revolutionary era after 1918, these confrontations were spectacular and even seemed to presage a revolutionary transition to a new society no longer ridden by class divisions. At other times, the struggles were contained within a framework of peaceful coexistence, as during the First World War, when labor, capital, and state saw a measure of reform to be in the interests of all. Whether through spectacular conflicts or in "quieter" give-and-take, workers and their political and economic organizations at Daimler contributed to shaping the structures of power in German society.

The Daimler facility was a cluster of thousands of individuals—workers, managers, and owners—with differing degrees of power and sharply conflicting interests. This work does not claim that the study of this one complex, no matter how important it may have been, is of the same order as the study of the whole of industry or the working class. Nor does it hold that the plight of Daimler workers is somehow representative or symbolic for that of others. Rather, this essay is a bit like a good biography, an exploration of a particular entity which was swept up in wars and revolution and which emerged transformed. The point is to integrate labor's experience at Mercedes into the broad structures and processes of change. As the author of an exemplary local study has observed, "It is a question really of asking how and in what ways the experience of the local community fits into the national experience and how, in what ways, and to what extent local areas participated in, contributed to, were effected by, and reacted to the large-scale, economic, and political transformations that changed much of Europe during this period."[3] Indeed, as of the writing of these lines, I know of no other work which illuminates wartime and revolutionary events from the perspectives of conditions and conflicts within a factory.

Researchers usually feel pressed to choose their subjects based on what might be available in archives. I wanted to examine Daimler from the start. First, I wanted to study a factory which played an important role in the political events of 1918–1920. Daimler's work force had, and was even dubbed the "shock troops" of the revolution in the Stuttgart area by the last interior minister of the *ancien regime* in Wuerttemberg. I sought an industrial facility in which rationalization and technical change were important, so I reckoned that an automobile factory would be the best place to look. I thought that a facility outside of the densely industrial Ruhr and Berlin regions would serve better to highlight the role of the factory in the labor movement, and Daimler-Untertuerkheim was one of the largest factories in southwestern Germany, a region with a mixed agricultural and industrial base. At the same time, the existence of a study by the *Verein fuer Sozialpolitik* from the prewar years was attractive and indicated that there might be a starting point for my own efforts.

The first chapter is a general introduction to the history of the Daimler-Motoren-Gesellschaft, the development of the German automobile industry, the economic and political history of Wuerttemberg, and the political economy of Stuttgart. Chapter 2 is an essay on the production processes, the varieties of workers at the Untertuerkheim factory, and their relationship to work. Although it has not seemed obvious to other historians that the study of work is critical to any account of the men and women who worked, the study of industrial labor processes must become a part of the social history of labor. This essay seeks to concretize work at Daimler and to integrate it into the social history of the work force. The focus for the chapter is the decade from the opening of the factory in December 1903 to the outbreak of the First World War.

Chapter 2 also examines the situation of the exclusively male work force of the prewar years and working conditions at the factory. Critical to it is the investigation published by the *Verein fuer Sozialpolitik* in 1911, which gathered much information at the firm from factory records which have mostly been destroyed or have disappeared in the subsequent 70 years. However the significance of the study undergoes a major theoretical transition here. Whereas the *Verein* study looks at the workers exclusively as objects, the intention here is to use it in order to understand the workers as subjects, as active participants in production, industrial disputes, and politics.

Chapter 3 introduces two of the book's most important themes, the labor movement and industrial conflicts, in the decade before World War I. The history of Social Democracy and of the big metalworkers' trade union is the backdrop for this discussion. The chapter also relies on the press and on documents and reports from state archives to reconstruct the disputes between the workers and the firm's direction.

Chapter 4 is a chronicle of the First World War years. It contains sections detailing the new era of war production at Daimler, as well as the economic and political measures the firm took to expedite its contribution to the war effort, especially the employment of female workers, and, crucial to the development of the intra-corporate division of labor, the opening of a new plant at Sindelfingen in 1915. The chapter contains one of the first accounts of the Daimler Affair, perhaps the most revealing corporate war-profiteering scandal in Germany during World War I. This scandal, it argues, is important for understanding the subsequent development of relations between work force and direction. A major section of the chapter details and analyzes the reaction of trade unionists at Daimler to the new situation at the plant. It concludes by analyzing fragmentary evidence which points to the radicalization of the work force in the closing months of the war.

Chapter 5 views events of the November revolution and the subsequent eighteen months—until March 1920, with the Kapp putsch and first Betriebsrat elections—from the shop floor. It portrays the new relations of authority which emerged for a time in the postrevolutionary period and speculates on their significance for understanding the dynamic of the revolutionary process in 1918 and 1919.

But the revolutionary period at Daimler (and in Stuttgart as a whole) ended with a bang in the late summer of 1920 with a bitter lockout and the subsequent dismissal of most of the work force. Chapter 6 provides a study of the climactic events of the lock-out and the aftermath of labor's shattering defeat. It also offers a tenative examination, based on scarce evidence, of technical and production-related developments at Daimler-Benz during the rationalization movement in the Weimar republic.

Chapter 7 surveys developments at Mercedes-Benz during the world economic depression and the Third Reich, and here the emphasis changes. It broadly portrays the composition and plight of the workers under radically changed conditions during the 1930s and 1940s. My goal is to present a suggestive study of the history of labor and of state-company relations during the National Socialist period based on the experience of Daimler-Benz, presenting an unusual picture of a Nazi "Model Business," its blossoming during the Hitlerian military buildup, and its use of forced labor and concentration camp inmates in its frenzied production of weapons and material during World War II.

For the Germans, the history of the first half of the twentieth century was exceedingly bitter, although it was far more horrific for the European peoples visited by German armies. The enormity of the drama of German history often threatens to overwhelm historians. Hope and barbarism were mingled amidst the struggles of classes, interests, and parties. To gain a firmer footing for understanding the sweep of this awful past, I undertook this study. "In science, each of us knows that what he has accomplished will be antiquated in ten, twenty, fifty years. . . . Each scientific fulfillment raises new 'questions'; it *asks* to be 'surpassed' and outdated," Max Weber wrote.[4] If this history, constructed for the most part "from below," serves to illuminate unfamiliar features, and helps others approach the past in a new way before being eclipsed by fresh projects, it will have been worth the effort.

1

THE GERMAN
AUTOMOBILE INDUSTRY
AND THE DAIMLER-
MOTOREN-GESELLSCHAFT:
THE MERCEDES MYTHOS

THE Industrial Revolution marked the most profound transformation of human life in recorded history. Nowhere in Europe was industrialization quicker and more far-reaching than in the German Empire. Paced by mining, iron, and steel, and from the 1890s on by the manufacture of chemicals and electrical equipment, Germany became an industrial superpower, its rulers vying for continental leadership and a properly imperial place in the sun. At home, cities swelled with men and women from the countryside. Advancing industrial enterprises ploughed up the old society of central Europe. The disorder of bourgeois society frightened and repulsed an influential group of publicists, whose resentments—well-documented by historians—fueled flights into a mystical, soft-headed longing for a pre-industrial past which threatened to cut short any movement toward a more democratic political order if it could become any group's political agenda. But for most, more mundane matters prevailed: businessmen sought to make more money, workers strove to make a respectable life for themselves and their families, to be enriched at some future juncture, many hoped, by the new, more noble solidarity of socialism. The whirl of bourgeois Germany was marked by the unprecedented mobility of people, materials, and products via an efficient transportation network of railroads, steamers, barges, and animals. Into this *fin-de-siecle* world rumbled the new motor vehicles of Daimler and Benz, and as the new century dawned, a host of other engineers.

The automobile changed the way people in this century have lived and worked. In the United States, auto factories introduced mass production, and henceforth, millions of men and women stood or sat at moving conveyor belts for days, years, or even lifetimes, performing the work for their daily bread. The tens of millions of vehicles built by the wildly successful American automobile industry and the ribbons of concrete which were poured to speed them on their way changed the face of towns and countryside, and gave a wide-ranging mobility to many.

In Germany, on the other hand, where the first motor vehicles were built, the automobile brought few radical transformations until after World War II. Motorized transportation first became a cornerstone of governmental policy in the Third Reich, both for the consolidation of the regime and, later, for military expansion. The journey of German motor vehicle production from servicing the luxury and sporting clubs on the peripheries of Wilhelmine society to building the first air force during World War I to, finally, forming the center of the *Blitzkrieg* strategy for the conquering of Europe is a key part of the German history of the twentieth century. It is a journey which companies like the Daimler-Motoren-Gesellschaft and later Daimler-Benz helped to steer.

DAIMLER AMONG THE SWABIANS

The history of the automobile began in southwestern Germany—in the mechanical workshops of Gottlieb Daimler in Bad Cannstatt and of Carl Benz in Mannheim.[1] The Daimler company's lot was tied to that of the land of the Swabians, Wuerttemberg, where it grew and prospered. The Swabian dialect is often incomprehensible to other Germans. As anyone who lives among them soon learns, they consider themselves—and are widely considered by others—to exhibit certain distinguishing characteristics. As one historian has put it, "A Swabian is said to be tenacious or obstinate depending on the point of view: plain-spoken or rude; solid, robust, and hardy, or coarse, gross and uncouth. . . . [and] very suspicious of 'foreigners,' whom he believes to be mocking his own slow and somewhat old-fashioned ways."[2] Such traits were said to render Swabian workers immune to the "foreign" ideas of Social Democracy and class conflict.[3]

Daimler (later, Daimler-Benz) became a symbol of Wuerttemberg's economic success. Its well-built vehicles reinforced the reputation of the Swabians for fine, exact work, for its work force was drawn mainly from the small towns and villages around Stuttgart and Esslingen. Its own fate was tied to the changes in Wuerttemberg's labor market and to the general state of the region's economy, which were in turn affected by the conditions at Daimler.

From the beginning of the twentieth century until the present day, Wuerttemberg has served as a kind of model for regional development in Germany, with its mixed, diverse economy and its tradition of relatively liberal political rule. By the 1930s, on the basis of its economic success, the working group East Prussia-Wuerttemberg at the University of Tuebingen, headed by the economist Erich Preiser, even sought ways to export the "Wuerttemberg model" to underdeveloped East Prussia.[4] The group's investigation compellingly laid out the structural reasons for the relative prosperity of Swabia, and its echoes can be heard in the words of many contemporary authors who today laud the *Bundesland* which consistently has enjoyed the lowest unemployment rate in West Germany.

The region's economy has proved itself remarkably durable over the past century. It has shown a resistance to economic crisis which meant that the depressions and crises of the present century never ravaged Wuerttemberg quite as badly as they did other regions: the hard times which the First World War, the inflation, and the world depression visited upon Germany were less extreme in southwestern Germany. For one, the region's combination of agriculture and industry included a sizeable sector of efficient market-oriented agriculture, particularly the enterprising small farms which raised grains, vegetables and animal feed. Whereas a quarter of the German Empire's arable land consisted of large estates of more than 100 hectares, in Wuerttemberg they made up only two percent.[5] Meanwhile, there was a steady modernization of farming in the quarter century before 1914. In the words of a historian, "Yields rose, state encouragement was given to more effective and scientific means of arable farming, hop-growing, market-gardening, and animal husbandry; educational institutions were extended, along with the agricultural inspectorate; and land was reclaimed and improved." Almost 15,000 acres of arable and meadowlands were drained from 1881 to 1906. Hundreds of self-help farming cooperatives also sprang up.[6]

At the same time, the diversity of Swabian industries, such as metalworking, machine-building, and textiles—some oriented to exports, others to the domestic market—lessened the impact of the recurring business slumps which afflicted other regions more severely.[7] The social structure of Wuerttemberg combined stability with mobility, and cities and towns like Stuttgart and Esslingen experienced relatively slow, gradual growth, unlike the explosive urbanization which created whole new cities within a few decades in areas like the Ruhr in the late nineteenth century.[8]

Wuerttemberg was the largest state in southwestern Germany, both in terms of size and population. Yet relative to the rest of Germany, it held only a small proportion of the total population and land area, about 4.1 percent of both in 1919.[9] The region is dominated geographically by two central features: the Neckar River, which flows northwest through Stuttgart to meet the Rhine at Mannheim, and the Swabian Jura, an area of hills east of Stuttgart reminiscent of the Appalachians in the U.S.

Until the last half of the nineteenth century, Wuerttemberg, with its moderately fertile soil, had been predominantly agricultural. The region lacked sizeable deposits of the raw materials which were used to fuel industrial development in other areas, particularly in the Ruhr valley to the north. There were virtually no exploitable deposits of coal and iron ore.[10] Its towns and cities were primarily commercial and administrative centers. The first wave of industrialization, based on textiles, coal and iron, virtually passed by the region. Wuerttemberg's small industries, worked by skilled workers, produced high-quality goods such as harmonicas and accordions, felt toys, small arms, clocks, corsetry, surgical instruments, and jewelry.[11]

By the onset of the modern era, the city of Stuttgart had emerged as the most prominent urban center, especially because of its role as the home of the rulers of Wuerttemberg. Its population climbed steadily and reached 183,000 in 1910, having increased 8.9 percent during the previous five years.[12]

After the French Revolution and the Napoleonic occupation and wars, the monarchs in Wuerttemberg had gained the reputation of being among the most enlightened in Germany. The constitution of 1819 had instituted a bicameral legislature to help the rulers govern, including a lower house with 23 privileged and 70 popular deputies indirectly elected by the taxpaying citizens. During the course of the century, the Landtag acquired the power to approve the state budget every two years; indeed, the government could not continue to collect taxes without its approval. Civil liberties such as the freedom of assembly and association were recognized from 1848 on, but the government possessed broad powers of surveillance and repression.

Swabian political culture at the turn of the century was a strikingly heady brew of associations and political parties. To be sure, the labor movement made steady progress among the handworkers, servants, factory hands, machine workers, and journeymen who came to be subsumed under the name "worker," especially after the lapse of Bismarck's anti-socialist laws in 1890. All social groups participated in the burgeoning public activity, with the government in Wuerttemberg itself mentioning the agitations of the "homeopaths, the anti-inoculationists, the pro-cremationists, the agrarians, and the publicans." Teachers, workers, shopkeepers, peasants, pacifists, nationalist associations—"all were propelled into public life, in a period of unprecedented social change, by the spread of education, communications and the new means of political participation in the *Kaiserreich*."[13]

Political parties represented the hosts of interests in the state parliament. By 1906, the Social Democrats (SPD) received the most votes in Wuerttemberg (24.9%), slightly more than the Catholic Center Party (24.3%). The left liberals—in Wuerttemberg, known as the People's Party—and the national liberals split a third of the vote between them, and the agrarian conservatives booked 13 percent of the ballots.[14] Swabian politics exhibited the frustrations which plagued Wilhelmine politics as a whole. The Social Democrats in particular were increasingly rendered lame by the split between reformist politicans in the Landtag and the large, radical socialist clubs in towns and cities like Esslingen and Stuttgart.[15]

Although most historians today view Wuerttemberg as an enlightened antipode to Prussian illiberalism in Germany, an influential faction of Swabians held the opposite opinion. Men such as Robert Roemer, a Tuebingen law professor and member of the Landtag, welcomed Prussian leadership in order to stir the region, in one historian's words, "from its stagnation, from Ultramontanist influence, intellectual incapacity, industrial and military backwardness, antiquated laws and institutions, which contrary to the lies of the democrats, did not guarantee any freedom at all." [16] Consciousness of regional differences was strong among the people of Wuerttemberg, whether they were viewed positively or not.

During the late nineteenth century, especially after unification, Wuerttemberg, too, was profoundly affected by the economic and social changes which were forging a new Europe. The construction of the railway net commenced before 1845 and was essentially completed by 1891. Along the Neckar, in the Protestant communities from Ludwigsburg to Stuttgart to Esslingen, a host of small workshops opened, producing textiles, machines, and metal products. Many of these utilized the cheap water power provided by the swiftly flowing Neckar. After 1895, electricity was also available, and with this energy source came an impulse to further capital investment in the region's industries and an extended period of industrial growth.[17]

As in many regions of Europe, but considerably later than in these other areas, the production of textiles was the first sector of industry to experience large growth. Nevertheless, the textile industry never provided the livelihood for much more than one-seventh of the wage-earning population. Indeed, the economy never became fully dependent on a single dominant industry.

By 1900, the metal and machine-building industries had emerged as an important pillar of the economy, providing grounds for Wuerttemberg's renown as a producer of quality goods. Relying on a well-educated work force for success rather than on cheap and copious supplies of raw materials, the region developed a core of high-performance industries. By the twentieth century, Graf Zeppelin's airships, Daimler's Mercedes cars, and Voith's turbines enjoyed worldwide fame. The economic transformation of Wuerttemberg was certainly impressive, but not as thoroughgoing as in parts of northern and central Germany. In 1907, for example, nearly two of every five residents of the small kingdom (37.8%) were still employed in agricultural occupations, a figure 9 percent higher than for the Reich as a whole. Many urban residents kept small gardens on the outskirts of urban areas, and their produce provided some with an added source of food. Even some industrial workers retained a tie to the land as late as 1920, and owned plots in the countryside.

After the turn of the century, the neighborhoods near the Neckar— Ostheim, Wangen, and Gaisburg in Stuttgart, as well as Bad Cannstatt, Untertuerkheim, Obertuerkheim, and Esslingen—filled with men and women who worked in the burgeoning metal and machine-building factories and workshops. Many were accompanied by their families. Bosch's spark plugs, Daimler's cars and engines, and the Esslingen machine factory's locomotives set in motion the urban and social transformations in greater Stuttgart. The population of many neighborhoods doubled within a quarter century, with resulting overcrowding and skyrocketing rents.[18]

Nevertheless, these neighborhoods retained their special Swabian flavor. Many observers remarked how unlike the proletarian quarters in Berlin or the Ruhr they seemed. The new residents on the Neckar came from the villages of Swabia, and many of them sought to retain their tie with the land by working plots or gardens in the countryside. A few years before the war, an observer of Daimler's workers asserted that the average worker at the Untertuerkheim factory "showed less understanding for the . . . class struggle than his colleagues outside of Wuerttemberg. . . . His general bearing [Gesamthabitus] is petty-bourgeois."[19]

Appearances were, in this case, remarkably deceiving. If one went beneath the Swabian Dialekt, and looked at the groups of working men and women who hiked year round through the vineyards and orchards, one confronted the tough-minded Germans who had made Stuttgart a cradle of the German labor movement and of Social Democracy. A vibrant network of working-class organizations—housing and consumer cooperatives; hiking, sporting, and cultural clubs; a lively social-democratic press—provided a foundation for social-democratic development.[20] The first local organization of the most powerful trade union in Wilhelmine Germany, the German Metalworkers' Union (DMV), was founded in Stuttgart in 1891.[21] Indeed, the vitality of the trade unions, Social Democracy, and workers' culture in greater Stuttgart made the area a Hochburg of the labor movement in Swabia.

Many workers in Wuerttemberg belonged to a trade union, and their proportion in the national unions corresponded to Wuerttemberg's share of the German population. The vast majority of organized workers were members of the social- democratic league of trade unions, while one-fifth as many belonged to the leagues organized by the Center Party. An insignificant handful belonged to the Hirsch-Duncker groups sponsored by the German liberals. Although most workers did not belong to a union, the number of unionized workers grew steadily until the last years before World War I.

Membership in a political party also serves as an important means for gauging the political self-assertiveness of a social group. On the eve of the First World War, the Wuerttemberg SPD had 39,930 paid members. By the end of the war, only 5,603 were left, but membership rebounded ninefold in the next months. According to the best estimates, the SPD in 1920 had 33,427 members, the USPD around 14,000 and the Communist Party 4,636. Thus, one out of every ten workers in Wuerttemberg may have belonged to one of the socialist political parties following the end of the war.[22] In addition, an unknown number belonged to the Catholic Center Party, although the Christian labor organizations were very weak in Swabia.

THE GERMAN AUTOMOBILE INDUSTRY: PRELIMINARY OBSERVATIONS

The general pattern of German industrialization within European development is clear enough and can be described to a significant extent by four words: later, faster, bigger, newer. The Industrial Revolution began much later in Germany than in pioneering Britain. Once economic change began in the German states, it surged forward with unique vigor in coal, iron, and steel, with the chemical and electrical industries kicking in decisively during the 1890s. Enterprises were larger, assisted in mobilizing capital by the German banking system and the spread of joint-stock companies. Mergers, takeovers, and cartels became common phenomena of economic life. German firms were often quick to adopt innovations in raw material preparation and manufacturing technology (including mechanization), as well as new sources of energy, even though most were not originally invented or worked out by Germans. Quickly, Germany emerged as the most advanced industrial power in Europe, and its trade appeared likely to keep pace in the years before World War I.

The German motor vehicle industry fell outside this pattern. Although several larger firms gained some success and renown for their cars, many modest workshops continued to construct small numbers of engines and vehicles well into the twentieth century. The industry was not particularly innovative as far as production technology and designing vehicles for a mass market were concerned. Auto producers remained on the periphery of Wilhelmine capitalism.

Surprisingly, although the history of the automobile began in southwestern Germany in the 1880s, the German industry blazed few new paths during the subsequent half century. There was no German counterpart to

Henry Ford, no technological visionary to launch the new age of mass automobilism in central Europe. While more than 4.4 million Americans bought automobiles in 1926, German car production totaled barely 32,000 in the 40th year after Daimler and Benz built their first vehicles.[23] Perhaps for this reason, the German automobile industry has attracted little attention from historians, and only nostalgic notice from car buffs and racing afficionados.[24] Nevertheless, car firms such as Daimler, Opel, and Benz employed thousands of workers; during the First World War, they assembled mammouth industrial armies. These companies provided an alternative path of industrial development, a way which passed on finally and for good with the assembly lines of the Hitlerian military buildup.

Well into the 1930s, much of the German automobile industry—including even many of its biggest firms—was labor-intensive and conservative. As late as 1925, the production of vehicles consumed vast quantities of labor. While the American Ford Motor Company employed the daily labor of five and three-quarters workers to produce one of its cars, Daimler needed 1,750 to build one of its top-class automobiles.[25] The revolutionary Model-T had no counterpart in the German industry, whose offerings were usually custom-made coupes well into the 1920s. Mass production came to the German auto industry only with the construction of tens of thousands of airplane motors in its factories at Daimler, Benz, and Opel during the First World War, and left once again quickly in its wake. At Daimler, which built both the motors and car bodies, customers could order a vehicle tailored to their every wish, from the power of the engine to the shape and design of the body or even any of its components. This customizing may have kept the industry's elite clientele satisfied but proved to be an insurmountable obstacle to the progress of the industry in reaching wider circles of consumers. It also prevented the revolutionizing of the production process and preserved the key role of skilled workers in the manufacturing plants. By the 1920s, with bankruptcy looming for many of the remaining firms, the German

TABLE 1.1
Auto Production in Germany and the U.S., 1913 & 1925

	Germany	USA	Daimler	Ford
1903	1,310	11,235	232	1,708
1913	17,162	461,500	1,567	248,307
1925	38,988	4,312,456	1,406	1,587,821

Sources: Kugler, *Arbeitsorganisation und Produktionstechnologie*, p. 110; Seherr-Thoss, *Die deutsche Automobilindustrie*, p. 551; Daimler-Benz Historische Datensammlung; Oswald, *Mercedes-Benz Personenwagen 1886–1984*, p. 69.

industry as a whole sputtered along like an old clunker struggling up the entry ramp onto a new Autobahn.[26] It was not until Adolf Hitler symbolically committed his government to the motorization of Germany, during his opening of the International Auto and Motorcycle Exhibition in Berlin only twelve days after becoming Reichskanzler, that the future of the German industry finally seemed secured.[27]

THE MERCEDES MYTHOS

The history of the automobile is tied to the engineering wile of Gottlieb Daimler and Carl Benz in the 1880s, but parted with their progeny at the turn of the century. The Daimler-Motoren-Gesellschaft, founded by Daimler in 1890 in Bad Cannstatt a couple of kilometers from the center of Stuttgart, employed several hundred mechanics and metal workers during its first decade who built a handful of expensive but beautiful driving machines.[28] The company was the kind of small, unpretentious unit which makes up the picture of the industrial revolution: clever, knowledgeable engineers and technicians who made a name for themselves with their clever applications —in this case—of internal combustion engines. Their early designs are noteworthy and were exported to France and England. In 1891, Panhard and Levassor used a Daimler engine in their pioneering car in France, while the firm erected an independent company in Coventry, England in 1896.[29] When Gottlieb Daimler died in March 1900, the company had already attained world-wide renown for its vehicles.

By the turn of the century, the Daimler workshop in Bad Cannstatt was thriving, employing nearly 300 highly skilled workers and engineers. The production of the Mercedes car in 1901, a vehicle named after the young daughter of the Austro-Hungarian consul in Nice, Emil Jellinek, and the mounting record of racing triumphs won by Daimler vehicles, gained a solid reputation for the company and stoked the demand among racing drivers for its motor cars. At the same time, the German army showed increasing interest in the potential benefits of using motor vehicles to transport officers, at least, in maneuvers. Daimler soon needed a new, larger factory in order to service the market for luxury, racing, and military vehicles.

In 1903, DMG purchased a large tract of 184,700 square meters of land in Untertuerkheim, about two kilometers from the original workshop. In the first of many favors which Daimler received from the public authorities at all levels, the village's municipal officials sold the property to the company for a low price and provided the riverside site with access roads. The firm began to build a factory there in 1903, shortly before a fire razed the Bad Cannstatt facility. A number of expensive racing cars were destroyed in the inferno, hindering the company's plans to enter a number of new cars in the prestigious Gordon-Bennett race.[30] The fire pushed forward the move to the new factory and opened an era at Daimler. Through two world wars, two empires, and two republics, the seat of Mercedes lay in Untertuerkheim.

The site of the new Daimler factory commanded a view of the Neckar valley on the main south German railway route connecting the major cities along the Stuttgart-Ulm-Augsburg-Munich southern tier. Here, an earlier transportation revolution had made a historic debut, when a locomotive powered its way along a stretch of tracks between Bad Cannstatt and Untertuerkheim in 1845.

TABLE 1.2
Production at the Daimler-Motoren-Gesellschaft, 1903–1926

	Cars	Trucks & Buses	
1903 (Cannstatt)	232		
1904 (Untertuerklheim)	698		
1905	863		
1906	546		
1907	149		
1908	109	122	
1909	671	158	
1910	1,106	199	
1911	1,490	291	
1912	1,866	317	
1913	1,567	358	
1914	1,404	568	(From 1914 to
1915	1,302	605	1919, DMG
1916	428	718	built 19,876
1917	401	792	airplane
1918	108	996	motors.)
1919	621	550	
1920	1,616	536	
1921	1,581	294	
1922	962	380	
1923	1,020	449	
1924	1,333	543	
1925	1,406	881	
1926	2,169	1,545	

Sources: Daimler-Benz Museum, Historische Datensammlung 1886–1980; Werner Oswald, *Mercedes-Benz Personenwagen 1886–1984*, p. 69.

TABLE 1.3
Daimler Cars, 1904–1926

Mercedes-Simplex	18/22 horsepower	1902–1905
Mercedes-Simplex	28/32 hp	1901–1905
Mercedes-Simplex	40/45 hp	1903–1905
Mercedes	45 hp	1905–1909
Mercedes	26/45 hp	1909–1910
Mercedes-Simplex	60 hp	1902–1905
Mercedes	36/65 hp	1905–1909
Mercedes	15/20 hp	1905–1909
Mercedes	10/20 hp	1909–1912
Mercedes	10/25 hp	1912–1915
Mercedes	14/30 hp	1909–1912
Mercedes	14/35 hp	1912–1915
Mercedes	35 hp	1905–1909
Mercedes	22/35 hp	1909
Mercedes	22/40 hp	1910–1912
Mercedes	22/50 hp	1912–1920
Mercedes	55 hp	1905–1909
Mercedes	31/55 hp	1909
Mercedes	28/50 hp	1910–1912
Mercedes	28/60 hp	1912–1920
Mercedes	38/70 hp	1910–1912
Mercedes	38/80 hp	1912–1915
Mercedes	37/65, 37/70 hp	1906–1910
Mercedes	39/75, 39/80 hp	1906–1910
Mercedes	37/90, 37/95 hp	1910–1914
Mercedes	38/100 hp	1915
Mercedes	8/18 hp	1910–1912
Mercedes	8/20 hp	1912–1913
Mercedes	8/22 hp	1913–1921
Mercedes	12/32 hp	1915–1919
Mercedes-Knight	10/30 hp	1912–1915
Mercedes-Knight	16/40 hp	1910–1916
Mercedes-Knight	16/50 hp	1924
Mercedes-Knight	25/65	1912–1915
Mercedes	28/95	1914–1915, 1920–1924

Source: Oswald, *Mercedes-Benz Personenwagen 1886–1984,* pp. 91–130. Photographs are in AGM DBAG Fotoarchiv.

The first shops at the Untertuerkheim facility opened in December 1903. During 1904, the construction of the new factory went on at a rapid pace. The complex of workshops and storage areas was hailed at the time as one of the most modern in the world. The *Allgemeine Automobil-Zeitung* proclaimed the new facility to be "the auto factory of auto factories. . . . The sign that [Daimler's] glorious tradition has finally found a worthy production facility."[31]

When it opened, the plant complex consisted of five main buildings: the forge, the administration building, the facility housing the machine park for the metalworking trades *[Saegedachbau]*, the testing and control shops, and a concrete structure housing the workshops of the woodworkers and upholsterers who built the auto bodies.[32]

Quickly, the company assembled a work force 2,000 strong—roughly three times as many as had been employed in Cannstatt—most of whom were skilled metal workers, drawn from the small Swabian towns and villages in the area. They fashioned the motors, chassis, and bodies for the Mercedes cars in the dozen workshops and machine parks located there on the grounds. Over 600 machines, including many of the most advanced German and American models, were at their disposal in the complex; by 1911, that number would increase to more than 900.[33]

During the plant's first decade of operation, the company increased the number of types of luxury cars it offered for sale. By 1910, the number had grown to ten different models, powered by engines rated between 18 and 80 horsepower. Thus, with not many more than 1,000 cars being built annually, there was little room for standardizing models as a way of cutting costs. While Ford was building hundreds of thousands of a single basic model, the Model T, Daimler built no more than a couple hundred of each of its offerings, and could not readily benefit from an economy of scale.

Nevertheless, auto racers and wealthy consumers who wanted to own the finest of luxury coupes kept the demand for the small number of Daimler cars strong until the outbreak of the war, although foreign sales declined in the business years 1912 and 1913, apparently due in part to heightened international tensions resulting from the conflicts in the Balkans. At the same time, the Prussian War Ministry, procuring agent of military materiel for the imperial army, began to subsidize the production of large utility vehicles at a smaller factory in Berlin-Marienfelde which Daimler had acquired in 1902.[34] Indeed, Daimler's automobiles had already acquitted themselves well during the army's general maneuvers of 1900, achieving what one author has termed a "breakthrough" in the military application of motor vehicles. By 1910, none of the upper echelon of German officers rode on horseback during maneuvers—all sat in the back of automobiles.[35] The partnership between Daimler and the German military remained a key factor throughout the history of the corporation.

THE AGE OF BERGE AND VON KAULLA

The duo of Ernst Berge and Alfred von Kaulla—one a shrewd businessman, the other a banker connected to the highest levels of high finance—shaped the development of the Daimler-Motoren-Gesellschaft during its first two decades on the banks of the Neckar at Untertuerkheim.[36]

In 1905, the Hamburg businessman Ernst Berge arrived in Untertuerkheim. From his office in the *Fabrikstrasse,* Berge dominated the company's day-to-day operations for the next two decades. Born in the summer of 1868 in Lueneberg, Berge lived for the first thirty years of his life in Hamburg and became a merchant. In 1902, he received his first post at DMG. He journeyed to Vienna to take up the post of chief business executive at Daimler's branch in Neustadt. He received the call to Untertuerkheim in 1905, and became an assistant member of the board of directors. Within two years, he had become a full-fledged director of the firm, in addition to being the business manager in Stuttgart-Untertuerkheim. Until he was deposed in the wake of the first merger arrangements with the Benz Company of Mannheim in 1925, Berge remained the leading figure in the daily operations of the Daimler-Motoren-Gesellschaft. As the company later asserted, "The development of DMG into a world-class firm is closely associated with his name."[37]

During World War I, Berge was officially named General Director and clashed fiercely with the German authorities who had acquired a leading interest in the firm's affairs by virtue of the huge military contracts they had bestowed on it. Berge was the central figure in the Daimler Affair of March 1918, and charges of war profiteering, the falsification of price documents, and treason swirled around him for the rest of the war. His fellow employers in the metal and machine-building industries in Wuerttemberg were nevertheless impressed by his aggressive stand against the government's wartime industrial policies, for they named him head of the League of Wuerttemberg Metal Industrialists in 1919.[38]

From Berge's surviving business correspondence, the picture emerges of a deliberate businessman who on occasion could be ruthless, be it with the state or with his workers. Ironically, his prewar willingness to compromise occasionally with labor was eroded as the institutions of labor obtained a measure of security during World War I and the Weimar Republic. The exceptionally tense state of labor relations at DMG after 1918 bears witness to his inability to adapt himself to the new conditions, which demanded flexibility and a readiness to compromise, or at least the appearance of being willing to do so.[39] The poor state of the firm's economic health after 1918 likewise showed his lack of vision. He insisted that the firm stick by its production of large luxury autos at a time when the automobile revolution, with the mass production of smaller, inexpensive vehicles, was moving ahead rapidly in Germany's competitor nations.[40] The making, and after the war the unmaking, of the Daimler-Motoren-Gesellschaft was above all Berge's achievement.

A second personnel change also contributed mightily to the subsequent development of the company and reflected the growing influence of the southwest German banks on Daimler's affairs. Shortly after the turn of the century, the banker Alfred von Kaulla, who had close ties to the Deutsche Bank, joined the board of trustees. He was not the only man from the world of high finance to supervise DMG's affairs. Kilian Steiner, Kaulla's prominent comrade at the Wuerttemberg Vereinsbank in Stuttgart, also sat on the firm's board of trustees in the early 1900s.[41]

Kaulla had achieved a considerable reputation for his exploits in extending German financial influence into the Ottoman Empire in the late 1880s. Born in 1852 to a doctor's family in Strassburg, Kaulla quickly moved up in the banking profession he had chosen for himself. By the 1880s, Kaulla, described by a historian as an "enterprising, bright, robust man," became a director of the Wuerttemberg Vereinsbank.[42] In the spring and summer of 1888, Kaulla was approached by Turkish officials who, mistrusting French and British meddling in Turkish affairs, wanted German banks to step in and finance a large railroad building project in Asia Minor. Although the Stuttgart-based Vereinsbank was too small to handle the transactions, Steiner, its chairman, used his connections to get the Deutsche Bank to support the project. Chancellor Bismarck gave his lukewarm approval, and Kaulla soon journeyed to Constantinople to take control of the byzantine business negotiations between German, French, British, and Turkish interests.[43]

After months of talks and several turns in the difficult negotiations, which quickly took on political connotations, Kaulla and the Germans extended a large loan to Sultan Abdul Hamid II, even though the Bank Imperiale Ottomane, dominated by French and British financial interests, had refused to finance the railroad project.[44] Soon, work began on the Near Eastern Railroad, providing German firms with large orders for tracks and railroad equipment, and increasing German influence in the Near East.

Kaulla's success in Turkey secured a handsome profit for both the Deutsche Bank and his own institution, the Vereinsbank. Since 1870, the two banks had worked together closely. When the Vereinsbank's chairman Steiner died in 1909, Kaulla became the key figure in the cooperation between Berlin and

Stuttgart. As the historian of the Deutsche Bank wrote, "the connecting link was Kaulla . . . , one of the last from the epoch of the great projects."[45] Thus, Daimler's approach to Kaulla won for it a banker with a solid reputation and with ties to high finance.

By 1910, Kaulla had become chairman of Daimler's board of directors. On the basis of the remaining materials in the Daimler-Benz archive, it is not possible to trace his influence comprehensively for much of the period. Bankers sat on the boards of trustees of many German companies: these bodies often did not convene regularly enough to control corporate affairs.[46] Nevertheless, if the extensive correspondence between Kaulla and Berge during 1918–19 is any indication, Kaulla's influence was great, extending to many details of the firm's operations, including arrangements with the states, banks, and unions.[47]

With the general proliferation of interest groups in Wilhelmine society, the Daimler-Motoren-Gesellschaft quickly cemented political contacts with other companies in the Stuttgart area and in the Reich at large. Nationally, Daimler was an obedient member of the League of German Metal Industrialists (VDMI), and joined in the campaign which the league mounted against North Sea and Baltic dockworkers in 1910, even threatening to lock out its own workers as part of a general anti-union offensive. Regionally, Daimler and other metalworking and machine-building businesses formed the Association of Wuerttemberg Metal Industrialists (VWMI) in 1897. In the first 23 years of the organization's existence, the company played an important role in its affairs. Two of DMG's most prominent managers, Paul Daimler and Berge, served as officials of the association during this period.

Nevertheless, the association's effectiveness was limited. The VWMI tried but, due both to internal dissension and to the decentralized regional labor market, could not erect a labor exchange to keep outspoken social democratic agitators out of area factories. In late 1913, such an exchange came into effect over the objections of the local unions, but within months, the world war had neutralized its impact. In 1907, the association drew back from supporting the foundation of company-supported "yellow unions," which, it knew, had very little support in the Stuttgart-area metalworking and machine-building industries. On the basis of the few surviving accounts, it seems clear that Wilhelmine "organized capitalism" gained a certain efficacy among Swabian industry. The motor vehicle industry at least was free of the cartelization which marked the German coal, steel, and iron industries. Of signal importance to the quest for economic stability and to its calculation of business opportunities, Daimler's most important connections eventually proved to be those with financial institutions and with the military.[48]

DAIMLER'S CONTROLLING BODIES

The Daimler-Motoren-Gesellschaft, like all other German joint-stock companies, was run by two councils, the board of trustees and the board of directors. According to the corporate statutes, the board of directors conducted "the affairs of the firm according to the law, statutes, and service contracts and according to the instructions given by the board of trustees."[49] Daimler's board of directors consisted mainly of engineers and businessmen. The board of trustees, which laid down the law to the directors, was chosen by ballot at the general shareholders' meeting of the corporation for a term of three years. Members could be (and usually were) reelected. Lest one assume that the assembly of shareholders was a democratic council, the power of the individual voters varied widely: a preferred share conferred sixteen times as much power as a share of common stock. The chairman or vice-chairman of the board of trustees presided over the stockholders' assembly. Although the control of the firm's daily business may have passed increasingly to "managers" and other paid employees during the course of the twentieth century, the trustees always retained the leading role in setting the general outlines of the financial and industrial policy to be carried out by the directors and managers.[50] While for other companies it may have been true that "the most important task of the board of trustees is to appoint good directors,"[51] the chair of Daimler's trustees did not shy away from taking the wheel at critical moments in the firm's dealings. Whether in war or in peace, good times or depression the trustees and directors ruled Daimler.

Clearly critical to assessing the economic interests represented in a firm is an analysis of the board of trustees and the firms and banks it represents. As a full-scale investigation of this sector of the German economy after World War II demonstrated, "the most important single element of influence or control [of a corporation] probably is that of personal ties in the form of interlocking directorships."[52] Particularly important were the offices of chairman and vice-chairman of the board of trustees: "these surely were not routine or courtesy positions." After all, at the very least the executive officers of the board of trustees set the "business guidelines" for the firm.[53]

An assessment of the business connections of Daimler's board of trustees shows a clear movement toward the domination of the corporation by large German banking interests after 1920, particularly those related to the Deutsche Bank.[54] These interests were borne in the persons of Kaulla and Steiner, and from 1920 on by one of the most prominent German bankers, Emil Georg von Stauss. By 1924, a host of big bankers dominated the firm's board of trustees. They worked openly for a grand merger of German auto companies, including in the best possible case the large-scale fusion of Daimler,

Benz, Magirus, BMW, and Opel into a kind of I.G. Auto. These motor vehicle companies had launched the German military into the aerial theater of combat in World War I, building almost 50,000 airplane engines for the German air force. There is evidence that Stauss, who was something of an eccentric visionary, wanted to secure the future of German air power through his promotion of a grand merger of German motor car companies.[55]

In any event, the Deutsche Bank dominated the Daimler-Benz company formed by the epoch-making merger which Stauss presided over in the summer of 1926. Officers of the bank held all of the top positions in the new firm's board of trustees. In addition, it ruled the shareholders' assembly. At the December 1932 stockholders' meeting, officers of the bank represented 68 percent (313,730) of the eligible votes.[56] Mercedes chairman Wihelm Kissel expressed it clearly in his business correspondence: Daimler-Benz "is, yes, bound to the Deutsche Bank."[57] By the 1930s, Daimler-Benz was becoming the flagship of the Berlin-based bank.

■

To build its engines and vehicles from 1903 to 1945, Daimler assembled armies of workers—from German skilled workers to, finally, concentration camp slaves. This work seeks to discover how much can we learn about these men and women, who they were, and how they worked, struggled, and lived. It is a history which is interwoven with Daimler and Daimler-Benz's journey to the center of the German military-industrial complex in the First World War and again during the Third Reich. The tension between the history of the company and its ties to the German state and economy on the one hand and the social being and political practice of labor on the other builds the analytical framework for writing this social history of the workers at what is today one of the largest industrial corporations in Western Europe, Daimler-Benz.

2

WORK AND WORKERS
AT DAIMLER, 1903–1914

D AIMLER produced automobiles, and, after 1911, airplane motors, at its
Untertuerkheim factory. This chapter will examine the nature of work
at Daimler-Untertuerkheim during the factory's first decade of operation,
the conditions under which workers labored, as well as the relations of
authority between workers, and owners and managers. These concerns are
the starting points for a portrait of the Daimler workforce.

The production processes at the plant during its first decade of operation
straddled two distinct types of industrial work. The one was characterized
by skilled handworkers and machinists, professionals working without constant supervision and direction. Skilled workers infused their work with
their knowledge and experience. Such workers remained important to Daimler despite the new industrial situation created by the growth of larger units
of production, the increasing use of machinery which dispensed with many
of the skill requirements in many metal trades, and the challenge posed by
foreign and domestic competition to cut costs.

The other variety was machine work, a distinct product of the development of industrial capitalism in the late nineteenth and early twentieth
centuries. Machine work at Daimler and elsewhere was characterized by
"the rise of a large class of semi-skilled machine operators mainly paid by
results."[1] The specialized machines set the pace and drove the operations
onward. The knowledge of the operators was of a different kind from that

of the skilled workers. The machine workers had little control over and only a partial conception of what they did. To paraphrase Marx, the imaginative structures they had raised in their minds before their work were limited to a small portion of the whole labor process and did not require a great deal of knowledge and creativity.[2]

The Daimler factory was the seat of both kinds of labor processes. Nearly 70 percent were skilled workers, while 12 percent were machine tenders and 19 percent unskilled laborers of the " 'fetching and carrying' kind."[3] Nonetheless, more than a fifth of the skilled workers were turners, working new machines from Germany and the United States which would have baffled metalworkers only a few decades earlier. Indeed, the clichéd couplets which associated "skilled" with "handworker" and "semi-skilled" (or "unskilled") with "machine worker" do not go far to explain the realities of the production processes at Daimler.

This chapter will explore the world of industrial work at Daimler, analyzing what was done and by whom. It will sketch the contours of change in these areas and suggest categories to explain these changes. Then, it will examine how work was rewarded and will probe the texture of the relations between workers and managers and between groups of workers within the work force. Finally, it will explore what is known about Daimler's work force during the years before World War I.

TYPES OF WORKERS AND MACHINES

Skilled workers in the decade before the war usually directed the labor process in which they were involved, whether it was at a machine, or done by hand aided only with a tool. They had received a vocational education in a workshop or factory and usually possessed a document certifying their achievement in their chosen occupation. Their mastery of a craft was the most important attribute they brought to work with them. Most of them were able to envision exactly what it was they were doing on the job; they worked consciously on the tasks they performed. They took pride in what they did and in what they produced. Reports of jubilation among the workers at the Untertuerkheim factory after one of the long string of Mercedes racing victories do not seem exaggerated; indeed, it would have been surprising if Daimler's skilled workers had not been proud of the triumphs of the vehicles they had built.[4]

Among the skilled workers at Daimler were contingents of fitters, tool makers, smiths, foundry form-makers, carpenters, upholsterers, and painters. Mostly, they worked with hand tools or with the help of machines. In addition, the turners working the hundreds of lathes in the plant were highly skilled professionals. A turner not only had to know how to use the machine and to install the metal pieces to be worked in order to cut the metal parts, but also needed to be able to respond and to adjust his work, like a skilled handworker, to a slew of variables: the hardness of the metal, the material used in the cutting tool, the shape of the tool, the depth of the cut, which coolant to use, the pressure, "speeds, feeds, and pulling power of the machine."[5]

The turners of the early twentieth century were, however, skilled workers of a special kind. Their skills could not be performed without expensive technical equipment, while a fitter or a carpenter needed only a few simple tools. A turner's equipment thus could normally be supplied only by an employer commanding considerable capital. Lathes were quite expensive—Daimler paid about 5,280 marks for each in 1910.[6] In addition, they used large amounts of energy (usually electricity) and required constant maintenance. The forged or cast pieces of metal to be worked were also quite expensive.

Nevertheless, the lathes of the turners and the tools of the fitters or carpenters were similar in an important respect: they were universal. All were employed in a broad range of operations and had not been adapted to performing a specialized function repeatedly. Lathes could cut and finish all kinds of metals to make almost any conceivable type of component. Similarly, the wrenches of fitters or the hammers of carpenters had an enormous number of uses, both at the Daimler factory and outside in the community.[7]

New types of machines—special machines—were appearing during the late nineteenth and early twentieth centuries in German industry and slowly beginning to replace universal devices. In the decade before the First World War, observers noted several trends in the utilization of machinery at Daimler (see table 2.1). Lathe-turning machines had been the most used machines at the plant since it opened it gates in December 1903, but grinding machines were being more widely employed for certain tasks, especially to provide the tools needed in the mass production of certain small parts. For these uses, the cylindrical grinding machine required less labor: the work operation dispensed with the chipping, smoothing, filing, and rubbing with emery cloth which were part of the cutting operation. Labor costs and time therefore decreased.[8]

The milling machine also acquired a growing prominence in the production process at Daimler at the expense of the planing machine. With proper maintenance, the milling machines cut good surfaces on metal parts, which afterward required little or no filing.

These special machines could be operated with ease by any reasonably intelligent, dexterous worker. Milling and grinding machines performed only one kind of metalworking operation, as their names indicate. "Trained" or machine workers could effectively operate these machines without expending the years of study and practice it took to learn a craft.[9] Usually, a few months training on the machines were sufficient for a machine worker, who would later gain speed through repeated performance on the machines.[10]

According to Daimler's leading engineers, the growing use of special machines in Untertuerkheim was the key to the firm's effort to cut its production costs. In line with this goal, the campaign to improve the efficiency of Daimler's machine departments led to a declining role for the turning machines in the production processes.[11]

The development of these special machines marked a watershed in the history of labor in the metal industry, and it had complicated ramifications for the labor processes at Daimler. The workers tending the milling, grinding, and planing machines at Daimler exercised little control over what they did, save for starting up and shutting off the machine, for loading the pieces to be cut, and for guiding the machine through its preset paces. To be sure, dexterity and experience were still important, but there was no longer much room for exercising independent intelligence and creativity in the labor process in the machine departments. What may have held the attention of the trained employees above all else was the struggle to pile up the pieces for the weekly piece-wages.[12]

Much of that which may have been lost in the craft was made up for by the elimination of strenuous and unpleasant work. If the new labor processes, still only a small if increasingly significant part of the work at the plant before World War I, took away some of the workers' initiative, many of the jobs became physically easier to perform. Observations to this effect by contemporaries seem to have later been confirmed when large numbers of women and girls, few if any with prior training, moved into the machine

TABLE 2.1
Daimler's Machinery Acquisitions 1910, 1911, 1914

	1910	1911	1914
Lathes	9	41	89
Automatic lathes	–	7	–
Turret lathes	–	–	26
Drills + Milling machines	29	49	94
Planing machines	4	–	5
Grinding machines	10	17	49

Source: AGM DBAG Daimler-Motoren-Gesellschaft. Pruefungs-Bericht der Deutscher Treuhand-Gesellschaft. Berlin, 1910–14.

departments at Daimler during the war, tending 40 percent of the machines in some departments.[13]

The low men in the factory order were the unskilled, the "day laborers." Nearly all of these worked according to the directions of foremen and skilled workers and were often called "help workers." Many carried work-pieces back and forth between the workshops. With patience, some of these might obtain the chance to become machine workers, but their lot seems to have been difficult, and they were often ill or missing from work. In the firm's records and in the documents of the labor movement at Daimler, there are few traces of these hundreds of laboring men—usually 15 to 19 percent of the total work force—except for the numerous notations of their dismal wages.[14]

Daimler also maintained a handful of apprentices—27 in 1909. All but one at that time were studying to become turners or fitters. Most were relatives of men working at the plant. They learned their trades by performing work alongside the skilled workers at the lathes or as members of gangs of fitters. At the outset, they could be a burden to those with whom they worked, but became a help to the others the more they learned. The apprenticeship at DMG lasted four years. During the first two years, the young man (they were always males) received a small hourly wage. During the last two years of his *Ausbildung,* he participated in the piece-wage system. His share was deposited for him in a factory account, which was given to him at the end of his apprenticeship.[15]

DAIMLER'S SKILLED WORKERS AND THE PRODUCTION PROCESSES

DMG employed a dozen varieties of skilled workmen in Untertuerkheim. Most of these—nearly 1,000 of 1,175 in 1909—were engaged in the metal professions, while a hundred or so were carpenters and woodworkers.[16] The production processes in which they were engaged were organized into workshops. Simply put, these workshops grouped together similar production processes. In the metalworking departments, which turned pieces of metal into components for motors and chassis, machines were generally grouped by types. Lathes were located in one department; milling, planing and grinding machines in another. Fitters worked together in assembly workshops for engines, chassis, and the complete vehicles. Pieces were moved from one department to another until they were finally brought together for fitting in the assembly halls.

This mode of factory organization offered important advantages. According to the factory engineer, Richard Lang, machines could be utilized fully and efficiently, while the company saved on "their numbers, on space and on skilled supervisory personnel." As long as the production volume of Daimler's luxury vehicles remained limited and the firm did not have to set up huge departments at considerable distances from one another, this factory arrangement seemed economically efficient.[17]

Nevertheless, the distances involved in transporting pieces from one department to the next were considerable in a factory complex spreading as inexorably across the Neckar *Wasen* as Prussia had across the map of Central Europe a half century before. Day laborers had to move parts to other buildings for the next state of their transformation into automobile components, a task made easier by the network of railroad tracks which bound the buildings.[18] With the expansion of the Untertuerkheim factory complex, the need to transport parts around the grounds became a major problem, especially during the war, when thousands of heavy engines were produced annually. In early 1919, Daimler reorganized its factory, bringing together into new departments the various labor processes required for working pieces of metal into complete components.[19]

During the first years of the plant's operations, Daimler built custom automobiles according to the wishes of its wealthy customers. The severe slump in the automobile industry in 1907–8 brought the first changes. This fledgling sector was shaken by the crisis, and Daimler acutely felt the pressure. The bank crunch in America had plunged the industry into a period of drastic retrenchment and readjustment. In Untertuerkheim, one third of the work force was given its walking papers, as the bottom fell out of demand and production. Throughout Germany, the surviving firms moved toward producing somewhat smaller automobiles with large standardized sections which could be manufactured in large lots by serial production.[20]

At Daimler, several new types were introduced in the wake of the crisis in 1908. They utilized the Cardan chassis. The importance of this for the organization of the production process was considerable. A large section of the firm's autos was thus standardized and could be produced according to a set design. The increase in the production of standardized parts set the stage for a push to reorganize and to rationalize the production processes.[21] The drive to lower costs in the next few years meant cheapening the outlays for production through a variety of methods: by increasing productivity through the introduction of more special machines wherever possible and by tightening the controls over expenditures by improving the central supervision of the acquisition of raw materials, the hiring of laborers, and the setting of wages and piece-rates (table 2.2).[22]

The result is apparent in the doubling of productivity between 1909 and 1913: in 1909, it took three workers to build one auto; in 1913 three built two cars.[23] Nevertheless, Daimler's success was far more modest than that achieved by Henry Ford's revolutionary innovation of the assembly line at his East Lansing operation.

The following section will examine the work performed by the skilled trades at Untertuerkheim in the decade before the war and will suggest the ways in which these professions were changing. The order in which the groups are examined here will roughly correspond with the progression of the production process for cars and engines at Daimler, beginning with the foundry and smith, proceeding to the metalworking departments with their banks of thundering machines, and finally to the various building, assembly, testing, and finishing departments.

FORMERS

In the foundry, liquid metals were poured into molds to produce the basic outlines of parts with clear geometrical lines. All things considered, casting was one of the simplest and cheapest ways to shape metal parts. The casting operations were done in a building which was opened in November 1906, outfitted with the latest high-quality equipment.[24] The foundry hall was a sprawling, two-story building, 132 by 30 meters. It contained the facilities for molding the bronze, brass, and aluminum parts.[25] The new foundry gave Daimler more flexibility in the production of these metal parts, most of which could now be formed at the plant by its own workmen according to its own specifications.

The first steps in the casting of parts were undertaken by designers and woodworkers. The designers, working closely with the factory engineers, produced technical drawings of the parts to be cast. These were then turned over to the model builders, skilled carpenters who built wooden models of the parts.[26] In the foundry itself, the skilled workers were the formers and

TABLE 2.2
Wages vs. Production and Sales at DMG, 1910–1914 (in Marks)

	A. Wages	B. Value of Sold & Unsold Products	A as % of B
1910	2,769,657	17,875,952	15.5
1911	3,187,104	21,725,534	14.7
1912	3,902,185	26,594,323	14.7
1913	4,092,885	32,665,202	12.5
1914	5,027,143	45,719,917	11.0

Source: AGM DBAG Daimler-Motoren-Gesellschaft Stuttgart-Untertuerkheim. Pruefungs-Bericht der Deutscher Treuhand-Gesellschaft. Berlin, 1910–1914.

the core-makers, who fabricated the molds for the molten aluminum and brass. The molds contained an outer portion, the form, and an inner one, the core. The form was constructed by embedding the wooden model in a large box of clay-rich sand and then coating the resulting mold with graphite. Similarly, the core was made by carefully packing sand into a conical core-model. After the core-model was removed, the core of sand was also coated with graphite. The casting of complicated pieces sometimes required several wooden models for the forms and cores.[27] Casting metals was no exact procedure, due to the inexactness of models made from technical drawings, the impossibility of precisely setting up forms and cores, and the propensity of liquid metals to shrink a bit while hardening.[28]

In the Daimler foundry, the formers worked alone in a separate area of the premises, on occasion with unskilled laborers at their disposal. The core-makers worked nearby, directly adjacent to the casting area. Formers and core-makers received piece-wages, figured by the size of the molds which they produced. On rare occasions, the casting of large and complex pieces required the building of teams of formers and core-makers. The resulting piece-wages were then divided among them.

The three other groups working in the foundry—the smelters, the casters, and the cast-cleaners—were trained workers. The cast-cleaners' job was the dirtiest and noisiest in the foundry. The power-hammers, chisels, and sand-blasting equipment, which were used to dislodge impurities from the surfaces of the cast pieces, raised much sand and dust. Dangerous lung diseases traditionally plagued these low-paid "semi-skilled" workers.[29]

The foundry master's office was adjacent to the area where the skilled core-makers, and the semi-skilled smelters and casters worked. From there, he could supervise the process in which the skilled workers set up the molds and the semi-skilled workers subsequently poured the molten metals into them.[30] Mistakes at this stage of the casting operation were costliest to the firm so the master strove, of course, to avoid as many of these as possible.

SMITHS

The smiths utilized heat and pressure to work pieces of metal into new shapes. Hand work, often with a hammer, survived in the smith and was perhaps the clearest example at Daimler of the persistence of techniques from an earlier age of the metal industry. Hydraulic presses and power hammers began to appear in their workshop, located in a separate building that opened in January 1907, and were indispensable for forging larger metal parts or pieces made of the harder metals used in the motor and chassis, such as the crankshaft. In all, 60 fires and furnaces blazed in the smith. Most of the work in the Daimler smith was done by gangs, which were typically made up of a head blacksmith, one or two young smiths, and several unskilled laborers. The blacksmith's quick, easy gestures directed the gang members.[31] An observer could easily have thought he or she was watching a master-artisan at work with his journeymen-smiths and apprentices:

> The head blacksmith stands behind the anvil, holds the work-piece with his left hand and grasps a light hammer with the right. His task is to lead the forging operation, to turn the work-piece and to give the other smiths the signs where they are to strike [with their hammers] and when they are to begin or to stop. . . .

Because of the din in the smith, the head blacksmith used a set of traditional, standard signs and gestures to direct his crew:

> The beginning of the forging was signalled by three three ringing hammer blows. Stop! [was signalled] by a hollow and a ringing blow. . . . [Other signs were given] by nods and turns of the head.[32]

The blacksmiths at Daimler were generally older men, and exhibited a paternalistic, authoritatian manner—only too understandable, since their own individual earnings depended on their success in directing the work of the gang forging its prescribed pieces. About one of three smiths at Daimler was a blacksmith. "Well-forged is half filed," declared an old maxim, emphasizing the importance of good work by the smiths for saving labor-time and effort in other departments.[33]

By the early 1910s, an observer noted that the open fires had been replaced by 15 reverberatory furnaces fired by coal, coke, and natural gas, which were far more efficient for heating iron. More important by that time were the powerful mechanical hammers, powered by steam and compressed air, which produced pressures of up to 2,450 kilograms for the hammerhead to work the hot iron and steel. For finishing the job, the smith was outfitted with a dozen trimming presses and metal saws. Thus, by the outbreak of the war, the smith (if not the smiths) had lost much of its old-fashioned flavor.[34] "These smiths, these formers [at Daimler] were hard workers," an observer recalled. "They kept company with steel, and their language did, too . . . their coarse, blunt language."[35]

TURNERS

Turning is the most fundamental cutting operation in metalworking. The name comes from the rotation of the piece of metal on the lathe as it is being worked. This spinning workpiece is addressed by the cutting tools, usually of steel, which are attached to the tool support.

The large contingent of skilled turners (243) was the backbone of the machine departments at Daimler. These precision machinists had mastered a wide range of cutting operations for turning sections of metal from the foundry or forge into parts with elaborate shapes. Their task was to cut away unnecessary material from the workpieces, to give them their exact form, with the necessary notches as well as screw and thread fixtures. Multiple cutting operations—roughing, facing, inside turning, smoothing, threading, or parting, each a separate procedure in itself—might be required to complete a single side of a component. At each stage, the turner might have to remount the work-piece onto the machine, and choose and clamp a new cutting tool, with the appropriate cutting face for the operations, onto the machine at the right angle.[36] The operation of the machine and the adjustment of its speed, the use of coolants during the cutting, the variables affecting the work process present in the materials which the tool and work-piece contained all had to be commanded by the turner. As with skilled handworkers, a wide range of initiative and variety characterized the job of the turner.[37] In addition, they worked constantly with the risk of a mistake that might lead to the loss of thumbs or fingers. Turners almost always received piece-wages at DMG, and were among the best paid professionals at the plant.[38]

The turners, along with the semi-skilled machine tenders, worked in the vast *Saegedachbau*, a complex 150 by 130 meters, enclosing about 20,000 square meters of floor space. The sprawling machine park housed a mass of machinery—600 units in 1905, 1,200 in 1912, and 1,500 in 1915—which "represented the best German and American [machine-building] factories."[39]

FITTERS

The largest group of skilled workers at Daimler was the fitters. There were, however, many different types of fitters at Daimler and in Germany in the early twentieth century.[40] What these metal workers had in common was that their assembling, adjusting, repairing, and maintenance relied on hand work and tools, save for an occasional drill, lathe, or welding torch. The most important fitters in Untertuerkheim were the assemblers, toolmakers, and mechanics. These were grouped in separate workshops, in which they were assisted by unskilled day laborers.

Before the adoption of fine precision standards in the metal industry, assembly work was an exerting task. Fitters using hammers and drills cajoled and coaxed together parts which were only approximately compatible.[41] At Daimler, the most elite fitters, the final assemblers, formed gangs, heading up groups of five to ten workers, along with an apprentice or two. Each gang assembled two or three cars at a time. Meanwhile, a foreman looked on, suggesting improvements in the procedures and plans which the gang was following.

Riveting gangs, with three or four fitters in each, were less supervised, for their jobs were regulated by a strict division of labor dictated by the drills and tools they utilized. One of the fitters headed up each gang, but usually encountered few problems. Although one observer attributed the smooth operation of the riveting gangs to the "sociability" of the Swabians,[42] the reason lay more likely in the established and stable division of labor inside the small group of fitters. Assembly teams at DMG were generally paid by the piece, and the wages were subsequently divided among the members by the head of the team.

The assembly halls were outfitted with cranes, and were, of course, well stocked with a variety of tools, screws, and bolts, mostly made there at the factory. A minimum of a month was required for the assembly work, including an estimated 8 to 14 days for trying out the components and then testing the finished motor or vehicle.[43] In the *Bremserei*, where the motors were checked and carefully tuned after assembly, skilled mechanics performed a minimum of two hours of exhaustive tests on engines clamped onto elaborate testing stands. Their goal was to insure that "the heart of the machine must be 100% healthy: that is the principle of the whole *Bremserei* operation."[44]

There is evidence of important developments in the work of assembly fitters at DMG in the last years before the war. A report of the technical engineers from early 1911 noted that the assembly of the chassis had been reorganized so that each fitter mounted only a single specific section of the chassis, instead of working with a group on the whole unit. The engineers listed two immediate benefits of this articulation of the division of labor: "an exact control" over the labor process and the longer retention of fitters at the plant, since they "are no longer so well suited for the chauffeur positions" and other more pleasant jobs in automobile plants which highly skilled fitters and mechanics coveted.[45]

THE TOOLMAKING SHOP AND OUTFITTING OFFICE: THE DESIGN OF PRODUCTION

Another domain of the fitters was critically important to the operation of the whole factory: the toolmaking shop, where the special tools and machine parts needed for executing the firm's designs were crafted. By the firm's criterion, the whole operation was "unproductive," for it did not actually produce commodities, but was nevertheless crucial for the operation of the factory. As an engineer wrote after the war about the unique role of this department for the industry, "From a poorly functioning toolmaking shop, paralyzing poison oozes out like a sickness through the entire factory. . . . If we look at the most successful factories, we find that the successes are accomplished . . . alone through a well-equipped and well-staffed toolmaking shop."[46] Daimler referred to its toolmaking shop as "the soul of the whole factory."[47]

Daimler's toolmaking department was located in the middle of the large *Saegedachbau*. It contained its own lathes, milling machines, grinders, saws, presses, forging furnaces, and measuring devices. One of its two key functions was to keep the machinery at the Untertuerkheim factory supplied with tools. The other was to work out more rational production processes, and to devise the suitable tools and equipment needed for them. An engineer who had discussed Daimler's affairs with the direction expressed the prevailing mentality in Untertuerkheim: "If a small improvement on a piece of equipment leads to a quicker completion of the work which brings a saving per piece of 20 pfennig, a profit of 2000 marks would be attained with the yearly production of 10,000 units."[48]

The tookmaking shop enforced exacting degrees of precision in its designs. It estimated the precision of its work at one thousandth of a millimeter. A pickup and dropoff office for tools was part of the effort to control precision and to engage less skilled and thus cheaper labor. This central control of tools, which spread through the auto industry in the early twentieth century, marked the passing of an industrial era in which the skilled workers themselves had responsibility for the maintenance of their tools. Indeed, the promenade of skilled workers to the tool-grinding machines had been a bit of the daily ritual of professional machinists around the turn of the century.[49]

This degree of precision in metalworking helped to reduce the need for expensive refinishing and touching up work during the assembly stages of the production processes. In addition, it simplified the maintenance and repair of the Daimler automobiles, for the substitution of exactly constructed standardized parts became possible.[50] An inspection station in the middle of the sprawling machine park "through which every part must pass" enforced the firm's strict standards.[51]

With the stabilization of the firm's offerings, the factory engineers devoted their efforts to improving the production processes in a variety of ways.[52] The special "outfitting office," part of the toolmaking shop, turned out designs for special equipment and tools which would facilitate carrying out the production processes in labor-saving ways, involving as far as possible uninterrupted work operations on the machines. One aim of the outfitting office at DMG was to lower the production costs of components. At the same time, the firm hoped to guarantee the exchangeability of its tools and auto components through precision production and supervision. The final goal of the direction of the machine toolmaking shop would be achieved only by the success of meeting the first two, to wit, the ability to use "less skilled and therefore cheaper labor power" on its special machines, with the worker increasingly assuming the responsibility of working several machines at the same time. "Thereby, one is less dependent on the skill of the workers; the machines are more fully utilized, and time is saved on labor—all points which together further the highest achievement in quality and quantity."[53]

Thus, the firm produced not only nearly all of its own parts,[54] but also the cutting tools which worked them according to its designs. This was perhaps the most important task which some in Daimler's large contingent of fitters performed.

The departments and workshops at Daimler were the scenes of moves in the years before the war toward greater control by management over the production process, especially after the dramatic crisis in the automobile industry in 1907. The charge of the toolmaking shop to devise labor-saving and machine-maximizing ways of building Daimler's products shows the extent to which the new ideas of controlling the work force had begun to take root. Only decades earlier, managment's right to control its labor force in the metal and machine-building industries had meant in reality only the general setting of tasks. Rarely had managers intervened to direct the workers' ways of executing them, preferring to let the skilled work force take the responsibility in performing its jobs. By the early twentieth century, in the wake of the movement for "scientific management" pioneered by Frederick Winslow Taylor in America, management's right of control extended to directing the actual mode of performing every job, from the simpliest to the most complicated.[55] There is no evidence the DMG followed a rigid Taylorism in its design of the production processes in the years before the First World War.[56] Nevertheless, the arch-principle of "scientific management" —the dictation to the worker of the detailed manner in which labor was to be performed—was enshrined in the guidelines for the "soul" of the factory, the toolmaking shop. Above all else, Daimler strove to develop the division of labor ever further in its plant, although emulating the Ford revolution was out of the question for this producer of luxury and racing vehicles.[57]

At the same time, Daimler sought to extend the piece-rate system as far as possible, as a spur to productivity. Although quantitative evidence is almost wholly lacking, the intention of DMG's technical direction is clear: "We have turned our entire attention . . . to the general introduction of the piece-rate system."[58]

THE MASTERS

The control over the work force which was being built into the labor processes at Daimler was reinforced by the organization of authority at the plant. Each department was headed by a master. Clad in his customary status symbol, black trousers,[59] the master oversaw production in his workshop and maintained work discipline. Having been a worker himself, often in the very same department, the master was intimately acquainted with the kind of work being performed. By enforcing a rational division of labor and by proposing improvements in his department's operation to the Daimler's engineers, he played a key part in making work methods cheaper and better.[60]

At Daimler-Untertuerkheim, as in most of the metal and machine-building industry, the master had considerable prerogatives in the shaping of the work atmosphere prevailing in his workshop. What an observer of the Berlin metal and machine-building industry noted was also true for DMG: whether a warm and personal, or a no-nonsense, business-like regime prevailed in the department depended to a large degree on the individual personality of the master in charge.[61] At Daimler and elsewhere, he could reward a personal favorite with good, highly paid work or penalize troublemakers with strenuous, poorly paid work. One worker described the Untertuerkheim factory as a "federation of independent master republics,"[62] with the masters controlling piece-rates and the preparation, assignment, and supervision of work. Workers at DMG often complained that the masters abused their positions to make work in their departments unpleasant or too difficult. Among the most important of the workers' grievances against Daimler's masters in the period 1905–1920 were the setting of piece-rates at low levels in order to force the workers to produce more and during the war reporting complainers to the army authorities for induction into the military.[63]

Nevertheless, there is evidence that the prerogatives of the masters were shrinking in the last years before the war. By 1911, the masters of the Daimler departments often set piece-rates with the *Akkordbuch* which they kept in their office. This catalogue of piece-rates was issued and kept up by a central bureau at the factory. It marked a certain centralization of authority and control at the plant.[64]

The masters in Untertuerkheim received a salary, and were rewarded with bonuses set according to the length of their service, the breadth of their responsibility, and their overall effectiveness. In addition, they benefitted from the overall profitability of the firm, receiving more during business booms. They were assisted by vice-masters, skilled workers who wandered from machine to machine and helped set them up for the employees.[65]

THE SPECIAL MACHINES AND THEIR TENDERS

The introduction of the revolving turret lathe at Daimler and elsewhere altered the way standardized metal cutting was performed in many operations. The first generation of lathes held only one cutting tool. If the turner needed to carry out a series of cuts on the work-piece, he had to find and to clamp into place each new cutting tool by hand, procedures which were time consuming. The turret lathe eliminated this loss of work time. Its new feature was a turret which held up to six of the tools needed for a standard sequence of metal working procedures. The turner could mount the next tool he needed easily and quickly; indeed, at his command, the machine did it for him. "The loss in time in changing the tools is eliminated with these turret lathes. The task of the worker is simplified; in a real sense it is limited to the supervision of the machine."[66]

Fully automatic lathes also began to appear at Daimler in the years before the war. They performed a standard set of cutting operations, moving from one tool to another automatically. These were suited for the mass production of small, standardized parts which could be produced in large quantities with little effort—screws, for example. A visitor to Daimler observed that "the worker has only the need to put the material into the machine; all else it does itself, more exact than could be done by hand, and cheaper." The department made "an overpowering impression. . . . As if by the hands of spirits, everything proceeds."[67]

New milling machines at Daimler made the production of cogwheels and gears easier. With the old milling machines, the miller had to notch and cut each individual tooth of a gear and then move the piece for the notching of the next tooth. The new machines did everything; the worker needed only to insert a metal disc which was cut into a gear by the machine. "These milling machines work fully automatically except for the mounting of a new work-piece, which had to [be done] . . . by hand," reported an engineering correspondent who visited the plant. Thus, one miller could tend several machines at the same time. The first miller at Daimler operated all three of the milling machines at the earlier Cannstatt factory in the late 1890s.[68]

The milling and grinding machines, and the revolving and automatic lathes, changed the shape of work for those operating and tending them. These workers were themselves moving to new repetitive rhythms on the job. As one observer noted, "A worker must turn a lever the whole time in order to grind out machine parts. The perpetual, regular turning motion becomes a habit for him; he performs 30 or more turns to the right and left per minute for hours on end."[69]

Drilling was also simplified. Drillers had to be extremely attentive; they had to carefully mark each position for a hole with chalk and then bore each slowly at the proper angle. The skill and attentiveness of the worker were important in what could be a slow, painstaking job. The introduction of the jig [Bohrlehre] quickly changed all that. This device was a hard-steel pattern which fit over the part being worked on to guide the bit. The result was that dozens of holes could quickly be drilled by unskilled workers, even by women, as one observer marvelled.[70]

The acquisition of more special machinery was central to the firm's cost-cutting strategy before 1914. When Daimler prepared to increase the production of its smaller Cardan auto in late 1909 and 1910, the engineers saw the procurement of new turret lathes, special drills, and grinding and milling machines as critically important, "if we do not want to revert to expensive turning work." An additional order for 15 special machines was approved six months later.[71]

Despite the innovations of the first decade of the Untertuerkheim operation, skilled workers performed the most important functions throughout the production process. Especially important were the turners and fitters who prepared the work-pieces and machines for the procedures to be performed. The so-called Anreisser indicated which labors were to be carried out to produce the parts with the proper specifications, while the Einrichter accordingly set up and mounted the pieces to be worked on with the machines.

Likewise, in the final stages of the production process, skilled fitters and mechanics remained the backbone of the process of assembling motors, chassis, and vehicles into the 1920s. This was no doubt due in part to the nature of the luxury automobiles and high-performance engines which the firm turned out. The company repeatedly contrasted the careful hand work which went into its products with the shoddy, "husch, husch—fertig" work methods allegedly employed in the United States.[72] At the same time, however, any notions of moving in the direction of such a truly radical innovation in the production processes as Henry Ford's assembly line were hampered by the absence of a mass market for Daimler's vehicles, by the lack of vehicles suitable for a mass market, and by the presence of a force of mainly skilled workers organized in an effective trade union movement.

OTHER SKILLED WORKERS

A relatively small group of skilled workers from other trades—about 100 strong—also worked at Daimler. A group of skilled carpenters built models for the foundry, as mentioned above. In addition, another group of woodworkers carved and fashioned the auto bodies. These used machines for their work, including an American-made wood-bending machine which molded the planks for the bodies. They formed a small contingent of woodworkers organized into the German Woodworkers' Union.

Forty or so upholsterers stuffed and sewed the seats for the autos. A contingent of 20 painters and lacquerers finished off the body with paints and varnishes. In the early 1910s, most of these workers had shifted from brushes to sprayguns, a development which slashed the time necessary for their work by two-thirds.[73]

Nearly all of the non-metal workers—with the exception of the model builders—were involved in the construction of the coach. A description of this process survives from the post-World War I period, after the Daimler body operations had moved to the new plant at Sindelfingen, but before any fundamental change in the production processes had been implemented.

Before Daimler introduced a number of standard auto bodies after the war, the coach builders worked each new one individually, according to the wishes of the customer. The so-called cabinet-maker [Kastenmacher], a woodworker with one or two assistants, began executing the first rough designs of the coach according to the drawing, choosing the wood from storage where it had been aging and drying for about four years. Carefully following the drawing the woodworkers cut and finished the pieces of wood with saws and bending, planing, and milling machines. The Flaschner produced the clasps for the carriage from metal and then clamped the various pieces together. A small group of smiths and fitters fit the coach to the chassis, making the alterations necessary for a clean fit and bringing the first stage in building the bodies to a close.

Workers lifted the coach off the frame, and installed the windows. Then a group of four workers descended on the auto body, cleaning, grinding, spackling, and finally applying a coat of paint. The next stop was the upholstery department, where seats and other fixtures were fashioned and installed. The body was subsequently sent back to the painters, who administered three additional coats of paint. The last stop was the final assembly room, where fitters joined together coach and chassis.[74]

THE FACTORY REGIME

Thus, a dozen types of skilled workers, along with a complement of trained machine workers and unskilled day laborers toiled in a dozen workshops in eight main buildings on the Neckar. The Daimler factory was not, however, a collection of independent workshops, but a cohesive factory mechanism, ruled by a central order which was dictated by the owners of the firm and their managers. This order was embodied in the factory's work regulations.

According to a national statue adopted in 1891, after the bitter miners' strike of two years before had agitated public opinion and demonstrated a need for an effective regulation of conditions in German's workplaces, all industrial concerns with 20 or more workers had to establish and maintain work regulations. These were legally binding on both employers and employees.[75] All personnel had to agree to this collection of ordinances in order to work at Daimler.

Control over the work regulations was almost always safeguarded by the management of German firms in the *Kaiserreich*. This right was, after all, a prerogative of the *Herr im Hause*, the owner who considered himself to be "master in his own house." As H. A. Bueck, a general secretary of the Central Association of German Industrialists declared in 1890, "To enact [the regulations] is the right of the employer, who . . . alone [is] responsible for the industrial enterprise."[76]

The factory regime prevailing at Daimler before the revolution was defined in two sets of work regulations, one promulgated after the industrial conflict of 1906, the other dating from the industrial unrest at the end of 1910. A copy of the second, which went into force on January 9, 1911, and which probably differed from the earlier version only in one main point, survives.

The ordinances specified the relations of authority which insured the maintenance of industrial discipline—"keep[ing] factory employees at their job tasks."[77] According to the rules, the workers' superiors in the plant included masters, foremen, and "those persons designated by the factory directors."[78] Among those included in the last category were engineers attached to the various departments and factory officials with tasks such as the setting of piece-rates. In general, it was the worker's duty "to carry out the assigned work with diligence and care, to look after and to promote the good interest of the factory to the best of [his/her] abilities, and to avoid everything which could be disadvantageous to the factory." The Daimler employee "must follow the orders of his superiors immediately, and make all of his declarations and statements to fellow workers and superiors dependably and truthfully."[79]

In early 1906, the length of the work day was shortened by an hour, to nine and one-half hours daily. Until the war, the six-day work week remained 57 hours, including three hours weekly divided among 12 short breaks. From May 1 to September 30, the departments commenced operations at 6:25 A.M. The workshops broke for the one hour and 50 minute lunch break at 11:55. The afternoon work began at 1:45 and lasted until 5:45. From October 1 until the end of April, the start of the work-day was shifted back by 25 minutes, to 6:50 A.M., with closing set for 6:05 P.M. Management pegged these starting times to the arrival and departure of trains at the Untertuerkheim train station, which lay ten minutes by foot from the east gate of the factory grounds. On Sundays, nine holidays, and two half-day fests, the plant was closed. Workers were often directed to perform certain jobs connected with factory maintenance and safety on these days. For their efforts on such occasions, workers who were paid by the hour received a 50 percent bonus, although those who worked by the piece received the normal rates. Workers received their wages in cash every Friday.[80]

Overtime work was not a rarity at Daimler. Some workers even performed it during the lunch break, especially if they lived too far away from the plant to go home for lunch and had to eat at the plant. Because of the length of the work day and the commute to and from work, it would be fair to say that most workers had an adverse view of overtime, although some felt that the extra pay compensated for at least a part of the resulting exhaustion. Nevertheless, the direction's policy of requiring overtime work precipitated a number of clashes between the labor movement and the direction at Daimler from 1906 to at least 1920.[81]

Most workers in Untertuerkheim were piece-workers [Akkordarbeiter], meaning that they were paid for each piece which they themselves produced or worked on. Many received individual piece-rates for the labor they performed, while others, who worked as part of a gang, earned group piece-rates—shares of the gang's earnings.[82]

The procedure for setting piece-rates was carefully outlined in the work rules, for disputes between workers and management on this score were frequent. It generally corresponded to arrangements which were more or less standard in the German metal and machine-building industry.[83] The individual rate was fixed according to the guidelines in the master's Akkordbuch. The worker had the right "to convince himself that the piece-rate offered to him agreed with the price set down in the guidelines."[84] Since the rates for many of the possible jobs could not be set beforehand, and since piece-rates were subject to change, the worker could consult with a representative regarding the rightness of the proffered rate. If a worker refused the scheduled piece-rate, he had the right to appeal to the plant workers' committee to bring up the matter with management. In such cases, the work rules were clear: "With differences of opinion, management decides." The worker always had the option to work for the almost always lower hourly rate. If a group of workers were involved together in turning out or mounting a part, as a gang, the total amount to be paid to each was to be arranged by all the parties beforehand.[85]

The masters' prerogatives were braked further in the spring of 1909 with the introduction of a complicated card system, which served to keep the plant management constantly informed of the current status of materials, labor, and wages in the workshops and departments.[86] In addition, in 1911,

DMG brought in an outside engineer from Frankfurt to regulate the piece-rates at the factory more closely.[87]

The Daimler direction enforced the principle of piece-wages whenever possible simply in the hope of boosting production. Their brand of economic orthodoxy held that workers would do more if paid according to what they did. The survival of the piece-rate in factories like Daimler was probably partly the result of the presence of the highly skilled workers needed to perform many of the tasks in the building of engines and motor vehicles. In a sense, the trappings of an earlier subcontracting system, by which independent artisans had once made a living, were preserved. In the new setting of the modern factory, the wage laborers contesting the piece-rates challenged their own subordination within the world of the workplace, but their subordination was almost always reaffirmed: the master and his *Akkordbuch* ruled. Demands for the abolition of piece-rates were widespread in the metal and machine-building industries, and had an important place on the Metal-workers' Union's agenda.[88] Daimler's direction believed that many of its workers wanted the abolition of the piece-rate system.[89]

Whether paid by the piece or by the hour, the worker had to be at his proper place daily at the appointed time, and had to remain there until the end of the work day. If someone arrived late, he had to report to his superior immediately on his arrival. Except for the lunch break, exit from the plant before closing time was possible only with the special permission of the master. The regulations expressly forbade noise, dallying, "idle conversation," and the reading of books and magazines. Drunkenness within the confines of the factory was an offense which could be punished through the imposition of fines. In addition, thirty-odd regulations attempted to diminish the incidence of accidents and to instill an awareness of the importance of safety in the employees. Smoking was forbidden in many areas of the plant, and precautionary directions for using certain machines were spelled out in the hope of preventing workers from getting limbs caught in them.[90]

The master and his superiors could deal with breaches of the labor discipline described in the work rules in two ways: through fines or through dismissal. Infringement of the ordinances could be punished by a fine of half the daily wage. In addition, "acts against fellow workers, major contraventions against good morals and against the maintenance of the good order of the factory for the purpose of a safe factory . . . can be punished with a fine of up to the full amount of the average daily earnings of the last wage period." Fines of up to a day's wages could also be levied for unexcused absences. The directors determined fines in accordance with the responsible master's recommendations. These exactions flowed into the factory's relief fund. Appeals could be made to the workers' committee, and the firm promised, at least, to take its opinions into consideration. Dismissal remained within the province of the owners. "The work relationship can be refused at any time by both sides. The exit then follows immediately." "Workers who, despite repeated warnings, contravene the already standing orders can be dismissed before the expiration of the contractual time without refusal."[91]

Nevertheless, relations between workers and their superiors at the Mercedes factory had a personal quality before the war which later could never be recovered. "The engineers spoke with the skilled workers often . . . with *Du*, for they were dependent on their ability and skill," recalled a worker, whose father was a Social Democrat and a master in Untertuerkheim after 1907. "The rack of beer always stood nearby, and when a motor was finished, masters and engineers drank with them. They loved their work. They also knew for whom they were building the car."[92]

■

In the prewar decade, skilled workers dominated the world of production at Daimler-Untertuerkheim. They formed the large majority of persons employed there. Nevertheless, there was a growing lot of special machines with preset functions, worked not by skilled employees but by men who had been trained to tend them. The factory organized all of them—skilled or merely trained—into workshops according to the labor processes they performed, not according to the parts they produced. Thus, the factory was a collection of smaller communities of workers, who in their daily labor had few direct connections to other groups of workers within the plant. These occupational groupings within the workshops were the focus of their on-the-job experience.

Masters, who had themselves been skilled workers, were the direct agents of the Daimler owners and top managers in the workshops, and were generally the only persons in authority with whom workers had regular contact. The functions which these hand-picked agents carried out were supervisory, regulatory and administrative. They supervised and helped to set up the work being done. They kept law and order, enforcing the work ordinances and keeping their superiors in the central administration offices informed on developments in the workshops. Using standardized rate books, they set the price-rates for their workers, and often quarrelled with doubting employees in the process. The use of these rate books, along with the role of the central offices for production techniques and for distributing tools in the toolmaking department were the most important limitations on the prerogatives of the masters at Daimler.

These rather modest administrative and productive practices formed the basis for the tentative, undramatic moves in the direction of rationalizing both control and production in Untertuerkheim. It should not be surprising then that they would also be the focus for the industrial conflicts of the prewar years.

THE *VEREIN* STUDY AND THE WORKERS OF DAIMLER

Daimler and the others drew a labor force from the Swabian towns and villages near Stuttgart. It is possible to draw a social portrait of the pre-war Daimler workers. The most valuable source of information for such a project is the work by the researcher Fritz Schumann, *Die Arbeiter der Daimler-Motoren-Gesellschaft*. Schumann was a member of the research project created by the *Verein fuer Sozialpolitik* in September 1907 to survey the impact of factory work on the lives of working people.[93] In reality, the mentor of the study was Max Weber, although the investigations themselves were carried out by German social scientists. Ten others were published between 1910 and 1912. Weber spelled out the purpose of the project in 1908:

> The present survey aims to establish the following: on the one hand, which influences the large-scale industrial enterprises exercise upon the individual character, the occupational fate and the style of life of its work force, which physical and psychical qualities it develops in it, and how these express themselves in the daily life of the workers; on the other hand, how the development and the potential future development of large-scale industry is limited by those characteristics of the workers which are a result of their ethnic, social and cultural origin, of their traditions, and their standards of life.[94]

Rather than seeking to formulate and propose specific remedial legislation to benefit the workers, Weber considered the surveys purely "scientific" and thus strove to gather knowledge about the occupational mobility of workers, their life styles, and their productive life within the factory. An important source of data for the survey was a questionnaire which researchers asked the workers themselves to complete. Supplemental information came from the researchers' analysis of factory office records and their scrutiny of the workers both on and off the shop floor.

As intriguing and useful as the group's factory studies are, they are marred by their strict avoidance of political issues and their neglect of the labor movement both within the confines of the factory and in German society at large. The one-dimensionality and passivity of their subjects is striking. In these works the factory is a jail, with "its hierarchic authority structure, its discipline, its chaining of the men to machines, its spatial aggregation and yet isolation of the worker . . . , its formidable accounting system that reaches down to the simplest hand movement of the workers."[95]

But labor is an active subject, not a passive factor of production. "It has a mind of its own, it resists as well as responds. Its performance . . . is not easily calculated."[96] Indeed, to a great degree, the rhetoric of the German labor movement actively espoused the dignity of industrial work and the creativity and political potential of working people. Even Marx, with whom one might be tempted to associate Weber's portrait of an alienated world of work, did not condemn the factory system as such—only an industrial system whose *raison d'être* was the production and private appropriation of surplus value. The *Verein*'s workers are like passive laboratory animals, objects of a researcher's too detached clinical gaze; certainly not the ebullient, individual, and complex legions of men and women who provided the powerful German economy with so much of its dynamism during the *Kaiserreich*. Thus, the categories and sheer taxonomy of the *Verein*'s industrial surveys, while providing valuable evidence for historians of the period, cannot compensate for the lack of an understanding of the historical and political issues raised in their accounts.

Fritz Schumann first visited Daimler's facility in Untertuerkheim in 1909. He noted that the Daimler workers were suspicious of his project to collect data about them, since they had seen him in the factory with members of the company's board of directors. Some thought that he was compiling "black lists" of employees for the owners or was part of an attempt to raise their taxes.[97] The workers' suspicion, which Schumann had to overcome, was a manifestation both of the difficulties involved in this kind of research and of the gulf between workers and owners in Untertuerkheim.

Nevertheless, the unions at Daimler, especially the German Metalworkers' Union (DMV), cooperated fully with Schumann, although he initially received only three dozen questionnaires back from the workers. He explained this by noting that the "average worker has a hard time expressing his thoughts in the orderly form of the written language."[98] Indeed, the workers in Wuerttemberg seemed to Schumann to be "mentally less active" than workers north of the Main, and accordingly seemed less interested in the "modern class struggle."[99] After concerted attempts to reach workers, which the unions furthered, Schumann managed to coax 173 questionnaires from workers, 72 from low-paid workers and 101 from relatively well-paid ones. This result led Schumann to suggest that the "trade union organization in factories like the Daimler-Motoren-Gesellschaft embraces the better paid workers in greater measure than the more poorly paid ones."[100] Still, the return of 173 of the 1,800 which had been distributed was a severe disappointment, but one which was repeated in nearly all of the other dozen surveys. Only the project researcher Marie Bernays, who actually worked for a time in a textile mill, succeeded in getting questionnaires returned from most of the work force.[101]

Schumann divided his report into two parts: the first consisted of a description of the Untertuerkheim factory and a perfunctory sketch of the production process; the second contained one section describing the work force itself and another detailing the life style of the Daimler workers. These latter sections, derived from factory records to which Daimler gave Schumann access and from the returned questionnaires, are an especially important source of information regarding the Daimler workers. In the turgid prose and wealth of tables, a portrait of the Daimler work force emerges which is impossible to duplicate for other periods of the company's existence. The next section, along with the accompanying tables (2.3–2.9) describes the findings in detail.

WAGES, AGE, SENIORITY

The best paid workers at Daimler were small groups of skilled metal and wood hand workers, such as metal-platers and model-builders (see table 2.3). Turners, the second largest bloc of skilled workers at the plant, received relatively high wages, 5.22 marks per day. The most numerous category of skilled workmen, the fitters, had to settle for 27 pfennigs a day less. The large group of smiths, on the other hand, were among the lowest paid professionals at the factory. A comparison of the wage levels of the three largest occupations at the factory, accounting for almost three-quarters of the skilled workers in Untertuerkheim, indicates that the machinists at the lathes were the best paid, while the smiths, many of whom still worked with hammers, made do with wages which were only 21 pfennigs more than those of the semi-skilled machine tenders. The fitters, who worked with wrenches and other hand tools and occasionally with machines, were moderately well-paid, ranking between the turners and the smiths on the pay-scale. Nearly all of these skilled workers had learned their professions from a craftsman or in a factory.

The trained machine tenders and the unskilled day laborers were among the two most poorly paid contingents in the Stuttgart automobile plant. Almost as poorly paid was the small group of painters and varnishers, the only skilled workers who earned less than the plant average.

It is not possible to compare the earnings of workers paid by the piece or by the hour for 1909. Nevertheless, the majority of all skilled and trained workmen in all categories were paid by the piece, from those groups which earned most to those who earned least. Most low-paid painters and well-paid carpenters alike received piece-wages.[102]

The oldest workers at the factory on average were found in the departments in which the machine tenders, the unskilled day laborers, and the tool makers labored. As a whole, the departments housing the older workers also tended to be those which had the employees with the most seniority in the factory. These departments were also generally those with the unskilled categories of workmen, with wages below the average wage-rate for the plant. Thus, skilled workers at Daimler changed jobs more frequently than did those belonging to the other categories.

In comparison, the best paid workers were the metal platers and the precision smiths who were in the factory's medium-aged range (31.3 and 32.9 years respectively). These skilled workers pocketed high wages although they had relatively little seniority at the plant. In general, workers at Daimler generally tended to earn less than the plant average until they reached age 25 and attained their maximum earnings potential before the age of 35. Beyond this age, the older one was, the less one tended to earn.

This statistical picture of the work force was the result of a complex of factors, which Schumann did not weight. For one, the occupational category into which one fell was clearly important in determining the magnitude of one's wage. Second, since most metalworkers at DMG at the time worked according to a piece-rate, the younger and more vital one was could mean higher earnings—if one had attained the dexterity that came only with job experience. Nevertheless, the level of skill involved in a particular occupation was a central feature of the hierarchy of wages, as is shown by the lower wages of the younger workers who were trained machine tenders, not professionals, and who also received piece-wages.

ORIGINS AND EDUCATION

The overwhelming preponderance of Daimler workers (86%) hailed from Wuerttemberg.[103] Using the factory records, however, Schumann determined that few Daimler workers were born in Stuttgart or other large cities (see tables 2.4 and 2.5). Nearly 45% came from villages with fewer than 2,000 residents and rural areas, while about 30 percent were born in small and medium-sized towns and cities (2,000–20,000 inhbitants). When one breaks down the statistics according to the major occupational groups, the rural and village background for woodworkers, carpenters, and smiths is striking. These occupations were traditionally associated with the small-scale industries which continued to thrive in Wuerttemberg well into the twentieth century. Daimler's mechanics had the most heavily urban origins: fewer than 30 percent came from the land, while 70 percent were born in cities and towns of more than 2,000 inhabitants. The unskilled workers, the machine-tenders, and the grinders—who generally had only the minimal amount of factory training—had more pronounced rural roots than most other groups of metalworkers. These types of industrial workers required dexterity and practice more than skill in order to perform their tasks well.

These workers were also among the oldest employed in the Untertuerkheim facility.[104]

Schumann found that most Daimler workers had been born within 25 kilometers of the factory, with the majority in occupations like forming, turning and machine-tending coming from within 10 kilometers of the plant. Given the industrial character of Stuttgart, with numerous small foundries and metal-working shops, this was not surprising. Almost a third of Schumann's sample came from parts of Wuerttemberg more than 25 kilometers distant from Daimler (see tables 2.6 and 2.7). Their daily trek through the Untertuerkheim railroad station, the oldest in Wuerttemberg, produced what one chronicler has termed "rush hour traffic" conditions as early as 1906 for the first time in Germany.[105]

As table 2.8 shows, the large majority lived close to the factory. Almost half walked to work daily and 80 percent of the employees required less than a half hour to get to work. The bulk of the work force lived in Cannstatt, Untertuerkheim, Ostheim, Wangen, Obertuerkheim, and other predominantly working class districts within three kilometers of the factory. These were classic proletarian quarters, crowded with workers from Daimler, Bosch, and the host of smaller works in Cannstatt, Wangen, and Untertuerkheim.[106] One of every eight Daimler workers lived in central areas of Stuttgart and Esslingen.

Slightly fewer than two fifths of Mercedes' employees came from proletarian families (see table 2.9). About 30 percent had fathers who they described as independent, including artisans, shopkeepers, and retailers. Twelve percent came from an agricultural backgrounds, while a slightly smaller portion described their fathers as clerks. When we consider the previous generation, the results confirm the historical portrait of the Wuerttemberg working class as "one drawn from the agricultural professions." Schumann himself described the workers as hailing from the "formerly agricultural, especially wine-growing population of Wuerttemberg."[107]

Most Mercedes workers had received an education beyond the required *Volksschule* (or for the handful from outside Wuerttemberg and Bavaria, the *Realschule*), although slightly more than a third possessed only the minimum required education. About 45 percent of the workers, mostly the skilled fitters, had received their occupational training from an independent craftsman, and a similar percentage, mainly lathe workers, had been trained within a factory. Only 12 in the survey had visited a technical institute, and eight, mainly day laborers, had had no special training at all. Fully 80 percent had kept the same occupation from the start of their training, including all of the skilled mechanics.

Of those who had changed their occupations, the turners predominated.

Around half of them had switched to their current positions from such jobs as baking, cooping, serving, and shoe-making. The trained and unskilled workers had also generally entered their current jobs recently.

Schumann found that all considered themselves Christians except for two agnostics. Seven of eight were Lutherans; the rest were Catholics. There was no difference between the earnings of Protestants and those of Catholics, demonstrating perhaps that there was no Protestant ethic at work, at least not among the Daimler employees. Workers who had served in the armed forces generally earned more than those who had been rejected as "unfit" or deemed "conditionally fit" for service, proving only that healthier or more fit workers tended to earn more.

WORK-DAY AND PAY-DAY

Using both the returned questionnaires and his own observations, Schumann sought to describe the work day at Daimler. The employees' work day, as we have already noted, began at 6:50 A.M. and ended at 6:10 in the evening, except during the summer. The lunch period began at 11:55 and lasted until 1:45. In addition, there were two 15-minute breaks, one at 8:30 A.M., the other at 4:00 P.M. Schumann noted that the first break usually injected a bit of life into the workers who heartily consumed "a large piece of sausage, cheese, and a hunk of black bread washed down with . . . apple cider."[108] Married workers, especially those with wives who had been trained or worked as servants, boasted the most appetizing snacks.

Many of those living near the plant went home for lunch. The rest, especially those whose residences were a bit farther from Untertuerkheim and those who were married, ate in or near the factory. Some ate in local diners, but many picked up lunches and took them to the main dining hall. Local breweries operated several concession stands within the factory gates in order to sell lunches to the workers. The firm encouraged the workers to drink its own privately commissioned raspberry and lemon-flavored soft-drinks, which it sold at six pfennigs for .3 liters. (These two varieties of soft drinks are still served today in the Daimler-Benz *Kantine*.) The profits from these drinks flowed into the firm's relief fund, but many workers nevertheless preferred to drink the locally produced apple cider which they carried in with them.

Schumann observed that most workers walked silently along the boulevards on the way home or to the railway station after work. He thought he detected a poetic sensibility in the way most workers chose to walk along the main street to and from the plant, "where there was something to see."[109] Workers tended to cluster with others in their occupational groups in the dining hall and on the street. According to Schumann, occupations were often marked by distinctive uniforms, which helped identify the wearer. For example, the metalworkers typically wore the classic flat-top cap, while woodworkers were generally bare-headed. Skilled mechanics donned clean, powder-blue linen uniforms, while unskilled day laborers worked in shabby street clothes. During the winter, the skilled workers typically wore coats in transit, while the shivering day laborers warmed themselves by keeping their hands deep within their trouser pockets. In Schumann's view, this division of the work force into distinct "work-shop communities" was important in avoiding a feeling of anonymity. "It saves the worker from feeling that he is totally a number, that he is totally submerged in the mass."[110] The work-shops were also the basis for the solidarity workers displayed in their confrontations with management before the war.

Schumann found that workers were concerned with overtime and stress. More than two-thirds of those responding claimed that overtime work was "frequently" required of them. The lathe-turners, mechanics, machine workers, and unskilled day laborers reported frequent overtime, whether their earnings were above or below the factory average.

Most respondents reported that their labor was "especially strenuous." Here, the criterion was exceedingly vague: namely, if a worker felt his job was strenuous, then it was. The reasons offered most frequently were the intensity of the labor, the strain on the eyes, nerves, and spirit, and the heaviness of the tools and materials with which they worked. Smoke, fumes, dust and changing temperatures were also the source of complaints. Schumann cited one worker's reasons: "Because one is continuously spurred on to produce more, and for the master, enough is never produced." Another complained that the bosses kept reducing the piece-rates, which made the work more strenuous. A machine tender wrote that overtime, and "having to work two machines" made his work more taxing. Schumann concluded that, "For 50 percent, the intensity of work is the chief cause for the strain. In other cases, external influences are more the cause."[111]

Most workers complained of chronic fatigue as a direct result of their work. Proportionately, the smith workers and the lathe turners reported fatigue most often, while, on the other hand, half of the mechanics claimed they were never drained by their work. The worst times of the day were the hour-and-a-half before lunch and the last two hours. By 4:00 P.M., most workers had already been at the factory for nine hours straight, although two of those hours were taken up by pauses and the lunch break. One worker wrote, "One is already tired in the mornings when you get up until you have reached your stride again; then [strength] wanes until 5:00 P.M., when one is really tired."[112]

The company itself reported that more than one-fourth of the 1,700 workers had been absent because of illness for at least a week during the course of 1908. Those with the highest incidences of disease were the smith workers and the machine workers, followed by the mechanics and the lathe turners. The unskilled day laborers had the best health and attendance records in 1908. The most highly paid skilled laborers, such as the metal-platers and touch-up smiths, were also blessed with reasonably good health. If one takes the age profiles of the various occupations into consideration, it seems that workers in the occupations which had older personnel were among the healthiest. The plant's younger workers, on the other hand, were those most likely to be absent from work, ostensibly due to illness.

Vacations were still a rarity for Daimler workers in 1908. A minimum of ten years' service with the firm was the prerequisite for a three-day paid vacation. An additional day could be gained for 13 and 14 years of service. The maximum vacation for workers was six paid days for 15 years of service.

Daimler workers, as most metalworkers in Germany, detested the practice of being paid by the piece. Whether one was paid a regular hourly wage or at a piece-rate was an important affair for the metal workers in Wuerttemberg, as elsewhere in the Reich. The elimination of the piece-rate had a prominent place in the Metalworkers' Union's program for industrial reform. Schumann managed to compile a useful cross section of workers' opinions at Daimler on the matter through his survey. The results are not surprising and demonstrate the disaffection of the workers with the whole system of piece-wages. Of the 53 responding to his queries who were paid hourly wages, all but two preferred this system. Of the 109 who were on the piece-wage scale and who generally earned far more than the workers in the preceding category, 84 would have preferred regular hourly wages to the piece-rates which they received. A fifth of those who favored retention of the piecework structure (of a total of 25) expressed this opinion only on the condition that their earnings continue to be superior. Eight of nine employees receiving part hourly and part piece wages preferred the hourly system. Of the fraction of Daimler workers who supported piece-rates, several did so because they claimed that this kind of labor made the day go more quickly and in a less boring manner, apparently because one strove to work harder and thus to earn more money.

In the last section of his investigation, Schumann turned his attention to the life styles of the workers outside the factory, using his sample of the 170 workers who returned the questionnaire. He learned that a fourth of the workers relied at least partly on the earnings of their spouses. This figure represented 36 percent of those who were married. The wives performed jobs such as delivering newspapers, beer, or milk; cleaning and servicing houses; taking on extra washing and ironing, and working in another factory. Seven-eighths of the workers had children, with the preponderance reporting from one to three children. The upper wage groups, filled mainly by older workers, had the most children; younger workers, who also earned average or below average wages, had fewer offspring. Over half of the Daimler workers had married only after first having conceived a child. The visiting social scientist did not believe that this in itself was an affront against bourgeois "good morals". Rather, it was the result of the rural origins of many of the workers: in the countryside, Schumann believed, "extramarital [and premarital] sexual intercourse was considered natural; the Swabian peasants often said that they " 'buy no pig in the sack.' "[113] The workers in the sample reported having 235 living children, and 35 who had died. Thus, at least 13 percent of children born to the families of the Daimler workers participating in the survey died before reaching maturity.

Very few of the next generation had as yet entered the job market, but of those who had, most were employed in the mechanical or commercial trades. The parents strove to give their children "the opportunity to become more than the father himself was," Schumann found.[114]

Few reported maintaining a household book for keeping track of expenses. Typical responses to Schumann's query on this count were: "not necessary;" "no, because nothing is left;" and "no, because nothing from nothing leaves nothing."

Daimler workers spent their free-time relaxing in much the same way as their successors do today. Most listed "walks" capped off with a glass of good beer as their chief means of unwinding. Others cited more sedentary pursuits, such as "smoking and reading the newspaper on the sofa," or "best of all, attending to my wife."[115] A handful listed the theater and concerts as their favorite entertainment. About a half of those answering asserted that they regularly enjoyed athletics, with most listing gymnastics [Turnen] and football as their favorites.

More than half of the Verein's survey belonged to a club, with the largest contingent in the singing associations, and another large representation in the sporting clubs. A whirl of singing clubs had sprung up in the communities making up east Stuttgart. Untertuerkheim could boast at least nine during the first decades of the century. Four clubs, dating from the years 1901–1907, catered to a working class clientele, which took its music seriously. One of these, the Lassalia, even performed the choral movement of Beethoven's ninth symphony in a city concert hall on the 100th anniversary of the composer's death in 1927.[116] Many also reported enjoying hobbies such as collecting herbs and keeping an aquarium.

Most of the workers surveyed (89) reported regularly reading a newspaper, with more than half of them naming the Schwaebische Tagwacht, the Stuttgart-based paper of the Social Democrats, as their favorite newspaper.

Of the avid newspaper readers, one-third earned under the average wage, two-thirds above it. The skilled fitters, turners, and smiths predominated among those who followed the papers. Two workers named Bebel's *Die Frau und der Sozialismus* as their favorite text. The workers' favorite general authors were, in order, Schiller (who came from the nearby village of Marbach), Zola, Heine, and Freiligrath. Goethe was far down the list, named by only two as their favorite author.[117] One need not be surprised by this fondness of working people for what today, amidst the refuse of corporate mass culture, is termed high-brow culture: access to science, literature, and art was one of the most prized demands of the European labor movements at the beginning of the twentieth century.

THE FINDINGS OF THE STUDY OF THE
VEREIN FUER SOZIALPOLITIK (1909):
FRITZ SCHUMANN, *DIE ARBEITER DER*
DAIMLER-MOTOREN-GESELLSCHAFT, 1911

TABLE 2.3
Age, Seniority and Wages at DMG by Occupation, 1908

	No. of Workers	Age (Yr., Mo.)	Seniority (Yr., Mo.)	Daily Wage (Marks)
Metal-platers	7	31,3	1,9.5	5.68
Joiners (W)	52	33,1.5	4,4	5.36
Tinsmiths	51	32, 5.5	4,9	5.26
Turners	243	29,9	4,5	5.22
Former	43	33,4.5	2,1	5.21
Carpenters (W)	47	28,10.5	2,3.5	5.20
Upholsterers	40	31,3.5	3,6.5	5.00
Fitters	503	29,4	3,11	4.95
Coppersmiths	29	34,2.5	5,4	4.94
Toolmakers	18	36,3	4,9	4.77
Smiths	109	30,7	3,8.5	4.77
Machineworkers	151	37,3.5	5,3.5	4.56
Painters	20	30,10	3,5.5	4.40
Grinders	41	35,2.5	4,7	4.02
Day laborers	323	36,4.5	3,6.5	3.77
(W = Woodworkers)				

TABLE 2.4

Origins of the Work Force

Size of Settlements	No. of Workers	%
over 100,000	92	5.4
20,000–100,000	288	16.9
5,000–20,000	227	13.4
2,000–5,000	337	19.8
under 2,000	736	44.5

TABLE 2.5

Origins by Occupation

Size of Settlements	Toolmakers & Fitters (521)	Turners (243)	Machine-workers (192)	Smiths (132)	Formers (43)
over 100,000	8.3%	5.0%	2.1%	3.9%	7.0%
20,000–100,000	22.5%	25.9%	13.5%	4.5%	27.9%
5,000–20,000	18.2%	7.8%	12.5%	9.1%	13.9%
2,000–5,000	21.1%	14.0%	24.5%	17.4%	16.3%
under 2,000	29.9%	47.3%	47.4%	65.1%	34.9%

	Woodworkers (99)	Body Workers (147)
over 100,000	3.0%	6.1%
20,000–100,000	20.2%	13.6%
5,000–20,000	4.0%	12.9%
2,000–5,000	16.2%	17.7%
under 2,000	56.6%	49.7%

TABLE 2.6
Geographical Origins of Work Force from Wuerttemberg in Relation to DMG-Untertuerkheim

Occupation	Wuertt.	w/in 10 km.	10–25 km.	Rest of Land
Fitters & Toolmakers	454	207	95	152
Day laborers	294	138	51	105
Turners	216	137	38	41
Machineworkers	159	79	26	54
Body makers	122	48	37	37
Smiths	105	21	19	65
Woodworkers	77	35	19	23
Formers	35	24	2	9

TABLE 2.7
Workers' Homes in Relation to DMG-Untertuerkheim

Workers live:	No. of Workers
0–2 km from Ut.	488
2–3 km from Ut.	647
3–5 km from Ut.	207
5–7 km from Ut.	48
7–10 km	242
10–15 km	17
15–20 km	32
more than 20 km	19

TABLE 2.8

Time to Get to Work:	By Foot	By Train	By Foot & Train	Together
to 15 minutes	646	31	–	677
15–30 minutes	38	632	136	806
30–45 minutes	47	26	21	94
45 min.–1 hour	26	21	9	56
1–1½ hours	6	16	25	47
1½–2 hours	–	6	7	13
more than 2 hours	2	4	1	7
Total	765	736	199	1,700

TABLE 2.9
Positions of Fathers & Grandfathers of Daimler Workers
(from Questionnaire)

	Fathers' Positions	Grandfathers' Positions
Proletarian	63	45
Mittelstand	50	77
Land	23	125
Clerks	19	20
"Better Occupations"	6	15

3

THE WORKERS' MOVEMENT
AT DAIMLER, 1903–1914

I N the German Empire, the histories of the German working class, Social Democracy, and the trade union movement were virtually entwined. The Social Democrats found fertile ground for their brand of politics among the industrial workers of the burgeoning industrial economy. During the reign of Bismarck, the SPD became the largest party in the empire in terms of the number of votes it received. Following the relegalization of the party, the synthetic Erfurt Program of long and short-term goals authored by Social Democracy's leading theoretician, Karl Kautsky, helped the SPD's expansion continue. Each election brought new gains, although the "Hottentot election" of 1907 dealt the party a short-lived setback. In 1912, the SPD amassed the votes of over a third of the electorate. Meanwhile, the Free Trade Unions, associated with the SPD, recruited members from the working population, reaching nearly 1.7 million members in 1907. The much smaller Christian and the liberal Hirsch-Duncker associations also appealed to a number of workers, although both were of decidedly minor importance for the Stuttgart labor movement.

Alongside this success story, a war of position between party and union factions raged in the shadows. The party was split into revisionist and radical wings, with the Marxist center around Karl Kautsky straddling the conflicting camps. The leadership of the Free Trade Unions, claiming to be interested above all in "positive work" and "practical little tasks" to secure a degree of economic and social security for the working class in the present, sided with the revisionists. The unions' rank-and-file was less conservative, often providing the shock troops of radical social democrats. The great church of prewar German Social Democracy was filled with rancorous, dissonant choirs.[1]

This history has often been told, but one of its decisive battlefields was Stuttgart and Wuerttemberg. Here, as in Hessen, Baden, and Bavaria, the revisionists held sway, cementing their power with a state [Land] party apparatus and an organizational "doctrine of state's rights" which they pushed within the party. Under the hegemony of the revisionists like Wilhelm Keil, Berthold Heymann, Karl Hildenbrand, and Hugo Lindemann, the Wuerttemberg SPD steered a course of legislative cooperation in the Stuttgart Landtag. The party voted for the state budget, and its deputies were even received by King Wilhelm at court or attended official state banquets. Prominent party spokespersons from Wuerttemberg pushed some of the most abject positions which existed within prewar Social Democracy, including for example, support for German imperialism and colonialism. In what may have been a reaction to such policies, the party's share of the Wuerttemberg vote ran 5 percent behind its national totals.

Given the SPD's principled opposition to cooperation with imperial authorities, the moves and pronouncements of Wuerttemberg's party leaders stirred bitter dissension among rank-and-file Social Democrats, especially in cities like Stuttgart, Bad Cannstatt, Esslingen, and Goeppingen. The large local organizations were rife with Social Democrats—party moderates and radicals, sometimes members of the organization of the youth movement— who opposed the regional bureaucracy's growing détente with the authorities. The revisionists held onto power by insuring the representational predominance of rural and small-town clubs and by deftly wielding the SPD's state organization. As Schorske wrote, the Land organization of Wuerttemberg provided "an extreme example of how the regional leadership built its organization on the small town membership as a weapon against urban radicalism." The revisionists' manipulation of the state's party congresses aborted intra-party democracy, all in the name of a devotion to a higher "democracy"—the quasi-parliamentary institutions in Land and Reich.[2]

The German Metalworkers' Union (DMV), the largest of the big four unions (the other three were building, mining, and woodworking) that constituted the confederation of Free Trade Unions, was founded in Stuttgart and organized large contingents of workers in the metal and machine-building enterprises along the Neckar. Daimler and Bosch were the bastions of DMV strength in Stuttgart. The sites of DMV strength in Wuerttemberg —especially Stuttgart, Bad Cannstatt, and Esslingen—were the strongholds of the radical wing of the SPD in southwestern Germany. Confronted with the obstinacy of the machine politicians, these socialist clubs in urban Wuerttemberg were the "breeding ground" of the future revolutionary leadership in Germany. In the last prewar years, Friedrich Westmeyer, the brilliant chairman of the Stuttgart SPD, and Clara Zetkin, the editor of the socialist women's newspaper *Die Gleichheit,* became leaders of the area's Social Democrats. Wuerttemberg's organization may have been in the hands of the revisionists, but the party base, especially where metalworkers were numerous, was staunchly socialist.[3]

In addition to the presence of the trade unions in many workplaces and Social Democracy in the spaces open to political activity in the Reich, the leisure time social lives of many workers were spent within the vast subculture of the labor movement. As noted in the preceding chapter, workers belonged to a myriad of societies, which enriched their leisure and recreation. In the words of Richard Evans:

> A member of the party could read Social Democratic newspapers and borrow from a Social Democratic library books which covered every aspect of life from a Social Democratic point of view; he could spend his leisure in Social Democratic pubs, or gymnastic clubs, choirs, or cycling societies; he could enrich his life through Social Democratic culture and artistic associations; his wife could enlist in the Social Democratic Women's Movement and his son in the Social Democratic Youth Movement; if he was injured or fell ill, he could call upon the Working Men's Samaritan Federation to help him; if he died, there were Social Democratic burial clubs to see he received a decent burial.[4]

The labor movement in greater Stuttgart was characterized by powerful unions entrenched in the area's large and mid-sized workplaces, by tough-minded local Social Democratic clubs vigorously opposed to the far-reaching revisionism of the party's leaders at the *Land* level, and by a thick "social-cultural milieu" of recreational and educational societies.[5] Both the density and effervesence of the workers' movement in the communities along the Neckar River virtually insured that Daimler's large new works in Untertuerkheim would be caught up in the forward march of German labor.

THE LABOR MOVEMENT AT DAIMLER

ORGANIZING AUTO WORKERS

Hundreds of members of the German Metalworkers' Union took jobs at Daimler, and hundreds of Daimler workers joined the DMV during the first two years of the Untertuerkheim plant's operation. By early 1906, 1,500 (68%) of the 2,200 workers employed at Daimler were members of the DMV. Thus, Daimler's DMV contingent included one out of every four metalworkers who were organized in the DMV in the Stuttgart area.[6] In addition, another 400 or so Daimler workers were members of other Social Democratic unions in the Free Trade Union confederation, particularly the Woodworkers' Union. Only two years after the opening of the new factory, the stage was set for the first campaign by the unions at Daimler.

The decisive push to improve working conditions at the Untertuerkheim plant took place in early 1906.[7] The DMV's *Metallarbeiter-Zeitung* reported that a "wage movement" was spreading at the factory in February 1906, but in reality it was much more than that.[8] Led by the area chairman of the DMV, Karl Vorhoelzer, the movement strove to "attain up-to-date working conditions" at the largest factory in Stuttgart. The campaign centered around three central grievances, standard for the German metal and machine building industries in the decade before the war. The Daimler workers criticized the firm's practice of requiring personnel to perform long overtime hours, especially since "hundreds" of employees had to commute for more than an hour every day to get to the plant. The auto workers also blasted the masters' widespread practice of "regulat[ing] wages" by imposing arbitrary piece-rate schedules on their departments, which served to limit workers' earnings in the interests of keeping departmental costs down. In addition, the overwhelming majority of the work force complained of the excessive length of the work day, which averaged 10 1/2 hours not counting overtime in early 1906. Thus, the work week lasted 63 hours or more, while many workers faced lengthy commutes of up to an hour or more in each direction.

These complaints were voiced at a general factory assembly on Friday, February 9, 1906, attended by an estimated 1,700 of the firm's 2,200 workers. The mass meeting, which DMV chairman Vorhoelzer presided over, formulated a list of demands amid "stormy agreement" to redress the conditions prevailing at the factory during its first two years of operation. For one, the mass of Daimler workers demanded that their supervisors treat them "respectfully." To eliminate the discontent over the setting of wage rates, the employees asked the corporation to compose typed schedules of the piece-rates which would be readily made available to the workers at their request. This would prevent individual masters from imposing lower wage rates in order to trim departmental costs, those attending the meeting hoped. "Changes in the fixed piece-rates will only be made because of technical improvements and will be negotiated with a representative selected by the workers of the affected departments," according to the workers' proposal.[9] If an agreement between a master and a worker on a piece-rate could not be reached, the workers' committee should receive the right to take up the matter with Daimler's central direction. The workers also wanted an across-the-board 10 percent wage hike, as well as parity between piece- and hourly wage rates in certain types of assembly work in which the earnings of hourly workers were falling far behind those of their counterparts working in *Akkord*.

The mass meeting also proposed the limitation of overtime work "as much as possible" and the total elimination of the overtime work which was being performed during the mid-day break. The work day should be limited to nine hours, instead of the prevailing 10 1/2 hours.

The company appeared ready to negotiate. On February 16, Vorhoelzer and another DMV official, Wilhelm Bremer, met with Director Paul Daimler.[10] Although Daimler received them very politely, he told them that any agreement on changing conditions at the plant would have to receive the approval of DMG's six directors. Later the same day, DMG informed the union officials that it would not deal further with them but would talk with the workers' committee at the plant. Within days, the unions' shop stewards in the Untertuerkheim factory agreed to give the workers' committee the chance to conduct talks for the DMV. When confirmed on February 23 by another mass meeting of employees, this marked a major widening of the prerogatives of the plant's workers' committee, which had not hitherto ventured onto the terrain of the trade unions. Two sessions were needed, but the parties hammered out an agreement, the first ever at Daimler in Untertuerkheim, during the last days of February.[11]

The agreement between the parties regulated working conditions at the plant until the outbreak of the war, and is the single most important bellwether for assessing the achievements of the trade union movement at the Untertuerkheim factory during the last peacetime years of the *Kaiserreich*. The pact afforded the work force real improvements. Piece-workers won the right to check whether the rates in their departments agreed with the piece-rates set for similar work in the rest of the factory. Here the Daimler workers won a clear victory: in the event of disputes, a shop steward was entitled to confer with the master of the department. If the disagreement could not be resolved at this level, the workers' committee would be entitled to take up the matter with the direction.

The work force also made a major breakthrough in the campaign for a shorter work-day. Beginning on April 2, 1906, the working hours were to be set at 9 1/2 hours daily, with no loss in earnings for the workers. The new working hours were to run from 7:00 A.M. to 6:30 P.M. from Monday through Saturday, with a two-hour lunch break from 11:45 to 1:45 and fifteen-minute breaks at 8:00 A.M. and 4:00 P.M. The agreement also brought shift work to Daimler-Untertuerkheim for the first time. In the smith and in the big departments which performed most of their tasks on banks of machines—the turning and milling departments, for example, the pact paved the way for the introduction of two eight-hour shifts, with no subsequent loss of earnings for the workers. The double shifts in the smith and in the machine shops were to begin at 6:00 A.M. and 2:25 P.M. To minimize problems which might arise by forcing people to work the evening shift, the personnel working these shifts were to be rotated on a weekly basis. In addition, overtime was to be avoided if possible, although here the firm avoided making a firm commitment. Double shifts—forcing employees to work back-to-back shifts because of scheduling problems—would not be required of shift workers.[12]

This section of the agreement gave both the firm and the Metalworkers' Union an important victory. Daimler could now utilize its new machines and its modern forge with its complement of metal presses sixteen hours daily instead of ten, while the DMV gained an initial, partial recognition for its demand for an eight-hour day. It also wrested the firm's accession to similar wages and working conditions in any other department which converted to shift-work.

On March 2, 1906, an assembly attended by more than 2,000 workers voted nearly unanimously to accept this agreement. As the metalworkers' newspaper rejoiced, "In the largest factory in Wuerttemberg, the nine, in part the eight, hour day exists, with the preservation of the previous wage payments." Although the conflict had threatened to become "very serious," the union concluded that the "skill" of those sitting on the workers' committee in controlling the work force and the "discipline" of the unions' shop stewards at the plant had in the end contributed mightily to the achievement of this triumph.[13] The movement was thus a confirmation of the practical effectiveness of the organization.

Nevertheless, only three days after the mass meeting, 60 workers staged a job action in the turning department. The members of the DMV walked off the job following the promotion of a nonunion worker to the post of master of the department. The new appointee voluntarily resigned, and the turners resumed work after a two-hour strike. It is unclear whether the turners' action had been sanctioned by the union leadership. The annual report of the factory inspectors interpreted the action as an attempt by the union to spread its influence at the plant, but it appears much more to have been a spontaneous reaction to the appointment of an unpopular master than a well-planned action to wring new concessions from management.[14] The union did not even mention the dispute in its newspaper or in its yearbook.

In the wake of the struggle, the union also paid tribute to the sense of responsibility displayed by the Daimler management. But the most important factor in the triumph was the "reality that of the approximately 2200 workers at the factory, nearly 1900 are organized in the free trade unions, of whom over 1400 are in the DMV."[15] The firm had recognized the organizations of the work force in the course of the struggle and had officially recognized the agreement. The Metalworkers' Union hoped that its success at Daimler would serve as the model for breakthroughs at other smaller plants in the region.

In reality, working conditions at Daimler still lagged behind those at the Bosch factory in Stuttgart. Under the progressive leadership of the remarkable Robert Bosch, who knew Kautsky and was open to Social Democratic ideas early in his life,[16] the Bosch factory for electrical ignition systems had already instituted an eight-hour working day. Despite the comparatively short 48-hour work week, the 580 Bosch workers earned about as much as their counterparts at other firms in Stuttgart, no matter whether they worked for hourly wages or by the piece.[17]

Only 18 percent of the Stuttgart metal workers in the factories surveyed by the DMV put in longer hours than Daimler's set 54-hour week. The weekly wages paid by the Swabian auto giant were roughly on a par with those paid by other firms in the Stuttgart metal industry, although there are indications that they may have lagged behind the pay levels for 48 hours' work at Bosch, at least in several departments in 1906.[18]

Nevertheless, the gains made by Daimler workers in 1906 were real and important. Evaluating the situation in Untertuerkheim six months after the pact was reached, the DMV judged it a major success. Workers' earnings from the new 54-hour week were at least as high as those previously, and often higher. "This once again confirms the old lesson, that the shorter the work week, the higher the productivity and the earnings." Life in the individual workshops also seemed better, with fewer complaints about the capricious setting of piece-rates. Indeed, with the more orderly system of setting them, "the workers [have managed to] secure a certain co-determination right," the union concluded.[19]

An important result which passed unnoticed was the new prominence which the plant's workers' committee won as a result of the role it played in settling the dispute. The committee, which had existed prior to the newly won prominence of the union at DMG, consisted of representatives of the individual workshops at the factory. According to the body's statutes, each department had at least one seat on the panel, while larger workshops sent a representative for each 150 employees. While the workers' committees in nineteenth-century Germany had developed as bodies to assist management in administering certain social benefits for the work force, these organs were beginning by the turn of the century to articulate the growing aspirations of many workers to protect their interests in their places of work and to claim a right to have a say in the administration of the factory.[20] At Daimler, the workers' committee, which existed from the beginnings of the new factory, played a role in shaping the new factory regime in early 1906.

The DMV considered its victory at Daimler the most important in its campaign to organize the Stuttgart metal industry. The gains made by the Daimler work force were nonetheless fragile and had to be defended repeatedly in the coming years. Although the agreement on working hours at DMG lasted until the war, other parts of the agreement quickly became frayed when the general economic downturn severely ravaged the German automobile industry in 1907 and 1908 and threw a third of the Daimler work force on the unemployment lines.[21] Early in 1907, there were already the first reports of numerous layoffs at the plant, along with a rash of new complaints about declining piece-rates. The metalworkers' newspaper reported that a similar situation prevailed throughout the rest of the industry and urged its members "to avoid the area Stuttgart-Cannstatt-Untertuerkheim."[22]

The full force of the slump, however, struck DMG at the end of 1907. The maximum number of daily working hours was reduced to eight temporarily, while a total of 450 workers were laid off on consecutive Saturdays in early and mid-December. Soon, the firm was forced to increase working hours again to earlier levels so that "the best people"—as the union termed the firm's corps of skilled workers—would not wander away to seek work elsewhere.[23] In 1908, the size of the work force stabilized at 1,700 to 1,800 workers. By 1910, Daimler was rehiring workers as the demand for its products again increased.

1910: A LOCKOUT THREAT, OVERTIME, AND WORK RULES

By the end of 1910, disputes over overtime and piece-rates were flaring once again. This time, the unrest was precipitated by events taking place far away from Daimler and Stuttgart: on the wharves of Hamburg and other German ports. The dockworkers of the Hanseatic ports, organized in the Metalworkers' Union, had raised the banner for a nine-hour work day and a fairer regulation of piece-rates. The shipping companies, including the Krupp Dock, saw the movement as a threat to their prerogatives and locked out 60 percent of the workers. Rather than caving in, the rest struck.

The dockworkers' action came on the heels of the largest labor struggle in Germany to date, when the biggest building firms locked out hundreds of thousands of construction workers all across the Reich in a futile attempt to break their union. Threatening yet another nation-wide employers' action, Buerger, the chief of the Association of German Metal Industrialists (VDMI), announced in Berlin in late September that its members would lock out 60 percent of their workers to retaliate for the paralysis of the loading and shipping companies on the waterfront caused by the members of the Metalworkers' Union. Daimler, a member of the industrial organization, immediately notified 60 percent of its employees that they would be dismissed in two weeks.[24] This notification was necessary: under the work rules in effect at the plant, either the direction or the employee had to give two weeks notice of intention to terminate the employment contract.

In response, an aroused work force agreed to refuse all overtime work. In the final days of September and the first week of October, many workers in Daimler departments—particularly in the turning and milling departments—disobeyed the orders of the masters and refused to work overtime. Faced with the complete idling of the plant in fourteen days, the corporation threatened to fire immediately anyone who refused to work overtime. The workers charged that the firm wanted to hastily complete as much work as possible before the lockout, and they would not cooperate.[25] The company took no action against any of its rebellious employees.[26]

The employers in the shipping and metal industries shied back from the brink, reaching a settlement with the dockworkers on October 6 and rescinding the threat of a national lockout.[27] Daimler, too, took back its threat to lock out its employees, who, for their part, agreed once again to work overtime.

The incident, however, disconcerted the DMG management. Because of its requirements under the work rules, it had been forced to "tip its hand" to the workers fourteen days before it could actually mount its attack. To Berge and the Daimler company, it was clear that the notification requirement had to be excised form the rules—something that could be accomplished simply by inserting the words "if possible" after the provision in the work rules.[28] The purpose was simply to increase the firm's freedom to lock out its work force and to deal with troublesome employees. When the subject was broached in talks with the workers' committee, the members were adamantly in favor of retaining the notification clause. At a mass meeting on December 12, 1910, at the *Saengerhalle* in Untertuerkheim, the rank-and-file also demanded that the two-week notice be preserved.[29] The unspoken factor which probably influenced the work force in demanding retention of the notification period was the high unemployment prevailing in Stuttgart, where 9,000 men and women were looking for work during 1910.[30]

During the ensuing round of talks on December 23, the direction rejected the workers' committee's claim to speak in the name of the whole work force, since some workers had stayed away from the assembly in order to work overtime. The committee members replied with a request that Daimler poll its employees to show the overwhelming sentiment on behalf of retaining the notification requirement. The management rejected this, declaring that if "99% of all workers are for the retention of the notification, [the matter] remains at our disposal." Troubled by this attitude, a committee member asked what use it had if Daimler was not interested in consulting it on important factory issues. A director responded, "It has the right to express the wishes of the workers."[31]

Later the same day, notices were posted on bulletin boards announcing the end of the two-week notification requirement for dismissal, effective on January 9, 1911. Since the next day was Christmas eve, when the factory was on a partial schedule (it was closed on Christmas), the abrupt timing of the announcement seemed clearly intended to defuse opposition to the move.

Yet after the holiday, the employees mobilized to meet the challenge, and the workers' committee announced plans to hold mass meetings in the workshops at the close of work on Friday, December 30, 1910. So that all could attend, the committee urged all of its constituents to turn down any orders for overtime on the day of the assemblies, and informed management of its intentions. On the day of the scheduled assembly, the committee asked the firm to alter the working hours so that the assemblies could occur without any disturbance.

Berge and Daimler responded by denouncing this attempt "to break the [work] rules and to disturb the factory." Any assembly should be postponed and held at the close of work on Saturday, the firm maintained. Appealing to the "feeling of responsibility of our workers," the firm insisted that overtime work had to be performed.[32]

Nonetheless, the Daimler trade unionists and workers' committee, firmly backed by the local office of the DMV, pressed on with their plans. At 6:15 P.M., three assemblies of workers convened, one in the *Saengerhalle*, and the others in two pubs [*Kneipen*] in Untertuerkheim, the Rebstock and the Krone. According to the leaflets distributed at the plant, the main business was the "report of the workers' committee about the negotiations with the direction regarding the abolition of the notification period and the introduction of a work-free Saturday afternoon."[33]

Of 250 men ordered to work overtime on Friday, December 30, approximately 100 refused. Nearly all of them were from the milling shop and the department with company's automatic machines, with its large complement of trained machine workers. The turning shop, thought by management to be potentially one of the most troublesome departments, saw no concerted refusals to work overtime. There, apparently only the shop stewards turned down overtime, although all workers later joined the mass meetings, which were already in progress.[34]

The workers rejected the company's attempt to rescind the notification period. The assembly also voiced its sharp objections to what had once again become a widespread practice at Daimler—the lowering of piece-rates by individual masters "in a totally frivolous and unashamed fashion" to lower the costs of their departments. Workers at the meeting testified that masters invoked the threat allegedly posed by competing firms, asserting that production must become cheaper "even if everything could not be so carefully produced." Some alleged that masters even received bonuses for lowering the costs in their departments and thus "proving their abilities as masters." These masters often dealt quite abruptly with those shop stewards "called by the workers to have some say in setting the piece-rates." The Metalworkers' Union bemoaned the prevailing attitude of Berge and his colleagues at the factory, which represented "the masters as the purest angels, the workers as the worst lot who are always trying to damage the firm and to grab a lot of money for [doing] nothing." According to one account, the tenor of the workers at the meeting was "Yes, the time is coming when our patience will run out."

The open meetings approved a resolution—obviously prepared by the DMV—protesting the "unjust reduction of piece-rates" which had led to a "worsening of working conditions": despite long hours and grueling labor, "an acceptable earning cannot always be achieved." Technical improvements or simplification of the labor process might be reasons for lowering the piece-rates, but in such cases it was imperative that the rates be set "so ... that for the same level of work, at least the same earnings could be achieved." All should feel free to reject any rate which had been "set too low."

In addition, the Daimler assembly agreed that Saturday afternoons should be free time for the workers in the future. It was not uncommon for employees to toil overtime in the workshops until 11:00 P.M. on Saturdays. Indeed, the whole question of overtime hours came in for sharp criticism. Overtime was the rule at Daimler, the union claimed. "To our knowledge, it is the case in no [other] factory in Germany that the firm demands overtime hours for the set mid-day break!"[35]

In the wake of the severe slump which had shaken Daimler and other auto firms in 1907–1908, no longer was the Metalworkers' Union speaking of the situation at Daimler as being a model for the rest of the industry. Now the union was claiming the right of Daimler workers to the same limitations on overtime work which were the rule in other German metal firms. According to the union, most other firms in Stuttgart worked until no later than 2:10 on Saturdays. Despite DMG's "secure world-wide reputation," the firm insisted on working its employees long and hard.

In the aftermath of the meetings, Daimler dealt quickly with those who had refused overtime to attend. Letters were dispatched to the individuals involved: "You are fined one mark because of unexcused absence from work on December 30."[36] The disciplinary action was measured: about 1 1/2 hours' wages for a skilled worker.

Nevertheless, 77 workers filed a complaint with the *Gewerbegericht* in Stuttgart, requesting repayment of the one mark fine. They charged that the firm's disciplinary action was based on an arbitrary interpretation of the work ordinance in question, which had not in the past been used to prevent workers from attending to their interests. How could they be charged with staying away from work, they asked, when they had already worked the required nine hours that day? "We only wanted to take part in a meeting for the protection of our interests, which would have been made impossible for us by overtime work." It had been the policy of the firm and of all others in the metal industry to forgo overtime on the days of scheduled factory assemblies, the plaintants maintained. They cited the words of the Daimler director Vischer, who had told the former head of the workers' committee, Schlenker, that "If the workers hold assemblies, naturally no overtime can be demanded" to support their contention. The firm had always acted accordingly in the past. A more fundamental consideration, the workers held, was the nature of overtime work. "Overtime is not our duty *[Pflichtarbeit]*, but rests on reciprocal agreement," they emphasized.[37]

Daimler officials, for their part, asserted that the overtime work was necessary in late December, due to a strike at one of its parts suppliers. As a result, the firm had fallen more than four weeks behind in the production of cylinders and other components. These now had to be made in Untertuerkheim, requiring overtime in the machine departments, "the first stage in the construction of [these] components." If the machine departments could not take up the slack caused by the strike, there would be insufficient work for other departments, which might cause extensive layoffs. According to the firm, this was because of "the peculiar nature of automobile components," which, because of their unique specifications, could not simply be brought in from other plants.[38]

On February 1, 1911, the *Gewerbegericht* handed the workers an unexpected victory, ordering the company to pay back the fine which it had exacted. The important factor in its decision, the court stated, was that "for a long time, the accused has made overtime the rule, while it should only be an exception, as is generally known. . . . The accused is naturally obligated, through its recognition of the work rules, to make overtime the exceptional case and not the rule."[39] However, although 77 workers were a mark richer, the corporation had successfully repealed the notification requirement in the work rules.

1911: MECHANICS AND PIECE-RATES

When Daimler's stockholders assembled in the spring of 1911, they had reason to celebrate. Growing profits and rising dividends signalled an excellent business year. Moreover, Daimler was embarking on a historic adventure which would have important ramifications, not only for the firm but also for the German military: the production of engines for that newfangled heavier-than-air craft, the airplane.

If the stockholders turned their attention to the state of industrial relations, they had fewer reasons to crow. Tensions remained between employers and workers after the clashes of the preceding fall and winter. The most recent skirmish had occurred only weeks before, involving the skilled mechanics who worked in teams assembling motors. When DMG began to produce a new type of motor in 1911 and slashed the piece-rates by which the mechanics assembling it were paid, they struck. Twenty-five of the 28 strikers were members of the DMV, and sought to enlist the support of workers in other departments for their action. They pressed the plant's trade unionists to shut down another workshop at the facility in solidarity with their walkout, in order to press management to open talks and to find a quick settlement. To the surprise of many, the firm's direction quickly agreed to begin discussions "from organization to organization" on the whole range of unresolved complaints.[40]

The two sides made quick progress in the talks and quickly worked out a new initiative to tackle the chronic friction over piece-rates. To take some of the pressure off of those in the *Akkordsystem,* both parties agreed to the adoption of an hourly rate for piece-workers *(Akkordstundenlohn)* based on 90 percent of the average earnings of the piece-rate workers in the individual departments. This was to function as a minimum rate below which wage levels would not be allowed to fall.[41]

In addition, management and labor at the Mercedes plant worked out a new schedule which would give the work force " a free Saturday afternoon." By eliminating the daily afternoon breaks and shortening the lunch break by 15 minutes, the workers would be able to go home at 1:30 on Saturdays instead of 6:30. The new arrangement meant the workers would spend less time at the plant, although the length of the work week would remain unchanged at 54 hours.

In order to resolve the strike of assembly mechanics, Daimler, while refusing to raise the piece-rates in question, nevertheless made a concession which would allow them to recoup their losses. A measure of so-called "secondary work" [Nebenarbeit] which each had to perform on work-pieces would be eliminated. Thus, the assemblers would benefit from a further subdivision of the labor they performed, shortening the time they spent on each piece a little.

Some of the assembly mechanics had doubts about this arrangement. According to a union observer, they nevertheless felt "obligated to the work force of the entire factory" to accept the outcome of the talks, since it afforded the thousand-plus piece-workers the benefit of an acceptable minimum for their earnings. They did so unanimously. The rank-and-file also accepted the new provisions, which Daimler trade unionists greeted as "a small step forward."[42]

THE LOCKOUT OF 1911: RESISTANCE TO OVERTIME AND FIRINGS

Within only a couple of months, the truce between the parties had broken down, and 2,600 workers found themselves on the street at the end of July 1911, locked out by Daimler. The confrontation began on Friday, July 28, as southwestern Germany was sweltering through a lengthy heat wave.[43] Two workers from the metal-milling department, a heavily mechanized workshop at the plant crucial for the production of most engine components, were dismissed by management as the result of an incident which the union considered a "trifle," but which the firm apparently saw as disruptive and agitational.[44] According to various newspaper accounts, the two had expressed their objections to Daimler's continuing practice of demanding overtime work during the lunch break. At least a portion of this overtime work was being carried out voluntarily by workers who lived too far away from the factory to go home for lunch. Several were willing to work at the milling machines instead of sitting around the cafeteria for the bulk of the 1 3/4 hour break and had reportedly asked the master to provide them with extra work.

This provoked discord among other members of the steamy milling workshop, who let their disdain for their fellows freely show. A shop steward from the union allegedly snapped, "It's all the same to me whether they croak or work." To which a miller chimed in, "To me, [overtime work during the lunch break] is a scam and a navish trick." At least one of the millers tattled, telling a supervisor that he had been insulted by the pair's remarks. The direction promptly fired the two, charging that they had verbally harrassed their fellow workers and were attempting to hinder overtime work. Although one of the two had been working there since the plant opened in late 1903, and the other for 18 months, management told the two to leave immediately.[45]

On Saturday, when the members of the 100-strong milling department learned what had happened, they sullenly stood around the shop, refusing to work. After a few hours, a handful started to work, but these soon quit again. By 10:00, the department was at a complete standstill. In other parts of the factory, protests erupted against the dismissals, and more workers stopped work.

Faced with this insurrection in one of its key machine departments and with the real threat of its spreading, the DMG direction decided to shut down the entire factory as work was ending at 1:30 P.M., locking out 2,600 employees. The firm told the press that its production schedule demanded that all workshops operate together at all times. Thus, because of the stoppage by the millers, the plant's functions had been completely disrupted. It is likely, however, the lockout was intended to prevent worker resistance from spreading further and escalating into a full-scale strike.

Daimler-Untertuerkheim remained closed for eight days. On Wednesday of the following week, negotiators from the Association of Wuerttemberg Metal Industrialists and the workers' unions finally began talks. The way to a settlement had been eased by the two dismissed workers themselves, who withdrew their requests to be reinstated, asserting that they would not last long at the plant if they returned to work. The parties reached a compromise settlement on Friday.[46]

The agreement sought to regulate the dismissal process in order to avoid future complaints. "Unanimous agreement was expressed on all sides that this incident would not have occurred if an authority chosen by the workers could have smoothly stepped in," the DMV reported. The innovation was the introduction of a three-hour grace period after the notification of a worker of his firing. During this time, the employees had the right to appeal, with the help of the workers' committee, to the firm's directors to reverse the dismissal. The workers' committee itself was to be democratized further, with plant elections forthcoming. This settlement, supported by the DMV, was ratified by the shop stewards and then approved at a mass meeting in Untertuerkheim attended by 3,000 locked-out workers and their supporters. Perhaps the pact was not overwhelmingly popular: the union newspaper merely mentioned that "a majority" of the millers had approved it.[47]

Reflecting on the affair, a union spokesman at Daimler laid the blame for the affair on the inability of the "northerners" in the management at Daimler to understand the "direct" and blunt manner with which the Swabian workers expressed their thoughts. "Outsiders" had disturbed the tranquility in Untertuerkheim.[48]

Ernst Berge, the factory's top officer, set a different accent. His company had successfully met the challenge posed by two "agitators," who had tried to "instigate" trouble. Nevertheless, in the last seven years, Daimler had "filled many of the wishes" of the work force. Although "employers and employees remain two economic opposites," and the "future will not be free of differences," Berge contended that industrial relations at DMG were reasonably smooth.[49]

For the firm, the experience of the previous five years had shown that profitability and concessions to the work force were not incompatible. For the powerful DMV and workers' committee on the shop floor, the lesson was that gains resulted from patient work and would have to be doggedly defended in order to be kept. Yet as ill- fated the strike at Bosch in 1913 showed to trade unionists in Stuttgart, one false step and nearly all could be quickly lost.

INTERLUDE: "LUGINSLAND" & HOUSES FOR DAIMLER WORKERS

It would be needlessly narrow to believe that the workers' movement labored solely on the classic terrain of the trade unions and the political organizations. Indeed, one of the striking achievements at Daimler was the successful endeavor by the workers themselves to build houses near the factory. Although this effort did not directly involve the organizations of the working class, it provided the opportunity for workers to build new living quarters and to build the framework for an autonomous proletarian community on the edges of bourgeois society for two decades.

Most immediately, however, the building project was the direct response by Daimler workers to the severe housing shortage in the area. By 1911, the Daimler-Motoren-Gesellschaft employed 3,000 workers, and the other industrial firms in Untertuerkheim and Bad Cannstatt provided work for another 2,000. One of the ill effects of this growth of industry along the Neckar was a shortage of affordable housing in eastern Stuttgart, Bad Cannstatt, and Untertuerkheim. The seriousness of this shortfall was documented by two investigations published in 1911, one by the Stuttgart branch of the Metalworkers' Union, the other by the Social Democratic League of the greater Stuttgart area. Rents in Cannstatt, Untertuerkheim, and Wangen reached 300–400 marks monthly for two-rooms and 400–500 marks for a three-room dwelling.[50] The trains which brought workers to and from Daimler were packed, and many others trudged to and from work with backpacks for carrying their food and drink for the day on their backs—Daimler's "Indians with back-packs [Rucksack Indianner]," the local inhabitants called them. The Metalworkers' Union estimated that Daimler employees lived in 100 municipalities throughout the area because they could not find housing in the immediate area, and that the trip to the plant often took an hour. Frequently, five or six people lived packed together in a one or two room flat.[51]

Neither state nor industry in Wuerttemberg moved to meet the acute need of working families for shelter. In Untertuerkheim in 1911, a group of nine Daimler workers organized a small discussion of the housing shortage. Out of it came the "decision to lead to the foundation of a building cooperative [Baugenossenschaft]." Those pioneering the idea appointed a three-member committee to work out the details and statutes of the group. By July, the building cooperative had set up a savings association. At year's end the group's savings totaled a modest 2,000 marks. The first year-end report noted that "these people gave us their money without any security." Since the group could not afford to hire a lawyer, the three-member committee hammered out the legal and financial details of the venture in the evenings after work.

The coop's first attempt to buy land in the nearby community of Muenster foundered when real estate speculators got wind of the project. Before the group of Daimler workers could purchase the desired tract of land, its price rocketed from 0.96 marks to over 2.00 marks per square meter. Rather than "benefit the land speculators," the group canceled the Muenster project.

Nevertheless, the dedicated group worked on. At a meeting of 19 workers on December 16, 1911, the members approved the founding statutes and chose five of their colleagues to sit on the board of directors and another six for a supervisory board. All of the members were skilled metalworkers from Daimler. Three assembly fitters, a metal-press operator and a lathe-turner formed the board of directors. Two mechanics, a machine-tool maker, a copper smith, and an assembly fitter constituted the oversight board.[52] Skilled metalworkers like these were the backbone of the labor movement in Stuttgart.

The goals of the cooperative were stated clearly in its first flyer: "We are determined to produce affordable housing." One of the statutes described the type of housing then envisioned: "single family houses with fruit and vegetable gardens, common facilities, in order to promote the bodily and mental soundness of the residents, and [a co-op] for the buying and selling of furnishings for the houses and gardens at cost."

Preparatory work proceeded slowly in 1912. Otto Hirsch, an official of the city of Stuttgart, gave the group legal advice before it formally filed its papers in Bad Cannstatt on February 5, 1912. Its official name was "Garden City Home of One's Own, a non-profit, family house-building cooperative." Two days later the group held an open meeting in the Daimler cafeteria attended by 600 workers. "Disappointingly little" came of it, for most workers doubted that their colleagues—who, after all, toiled full-time six days a week with them—could actually run such a project in their spare time.

Nevertheless, the dedicated group labored on, and was soon ready to bid for a tract of land in the nearby community of Heumaden, about four kilometers south of the factory. Here, too, their efforts came to naught. The plans were fought by a group of bourgeois residents in the village who saw the danger of "every kind of riff-raff [Lumpenpak] coming into the community." In addition, several members of the cooperative were dissatisfied with the new location. At the same time, the land speculators struck again, and the price for the tract soared from 0.70 marks to 4.00–6.00 marks per square meter. The coop soon broke off the negotiations.[53]

The coop finally procured a piece of land on its next try. An Untertuerkheim architect, Wilhelm Wacker, suggested that the directors look into a parcel of land on a hill north of the factory in Untertuerkheim. Bounded by vineyards and orchards, and with schools and the factory gates within a short walking distance, this was a prime piece of real estate. Within three days, a deal was worked out with the owners for the sale of the land at a price of 518,000 marks, (about 6.00 marks per square meter), a higher price than the coop members had wanted to pay.

Although it took considerable pains to work out the terms of the mortgage agreements for the purchase of the land, the coop finally succeeded on October 7, 1912. The funds were provided by an insurance company, two savings banks, the industrialist Robert Bosch, and the Daimler-Motoren-Gesellschaft.[54] The 100 comrades of the building cooperative provided 69,000 marks of their own savings.

Daimler's share amounted to approximately one-third of the mortgage money, lent at 4 percent interest. Ernst Berge and Gustav Vischer were key corporate supporters of the project. Daimler's support of the project was founded, in part, on its concern for the acute housing shortage which had a negative effect on the labor market in the area. Part of DMG's support, however, was politically motivated. Vischer's son, himself an engineer at the firm, later volunteered an explanation for the company's support of the Luginsland project: "My father said that the struggle against Social Democracy can best be waged if the people are allowed to get a little property because then they will become alienated from the social democratic movement and will become solid citizens [Buergerleute]."[55] A more immediate concern to the directors may have been a desire to improve relations with the workforce in the wake of the protracted conflicts and lockout of the preceding year.

Now that a parcel of land had been procured, the architect Wacker drew up plans for a colony of 342 houses and gardens. Once financing was obtained, construction began immediately. Although it was still unfinished (there were as yet no doors and windows), the first 55 families moved into "Luginsland" on July 1, 1913. In October, another 33 arrived.[56] The colony had a large communal canteen, which was the center of Luginsland's social life. A branch of the Cannstatt-Feuerbach consumer cooperative opened at the colony to procure food and other supplies for its families.

The total cost of the first Luginsland project was 852,757 marks. The average cost per house totalled 9,690 marks, approximately the cost of 13 to 14 years' rent in the Bad Cannstatt-Untertuerkheim area. For the money, a buyer received a two-story residence with two rooms on each floor. The reactions were generally favorable: "The inhabitants of our houses feel happy and satisfied in their own places," reported the coop's directors at the end of 1913.

The next project, designed by another local architect, Hermann Moser, began in 1914 but was interrupted by the start of the war. Anxiety about the war and the deteriorating economic situation of the populace took its toll on the cooperative; by the end of 1915, the number of members in the cooperative had fallen from 223 to 202. As scarcity, price hikes and the resulting distress spread, the directors concluded that "we have the best hopes and prospects for a secure and prosperous progress if the war comes to an end soon" and decided that "further construction during the war is ruled out." Construction of housing did not resume until 1919.[57]

The 500 residents of the community moved to meet the problems caused by the wartime conditions by aiding each other. On at least one occasion, enemy pilots hurled crude bombs out of their biplanes as they buzzed Daimler and Luginsland. They exploded harmlessly in nearby fields. A far more severe menace for the community was scarcity. The gardens proved to be a critical source of fruits and vegetables at a time when supplies of milk and meat were uncertain, and quite dear at that. In March 1917, several of the residents joined together to form a small enterprise to produce and sell apple cider. Others felt that the existence of such a private firm at Luginsland contradicted the cooperative spirit of the settlement. This view prevailed: the firm with all of its equipment was taken over by the whole cooperative after the war. Another product of the war years was a volunteer fire department, which consisted of 30 men. The whole community turned out to watch its first practice session.

When the war ended, plans for the construction of a group of row houses began immediately. Faced with a shortage of building supplies, the group produced concrete blocks from supplies of cinders—an industrial waste product—provided by Daimler and by the gas company in Stuttgart. Indeed, Daimler offered "broad support" to this new construction project at Luginsland, again lending financial assistance and giving the coop's chairman a four-week leave of absence to round up building materials. Berge even allowed him to use one of the firm's telephones. The revolution had had an impact. Soon, work on 61 more housing units, each with three, four, or five rooms and a kitchen, had been completed.

The postwar years were filled with political tensions between Social Democrats and Communists, which often erupted into arguments at the meetings of the cooperative's members. Yet these never crippled the social life of the community, which flourished as Luginsland slowly grew. By 1920, groups of gymnasts, athletes, nature-lovers, and gardeners were thriving at

Luginsland, and the annual garden show and the festival of children were the highlights of the colony's life. The *Saengerkreis Luginsland*, founded in 1920, was a well-known workers' choir in the area. A women's choir was added in 1924. In addition, the Socialist Workers Youth Group, tied to the SPD, organized an especially successful educational group. Soon, a kindergarten was also added.[58]

The slow expansion of the community continued through the rest of the Weimar Republic. Another 161 units were added before Hitler became chancellor in 1933. Although construction continued under the National Socialist regime, the life of the community was shattered by the arrival of the first Nazi settlers. Luginsland, which, with its strong socialist leanings, had seen little Nazi encroachment before the collapse of the republic, now endured the inevitable "coordination" of its board of directors and supervisory board in 1933. General meetings were no longer given over to lively discussion and debate; they were now vehicles for "leaders" to issue their orders to the inhabitants of Luginsland.

According to a chronicler of the "garden city," the new Nazi authorities and settlers were greeted with "dogged resistance." Another account mentions that the settlement was a center of Social Democratic and Communist opposition to National Socialism. The residents avoided mixing with the newcomers. Soon, the social network built up over the past two decades shriveled and died. The *Saengerkreis* was dissolved in 1933 and re-founded under Nazi sponsorship that December. By the time the 25th anniversary of its foundation was celebrated in 1936, the community's commemorative *Festschrift* heralded its new place in the National Socialist *Volksgemeinschaft*.[59]

Whereas nearly all of the residents in the 1910s and 1920s were industrial workers from Daimler, many of the newcomers were white collar workers. In 1936, 120 of the 467 members of the cooperative were white collar workers, officials, or independent small businessmen. Fully four-fifths of the 293 industrial workers living at Luginsland worked at Daimler-Benz. Luginsland's board of directors in its anniversary year included Georg Gienger, the local Nazi leader, as well as Wilhelm Hilzinger, a senior auditor in the regional government.[60] Workers had ceased playing a prominent role in directing the community's affairs; the working people of Luginsland were not to be trusted with leading roles in the Nazi *Volksgemeinschaft*.

■

In the summer of 1914, the Daimler-Motoren-Gesellschaft was a successful producer of automobiles and high-performance engines for airplanes. The company's factory brought together hundreds of skilled workers from nearly all branches of the metal and machine trades, along with contingents of hand workers, machine workers, and unskilled day laborers, who worked together to turn out some of the most highly renowned motors and vehicles in the world.

The friction over wages and working conditions typical of many factories in the German metal and machine-building industry marked relations between labor and management in Untertuerkheim. Nevertheless, the workers at Daimler confronted a management which, although sometimes loathe to cooperate with trade union representatives, never attempted to smash their organizations in the prewar years, in sharp contrast to the anti-union obstinence of employers in the mining, chemical, textile, and iron and steel industries.[61] The work force, organized by the DMV, DHV, and the tiny, barely visible, Christian and liberal unions, had managed to win recognition from the firm's owners, and the workers' committee at the plant, dominated by representatives who were near the DMV and the Social Democrats, helped to police a situation in which wages and working conditions were average for the area's factories. In the summer of 1914, despite a decline in the company's important export sales, the immediate future seemed rosy. The domestic market was bouyant and Daimler's share in it seemed secure. For the company, the July crisis and the outbreak of the general European war came like a bolt of the blue. The founding era of Mercedes—symbolized by the innocence of racing and luxury cars—was swept away within weeks, as Daimler became a major military producer in the Reich.

4

WORLD WAR I
AT THE DAIMLER-
MOTOREN-GESELLSCHAFT

IMPERIAL Germany went to war in August 1914. Her "grasp at world power" ignited a general armed conflict in Europe unprecedented in the age of industrial capitalism. As the struggle grew more desperate, reaching a new level of horror at the battle of the Somme in the summer of 1916, the continuation of the escalating terror necessitated the mobilization of the masses and the mass production of the new technologies of death on a unique scale. Total war strained imperial economy and society and highlighted the weakness of the Wilhelmine political system.

The war precipitated great changes in German society and politics, most of which directly affected the Daimler work force.[1] With the mobilization for war, the German Reich was recast, and new, militarized relations of authority emerged from the womb of the Kaiserreich. On Mobilization Day, the government invoked the Prussian emergency legislation of June 4, 1851, and proclaimed a state of siege. The legislation placed military officers at the head of the 24 army regions in Germany, who were responsible only to the Kaiser for preserving the "public security" in their districts. According to article 68 of the Reich constitution, the Kaiser could declare a state of war if the "public safety of the realm" was threatened. Until a law to suit the actual conditions could be drafted and approved—and, hardly surprising amidst the rush of events, one never was—the provisions of the Prussian law of 1851 for a military administration remained in effect.[2]

With such a vague mandate, the new authorities—the deputy command-ing generals, for the commanders were at the fronts—were in reality little dictators, intervening often in many aspects of society and politics "along-side or even against" the provincial and state authorities.[3] In Stuttgart and Wuerttemberg, which formed the Reich's district 13, General Otto von Marchthaler and, after 1916, General Paul von Schaefer were the command-ing officers.

After the German army failed to deliver the knockout blow against its enemies in the first weeks of the war, the important task for the Reich became the procurement of weapons, ammunition, and supplies for the armed forces on an unprecedented scale. Although the Prussian War Minis-try in Berlin had the task of coordinating the procurement contracts, the regional authorities generally saw their role as removing the obstacles to the necessary production of the wares of war. Workers and raw materials were industry's most critical needs. As one historian has asserted, "the responsible military authorities influenced to an increasing degree . . . the prerequisites for an undisturbed production. The general working conditions and wage relationships of the industrial work force, as well as the sufficient provision-ing with food and supplies but also the setting of corporations' prices were drawn into the authorities' field of activity." In other words, the require-ments of a war economy and the existing industrial economy did not entirely coincide. An official in the Prussian War Ministry expressed the sentiments of many officials when he declared: "War economy does not mean to run the economy in wartime in such a way as to create the least economic damage. War economy means much more to run it in such a way that one wins the war."[4]

The results were the unprecedented militarization of the German state, as well as the penetration of state power into most aspects of German society. Many contemporary analysts and historians conceived of this wartime situ-ation as marking a whole system of "war" or "state socialism."[5] The wielding of state power by military officers with seemingly open-ended prerogatives, who often did not hesitate to intervene in many areas of economic life to see to it that German forces received adequate provisions, supposedly produced far-reaching systemic changes, which saw army, indus-try, and labor movement bargain at the highest level of the German institu-tional edifice and set the stage for the social partnership of November 1918.[6] However, Wilhelmine capitalism—the most dynamic in Europe at the start of the twentieth century—had already developed into a cartelized and con-centrated industrial and financial ensemble.[7] Only after the summer of 1916 did emergency measures collide with the political-economic structure. The vigor and organizational adaptability of German industry allowed effective economic mobilization which could be translated into military power at the fronts.

The German authorities' opening to labor remained limited, and was unpopular with many representatives of German private industry. For example, as Gerald Feldman points out, "until October 1918 the leaders of heavy industry were, with few exceptions, adament in their refusal to accept collective bargaining."[8] In their opposition, they were joined by many workers who favored competing schemes of "co-determination" or even socialist revolution.

Therefore, we should resist the temptation to view the politics of 1914–1918 in an overly schematic manner which attributes a much more systemic quality to often improvised political developments than they can bear. To be sure, unions, industrialists, and army officers negotiated frequently during the war, and union officials achieved a position in these discussions which surpassed anything they had previously attained.[9]

Nevertheless, whether viewed from the angle of wages, working conditions, or workers' power in determining or even "co-determining" their economic fates, the results seem meager indeed, and are certainly difficult to package neatly as the coming of a new social partnership. State intervention (in the form of military power) did not alter the relations of production in the German economy during World War I, of course; nobody seriously makes such a claim today. Wartime governmental initiatives generally operated within the general apparatus of "organized capitalism" painstakingly assembled during the heady, self-satisfied decades of industrial expansion preceding the war. It was, more often than not, a welter of improvisations and pragmatic measures taken in a new type of wartime situation which no one fully understood. As we shall see, the result of the military's interventions at Daimler in Stuttgart-Untertuerkheim was usually the strengthening of the firm and its furious accumulation of profits, even when the army intervened in spectacular fashion to suspend the firm's manager and to erect a military supervision over the corporation in March 1918. Yet this was not the immediate intention of the authorities; indeed, as will be seen, it is wrong to attribute any motives to the military's intervention at DMG other than the removal of immediate obstacles to war production.

BUILDING THE ENGINES OF WAR

It is worth noting the new, central role which industrial corporations played in the first general European war in a century. This may seem at first an obvious point; yet when one recalls that political and military leaders had no experience in mobilizing for a war of this type and duration, their actions between 1914 and 1918 appear less systematic and more improvised. Total war, with an unprecedented reliance on weaponry and supplies made available only through large privately held industrial firms and their new production techniques, was new; the belligerents' perceptions of it dawned only gradually with the disappointments of indecisive campaigns in 1914.

The industrial revolution effected a major transformation in the conduct of war by the early twentieth century. Indeed, in the words of one author, "now the machine came to assist war, and war in return promoted the transition to the age of the machine." Warfare now necessitated unprecedented economic mobilization.[10] The railroad system was a critical element in the planning of military officers, both for the mobilization of men and material at the onset of war and for the resupply of the armies in the field. In addition, all of the industries which supplied equipment for the war had become dependent on the reliable transportation of their products by the railroads. With the onset of the age of motorization in the early twentieth century, the armies saw the possibilities inherent in the transportation of men and supplies with motor vehicles. Heavy artillery and high-level officers could both be transported around the fronts more easily with the new technology of the motor vehicle. In addition, the airplane and the submarine increased the possibilities of effectively attacking the forces and interests of an opponent. As one of the leading producers of motors in Wilhelmine Germany, it was inevitable that Daimler would become an important participant in war-time mobilization and production.

In addition to the new modes of transport and the new engines of war which industry in the early twentieth century could offer the military, the new production processes, especially mass production utilizing a highly developed division of labor and increasingly sophisticated machinery for taking over many tasks, proved critical to the war efforts of the participants in the carnage of 1914–1918. Ties between industrial firms and the military establishments had grown closer for decades before the war, with the powerful German fleet a result of the conjunction. On a much smaller scale, as we have seen, Daimler vehicles were being employed by the German army in its maneuvers by 1900,[11] and the company received military subsidies to develop new vehicles for the armed forces in 1910. Soon after the first successful flight of a heavier-than-air machine took place in December 1903, Daimler and the German army were already working together on an aviation development program. Indeed, Paul Daimler had taken up the design of aircraft motors after the Wright brothers' successful flight.[12]

Daimler eventually supplied a wide range of products to the war effort, including heavy transport vehicles and parts for submarine engines. In the early stages of the war, general director Berge reflected on the significance of the war for his industry: "The war may have shown us so many frightful [things], but for [motorization] it was the most excellent propaganda which one could think up. Through this war, the irreplaceability of the automobile has been shown to the whole world."[13]

Yet DMG's most important contribution was in its role as Germany's largest supplier by far of airplane motors. Indeed, during the war, 46 percent of all German airplane engines were provided by the Daimler-Motoren-Gesellshaft (see table 4.1).[14] The production of such motors was deemed urgent by the Prussian military authorities. The war ministry in Berlin gave DMG and other firms producing airplane motors special treatment in the provision of workers and raw materials from the early weeks of the war, a "Hindenburg Program from the beginning on," as the chief of the *Luftfahrabteilung*, Oschmann, described it before a Reichstag Committee in 1918. The industry's high priority status stemmed from the commission which met in the Reichstag on August 6 and 7, 1914, and gave the Reich's air force "a mandate from the German people."[15] In early October, the Prussian War Ministry ordered that the productivity of the airplane industry be raised in the "interest of the defense of the nation," and decreed that workers irreplacable to this effort be freed from military service.[16] As the top man at Daimler put it, "The airplane is the eye of the army,"[17] and many eyes were necessary for a two-front war.

The company produced numerous models of airplane motors during the war, but only five types in large quantities. The smallest was the DI, a 100 horsepower engine which Daimler was already producing in large numbers by 1913. At the outbreak of the war, the "catalogue price" for this motor was 11,500 marks.[18] Two other models were under development when hostilities commenced: the D II (120 horsepower) and the D III (160 horse-

TABLE 4.1
Largest German Producers of Airplane Motors, 1914–1919

	100 hp	150 hp	200 hp	300 hp	Total	% of Total
Daimler	1,727	977	12,163	5,009	19,876	46
Benz	–	505	3,162	7,693	11,360	26
Oberursel	1,391	834	707	–	2,932	6.7
Opel	–	–	2,260	–	2,260	5.2
Argus	390	837	–	–	1,257	2.8
Maybach	–	–	–	1,123	1,123	2.4

Source: AGM DBAG, K. Schnauffer, *Die Motorentwicklung in der Daimler-Motoren-Gesellschaft 1907–1918*, 1956, Anlage 63, unpublished manuscript.)

power). Two even more powerful engines were developed during the war: the D IV, at 220 horsepower, and one called the "new type" and the D IVa in the documents, a motor rated at 260 horsepower.[19]

The production of airplane motors was possible without drastically altering the production processes at Daimler. Simply put, the Daimler airplane motors resembled the Daimler auto and truck motors in their fundamental designs and components. Thus, metal workers in the foundry and smith fabricated the basic components from iron, steel, and copper. The workers on the banks of machines—both those skilled and those only "trained"— formed and honed them to a multiplicity of exact specifications, while fitters and mechanics assembled and adjusted the motors. During the whole process, day laborers provided critical support and moved parts and materials around the large (and ever-growing) plant.

Nevertheless, the enormous dimensions of the aeronautical production programs at Daimler made possible economies of scale unlike anything ever seen before in Untertuerkheim. For the first time, large-scale serial production by the thousands of a handful of set types—the basis, after all, for Ford's American success—came to DMG and to the German automobile industry. The Wilhelmine military and political system provided the spark, not the entrepeneurial vision of the company's management. Daimler merely organized the procedures, and reaped the benefits.

The outline of the transition to war production at Daimler and other motor-building factories was agreed to at a meeting on September 3, 1914 involving the representatives of the army and the navy, a commission of Reichstag deputies and directors from the companies which produced airplane motors. The meeting agreed on prices which the military would pay for the wares of the firms. Daimler would manufacture the engines for the army at a hefty 90 percent of the catalogue price "in view of the rising cost of raw materials." The price was generous; 55 of the DI motors were quickly provided for the war effort in the first weeks of the conflict, with 525 by the end of the year.[20]

One year after the first Berlin meeting, on August 28, 1915, the *Inspektion der Fliegertruppen* and Daimler officials met at Untertuerkheim and agreed on an upward revision of prices. In the following year's talks, Daimler agreed to give the air force an 8 percent rebate on its business volume in excess of 8 million marks monthly. By that time, the reduced costs and increased profits accruing from mass production were apparent in DMG's growing dividend payments to its stockholders.

By then, Daimler's production had begun to shift to the D III, 160 horsepower engine, which would become the staple of DMG's contribution to the air war. Daimler had constructed 1,169 of these by the end of 1915, as well as 1,681 of the smallest D I motors and 598 of the D II engines. In 1916 and 1917, the Daimler-Motoren-Gesellschaft built 6,494 of the D III's, as well as 2,881 powerful motors of the D IVa, 260 horsepower model. During the same years, it delivered only 50 of the small D I's and 92 of the D II's. The monthly production totals indicate that the firm delivered the most engines in January 1918 (735), before its production slumped drastically in February to 486 units, helping set the stage for the March 1918 crisis. The worst months were January 1917 (249), May 1917 (275), and June 1917 (293) (see table 4.2).[21]

Despite the production slump in January 1917 and its hefty dividends payments, Daimler requested a large 50 percent price increase for the spare parts it provided, which the authorities in Berlin quickly turned down.[22] By the summer, DMG was pressing for new price adjustments for airplane motors because of rising wage and material costs. In a forceful letter to War Ministry officials dated June 20, 1917, Berge cited wage increases granted to the work force in November and December 1916 and June 1917 which had made labor 33 1/3 percent dearer. According to the company, prices should also be increased 10 percent across the board. The firm even invited the *Inspektion der Fliegertruppen* to test its claims: "In case you have the wish to test [the situation] yourself, we ask you . . . to send a neutral man to our factory and we will gladly show comparable wage and price lists in the

TABLE 4.2
Production of Airplane Motors at Daimler, 1914–1918

	1914	1915	1916	1917	1918
January		163	257	249	735
February		295	257	444	486
March		213	211	508	449
April		270	352	402	590
May		221	348	275	602
June		171	332	293	595
July		259	362	406	598
August	36	233	382	622	694
September	85	320	458	591	n.a.
October	137	213	386	633	n.a.
November	133	327	489	679	n.a.
December	152	311	345	497	n.a.

Compiled from AGM DBAG DMG 17 (84), Produktion neuer Motoren . . . , and HStASt M 77/1 76, M.A. 265.

original from our purchasing office."[23] Berge's offer to allow inspection of some of the firm's books marked a notable change in Daimler's standing position.

On July 12, 1917, the *Inspektion* told DMG that its pricing requests would be referred to higher authorities in the war ministry. By February 1918, Daimler had not yet received a reply to its earlier request for the price increase. While thousands of Daimler engines provided the backbone for Germany's fleet of biplanes, the relationship between firm and military was becoming frayed over the issue of money.

Although Daimler's production schedule was dominated by the manufacture of airplane motors, it also produced motorized land vehicles for the war effort (see table 4.3). Many of these were produced at the works in Berlin-Marienfelde. Most were larger and heavier than the renowned automobiles for which Daimler had become famous. Some bore large artillery pieces; others moved men and supplies.[24] After the allies had begun to deploy tanks on the western front, Daimler became involved, at the behest of the military authorities in Berlin, in a project along with Krupp to build German tanks. For its part in this program, Daimler demanded a large sum of money from the military to cover its investment in the program in man-hours and expansion of the facilities.

During the war, Daimler received contracts worth hundreds of millions of marks from the army, astronomical sums for a firm which had averaged only a fraction of the wartime volume in the last prewar years. The Prussian War Ministry placed its orders with Daimler through numerous contracts for limited numbers of engines and vehicles. Even given wartime inflation, the magnitude of these contracts is indicated in a rare surviving document: in September 1917, DMG's board of trustees was informed that 385 million

TABLE 4.3
DMG's Production of Vehicles for the Ground War

Year	Cars Produced 1913 = 100	Heavy Vehicles Produced
1913	1,567 (100)	358 (100)
1914	1,404 (89.6)	568 (159.6)
1915	1,302 (83.1)	605 (169.0)
1916	428 (27.3)	718 (200.6)
1917	401 (25.6)	792 (221.2)
1918	108 (6.7)	996 (278.2)

Source: AGM DBAG Statistik.

marks of army orders were currently on the books, with 240 million for airplane motors and 86.4 million for artillery vehicles which Daimler was also building in a joint venture with Krupp.[25]

As a result, Daimler greatly expanded its facilities to handle these orders. Many firms were not enthusiastic about drastically enlarging their facilities, but during the first three years of the war, Daimler did not share their reticence. The factory in Untertuerkheim grew enormously, especially between 1915 and 1917, with new buildings going up on the land along the Neckar southwest of the Cannstatter *Wasen* which DMG had acquired.[26] The total work force increased four and one-half fold, to more than 15,200. A new factory was opened in Sindelfingen, an hour south of Stuttgart by rail, as was a much smaller facility in the workshops of a Stuttgart firm, Schiedmayer—both for the airplane projects. In addition, the number of machines and tools in operation increased markedly at Untertuerkheim during the 4 1/2 years of war. Nevertheless, this increase failed to keep pace with the expansion of the work force. In July 1914, the Untertuerkheim plant had one machine per 1.8 workers. By the fall of 1918, the ratio had decreased to one machine per 2.4 workers.

In addition, the trend of the last peacetime years toward deploying more special machinery worked by cheaper labor-power—automatic lathes, milling and grinding machines, etc.—slowed during the war. The proportion of special and automatic machines to lathes introduced at the plant in 1915, 1916, and 1918, a telling index of the mechanization of the labor process, decreased slightly from the prewar years, from 2.17 / 1 to 1.99 / 1. Thus, Daimler acquired proportionately more machines which required skilled labor for the labor processes in Untertuerkheim during the war than it had in the last pre-war years, reversing the trend to machinery which did not require skilled labor.[27] The privileged position of Daimler and its airplane motor production in the war economy helps explain why it could continue to rely on such skill-intensive production processes while skilled workers were in short supply.

Thus, at Daimler at least, the war saw no revolution in the production process. Legions of skilled hand workers and unskilled day laborers who had no machine duties were still essential to the firm's productive enterprises after years of war.[28] Economies of scale guaranteed by the state, not a revolution in the production processes, made possible huge profits at Daimler. By the end of the war, Daimler was the industrial Behemoth of the southwest, employing more than 20,000 workers in Wuerttemberg.

PROCURING WORKERS AND PRODUCING FOR WAR

The German authorities had to provision the armies at the front with military equipment, and the industrial firms crucial to the war effort had to be supplied with enough productive workers. These twin tasks—along with the procurement of raw materials the sinews of war for Imperial Germany —required the cooperation of owners, unions, and military authorities. The story of the cooperation of these three sectors of German society is one of the most important of the war. Indeed, whatever success the Reich had in maintaining its forces in the field in the face of Germany's geographical isolation and the Allies' blockade was due in large part to the difficult *modus vivendi* achieved by the three, and institutionalized in the provisions of the Auxilliary Service Law of December 1916. Yet this cooperation was often quite difficult, and came to the brink of breaking down at DMG in March and June 1918. Nevertheless, a functioning relationship (if barely, at times) was maintained, which worked well enough most of the time to allow Daimler to produce thousands of airplane motors and to pile up profits which the Prussian War Ministry estimated at 95 million marks or more.

In July 1914, DMG had 3,376 workers. The mobilization and the outbreak of hostilities drew hundreds of them, many of them skilled, from the plant.[29] As Daimler succeeded in attaining an important niche in the wartime military-industrial complex with the emphasis the army decided to place on the construction of airplanes, it became clear that these workers had to be replaced, and many more would have to be added to meet the army's demand. DMG gained new workers from other factories, attracted others with its competitive wages, and added large numbers of women to its work force for the first time. The army sent thousands of skilled workers, especially those who had already worked at the plant, back from the front to Untertuerkheim to build airplane motors (see table 4.4).[30]

By the spring of 1917, the firm's work force in Untertuerkheim had grown to 9,100 industrial workers, of whom 1,100 (12.1%) were women. More than half of the males had been sent back from the front to work at Daimler. Over 60 percent of these were still considered fit for combat, and others for garrison duty.[31]

The vast majority of Mercedes' workforce—more than two-thirds— belonged to the age cohorts which fought the war in the trenches. More than 500 boys and young men 16 years and younger worked in the plant. Although this total seems large, it amounted to only 6 percent of the male work force. Almost a thousand men were 48 years of age or older, including a handful of senior citizens.

On the basis of the available evidence, it seems unlikely that Daimler seriously tried to cover a significant portion of its need for labor power during World War I by using foreigners. There were only 125 foreign workers on hand in mid-1917, not much more than 1 percent of the work force. Their nationalities, methods of recruitment, and working conditions cannot be determined, but it is possible that they included a contingent of Italian POW's.[32]

DMG's need for new workers became even more pressing, as it built up its facilities in Untertuerkheim to produce 750 airplane engines a month and prepared to open the new facility in Sindelfingen. In January 1917, it pressed the military for 1,381 new workers to help it meet its contractual obligations to the War Ministry. Only 646 eventually arrived to fill the company's request.[33] At the same time, an exceptionally high turnover rate for workers plagued the firm. In 1917, at a time when the Auxiliary Service Law was supposed to stem the mobility of the work force, more than 4,400 employees quit the Untertuerkheim plant (of an average work force of 10,248 for the year). DMG blamed this exodus on "war-time conditions."[34]

On the other hand, the Auxiliary Service Law did have an effect—however limited—on worker mobility at Daimler, as the following example shows. Many Daimler workers lived far from Untertuerkheim, and required lengthy train rides to commute to and from work. The experience of a contingent of workers recalled from the front who lived in the town of Eislingen shows the difficult conditions many wartime workers had to en-

TABLE 4.4
The Workforces at Untertuerkheim and Sindelfingen

	Untertuerkheim		Sindelfingen	
	Workers	Clerks	Workers	Clerks
July 31, 1914	3,376	379		
Dec. 31, 1914	4,376	341		
Dec. 31, 1915	5,159	368		
Dec. 31, 1916	7,500	465	226	–
February 1917	7,675		386	
October 1917	9,741			
Dec. 31, 1917	11,478	624	1,435	95
June 1918	13,223			
Nov. 10, 1918	15,130	869	5,068	381
Dec. 31, 1918	11,889	875	1,823	374

Sources: AGM DBAG DMG 17 (83–85) & Ut. 6; HStASt M 77/1 76 M.A. 223)

dure. For years, these workers had to set off by foot by 3:30 A.M. in order to catch the 4:35 train from Goeppingen. After work, the train dropped them off in Goeppingen at 7:56 P.M., and they did not arrive back home until 9:00 or later. These men, on leave of absence from the front, were not allowed to change their place of work under the terms of the Auxiliary Service Law.[35]

Daimler managed to assemble the largest industrial army in southwest Germany. When the military overseers moved into Untertuerkheim in March 1918 and Ernst Berge departed, the firm employed more than 12,900 workers, all but 1,700 of them at the main works on the Neckar. Over the next seven months, more than 6,000 workers were added to the work force, of whom a third or so were females. The evidence indicates that neither Daimler or the military had any medium- or long-range plans for provisioning the facilities in either Sindelfingen or Untertuerkheim with the necessary complement of skilled workers. Rather, the record indicates that the firm and the overseers put forward a host of small requests for skilled workers to the responsible military commanders in Stuttgart and Berlin.

On March 28, 1918, for example, the firm requested the immediate hiring of 350 skilled workers for Sindelfingen. "For the time being, the hiring of fitters can be dispensed with; we need lathe-turners."[36] In early April, the firm asked the military for quick action on a request for skilled workers "so that we can train more unskilled workers for production with the help of these workers."[37] Three weeks later, an "urgent" request went out for 150 fitters, as well as 162 other skilled and machine workers. In May, 304 more fitters and lathe-turners were ordered.[38] Yet neither the firm nor the military displayed a clear sense of their ultimate need for more workers to execute the production schedules. The pattern, for 1918 in any case, is quite chaotic, with frequent requests for workers, and no target for the size and composition of the work forces at Untertuerkheim and Sindelfingen. This was no doubt due in part to the firm's inability to estimate the effectiveness of the less trained men and women it was forced to employ in the works. Yet, the picture for 1918 approaches total improvisation, with the military often expressing its exasperation.

On July 18, for example, an army supervisor informed Paul Daimler that the military had secured the allocation of 1,000 skilled workers for the firm. Nevertheless, the military felt it necessary to warn the firm that the "considerable increase in the number of workers in the last three-fourths of a year had not resulted in a corresponding increase in performance." The officer backed up this charge by presenting calculations which he alleged demonstrated that the firm already "either produced 130 fewer airplane motors than it could have, or employed today around 2000 workers too many." If one assumed an annual "average earning of M 3500" per worker, then

Daimler was paying out 7 million marks too much in wages, "for which there was no corresponding increase in output."

In fact, the army official complained, the "performance" of the factory had sunk in recent months. In the *Bremserei*, where motors were closely checked and finely tuned, the amount of time spent on a motor had risen 70 percent since the abolition of the piece-rates and the introduction of a flat hourly wage in the department, according to the military overseers. These reckonings, the officer added sarcastically, applied only to the Untertuerkheim plant, for the new Sindelfingen plant as of July 1 had "not yet produced anything." In addition, the firm had not yet finished setting up the "training workshops" for women, despite repeated promises made to the military.[39]

Confusion and delays also ruled in the procurement of machinery for the expanded production process, and added to the company's difficulty in meeting its production schedules. It is clear that the firm would have preferred to import superior American-made special machines before the U.S. entered the war but was prevented from doing so by the British blockade.[40] As a result, the firm had to order German makes.

The orders for new machinery which Daimler placed with German firms were never delivered on time; often they were many months late. These delays contributed to the spectacular decline in the firm's delivery of motors in February and March 1918. In July and August 1917, for example, Daimler had placed large orders with A. H. Schuettle of Koeln-Deutz for milling, polishing, drilling, and shaping machines, which were to arrive at Daimler in October and December. DMG had also ordered tens of thousands of drill bits and other machine tools from Schuettle. In addition, large orders for polishing machines and lathe-banks had gone to the Werner factory in Berlin and to the Schuettoff-Baessler works in Chemnitz. Finally, in April 1918, with all of these and a host of other orders for machinery and tools long past due, the new military overseers in Untertuerkheim dispatched blunt letters to the firms, notifying them that the delays were impeding Daimler's delivery of airplane motors for the war effort and strongly requesting the shipment of the outstanding orders. These interventions by the military usually elicited protestations regarding raw material shortages, and promises to proceed with the orders with all due speed. This military pressure on Daimler's contractors was an important benefit which the firm derived from the existence of the military supervision in the wake of the Daimler Affair of March 1918.[41]

Similarly, Daimler experienced long delays in receiving many of the orders for axle parts and other components which it had placed with subcontractors. For example, in April 1918, the firm had not yet received shipments of parts it had placed up to a half year earlier.[42]

Nevertheless, the battle for the vast amounts of labor-power needed to fulfill the commitments made to the military was the most important the firm fought. Here, it enlisted large numbers of women for the first time in its history.

MERCEDES' SISTERS: WOMEN AT DMG

Before 1914, women were of little direct use to the Daimler-Motoren-Gesellschaft. Although a handful of firms in the metal industry had begun to employ women in the production process in the last years before the war (Bosch in Stuttgart, for example), DMG was not one of them. In general, the skilled metal trades were off limits to German women, and women were deemed unfit for employment as unskilled labor in most firms because of the physical demands of much of the work. At the same time, of course, large numbers of women toiled in the textile mills of Wuerttemberg, as well as in its fields and vineyards.

Even though the prejudices about the fitness of women for work in the metal industry have been slow to die to this day,[43] the wartime situation quickly changed the role of women, if only for the duration of the conflict. Mobilization in August 1914 drew many skilled and unskilled workers from the work-force of the metal industry at a time in which its especially critical role for the war effort was being recognized. Not only were replacements needed for the men at the front but large numbers of new employees were also required to work in an industry central to the whole war effort.

To facilitate the provision of labor-power in industry, the government suspended the regulations which determined working conditions in August 1914. Among them was article 137 of the industrial code, which barred women from working the night shift or from being employed in mining pits, cokeries, or hauling operations. The regulation entitling pregnant women to an unpaid eight-week leave was also suspended. Thus, the stage was set from the very beginning of mobilization for the entry of a host of new women workers into German industry.[44]

Millions of women took jobs during the four years of the war. In 1916, the Metalworkers' Union reported that the number of women employed in industry, business, and trade had increased by more than 50 percent from 1914 to 1916, to a total of 4.1 million. The authorities concluded that the number of women working in the metal industry in Stuttgart grew by 361 percent during the war to 29,114.[45] At Daimler in Untertuerkheim, there were 678 women workers in the plant in October 1916, and 2,733 in October 1918, compared to virtually none in July 1914.[46]

According to one study, the women who were drawn into the metal factories in Stuttgart came from a variety of backgrounds and social situations. Some were women whose husbands were serving in the armed forces and who had to support themselves and their families by getting a job.[47] Others were women who had been working in the textile industry in Wuerttemberg and now found themselves unemployed and in need of work because of the extraordinary contraction of that industry during the war. Others were young, single women who had never worked before. They came to the factories "because one could earn nice money there and live well. This consideration drew especially the younger women into the factory."[48]

The longer the war lasted, the more men were needed to serve at the front, and the greater the possibility for the employment of women in the factories. By 1917, more than 300,00 members of the Metalworkers' Union had been drafted for military service. An investigation by the DMV in 1916 revealed that women were employed in more than 66 occupations in the industry.[49] According to the Wuerttemberg factory inspectors, women were "checkers, they were used on the banks of lathe machines, the automatic machines, the grinding, drilling, and polishing machines; for annealing (tempering) metals, welding, smith work, etc."[50] The use of women on the banks of machines was particularly striking. Indeed, by 1918 at Daimler, 40 percent of the machines in many departments were run by women.[51] "The employment [of women] on machines was partially possible only because of the greatly expanded division of labor, by the utilization of help-machines and through the preparation of work by technically skilled *Einrichter*," the factory inspectors concluded.[52]

Women were not employed only in the machine shops of area metal factories. "They were also used in [jobs] which only skilled mechanics carried out, . . . even as crane operators and at the steam hammers."[53] By October 1918 women were employed in all sizeable departments except the smith, including departments of skilled workers.[54] Most of the Daimler women (1,498 or 55%) worked in the machine workshops, including those with mainly turning machinery. Four of five women performed what the company called productive work, meaning that they were actually involved in production jobs. In the machine department, all but 98 women —more than 93 percent—were productive workers. On the other hand, few if any Daimler women worked in the smith or woodworking workshops. Of the nearly 2,400 workers in the fitting and assembling departments, 15 percent were women. Only two-thirds of the women were performing productive work. About 10 percent of the toolmakers were women. Thus, in the two major sections of the plant worked by fitters and mechanics, women were underrepresented.[55]

The training Daimler gave its women workers paled in comparison to that offered by the other Stuttgart giant, Bosch. While Bosch set up special workshops and eight-week courses for training women employees, Daimler offered a more limited training program. A woman's first days at DMG consisted of learning the "necessary concepts, terms, and tools" and of observing the work going on around them. Then, she tried her hand at a job. If she could not show that she could perform it adequately, she was moved to another job to try again.[56]

Nearly all reports agreed that women in the Stuttgart metal and machine-building industries performed first-rate work. "The 'trained' woman performed very well; some achieved astounding skill in their job." In the words of another observer, "the judgments of the individual factory heads and managers . . . which I heard about the work of women coincide almost completely." Women performed jobs requiring "dexterity" and "skill" in an "amazing" manner. Their "agile, slender fingers" even permitted them to "surpass" the performance of men in certain tasks. Their "zeal" and "punctual work" were also noted. In departments paying piece-rates, in which many women worked, "one tried to surpass the other; each wanted to bring home the highest 'pay day.' "[57] Despite the enthusiastic reviews from many industrialists, the factory inspectors noted that women sometimes had problems "in very hot rooms, moving heavy loads, and [with] work which had a high danger of accident."[58] By the summer of 1918, female employees of the Ministry of Labor in Stuttgart demanded that women be spared after the war from performing certain kinds of work at Daimler because they were "particularly damaging to their health." These included foundry-work, welding, and the hardening of metals.[59]

At Daimler, the only surviving company report on the performance of women, dating from the end of 1917, drew a generally favorable, if unenthusiastic, balance. On simple jobs, Daimler's assessors held that women worked about as well as men. On complicated jobs, in which the overall division of labor was not so advanced, on work with heavy pieces, or on tasks which placed "too high a demand . . . on [their] strength," the performance of women was inferior to that of men. Daimler asserted that more supervisory personnel, foremen, and skilled workers had been assigned to the departments with large numbers of women.[60] Rather than gender, the most important factor explaining the need of extra supervision may have been the unskilled and untrained nature of the available female labor.

Females provided an obedient, compliant work force. "There was no talk" of intentional slowdowns or other job actions to force the piece-rates up. The lack of militancy among these new workers was not unusual, but in this case the fact of gender seems decisive. The Metalworkers' Union complained that it was difficult to interest women in its campaign to improve their working conditions, although the union did not suspect that its own mainly male organization and the hostility of many unionized male workers to the influx of cheap female labor might have contributed to the aloofness many women demonstrated to the DMV.[61] Indeed, a report by the Berlin *Buero fuer Sozialpolitik* done for the military authorities concluded that "from experience, women workers represent the least reliable element in the trade unions."[62]

The most important reason for the limited participation of women in the labor movement may have been the temporary nature of female employment in the industry. These replacement workers had limited prospects in the industry and could not expect to reap the fruits of a steady membership in the unions.[63]

In jobs where teamwork was essential, women never left their assigned places, several managers noted. Some adjustments had to be made to the "physical constitution of the woman": women allegedly worked better sitting than standing.[64] And Daimler complained that a number of its married female employees skipped work on occasion to care for the family responsibilities.[65] This is hardly surprising, since many women had to work a "second shift" at home, caring for family members. True, the food supply in Wuerttemberg and greater Stuttgart was never destabilized by the critical shortages which plagued most other parts of the empire. Nevertheless, shortages were rampant and made the provisioning of households—overwhelmingly the responsibility of women—more difficult and time-consuming.

Although women served the German war effort well by toiling in the factories and generally keeping civil society together, their efforts were not rewarded in kind. In a description of the working conditions for female labor, *Die Gleichheit,* a socialist women's newspaper, observed, "Women stand at banks of metal polishing machines and lathes, they are employed in the smith and at cranes, even digging. Since the protective regulations for women and youths are cancelled, the women must work overtime and at night. For women who work at a piece-rate, the rates are lower than for men; many times they amount to only half."[66]

In addition, there is evidence to suggest that working conditions took their toll on the health of women in the Stuttgart area. The rate of illness increased by 45 percent between 1915 and 1917, in part according to observers like the Metalworkers' Union because of working conditions which were no longer officially regulated.[67] The DMV lamented that "Today, the missing protection means a danger to the vitality and health of the people," and petitioned the Reichstag in March 1916 for the institution of an eight-hour day for women, "at least for those employed in heavy industry."[68]

Nevertheless, near the end of that year, the government recommended the wider utilization of women during the night shifts at Daimler. The main reason was simply the combination of expanding factories and the chronic scarcity of male workers. Most of the producers for the military were required to work long, even "unbroken" hours to meet the demand and to "make fullest use of the productivity of the machines." Firms using women for their night shifts, however, had to take the greatest care to look after their "health and morals." Employers also had to adhere to the eight-hour shift for female night workers.[69]

The use of hundreds of thousands of women in the industries producing for the war effort is an important factor in accounting for the massive wartime profits amassed at Daimler and elsewhere. Women performed many types of work, including advanced machine labor, widely judged to be of high quality, yet received only half the wages of their male counterparts. Simply put, the firm pocketed the half which the women did not receive.

The thousands of women who toiled at Daimler during the war shared the same fate as their colleagues throughout Germany after the armistice. They were dismissed *en masse* in November and December 1918. Some managed to find other jobs, but most were banished to the households to keep civil society together in a time of social turmoil and revolution.[70]

SINDELFINGEN

The opening of the Sindelfingen plant for the construction of airplane fuse-lages in 1915 had important ramifications for the intracorporate division of labor at Daimler. In the course of the war and its immediate aftermath, most of the skilled woodworking and nonmetal handworking occupations were moved out of Untertuerkheim to Sindelfingen. The motor-builders and metal trades remained at Untertuerkheim. The company also intended to move the production of its automobile bodies to the new plant when peace finally returned. Indeed, wartime expansion gave Daimler one of its most important facilities.

The site for the new factory was chosen because a small air field had opened between Sindelfingen and Boeblingen, which met the testing needs of the airplane motor producer.[71] Although the details are sketchy, the city of Sindelfingen was required by the military authorities to purchase and to secure the property for DMG before a contract between Daimler and Sindel-fingen would be worked out. On October 21, 1915, the operations at the plant commenced. Due to the scarcity of building workers, prisoners of war helped in the construction of Daimler-Sindelfingen. Soon afterward, work began on the production of airplane bodies in a large shed next to the airstrip. By the end of the war, 271 were completed. Wings were hauled in by horses from DMG's wood workshops in Stuttgart.[72]

On July 1, 1917, the War Ministry in Berlin gave the firm the historic commission to expand its operations and to build high priority airplane motors in Sindelfingen. Meetings between representatives of the firm and the state authorities that same month in Berlin set a provisional target of 750 motors per month for Untertuerkheim (up from 500) and 250 for Sindelfingen.[73] The deadline for delivery of the first motors from Sindelfingen was April 1918, with production to begin December 1, 1917, at the latest. The toolmaking departments at Untertuerkheim were to help provide the necessary machine tools. DMG also placed orders with other companies for machines and special tools, but many were reluctant to contract with Daimler because of the endemic shortages of steel and raw materials which hampered their own production schedules.

In addition, the military authorities agreed to provide 1,500 additional skilled metalworkers for the two Daimler plants in Wuerttemberg. The head engineer of the Sindelfingen project later charged, however, that "the provisioning [of skilled workers] remained in the main only promises." Included among the "skilled workers" shipped to Sindelfingen were many "completely unskilled people, who described themselves as skilled workers in order to get out of the military service." Those from other parts of the Reich, particularly the Rhineland and the greater Berlin area, exhibited a thoroughgoing dissatisfaction with the wages and the working conditions prevailing at Daimler-Sindelfingen once they arrived and proved difficult to manage.[74]

The engineers at the new factory sought to utilize what had already learned through the experience of the Untertuerkheim plant in their plans for the production process, especially in the layout of the machinery.[75] The point was to ease the path of the engines through the production process as much as possible by carefully arranging the placement of the departmental subsections. Delays, however, plagued the effort to bring the new plant on line. Not only machines and workers, but also doors and windows for the buildings were in short supply. On December 31, 1917, six months after receipt of the military's commission, 247 workers were employed in the motor-building department, far fewer than had been envisioned the previous July.

In the new year, operations expanded quickly. By mid-April, the work force had reached 800, and nearly 200 machines were finally in use. Over the next seven months, the size of the department's work force grew by 2 1/2 times, reaching 2,100 in mid-October. The percentage of women workers kept pace, at roughly 22 percent of the total. More than 40 percent of all machines at Sindelfingen were operated by women in April 1918, although the proportion declined slightly thereafter.[76] This marked the most extensive utilization of women in the production processes at Daimler during World War I.

Several categories of workers grew inordinately during the period, including the ranks of the so-called "help workers" employed either at machines or at the side of skilled labor. Both of these groups nearly quadrupled. Among the skilled workers, the complement of lathe turners, the skilled machine workers who were probably the most valuable single group for Daimler's production, increased proportionately the most, from 25 to 121. The number of machines drawn into the production process grew more than fourfold, from 194 in April to 820 in November. The tally of machines actually procured for the plant increased considerably less, from 539 to 877 (62.7%). In general, it is clear that immense progress was made in actually bringing machinery on line and into the production process, and that this progress was made by a work force in which women and unskilled workers predominated (64.9% in April and 58.3% in November). It was also made by a work force in which skilled workers were of questionable caliber: in August, 55 "skilled workers" sent by the army actually had to be shipped back because they were "totally incapable."[77]

Nevertheless, the final consideration for the Sindelfingen project must be the number of airplane motors actually delivered by the Sindelfingen facility to the military by the end of the war. Although a handful had apparently been completely assembled by the closing months of the war and 72 others had been repaired, not a single airplane motor had been delivered to the army by November 11, 1918.[78]

Daimler claimed that it had pushed its bloated production capabilities to the limit on behalf of the war effort, although the German army did not agree. Berge reported in early 1915, "Now we work with an exertion such as never in peace-time, with day and night shifts, if necessary also on Sundays, and it is our vaulting ambition to extract form the Mercedes works the last bit of energy."[79] What remained unspoken at the time was that Daimler expected premium prices for its efforts.

PRICES, PROFITS, AND PATRIOTISM: THE DAIMLER AFFAIR

On February 12, 1918, Ernst Berge, on behalf of the Daimler-Motoren-Gesellschaft, sent a letter to the firm's chief patron, the Prussian Ministry of War, once again requesting a price adjustment.[80] This was (and, indeed, still is) a common enough occurrence: a major military supplier claiming that cost overruns, in this case, mounting costs for wages and materials, necessitated an urgent price hike. Although the authorities had in the previous months repeatedly rebuffed Daimler's entreaties, the letter of February 12 did not have the desired effect of eliciting their capitulation. Instead, it opened the most spectacular corporate scandal of the war and let to an investigation into charges of treason against the leaders of one of the Reich's most important military producers. As such, it marks one of the most confrontational episodes in the relations between state and industry in Germany during the First World War. In retrospect, it is clear that the affair also contributed mightily to the deterioration of labor-management relations and to the radicalization of the work force at Daimler to a degree unmatched in the Stuttgart area. The Daimler Affair grew to become a symbol of the indecent, unbridled corporate lust for profits—and many on the shop floor in Untertuerkheim and Sindelfingen were paying attention.

Berge's missive, addressed to the Ministry's department A.7 L., which supervised the production of airplane engines, noted that since the last adjustment of prices for motors and spare parts on August 30, 1916, the costs of raw materials and labor had continued to increase. Seven times Daimler had requested higher prices; seven times the department had ruled against it. Meanwhile, the ministry departments overseeing the production of motor vehicles and trucks for the army had looked more kindly on Daimler's humble supplications and had approved several price hikes. "For my part, the wage controversies with the work force have been settled so steadfastly," Berge reminded the bureaucrats, "that in the interests of the leadership of the army, work has not halted once since the beginning of the war." Daimler's "protection" of the national interest had meant agreeing to considerable wage hikes, which "go into the many millions of marks."[81]

Now, Berge informed the ministry, pressure from the factory's workers' committee had led to the convocation of the Stuttgart Arbitration Committee to settle a host of wage claims by the workers at the plant (in line with the provisions of the Auxiliary Service Law). "It gave in to the wishes of the workers on most points," Berge dolefully reported. Eleven mass meetings had been held at the Untertuerkheim facility, and all had shouted their approval of the Arbitration Committee's settlement. It was "now up to you" to carry out "a revision of prices for the benefit of the Daimler-Motoren-Gesellschaft."

The letter also protested the department's requirement that copies of detailed calculations be submitted with each request for a price revision. "Such copies have never been claimed on the part of the land vehicle sections; and the right to demand these copies is disputed on the part of the Daimler-Motoren-Gesellschaft."

It was the concluding paragraph, however, which seemed to escalate the dispute to a new level of gravity:

> If a revision of prices is not effected within a very short time, I am obliged in the interests of the factory to take into consideration the introduction of savings, which first must consist in abolishing the unlucrative night shift and the just as unlucrative overtime work. Such cutting back of the factory

would of course not insignificantly influence the production schedule. Before I carry through on these measures, I hold it for my duty to ask you again for a revision of prices and gladly make myself available for verbal negotiations.[82]

As if to show the military authorities that he and the corporation were not bluffing, Berge sent one of the military engineers at Daimler a letter one week later, declaring that "in the event a prompt understanding cannot be reached . . . the night shift and the overtime will cease with the end of March. A correspondingly abbreviated production program will be set up and delivered to you."[83]

In the wake of DMG's initial requests for a 25 percent price increase, several Reichstag committees had already launched inquiries into Daimler's affairs. The investigating subcommittee of the Main Committee of the German parliament devoted two sessions to the question of "excessive prices, especially in the auto industry."[84] Daimler came up in the first of these, on January 14. At that time, the deputies questioned the pricing policies of DMG and other firms. While the prices for motorized vehicles may not have risen greatly since the beginning of the war, the mass orders for individual models had allowed firms to cut production costs considerably, and to reap windfall profits in the production of engines, several witnesses testified. Firms achieved these savings not by dramatically revolutionizing the production process in their factories, but by adopting serial production of a few models.[85]

Late in February, the chairman of the investigating subcommittee, the chemical industrialist Stoeve from the National Liberal Party, received the uncorroborated testimony of a Daimler clerk who charged that he had been directed to fake calculations for the firm's products so that "the new calculations agree with the prices which the Daimler works have made for the army administration." As a result of this news, the subcommittee requested that DMG be placed under the supervision of the armed forces, but confusion over whether the Berlin War Ministry or the military commander in Stuttgart should act delayed the move. In addition, military authorities at first feared that the workers would "declare themselves in solidarity with the direction" in the event of the imposition of a military supervision or might interpret such a measure as the militarization of the whole corporation. After considering the situation, the military overcame its doubts.[86]

The turn in the dialogue between firm and military in February—to wit, Berge's "threat" to cancel the night shift and his refusal to allow the military to inspect the company's ledgers—further alarmed the committee. Gustav Noske, the Social Democratic deputy, denounced the "blackmail and exploitation of the emergency situation of the Reich by large firms like Daimler, and the military's excessive patience with such practices."[87] Members of the committee pressed the government to make the firm pay back profits, while Colonel Oschmann from the *Luftfahrtabteilung* in the Prussian war ministry even suggested that it would be possible to force Daimler to work without profits if a military supervision were installed in Untertuerkheim.[88] Nevertheless, the government had taken no action against Daimler by late February, despite accumulating evidence that all was not well at the Swabian military-industrial giant, when an obscure clerk's account of pricing fraud finally pushed the issue to the forefront.

Barely two weeks after Berge's letter to the Prussian War Ministry, on February 25, 1918, Hans Wohnlich, who had been a commercial clerk at Daimler from October 1912 until the previous month, sat down with a member of the public prosecutor's office in Stuttgart and told a story of corporate intrigue and the falsification of documents which heightened the army's fears of what was going on in Untertuerkheim. Wohnlich, born in 1889 in Goeppingen and a resident, with his wife, of Bad Cannstatt, had enlisted in the army on August 4, 1914, but was released six weeks later because of "physical defects." He then returned to the calculation office in Untertuerkheim which was headed by Erwin Keim. By his own testimony, his responsibility there was to "work out the calculations for the contracts the firm had completed." This statistical work was distinct from the preliminary calculations *[Vorrechnungen]* which served as the basis for the prices charged by the firm; his figuring helped the firm to evaluate DMG's actual performance.[89]

On a day in early March of the previous year, Wohnlich asserted, Keim had handed him a "rough piece" of paper which had only the following entries on it:

Mat. 4532
—————
L 1995

As Keim handed Wohnlich the piece of paper, he instructed him to work out a set of calculations for a 160-horsepower airplane motor which arrived at the figures written on the slip of paper. Wohnlich recognized immediately that that figures stood for material and wage costs, respectively. Recalling that he had already done *ex post facto* calculations for such motors and that the figures being provided by his boss were far too high, Wohnlich told Keim that it was impossible to arrive at this set of numbers for the line of airplane motors in question.[90]

Keim reiterated his instructions, explaining that the director of Daimler —Ernst Berge himself—needed the new set of calculations quickly, for he expected a visit soon from a Reichstag commission which would be checking the validity of the prices being charged for airplane motors. He added these specific instructions: Wohnlich should use the engine series number 571 as the base for his calculations, alter the figures for the costs of the raw materials, and double the values for as many of the wage-totals as was necessary to arrive at the figures on the slip of paper. According to the clerk's testimony, Keim instructed Wohnlich to work alone on this project and to make sure no one else know what was going on.[91]

Wohnlich set about his new project in the following days. It was no simple task. First, he changed the prices for materials, substituting the highest price which Daimler had ever paid for an item for the actual costs of the material used in a 160 horsepower motor. His department chief returned his first efforts at calculations, declaring them worthless, and offered more "precise instructions" on how to come up with the magic numbers. Some time later, shortly after Wohnlich submitted his final doctored figures, Keim instructed him to create a set of "calculation cards" for the firm's files in case the Reichstag commission requested data to back up the firm's numbers. His supervisor subsequently retained the original cards.[92]

As a result of Wohnlich's testimony, the public prosecutor's office concluded that Daimler may have been making "excessive profits"—over and above those deemed proper—of up to 4 million marks on the 500 airplane motors which it delivered to the military every month. "The Reich is thus damaged by about 48 million marks in 12 months by the practices of the Daimler firm." The *Staatsanwaltschaft* speculated that "the sense and meaning of this falsification of the calculations . . . was to back up the right to a selling price of 15,200 marks. . . . One would compute a cost of about 10,500 marks for a single [motor] and with it substantiate the profit . . . as permissible, because it is [approximately] 33 1/3%."[93] This also explained the alleged falsification of the calculation cards, because they were supposed to serve as the basis for setting the actual prices of the airplane motors. They bore the prices of, typically, the cast-iron, aluminum, bronze and brass, steel, tin, forged iron and steel, brass and copper tubing, screws and nuts, and other miscellaneous items which went into Daimler's products.

As the high command began to consider these unsettling developments (as if they were not enough), the nagging irritant for relations between Daimler and the military—the firm's inability to meet production schedules —was intensified anew by a drastic 34 percent drop in the delivery of airplane motors from Untertuerkheim, from 735 in January to 486 in February. The goal was 750 per month. Although the military later found that the February production slump had been caused by "insufficient deliveries of coal, electricity, and material shortages at the subcontractors, as well as by occasional rail bottlenecks" and not by "an intentional slowdown on the part of the firm,"[94] the new figures heightened fears in the Berlin and Stuttgart commands about what was going on in Untertuerkheim.

While the probe was reaching fateful conclusions, the Berlin authorities alerted the army command in Stuttgart to Berge's threatening letter. In addition, they dispatched a commission to Untertuerkheim, which quickly forced Berge to rescind his threats of curtailing production and to agree to give the authorities documentation to back up the requested price increase.

Nevertheless, on March 6, in the wake of Berge's aggressive letter and of Wohnlich's tale of Daimler's statistical skullduggery, the authorities of the German army in Wuerttemberg, represented by the regional commander General von Schaefer, placed the Daimler-Motoren-Gesellschaft under military supervision. "Differences exist between the administration of the army and DMG which have led to the ordering of a military supervision for the management of the firm," the military's public statement declared. The operations in both Untertuerkheim and Sindelfingen were to continue as before, but when the military supervisors deemed it necessary to step in and issue orders, all employees and managers were obliged to obey. General von Schaefer emphasized that "the relationship of the work force to the firm is in no way disturbed by this action."[95]

At the same time, the army banned Ernst Berge from the firm indefinitely, for Berge, as chairman of the board of directors of Daimler, had precipitated the military's intervention and "is not to be expected" to "cooperate with the military supervision."[96] Lieutenant Colonel von Holzhauser would be leader of the military's supervisory commission.[97]

The government of Wuerttemberg did not move until the next day to protect the integrity of the firm's documents for the upcoming investigation of Daimler's purported fraud, a delay which caused concern in the Reichstag. Roth, the public prosecutor in Wuerttemberg, ordered the card file containing "calculations for the airplane motors" sealed. In addition, Erwin Keim, the chief of this bureau at Daimler, was not to take anything out of his office, and the duplicates of the original documents which he kept in his private quarters were to be secured immediately.[98]

The public prosecutor set out the charges against Daimler in a private memorandum on March 8. The firm had set "unjustifiable prices for its military production" and had falsified the documents which it had given the authorities to support its prices, "as far as its production costs are concerned." On top of these new charges, the prosecutor cited a "mistake" in the firm's records from 1915 which had caused it to overstate the value of the raw materials it had consumed that year by 440,000 marks.[99]

Yet the authorities could not comprehend why the falsified records bore the "real serial numbers and delivery dates of a line of motors" which could be easily checked and why they should have been "put under special lock and key." All later series of motors produced by Daimler actually had lower sums listed for material and wage costs, making the false records easy to spot. Keim of Daimler had speculated that the preparation of the falsified figures was probably intended for a planned investigatory committee of the Reichstag.[100]

Roth believed that the fears which had been expressed in the Reichstag that someone might have tampered with the unguarded records were groundless, for all the necessary documentation had been secured. In all, there were millions of cards in the central calculation office, but only those documenting a production series of about 100 motors were actually at issue. All of these had now been found. "The falsified [cards] were kept under special lock and key by Mr. Keim," who gave them up immediately at the request of the public prosecutor, the government reported.[101]

Five days after the military's intervention in Untertuerkheim, the Stuttgart police searched the houses and offices of Berge and the chairman of the board of trustees, Alfred von Kaulla, looking for "secret books" and documents. According to the subsequent police report, no "secret books" were found in the quarters of the Daimler officials five days after the military action and the talk of treason charges had begun. Nevertheless, the police confiscated a couple of calculation cards and correspondence relating to engine prices and the negotiations with the workers' committee over its demands for higher wages in February 1918 from a locked desk in Berge's office at Daimler.[102]

The reactions in the nation to the press reports of the "Daimler affair" (as it was dubbed) were mostly furious. Daimler itself later complained that because of the "false" reports about the scandal, "the voice of the people rose to a boiling heat [Siedehitze]."[103] The furor which swept Germany over the Daimler Affair should be placed within the context of the suppression of the mass strikes in Berlin at the end of January, which the army crushed by drafting thousands of strikers and court-martialing hundreds of "agitators" who allegedly helped to organize the work stoppages.

The leftist press, especially Vorwaerts, devoted extensive coverage to reports of Berge's threatening letter which were emerging from the committees of the Reichstag. The entire front page of the Saturday, March 9th edition was devoted to "The Daimler Scandal. How war profits are made. Debate in the Main Committee." In large, bold-face print, the paper condemned the "strike threat" which it said had been made by Berge and contended that if strikes by workers during wartime could be considered treasonous, the same must be true for the actions of a corporation which threatened to cut back the production and delivery of crucially needed airplane motors.[104]

The Daimler Affair dominated the proceedings of the Reichstag on the eve of the launching of the huge spring offensive. It was as if many legislators had transferred their frustrations with the conduct of the war and with the deteriorating home front to these new revelations of unbridled corporate greed. Speaker after speaker rose to condemn the business practices which led to large wartime profits. Gustav Noske, who, according to the socialist press, "played a leading role in the negotiations in Stuttgart . . . which led to the army decree of March 6," railed against "a part of German industry drowning in gold in the truest sense of the word."[105]

The deputy Stoeve, a Hamburg industrialist and member of the National Liberal Party, argued plausibly that Daimler's recent raising of its capital from 8 million to 32 million marks had been done "in order to disguise its profits."[106] The Center Party's Matthias Erzberger blasted the firm's submission of the figures for the airplane motors. "I do not hesitate to speak out that this calculation is to be described as a direct mockery of the War Ministry." According to Erzberger, the preparation of the data for the Reichstag underscored Daimler's derisory attitude to the German parliament: "Yes, one can submit anything to that collection of idiots [Idiotengesellschaft]."[107] He pressed for stronger action against Daimler and other firms suspected of war profiteering. For one, the government should send experts into the calculation offices of the large firms producing for the military. In addition, the government should resort to the militarizing of firms in cases of brazen profiteering at the expense of the Reich, not only as a weapon against strikes by employees or management. Third, Erzberger called for the formation of an authority to test the prices charged by firms producing motorized vehicles and airplane engines, along with the levying of fines against firms charging inflated prices.[108]

Amidst the furor, a few voices were raised on Daimler's behalf. In the business magazine *Handel und Industrie,* the reporter Kurt Wolff defended the firm. The DMG's reluctance to provide the government with figures on the airplane motors made sense because such "calculations are business secrets" which could not become "knowledge of the competition." Since the author had observed the development of the firm since its foundation "as an outsider" and knew "its general director . . . as the most noble of industrialists," he personally felt that "it is ruled out . . . that intentional falsifications were carried out." Indeed, the whole affair appeared to be "an agitation [campaign] staged by Social Democracy."[109]

Berge's fellow bosses in the auto industry expressed their solidarity with the beleaguered Daimler official by naming him to the board of directors of the Association of German Motor Vehicle Industrialists, a move described by one newspaper as a "manifestation of trust."[110] At the same time, Berge's peers in the Association of Wuerttemberg Metal Industrialists honored him in the subsequent months by naming him to the executive of that body.[111]

In the aftermath of Berge's suspension, the rest of the top leadership of the firm continued on as before. The DMG named no new director or replacement in the weeks following the outbreak of the scandal. Instead, the bulk of Berge's duties shifted to other top directors of the firm, Paul Daimler, Sekler, and Schippert. "A replacement . . . is not needed . . . for Berge was only *primus inter pares*." [112]

Several company officials defended themselves against the charges in their accounts of events. Erwin Keim, the head of the department, testified at least four times before the public prosecutor's staff.[113] His story contradicted Wohnlich's on several crucial points. "Berge said to me he would like to have a calculation about the 160 horsepower motor according to the state of affairs then in March 1917 . . . to lay before a commission which would be sent by the Reichstag." Keim denied that Berge had given him any untoward instructions. "I understood the mandate that the most recent prices of materials and the most recent wage totals should be in the calculation, as the most expensive instances, in order to get a clear picture about the upward movement of wage and material prices." [114]

In Keim's version, the figures on the slip of paper came from his own substitution of material and wage costs as given by the *Bewertungsabteilung* and the office of wage statistics for the corresponding figures on the final report for production lot "413 or 433—I don't remember any more." Seven months later, Keim changed his story. An investigator told him that if he had indeed followed this procedure, he would have arrived at different figures than the numbers on the slip of paper. Keim then said that he did not know how he came up with the figures. He could not explain how the very same figures appeared in Berge's letter to the war ministry of March 23, 1917 which had pleaded the firm's case for a price hike on its airplane motors. He consistently denied issuing any instructions to Wohnlich to falsify any data. "How Wohnlich came to such lies, I can't explain. I believe, however, that at the time he already had the intention to trip me up because he certainly knew I would not check his calculations. That never happens." [115]

In retrospect, the Daimler affair consisted of several sets of charges. Each brought into sharp relief the practices and indeed the degree of patriotic responsibility of the corporate stewards of the German economy. The most immediate was Berge's implied threat to cut back production which was contained in his letter to the office of the Prussian War Ministry supervising Daimler's production of airplane motors for the war effort. This led to the militarization of the plant from March 6 through December 1918 and the investigations into charges of attempted treason and blackmail against Berge and other DMG officials. After the Social Democratic leaders of Daimler's workers committee, Salm and Schifferdecker, interceded with the military officials in Berlin on Berge's behalf during the closing weeks of the war, Berge was reinstated.[116] The amnesty declared by the provisional government on November 15, 1918, quashed the investigations into the charges against him and the others.[117]

The second set of charges in the Daimler Affair centered on the clerk Wohnlich's testimony that he had falsified calculations at the behest of his superiors Berge and Keim which were used by the firm in March 1917 to press its case for an increase in the prices of airplane motors. Although the firm publicly denounced Wohnlich's tale as a collection of bold-faced lies concocted by an extortionist,[118] the testimony before the Stuttgart public prosecutors by Wohnlich and Keim does not support such a view. Keim, the head of the calculation bureau, admitted that he had instructed Wohnlich to produce calculations which did not actually correspond to the real production costs of the 160 horsepower engines. In addition, the discrepencies in his story—most important, his inability to explain how he arrived at the overall totals which served as the basis for Wohnlich's computations—indicate that there was more to the case than Daimler's heavy-handed public relations campaign suggested. The amnesty of November 1918 ended this investigation, too, before charges could be filed or the accused could be cleared of the allegations.

The charges which had the widest social and political ramifications concerned the allegations of excessive profit-making by Daimler from its huge military business. This theater of the Daimler affair, which began in the Main Committee of the Reichstag, soon became an important issue for the whole left and center of German politics.

The affair hung like a pall over the relationship between the company and its work force for years afterward. To many workers, it indicated that the firm was run by men whose greed knew no bounds. The implication—that an economic system based on such an all-consuming lust for profit was indeed unjust—helped win a hearing for the radical groups within the socialist movement among the work force.[119]

In its own defense, Daimler contended, simply, that its profits were justified by the indisputable fact that it provided larger numbers of airplane motors more cheaply than any other German supplier. An outsider might receive the impression of inappropriately high profits only if he or she weighed them against the public figures for the size of the firm's capital which dated from before the war. In reality, the firm contended, it had been required to grow enormously to meet the military's demand for its products —an expansion which held no promise of peacetime prosperity—and "received too little money for its products."[120]

DAIMLER'S WARTIME PROFITS

For its efforts on behalf of war, Daimler claimed as its real profits the 8.7 million marks paid out as dividends to its shareholders through the end of fiscal year 1917.[121] This sum was in reality all that was left after production costs, taxes, and the massive expansion it undertook during the war had been accounted for, according to DMG.[122]

In its own financial summaries, the firm defined its profits somewhat differently. In 1914, for example, Daimler claimed a profit *[Reingewinn]* of 4.15 million marks, and paid out 16 percent dividends on its 8 million mark capital (see table 4.5).[123] From the summer of 1914 on, DMG produced almost exclusively for the military. In 1915, "the sales divisions have . . . not worked," yet the official profits reached 6.1 million marks, with 28 percent dividends. The story was much the same the next business year, with profits and dividends continuing to climb. Dividends reached 30 percent in fiscal year 1917. Even in turbulent 1918, after a fourfold increase in its *Aktienkapital* to 32 million marks, the firm paid 6 percent dividends. That year, after numerous writeoffs as a result of the major enlargement of its Untertuerkheim facilities and the opening of the Sindelfingen works, the firm's 16 million marks in earnings were trimmed to 3.5 million marks of "pure profit."[124]

Daimler's figures were widely disputed, most adamantly by the Investigatory Commission of the Prussian War Ministry which had been appointed to investigate Mercedes' profits in the wake of the Daimler Affair.[125] Its report, completed in 1919 and leaked to the Social Democratic newspaper *Der freie Angestellte* in 1920, claimed that DMG's real profits from fiscal years 1914 to 1917 amounted to a minimum of 95,847,332.16 marks. The bookkeepers of the War Ministry, who had full access to Daimler's records for this period, believed that millions more had been "hidden" in numerous accounts and writeoffs which it could not fully trace. The corporate ledger for fiscal year 1918 also undoubtedly contained many additional millions of profits, but this had been outside its official charge. Caesar Loehde, a Hamburg bookkeeper who was a member of the commission, testified that the body had not looked into the earnings report for 1918, but he believed that DMG's actual profits in the last year of the war vastly exceeded those it had claimed. In addition, the commission concluded that there was "no doubt" the firm had communicated details about production costs which "diverged . . . considerably from reality" for the "purpose of increases of [its] prices." Whether this was a willful conspiracy or the outcome of innocent mistakes, the bookkeepers could not determine.[126]

Besides the ministry's report, there is other evidence that Daimler's war-

TABLE 4.5
DMG's War-Time Performance—Two Assessments

I. Daimler's Figures (in millions of marks)

	1913	1914	1915	1916	1917	1918
Share capital	8	8	8	8	8	32
Profits	2.7	4.15	6.1	7.7	4.8	3.5
Dividends	14%	16%	28%	35%	30%	6%

Source: AGM DBAG DMG 26 (131) Geschaeftsjahr 1913–1918)

II. Prussian War Ministry's Figures for DMG's Profits

1914	10,424,226 Marks
1915	22,165,556 M
1916	30,047,236 M
1917	32,210,313 M

Source: AGM DBAG DMG 228 *Bericht der Pruefungskommission des Preuss. Kriegsministeriums.*

III. Share Prices

	July 1914	August 31, 1918
Daimler	84	439
AEG	221	259.5
Deutsche Bank	223	279.5

Source: Emil Lederer, "Die oekonomische Umschichtung im Kriege," in *Archiv fuer Sozialwissenschaft und Sozialpolitik,* 45: 1918/19, p. 442

IV. The Balance at Other Companies, 1916

	Profits (Millions)	Dividends (%)
Benz	15.2	20
M.A.N.	7.4	18
Deutsche Waffen- u. Munitionsfabriken	12.6	30
Ludwig Loewe	3.7	32
Krupp	89	10

Source: Lederer, "Die oekonomische Umschichtung," pp. 436–37

time profits were enormous. While being interrogated by Stuttgart prosecutors on March 14, 1918, Berge admitted that he earned a base salary of 20,000 marks annually (to be raised to 36,000 marks on April 1), plus a commission amounting to "0.72% of the official pure profits [statuarischen Reingewinne]." For 1916, this commission amounted to between "200–300,000 marks."[127] According to Berge's formula, pure profits for 1916 amounted to between 14.4 and 21.6 million marks, and as the ministry concluded, probably totalled much more.

In reality, Daimler's staggering profits sprang from the Prussian War Ministry's generous prices combined with relatively cheap mass production. There was another reason, too: new, low-paid workers—women—who took up many tasks in the labor processes.

DAIMLER'S "MILITARIZATION" AND THE BATTLE OF THE SPARE PARTS

Once the military supervision was in place in Untertuerkheim, it sought to prod the firm to increase motor production, which it believed was slumping dangerously. For example, the military supervisors and officials of the firm sought to rectify a shortage of crankshafts for the 160-horsepower engine, as well as cylinders and linkage parts for other motors, by suggesting that Saturday work be instituted in the departments which worked only five days to make up for the slack.

Since the production of airplane motors was so important, the delivery of parts for these motors from other firms was placed under "Urgency Category Number 1." A military directive on March 26 sought to make up for a shortfall in the spare parts produced by DMG's own mechanical departments by bringing in components from other firms and to discover the reasons for this shortfall. Simultaneously, the military overseers sought to expedite the delivery of crankshafts which had already been ordered from subcontractors, for the "production of airplane motors last month and this month has fallen to two-thirds of the total ordered by the [War Ministry]." The Duesseldorf authorities quickly responded that a malfunction of the cooling systems had caused 40 of the crankshafts to crack. They would be delivered by the end of the week, if all went according to plan, with another 150 to follow by the end of April. The military had in the interim formally notified subcontractors of the "importance of the production of the Daimler-Motoren-Gesellschaft" for the fatherland.[128]

Yet the army's drive for the increased deliveries of motors from Daimler and its high-priority campaign to strengthen its air forces by getting damaged or broken motors back into the air were hampered ultimately by the firm's lack of the productive capacity to produce the parts required for the new motors and the spare parts required to keep the Reich's fleet of airplanes in fighting condition. The military authorities in Berlin recognized this and sought to rectify this shortcoming by having other firms produce some of DMG's customized parts. In March, the army demanded that blueprints of all bevelgears and cogwheels, as well as of the cylinders of four lines of Daimler motors, be turned over to it so that other firms could begin producing these Daimler-designed parts. "Production of these motor parts is urgently required and it will put the battle readiness of our air force at the front into question if Daimler does not deliver the drawings." It took nearly three weeks, until April 8, for the military oversight committee to secure the designs of the bevel-wheels and pinions. The next day, however, the supervision reported that the firm would not turn over the blueprints of the cylinders and would consent to handing them over only if the army command directly ordered them to. DMG was balking at delivering its designs to its competitors.

The military authorities at Daimler asked for further instructions, but indicated that they themselves would not order the firm to turn over the blueprints unless the Wuerttemberg commanders required it. Three weeks later, no progress had been made in coaxing DMG to turn over its blueprints. Yet the production situation had not changed. Daimler could not produce the spare parts needed by the armed forces. Therefore, in the urgent interest of the war effort, the Wuerttemberg command should order the firm to produce the drawings. On Daimler's part, the direction claimed that it simply could not hand over these drawings without obtaining the permission of the board of trustees and the general meeting of the shareholders, since it could be held "responsible for compensation for [economic] damages." [129] The military command in Stuttgart did not think much of Daimler's objections, and General von Schaefer ordered the delivery of the blueprints on May 24. Citing article 9b of the state of siege law, he asserted that the "interests of the safety of the Reich demanded this move. Failure to comply would mean a prison term of up to one year and a fine of up to 1500 marks." [130]

General von Schaefer's command settled the matter, and at least 24 drawings were turned over.[131] Yet it is worth noting that Daimler managed to delay the delivery of the blueprints for the production of the needed spare parts for more than two months, holding out for the military to sweeten the deal. The result was more bad feelings between state and firm. The withholding of the drawings was "unpatriotic," Major Wagenfuehr declared at a meeting of the top brass in Stuttgart. The air command would have been able to put the enemy in the "most difficult situation" if it had been able to obtain the needed spare parts. According to the minutes of the meeting,

Wagenfuehr charged that "no other firm had treated the matter of preserving its interests as irresponsibly as Daimler, and he [said] he would never forget this of the firm and its leaders." A fellow officer added that hundreds of damaged and broken motors were out of operation due to lack of spare parts.[132]

Daimler's problem with providing spare parts persisted through the summer. In late July, the military again pressed the firm to provide the replacement parts for its air fleet for which it had contracted, especially propellor hubs. A shortage of these parts was very damaging to the air forces. Recalling what he referred to as the infuriating "Brussels incident," in which parts shortages had let to the idling of a fleet of German planes for weeks and months, the official urged DMG "to dedicate yourself to the production of spare parts, which is an essential element for the readiness of the air forces."[133]

The tension between the military command in Berlin and Daimler boiled over again in the last days of September 1918. This flareup was prompted by the use of a portion of the workers who had been sent to Daimler to work on the high priority airplane motors in the manufacture of heavy trucks instead. The head of the *Inspektion des Flugzeugwesens* wrote, "This fact causes me to express unequivocally my standpoint toward the firm." His "standpoint" was simple: Daimler had refused to take seriously the shortage of laborers. Throughout the years, DMG had not moved quickly enough to replace workers with women "and [other] replacements." Now, "in the fifth year of the war, the manpower shortage was more critical than ever, and yet the firm still refused to cooperate." The personnel had been sent to Untertuerkheim to work for "strengthening our air force," not to be employed for other purposes. At the same time, DMG had brazenly refused to supply the information requested by the office detailing the number of male laborers born between 1894 and 1900. While all other firms had quickly complied with this request, Daimler had responded that the shortage of personnel on hand made it impossible to gather the information. "I will make it known to higher-ups, that Daimler [should] be forced to take the question of worker utilization more seriously."[134]

The firm denied these accusations. "We have not spared any effort to train replacements and women." Although the current rate of women in the work force at Untertuerkheim was 20 percent—"a little behind other motor firms" —the firm was preparing a new influx of women which would put Daimler "at the top." Rejecting any implication of a lack of understanding for the needs of the war effort, Daimler asserted that it was its concern for all of its contracts which had led it to assign to trucks many of the workers who had been sent to Untertuerkheim. It had not tried to hide this; indeed, the military overseers had known of the matter all along.[135] By this point, with the end of the war only one month away, the military authorities did not press their complete exasperation with DMG's performance.

Despite numerous disputes between Daimler and the military authorities which culminated in the establishment of the military supervisory board, DMG derived undeniable benefits from its role in the war effort. Huge contracts, correspondingly generous profits, and a privileged position in the procurement of new machines, raw materials, and workers outweighed the nuisances and indignities of the military's interference in many of the firm's affairs. As tiring and distracting as this may have been, the firm's officials were also forced to grapple with challenges to their daily hegemony from another quarter as well—their workers.

THE REINVIGORATION OF CLASS CONFLICT

German Social Democracy broke asunder during the war. The polarization in Wuerttemberg during the previous decade set the stage for the debate on support for the war effort, which broke out earlier and more intensely in Stuttgart. In 1914–1915, the party split, as the fault lines generated by earlier conflicts gave way. In the decisive confrontation, the party executive sought to end the anti-war editorial position of the Stuttgart newspaper, the *Schwaebische Tagwacht,* by summarily replacing the dissident editorial board with rabidly pro-war Social Democrats. Meeting in Wuerttemberg's first electoral district on December 6, 1914, a majority of SPD members in Stuttgart, Esslingen, Untertuerkheim, and other industrial Swabian industrial towns condemned the conservative executive's move, and their clubs mobilized to support the dissident editors from the *Tagwacht.* The pro-war Social Democrats, headed by Reichstag deputy Wilhelm Keil and numbering about a third of those present at the meeting, walked out. The anti-war majority quickly passed a resolution supporting Karl Liebknecht, who had cast the first vote against war credits in the Reichstag only four days earlier. Subsequently, the Independent Social Democrats, or USPD, grew out of the longstanding socialist groups in the urban areas along the Neckar like Stuttgart, Bad Cannstatt, and Esslingen, while the rump SPD supporting the war collected around the *Land* organizational apparatus in Stuttgart and the clubs in the hinterlands. Indeed, the events in Wuerttemberg presaged the national schism by more than a year.

The fracture of Social Democracy did not debilitate the labor movement at Daimler during the first years of the war. Anti-war and radical social democrats were quickly isolated, as many were called up for military service and the rest were muzzled by the police and the military authorities in

Stuttgart. The workers' committee inside the plant sparred with the firm and military over wages and working conditions. In this arena, the support of the chief organizations of the work force—particularly the Metalworkers' Union at DMG—for the war effort was never in doubt, as they maneuvered and negotiated to prevent the labor situation at the plant from unraveling in the face of wartime economic and political pressures. This bargaining usually never involved more than a handful of individuals from these organizations who had won acceptance from both the firm and the Wuerttemberg military authorities in the frequent rounds of talks held to improve the efficiency of the home front.

Yet as thousands of young Swabians fell amidst the horrifying carnage at the fronts, and as the people at home labored under growing shortages, another voice came to be heard, faintly at first, among the southwest German working class. Bitterly denouncing the "sell-out" of the SPD and trade unions to the Kaiser, capitalists, Junker generals and their war in August 1914, the socialist peace movement involved a meager handful of persons in Stuttgart, but they were isolated, hounded, on the run, and even sent to their deaths at the front for their efforts. These men and women operated in a shadowy, semi-underground world on the fringes of the urban Social Democratic clubs whose organizations shriveled in the wake of the schism, and did not surface often within Stuttgart factories until the late summer and fall of 1918. Their first goal was to spread resistance to the war. They were responsible for the anonymous leaflets which mysteriously appeared from time to time. They gathered on rare occasions for annual picnics, closely watched by the security police as they sang songs and renewed personal ties. Despite their impotence during most of the war, they were able finally to connect with the shop-floor in the closing weeks of the war. They and their comrades at Daimler helped set a new radical pace for labor there during the following two years.

INDUSTRIAL RELATIONS

Despite the *Burgfrieden* between socialists and government, and between labor and capital, industrial relations at Daimler were marked almost from the beginning of the war by disputes between the management and the work force. Berge remained the director in Untertuerkheim, and Kaulla continued to head the board of trustees. The leaders of the Daimler workers' committee were the moderate trade unionists Albert Salm and Wilhelm Schifferdecker, who had emerged as leaders of the work force following the confrontations of 1910–1911 and who usually supported the politics of moderate Social Democracy. Salm, who was 32 years old when the war broke out, was a fitter at Daimler who lived across the river in Wangen. Schifferdecker, a mechanic, was 33 years old.[136]

The issues at stake during the war were often the same ones—wages, piece-rates, overtime and working hours—which had triggered the previous disputes at the plant in 1905–6, 1910, and 1911. The parties in Untertuerkheim, however, were joined by a new participant intent on vigorously pursuing its interests of producing needed equipment for the war—the German military establishment.

The first incident which received widespread attention in the military regime began less than nine months after the start of hostilities and reflected practices which apparently began with the war. The Metalworkers' Union suggested on May 27, 1915 that the obstinacy which Daimler had displayed to its employees' grievances about wages and working conditions necessitated its intervention with the military authorities in Stuttgart.[137] Among the alleged abuses at Daimler which the union sharply protested were reductions in piece-rates in many workshops, Sunday work, and slipping wages for unskilled workers. The DMV pushed for the institution of bonus payments to those at Daimler working overtime and to those required to work on Sundays. The behavior of the masters of the individual DMG workshops came in for particular criticism. The DMV charged that many abused their positions of authority. Several had slashed the piece-rates in their departments during the last few weeks, provoking protest from the employees. The masters' response was invariably: Keep it up and you will be "sent out into the trenches." In addition, the union claimed that it was common practice at Daimler for masters to threaten those skilled workers who had been furloughed from the army to work back at the factory. "If the workers are not docile, they take the opportunity to have them sent back into the field." [138]

In general, the workers could no longer tolerate conditions at Daimler, the Stuttgart office of the DMV contended. "After they have been made over a long time to work regular overtime hours daily, they are then made to work on Sunday." By itself, this took its toll, particularly with the "intense production process" prevailing in the factory, but the impact was made worse because of the fact that many workers had to endure long train rides to get to work. Sunday work was now the rule, even in those departments which eschewed overtime work on weekdays. The DMV contended that the workers had the right to expect a bit of "rest and recovery" on Sundays, such as was usually afforded to troops in the field.

The wage rates prevailing for many workers also came in for criticism. Workers paid hourly wages were finding it increasingly difficult to make ends meet. "Up to now, the increase in earnings affects chiefly the skilled workers, while the most poorly paid helpers and unskilled workers" had to do without wage adjustments for the most part. Therefore, the union suggested that DMG initiate a supplementary payment to cover the rising cost of living for these workers, as "a large number of corporations" had already done. At the same time, Daimler should reward overtime work by piece-workers with a 25 percent bonus, with a 50 percent supplementary payment for labor performed on Sundays and holidays.[139]

The Daimler-Motoren-Gesellschaft bitterly objected to the union's complaints. On behalf of the firm, Ernst Berge and Paul Daimler wrote the Stuttgart commander, in a confidential letter, that "the union wants nothing other than to stir up our work force. . . . They want the right to interfere in our internal business."[140] As an example of the perfidy of organized labor at DMG, the firm cited a meeting at the factory on May 6, 1915, which had allegedly been manipulated by the workers' committee. Several of the workers, whose grievances were subsequently brought to the direction by the committee, later claimed that they had not actually given the committee their grievances. What few real complaints there actually were had already been settled. Complaints about piece-rates had been met with a renewed pledge to let shop stewards help settle disputed rates. In addition, the firm had agreed to pay bonuses to anyone working on Sundays. These would amount to 25 percent for piece-workers and 50 percent to those working for hourly wages.

Berge and Daimler judged the work force at DMG to be basically contented. Extra work and overtime "are willingly performed." "We have given all we responsibly can and will continue to do so in the future;" if the workers or their representatives had actually complained about the conditions at Untertuerkheim, they could not be serious. Rather, it was all part of the overall design to spread the influence of the unions. One of the leaders of the workers' committee had even allegedly said, "We consider any advance as only a partial payment."[141]

The Stuttgart army command asked the office for commerce and trade in Wuerttemberg to mediate the dispute.[142] Ten weeks later, it believed it had successfully resolved the dispute between corporation and union, at least "for the duration of the war." It reiterated Daimler's pledge to involve shop stewards in the settlement of disputes about piece-rates. Although DMG had denied that its departmental bosses had threatened in the past to have independent-minded workers sent to the front, it had since "strictly" informed its supervisory personnel to avoid such behavior.[143]

The question of work on Sunday was thornier, "because of the demands of the military authorities on the factory." Yet the firm pledged to be forthcoming, and to limit work on Sundays so that it would be required at most only twice every nine weeks. Daimler had denied that there was a need among its workforce for an increase in earnings, but pledged to set 44 pfennigs as the minimum hourly wage for unskilled workers who were over

21 years of age. It assented to a bonus of 25% for piece work both during overtime and on Sundays.

Nevertheless, the union was disappointed with these results and resolved to press its case. For one, workers who put in many overtime hours over six days could still be required to work on Sundays. In addition, it deemed "absurd" the prevailing manner of measuring wage rates by including the "considerable overtime work." How could the matter of bonuses for matching the increasing cost of living be handled fairly if now, in the wartime situation, workers were expected to perform long overtime and weekend work to earn a minimal subsistence? Progress on all of these points was needed to create "a just relationship for the work force in the factory during war-time." It would accept, however, the terms which had been worked out during the weeks of difficult talks.[144] In reality, the union displayed a thorough readiness to give in on such fundamental questions as the inclusion of long overtime hours in the standard level of remuneration during the war.

As the winter of 1916–1917, the bitter "turnip winter," settled on Germany, the urban population was plagued by a severe shortage of food and scarcity of heating fuels. According to some estimates, 700,000 Germans died from starvation or hypothermia, mainly the poor, the weak, and the elderly. In Stuttgart, the nutritional situation was dire, but not catastrophic. Daimler helped keep its work force alive by subsidizing meals in its cafeteria, where 5,200 workers ate dinner daily. The firm honored its workers' 70 pfennig ration coupons for meat and bread for 120 pfennigs, a large subsidy. The company served meat even during the "meatless weeks" of 1916 by procuring exceedingly rare large cattle. In addition, it distributed 199,606 marks to its work force in 1916 (about 27 marks per worker, or half a week's salary) to buy potatoes for their sustenance. By 1917, Daimler's own nutritional enterprises encompassed facilities for steers, pigs, poultry, as well as wheat fields, orchards, and a soft-drink factory. In one month during the winter of 1918, the company gave its workers five portions of meat and cheese.[145]

The workers were being kept alive to work, and problems flared anew on the job at Daimler during the "turnip winter." In November 1916, assemblies of workers in the Daimler departments requested "that a drastic regulation of piece-rates should take place."[146] With this rank-and-file support, the workers' committee sought to win the pricing of piece-rates so that an "average" skilled worker would make 1.50 marks an hour, while a trained machine worker would earn 1.30 marks an hour. Hourly workers were also to earn roughly the same wages, if the committee would get its way.

Quickly, Daimler informed the military that the stakes in this dispute were high.[147] If the firm gave in on these points when its wages were among the highest in Wuerttemberg, the result would be the destabilization of the wage structure in the whole region. Its average rates were already approximately 1.20 marks per hour. After a rugged six-hour meeting with the workers' representatives on November 23, 1916, Daimler told the military that the unrest among its workers was growing and the work force was "very inclined to strike."[148] It took another lengthy session on November 30 for the outlines of a settlement to emerge. The sides basically split the differences between them.[149] The goals were to be 1.35 marks for skilled and 1.15 marks for machine workers. The chronic problem of setting agreed upon piece-rates for jobs in the departments was again addressed, since this new agreement would necessitate a far-ranging adjustment of such rates. Departmental chiefs were to work with shop stewards and members of the workers' committee to agree on the new rates.

In the fall of 1916, the white-collar workers at Daimler joined the groundswell of protest against earnings and working conditions. After two years of war and upwardly creeping prices, the white-collar workers felt themselves to be the victims of a generally deteriorating situation. "Despite supplementary payments and limited salary increases, the earnings of white-collar workers remained . . . far behind the rising cost of living and also behind workers' wages," writes the historian of the *Angestellte*.[150] In the fall of 1916, white collar workers at Daimler claimed that their monthly earnings were less than those "of a middling worker."[151] To be sure, office workers suffered at the hands of the war economy, and did not recover their losses for at least a decade after the war's end.

Kocka's catalogue of reasons for the plight of the clerks is compelling. For one, the rising cost of living during the war hurt the more inflexible, less market-oriented salaries of office workers more than it did wages, which were constantly being renegotiated, according to Kocka. In addition, the strong organizations and radical oppositions which made the labor movement such a potent political force were lacking among the white-collar workers. Military and government authorities were not so adamant on behalf of clerks, because they rarely joined together in strikes. "Above all," Kocka concluded, "the corporations could make out in the labor scarcity of the war more easily with fewer office workers than with fewer [industrial] workers."[152] Wary and fearful of those they deemed beneath them on the social ladder, and distrustful of bosses who would not give them their due, they felt increasingly menaced on all sides. Although they eschewed the social democratic organizations and trade unions at Daimler and elsewhere, they nonetheless found themselves pressed to react as their living standards fell, and addressed a plea for assistance to the Daimler direction.

Finally, on September 25, 1916, Daimler announced that the firm was now willing to assist any of its clerks who had been working there for longer than six months. Individual clerks had to apply in writing to the firm for this support, giving "the number and birth dates of the family members and providing a short written explanation to the direction."[153] Such an attitude, patriarchal to the extreme, was indicative of DMG's handling of its white-collar employees during the war, and finally prompted the military authorities in Stuttgart to monitor the situation.

Two adjustments of clerks' salaries were necessary in 1917—a raise and a "readjustment"—but still the pressures persisted.[154] The leaking of the story about what became known as the Daimler Affair by a disgruntled clerk in early 1918 is perhaps the extent of the office workers' dissatisfaction with the firm and its inadequate response to their dire economic condition.

Disputes flared anew within most parts of the Daimler empire in the winter of 1917–1918. The works in Berlin-Marienfelde were the scene of work stoppages which led the Prussian army to militarize the facility in December 1917. The plant direction's practice of having uncooperative workers drafted into the army was apparently a major cause of the difficulties at the factory. The army cited article 9b of the Prussian law on the state of siege in order to militarize the plant, which was an important supplier of military vehicles. The new military command at Marienfelde forbade workers to change their place of work without the permission of the military authorities, to "stay away from work . . . , [or] to stop work without being demonstrably unable." Avoiding work or slowing the tempo were also forbidden. The military decree required striking workers to take up their work again quickly or to report to the commanding officer immediately: "Then it will be communicated to them whether they will find employment with the troops or whether they are to continue their work as a soldier, receiving soldiers' wages."[155]

The Berlin authorities were able to report favorably about the results of the militarization. "Order in the factory was immediately restored and the overwhelming majority of workers took up the work immediately with good will." Nevertheless, the calm was short-lived, as the factory was one of the seven in Berlin at the center of the mass strikes of January 1918.[156] The radical wing of the Independent Social Democrats and the revolutionary shop stewards' movement among the metalworkers had a powerful presence at Daimler in Berlin-Marienfelde.

Yet, as 1918 dawned, the main works in Untertuerkheim still remained virtually untouched by radical politics. The new year, the last one of the war, would see dizzying changes, and by October and November 1918, Daimler would be the seedbed of revolution in greater Stuttgart.

In February 1918, the employees of the small independent department of the DMG in Stuttgart, Flugzeugbau Schiedmayer, held a mass meeting to demand a 30 percent bonus for the base wages of skilled workers and wage increases for unskilled and female laborers. It took more than a month to arrange a settlement acceptable to both sides.

Meanwhile, unrest over wages spread through the factory work forces in Untertuerkheim and Sindelfingen in early 1918. The main Untertuerkheim factory was wracked by protracted disputes with both manual and white-collar workers. The conflict with the *Angestellte* was particularly bitter. A group of clerks petitioned Daimler on January 18 for an increase in the supplementary payment *[Teuerungszulage]*. They cited price increases within the past six months of 7–8 pfennigs per pound of bread, 10 pfennigs per pound of sugar, 2 pfennigs per pound of salt, and 5 pfennigs per liter of milk. "Monthly expenses in a small household are 10 marks more now than they were in June 1917," they calculated. The clerks' pension fund had also been adversely affected: whether because of their financial situation or not, certain groups of office workers were no longer paying into it.[157]

The firm responded brusquely over a month later: there would be no more money for the office workers, and the "setting of a meeting to discuss the situation in your letter appears unnecessary to us." Besides, "we ask you to avoid an unnecessary loss of time in the future by leaving [those office workers] out of your representations. . . . They do not belong to your responsibility."[158] This apparently referred to the vague pension matter. It should be noted that this abrasive response was delivered as the military authorities began earnestly investigating the charges of the Daimler clerk, Hans Wohnlich, who alleged that DMG had falsified pricing data sent to the military. There the matter remained.

The grievances over wages and hours in the factory remained unresolved and continued to simmer in early 1918. Salm and Schifferdecker, the staunchly moderate SPD-men who led the Untertuerkheim workers' committee, launched a new effort to win an improvement in wages and hours.[159] Once again, mass meetings in the departments and workshops reinforced the demands for a far-reaching revision of the pay scales and for an 8-hour limitation on the working hours for women at the plant. The workers' committee did not press the broader issue of overtime and weekend work this time. Instead, it assailed the piece-rates in place as inadequate and called for their revision so that the average skilled worker would earn 2 marks per hour with a 30 percent increase in the average hourly base-rate, while the typical machine worker would make 1.80 marks. Unskilled workers would make 40 percent more, women 15–20 percent more despite the proposed eight hour limitation on their daily work time. The workers' committee asked that talks between the parties on these issues should begin immediately, "in view of the great dissatisfaction of the work force."[160]

The engineer on the scene for the Berlin war ministry's air office, Dr.

Weisshaar, quickly communicated the scale of these demands to his superiors in Berlin. He reckoned they would amount to "around 15 million marks—that is 47% of the share capital."[161] The present wage rates at Daimler, Weisshaar contended, are "not that far from those paid in northern Germany, while on the other hand the living conditions [in the area] are definitely better." Daimler wanted to oppose this campaign by the union, but "from earlier experiences with the Wuerttemberg War Ministry, can hardly hope for support." The officers in the ministry acted only "in the interests of peace [Ruhe]" without regard to the industry. Nevertheless, the firm still held out hope for reaching an "acceptable agreement" with the workers' committee, Weisshaar reported.[162]

When the military officials learned of the workers' new claims, they pledged their support to the firm if it resisted them. The bill from the demands would reach 15 million, and "in the end, this increase [would] have to be paid by the army command." Nevertheless, the law clearly called for the submission of the matter to the regional arbitration committee.[163]

The arbitration process called for by the Auxiliary Service Law began on February 5, 1918, with a public session of the Stuttgart arbitration committee. Berge and Paul Daimler were the most prominent witnesses for DMG; Salm and Schifferdecker were the key representatives of the workers' committee.

Within days, the arbitrators had rendered a decision. The piece-rates for skilled and machine workers should remain about where they were—about 1.70 and 1.45 marks per hour on average. This was in line with the rates prevailing in the greater Stuttgart area. The hourly wages for piece-workers and for those skilled workers receiving an hourly wage should benefit from a 30 percent bonus and should be comparable to the earnings of piece-rate workers. Unskilled workers over 18 years of age should receive a 10 pfennig per hour raise. The arbitrators concluded that women should work only eight-hour shifts if possible, and that if paid as piece-workers, their earnings should amount to 85 pfennigs, about 60 percent of what males earned. For the second level of women workers—those paid by the hour as day laborers —the just rates should total 65 pfennigs an hour for married women; 60 pfennigs for single women over age 18; and 40–50 pfennigs for those under 18.[164]

In addition to all of the basic rates, the wage package should include two other elements. "In view of the especially prosperous conditions of the firm," a weekly bonus of eight marks for married male workers and five marks for single male workers and women should be instituted. Cost of living adjustments [Teuerungszulage] should remain reflections of the trends in the cost of living.[165] This compromise infuriated Berge.

The issue of piece-rates lay at the heart of the dispute at Sindelfingen in the late winter of 1918. On March 22, the workers' committee there called for the setting of goals for the hourly earnings of all piece-workers. Skilled workers should receive 1.75 marks, machine workers 1.45, and women 85 pfennigs. These should be paid out if piece-rates could not, for whatever reason, be set or agreed upon before the actual job began. The rates themselves had to be posted "in ink or typewriter." The committee also blasted the tendency for piece-rates to fall if workers "through [their] diligence and skill" attained higher earnings. It demanded a payment of 2 marks daily to those married workers who had been transferred from Untertuerkheim to Sindelfingen until they could locate a flat in or near the new factory.[166]

Fearing a disruption in the operation of its new factory at Sindelfingen, which had yet to turn out a complete airplane motor and for which it was desperately trying to obtain skilled workers through army channels, Daimler agreed to wage adjustments which were generally 7 to 10 percent below the figures presented by the workers' committee. Mass meetings of the workers were held on April 8 and 9. In their wake, the workers' committee expressed the work force's "regret" that the firm had not met their "justified wishes." Still, they reluctantly agreed with the Daimler proposals, "but only in the sure expectation that the firm fulfills the concessions restlessly and immediately."[167]

Within three weeks, this agreement was on the verge of breaking down. On April 29, Daimler told the military authorities that the workers' committee no longer accepted the wage rates for unskilled workers and for the building workers who were constructing the facilities at Sindelfingen. "We feel that the average of 80 pfennigs [per hour] represents a sufficient payment for a day laborer" and therefore rejected the demands. The dispute festered through the spring and summer, but without work stoppages or an escalation of the strife.

JUNE 1918: OPEN DEFIANCE

The most serious wartime confrontation, which grew out of the festering grievances in Untertuerkheim about lengthy hours and weekend work, flared up in June 1918. This time, however, the military was a key participant, providing the muscle to quash a job action. The history of this dispute provides a perspective for assessing the positive role of the military supervision for the Daimler stockholders during 1918.

In March and April 1918, the workers' committee had not seriously pressed the campaign to win a shortening of hours, particularly on the night shift. Still, after this round of negotiations, the workers believed that the firm would be forthcoming on the issue of long hours with the coming of the "hot time of the year." By mid-May, pressure from the shop floor again demanded action to shorten the work day. As a result, the workers' committee addressed the direction of the corporation on May 23. This time, Salm and Schifferdecker put forward proposals which would have permitted shortened hours without impairing production. For one, workers from "all of the mechanical workshops" had reported that "many of the machines are only singly utilized. Through a doubling of this utilization, a part of the lost production due to shortened working hours would be made up." This meant that, according to the workers' committee at least, machines were inefficiently used and managed at the Untertuerkheim plant. In addition, some of the repair procedures, often lasting four to six days, could be shortened to permit them to be used more.[168]

Whatever the means for improving the efficiency of working hours, the workers' committee believed it to be imperative that the late shift on Saturdays be suspended. "The largest part of the workers wish that in the future on Saturdays only one shift work, from 6:20 A.M. to 1:30 P.M." The most pressing reason, recognized by company officials, was simply the toll taken by the combination of the long hours during the week and the time needed for the daily commute to and from work. The workers could not "use the free time to rest." The time to settle the issue was at hand, the workers' representation declared, and negotiations should begin immediately.[169]

While the matter of exhausting working hours was once again being raised, the military authorities complained of production delays in the Daimler workshops. The testing of new engines in the *Bremserei* was proceeding too slowly, Captain Gross complained. The number of motors being adjusted there had actually declined by 75 from April to May, instead of increasing according to plan. The military supervision was growing noticeably testier. It also carried out a comparison of the average lengths of work time spent in producing the 160 and 260 horsepower engines during the previous 15 months. The results showed a considerable increase in the year between March 1917 and March 1918—from 43.8 hours to 80 hours for the 160 horsepower engine, and from 55.7 hours to 97 hours for the 260 horsepower model.[170] By early June, the situation had stabilized somewhat, due to a great extent to the military's attempts to eliminate production bottlenecks and to stabilize the provision of tools and machinery. Nevertheless, the productions of motors of these types required up to 55 percent more labor-power than they had in early 1917.

With army authorities exerting pressure on Daimler, the firm felt it could resist the demands being put forth by its work force. Its response to the workers' committee was to suggest the adoption of a single ten-hour shift on Saturdays, ending at 5:40 P.M. With this answer, the military supervision at Daimler intervened, addressing the War Ministry in Stuttgart on the full ramifications of the Daimler workers' requests.[171] If they were granted, the Daimler employees on the night shift would work 56 hours each week, the day shift 66 hours. For both groups, admittedly, "48 hours would be completely work free" on weekends. "Despite the accelerated installation of machines and the provision of more workers, the firm remains far behind the demands of the military aviation authorities." With such a situation prevailing, no shortening of the work week could be contemplated. Even if Daimler's proposal were implemented, the resulting slackening of production would be the equivalent of the loss of 2,000 workers.[172]

With both the firm's direction and military overseers unwilling to countenance the workers' demands, the workers' committee was unable to resist the growing pressure from the rank and file. Talks broke off on June 13, with the sides far apart.[173] At a mass meeting on Friday, June 14, the work force decided to press its campaign. The rank and file rejected a proposal by the workers' committee to seek a compromise settlement along the lines of one proposed by the company, which was presented by Schifferdecker to the mass meeting, and refused to wait for the arbitration committee to rule on the matter. Instead, it pressed for direct action to force an end to afternoon and night work on Saturdays.[174] Within hours, the workers' committee reluctantly issued the following leaflet: "Today's assembly has unanimously decided: The day shift on Saturdays ends at 1:30 P.M., the night shift is eliminated. This decision goes for everyone. The working hours for women remain unchanged."[175]

On Saturday, June 15, the workers for the second shift did not report as required. The employees' resolve initially caught the authorities off guard. In a secret communique on Saturday, the military command asserted that "For today . . . a response is no longer possible." It noted that the workers' committee had assured it that "it stands apart from this matter." The War Minister, von Marchtaler, later confirmed that the job action occurred "without the collaboration of the workers' committee."[176]

Nevertheless, the military supervision recovered quickly. Indeed, in these very days and weeks, the German army's "final offensive" was cresting along the Marne, only 56 miles from Paris. Preparations for the next stage of the offensive had begun. The final battle with the enemy had seemingly been joined, and swift, responsible action was now needed to secure the home front and one of the most important military suppliers. Plans for the full militarization of the factory were readied. Such a move would have permitted the swift induction of any member of the work force into the army. Once in the military, they could be sent to the front or commanded to work at Daimler for military pay. Two months earlier, General von Schaefer, the head of the army in Wuerttemberg, had issued secret guidelines in the event strife in important war-related industries necessitated the militarization of factories in order to restore military production. Bearing the designation "strictly secret," von Schaefer's instructions indicated that the military authorities would not needlessly seek a confrontation with the industrial work force. In the event of work stoppages, von Schaefer asserted that "the overwhelming majority of the workers" would "voluntarily" take up work again, and only a small handful would be subject to the military's punitive summons. The purpose for their mobilization into the army would clearly be to force them to take up their work again. The general stated his point clearly: "The militarization is not to be ordered for the advantage of the company, but for the best [interest] of the fatherland."[177]

Now, in line with this strategy, von Schaefer issued a strongly worded order which was posted at the plant gates by a policeman early on Monday morning.[178] "The war situation demands here . . . that the production of the Daimler factory be kept up with all means and if possible be increased. Every hour of missed worked is treason to the fatherland and endangers the lives of our brothers and sons at the front." Until now, Daimler workers had willingly performed the "difficult work" demanded of them. However, within the past weeks, a "change" seems to have occurred, General von Schaefer asserted. Now, the workers had undertaken "to set arbitrarily the work-time," thereby breaching the established rules. "I want to leave no doubt . . . ," he declared. "I will meet [attempts] to disturb the orderly operation of the factory with all legal means." He threatened to draft those workers "who do not punctually keep the set working hours" and to subject them to the "laws of war." The general spelled out the exact working hours on Saturdays with a peace-offering to the workers: one day shift lasting to 5:40 P.M., with no night shift. Any willful disregard of this command could also be punished by a minimum of one year's imprisonment or by a fine of up to 1,500 marks.[179] Thus, the workers secured the ending of the night shift on Saturdays, and Daimler won enactment of its proposal for the ten-hour Saturday shift. General von Schaefer had given both labor and management a concession.

Faced with this resolute action, and having won the abolition of the late Saturday shift, the work force was reluctant to press its challenge any further. On Tuesday, June 18, the workers' committee indicated to the chief of staff of the army in Wuerttemberg that it would ask the workers to obey General von Schaefer's order and to report for work at the newly set hours on the next Saturday. Nevertheless, the representatives repeated that the limitations on Saturday work desired by the work force could be implemented without a falloff of production if their proposals for "a greater intensity of work" were implemented.[180]

On June 21, the workers' committee formally asked their rank and file to heed the general's order and to avoid a confrontation. Afterward, it announced that "the direction of the workers' committee is authorized, together with the leadership of the [union] organization, to seek the rescinding of the order and a new regulation of the working hours in line with the request of the work force."[181]

The whiff of decomposition hung over the labor movement at Daimler during the summer of 1918. The chasm between the trade unionists on the workers' committee and the rank and file threatened labor. The danger was that an ossifying organization apparatus might come to lack the muscle of the masses in its dealings with military and firm, while the rank and file might lack leadership possessing the full confidence of those on the shop floor as the trials of the future clearly loomed.

Although the quick confrontation with the military ended open insubordination for the time being, the rate of absenteeism increased sharply in the following weeks (see table 4.6). Whereas approximately 3 ½–4 percent of the work force was absent on average in May 1916, and 6 percent in May 1918, the rate ballooned in the weeks after the job action, reaching 20 percent of the total work force on July 9.[182] Undoubtedly, the influenza epidemics which raced through the general population in the summer and fall of 1918 were partially to blame, but the military authorities pressed the Daimler hierarchy to do something about the growing numbers of workers staying away from work. DMG quickly instituted a new procedure for handling the absentee problem. It ordered a special clerk to gather the names of all those absent from the departmental chiefs each day. Those who stayed away for three straight weeks were to be reported to the *Kriegsarbeitsstelle,* as were those who were absent "twice within a short time."[183] By the end of July, despite the persistence of the grippe in the region, officials were hopeful they had the absentee situation at Daimler under control, as the daily lists shrank to less than 10 percent of the work force. Nevertheless, the military supervisors noted at the same time a growing tendency for the employees to avoid working overtime, despite the contraction of the working week made the previous month.[184]

The undeclared truce after the June job action lasted for nearly three months. The workers' committee tried again unsuccessfully in talks on August 17 and September 6 to win a further concession on Saturday work hours. Discontent erupted at Daimler on September 11, 1918, a few days after the last session, when an assembly of 10,000 workers in the bloated factory met to press demands for a 30 percent wage hike and a reduction in the night shift from 11 hours 20 minutes to 9 hours 40 minutes.[185] Following a two-week hiatus caused by the elections to the workers' committee, Salm and Schifferdecker (who ran unopposed for reelection despite a growing radical opposition) requested the urgent resumption of negotiations with the direction on a variety of issues, including wages. "We are no longer in a position to recognize the Arbitration Committee's decision of February 6, 1918."[186] Besides the important matter of wages, a number of other areas required attention. The workers in the revolving-lathe workshop had "grievances concerning the drop [in the number] of work-pieces [recorded] by the auditors." Two groups of unskilled workers from the mechanical department and the magazine also sought to be included for purposes of wages with the machine-workers. Piece-rate workers now wanted their piece-rate summary cards before they were paid in order to give them a chance to figure their correct wages before they accepted their money. In addition, in an indication of dissatisfaction with the direction's control of disciplinary matters, the workers' committee wanted to be consulted in cases of the

TABLE 4.6
Absenteeism at Daimler-Untertuerkheim, 7/3–8/2 1918

Date	Males Ill	Females Ill	Total Ill
July 3 (Wed.)	1,517 (13.6%)	491 (17.8%)	2,008 (14.5%)
July 4	1,653 (14.9%)	575 (20.9%)	2,228 (16.0%)
July 5	1,725 (15.5%)	626 (22.8%)	2,351 (16.9%)
July 9 (Tues.)	2,101 (18.8%)	651 (23.4%)	2,752 (19.7%)
July 10	1,845 (16.5%)	641 (23.0%)	2,486 (17.8%)
July 11	1,697 (15.2%)	603 (21.7%)	2,300 (16.5%)
July 12	1,540 (13.8%)	620 (22.3%)	2,160 (15.5%)
July 13 (Sat.)	1,716 (15.4%)	606 (21.8%)	2,322 (16.7%)
July 16 (Tues.)	1,263 (11.3%)	458 (16.5%)	1,721 (12.4%)
July 17	1,190 (10.7%)	460 (16.5%)	1,650 (11.8%)
July 18	1,211 (10.7%)	478 (16.9%)	1,689 (11.9%)
July 19	1,152 (10.2%)	439 (15.6%)	1,591 (11.2%)
July 20 (Sat.)	1,209 (10.7%)	459 (16.3%)	1,668 (11.8%)
July 22 (Mon.)	953 (8.4%)	376 (13.3%)	1,329 (9.4%)
July 23	913 (8.0%)	365 (12.8%)	1,278 (8.9%)
July 24	858 (7.5%)	370 (13.0%)	1,228 (8.6%)
July 25	817 (7.1%)	350 (12.3%)	1,167 (8.2%)
July 26	806 (7.0%)	347 (12.2%)	1,153 (8.0%)
July 27	902 (7.9%)	361 (12.7%)	1,263 (8.8%)
July 29 (Mon.)	749 (6.6%)	294 (10.4%)	1,043 (7.4%)
July 30	767 (6.8%)	312 (11.1%)	1,079 (7.6%)
July 31	772 (6.8%)	302 (10.7%)	1,074 (7.6%)
August 1	700 (6.2%)	290 (10.3%)	990 (7.0%)
August 2	718 (6.3%)	295 (10.4%)	1,013 (7.2%)

Source: Compiled from HStASt M 77/1 76. Percentages are based on totals for the Untertuerkheim work force, which changed weekly.

dismissal or punishment of workers before management took any disciplinary action.[187]

The most critical issue turned out to be wages. In talks with the workers' committee, the firm asserted that its financial balance had deteriorated sharply since March, and, thus, it could not give in to these demands whose costs amounted to around 22 million marks.[188] After all, it claimed that its wages were among the highest in the area.[189] When the workers' committee appealed to the military overseers of the firm and to the War Ministry in Stuttgart, they confirmed the shaky economic situation in Untertuerkheim. The workers' representatives protested that a pay increase was now badly needed and succeeded in getting the whole matter shifted to the War Ministry in Berlin for consideration by a commission which would examine Daimler's plight. Soon, during the first week of October, the leaders of the workers' committee traveled to Berlin, having secured vacation days from the firm.[190] They arrived in a capital astir in the wake of General Ludendorff's decision a week earlier that the war was lost, and that the Reichstag must now sue for peace.

The negotiations quickly encompassed more than just the wage issue. Salm and Schifferdecker, alarmed by the military supervision's neglect of the firm's financial planning since March 6, requested that the ban against Ernst Berge be lifted so that he could take the helm again for the critical transition period which lay ahead.[191] "The interest of the workers demanded measures to lead the operation into peacetime production after the cessation of military contracts. The military supervision had no interest in that. It was only empowered to watch over the handling of the war contracts; what came afterwards was not its task."[192] Yet the committee made no secret that in return it expected "a hastening of the settlement of the wage claims." "We long had the impression that the leading members of the firm had held back from making concessions to the work force, because they feared they could not justify concessions" without a readiness to compromise on the part of the workers.[193]

The ministry informed Salm and Schifferdecker that it was conceivable the charges against Berge would soon be dismissed due to lack of evidence. The delegation of Daimler workers' representatives made clear that they were interceding for Berge's reinstatement, "not on account of Berge but on account of the workers."[194]

The trip yielded immediate rewards, if not yet for the workers. The army lifted the ban against Berge. On October 16, he resumed his duties as head of the Daimler-Motoren-Gesellschaft, although the company remained officially under military supervision until at least December.

After the workers' representatives returned from Berlin, they announced their readiness to settle for a one-time payment to hold the work force over for the coming winter months.[195] This was the first time that the workers' committee had ever raised the question of a lump sum. As had become standard by now, the payment would be adjusted according to age and marital status, not according to level of skill. According to Daimler's estimate, such a payment to the Untertuerkheim work force would amount to six million marks.

The workers' committee also had a political interest in coming to terms quickly with the firm. In a telegram to military authorities in Berlin, Daimler asserted that the workers' committee now feared it would soon "lose control of the work force" and therefore wanted to settle on a sum of money quickly.[196] The company warned, however, that any settlement would force it to raise its prices.

Negotiations dragged on inconclusively through October. Once again, military intervention broke the logjam. Captain Letzgus, of the *Kriegsarbeitsstelle* within the Wuerttemberg command, chaired a session which was joined by legates of the VWMI and the DMV on October 26, 1918.[197] Letzgus succeeded in getting the parties to agree to his proposal for payments to workers amounting to 400 marks for those males or females who were heads of households, ranging on down to 100 marks for young men and women under 17 years of age. At the same time, the Daimler company, which was pleading grave financial difficulties "as a result of the events of March 1918 . . . [which have done] extraordinary damage,"[198] apparently succeeded in inducing the military to provide the funds for the payments, which would amount to six million marks for the Untertuerkheim works. The first installment, totalling three-fifths of the whole, was to be disbursed at the onset of the Advent season; the final payment was to be issued on the eve of Lent.[199]

Yet within weeks, the war was over, the revolution had begun, and the fashioners of this deal were obliged to leave the leadership of the workers' committee, victims of a shattering no-confidence vote.

From mobilization to the October 1918 crisis, the leaders of the workers' committee had steadfastly supported the war. They repaid the military for the attention it paid them. The Daimler workers' committee accepted an invitation from the assistant military commander in Stuttgart in mid-April 1918 to discuss the improvement of pro-war propaganda in the factories and helped prepare a two-day meeting of factory representatives. The receptivity of the delegates from the area factories pleased the military authorities, particularly their orders for "patriotic" posters and brochures. The Association of Wuerttemberg Metal Industrialists opposed the conference, protesting that the military commanders were responsible for the growing self-confidence of the workers and contending that it was unworthy of officers to sit at the same table with workers.[200]

RADICALS AT DAIMLER: LEAFLETS AGAINST THE WAR

The course of radical militancy at Daimler during the war is virtually impossible to reassemble fully. For one, in a world of military administration and prerogative, Stuttgart's radicals existed on the fringes of legality. In addition, they rarely turned their attention to organizing in the factories until late in the war. The host of reports received by the Ministry of the Interior traced the activities of a small group of men and women around Friedrich Westmeyer, Edwin Hoernle, and Artur Crispien—the so-called Westmeyer group —who were associated with the Social Democratic League of Stuttgart and the socialist youth movement in the greater Stuttgart area.[201] After the spring of 1915, these activists were outside of the official SPD. They often tried to hold meetings and to organize picnics and other outings, but the preponderance of these were banned by the police or the military commanders. Several activists sympathized with the revolutionary Spartacist movement. Nevertheless, in a secret report in April 1917, the Stuttgart police pronounced the situation calm and noted that radical leaders had left or been removed from Stuttgart via military conscription.[202]

The authorities considered even the radicals' attempts to distribute anti-war leaflets grave subversion. But even on this count, it is surprising how few incidents were recorded by the police. For example, in the aftermath of the militant strike movement in Berlin and elsewhere in January 1918, the Stuttgart police marveled that they "had not seen even leaflets [here], and this despite the fact Stuttgart was a *Hochburg* of radicalism before the war." They ventured an explanation for this unexpected calm, pointing out the "relatively better [food supply situation], as well as the fact . . . that the Stuttgart military workers are dispersed with residents of the neighboring locales who have a small plot of land, while the strikers in the north and in Munich are to a large extent a homeless people *[heimatloses Volk]*."[203]

Nevertheless, anti-war leaflets were spread on several occasions in the area. It is striking that most recorded locations where leaflets were posted or passed out were in central areas of Stuttgart, where one might have expected to find chiefly a bourgeois and *kleinbuergerliche* public.

There are several recorded episodes of the distribution of radical leaflets at the Daimler plant or by Daimler workers. In July 1916, the leaflet "2 ½ Years Prison," which protested the sentencing of Karl Liebknecht for anti-war activities, was passed out "in large numbers" at DMG by a youth "between 18 and 20 years old." Later three youths, 17 and 18 years old, were arrested for distributing the handbills.[204] Leaflets announcing a general strike on August 15, 1917 "for the achievement of peace" were "pasted onto the walls of much-visited areas—the guard house at the entrance, the cafeteria, etc." Two weeks later, two Daimler workers, 39 and 42 years old, married, and living in Bad Cannstatt, were arrested on charges of "attempted treason" for distributing leaflets.[205]

The great strike movement of January 1918 passed over Stuttgart and Daimler. The first clear indication of growing militancy at DMG was the rank-and-file attempt to cancel the Saturday afternoon and evening shift by not reporting to work in mid-June 1918. The ensuing mass absenteeism may have been a sign of a more passive resistance to the difficult working conditions, although this is more problematic. In any case, the new militancy at DMG was not the result of acute food shortages, but rather of growing anger with working conditions in the wake of the Daimler Affair and with the apparent connivance of the military supervision with management.[206]

What is clear is that when the anti-war Independent Social Democrats and Sparticists showed renewed interest in agitating among Stuttgart factory workers in the late summer of 1918, they turned their attention to DMG-Untertuerkheim.

5

RED STAR OVER MERCEDES:
DAIMLER WORKERS AND
THE REVOLUTION,
NOVEMBER 1918
TO JANUARY 1920

THE *ancien regime* slid into crisis as the allied forces hammered away at the German army in the late summer and autumn of 1918. The domestic front began to buckle at almost every point of the imperial edifice: shortages in food supplies for the population became more widespread and acute; raw material shortages led increasingly to production bottlenecks which further burdened the beleaguered economy; unrest and unease spread throughout the exhausted population; the political order was being re-drawn with the help of the SPD in October 1918 yet increasingly lost legitimacy. The spreading actions and demonstrations in late October and early November were demands for relief from unbearable political and economic conditions. At the moment Social Democracy finally made its way in—into government and into industrial negotiations through the trade unions—the bulk of the population looked to the SPD, the organization least discredited by the experience of the war in the eyes of many Germans, for a way out. Thus, as one historian pointed out, "The SPD in reality made revolution against itself. Social-democratic masses, led by Social Democrats, tore apart a lawful order, at whose head stood a government dominated by the SPD."[1] Yet within weeks, many life-long Social Democratic workers at Daimler and elsewhere cast their lot with the militants of the Independent Social Democrats or communists.

From Berlin to Stuttgart, from Hamburg to Munich, republican governments, led by men and women who had managed with great difficulty to cooperate within prewar Social Democracy, came into being. Almost without exception, they enjoyed widespread support among the populace during the first weeks. This grace period for the SPD, however, proved to be of very short duration, as radicals left provisional governments in late 1918 and 1919.

In the Daimler factory in Untertuerkheim, the period of grace was already long finished for the SPD. A shop-floor movement to the left of the established workers' leadership had emerged during the dispute over working hours in June 1918. The work force moved to the brink of confrontation with the military before General von Schaefer's stern warning deterred it from crossing the threshold into open disobedience. Three months later, the social democratic leaders of the workers' committee stood unopposed for reelection. Nevertheless, a powerful and growing radical opposition had moved with increasing confidence onto the political field at Daimler. Dissatisfaction with the way the committee had handled the negotiations for a pay increase in September and October and with its open intervention with the war ministry on behalf of Ernst Berge fueled the strength of the opposition, as yet only loosely associated with the independent social democrats and Spartacists. In a sense, the prewar domination of the local party organizations in greater Stuttgart by radical socialists was reasserting itself, as the work force rapidly moved leftward to embrace more or less traditionally militant Social Democratic positions now espoused by the USPD and Spartacists.

By early November the USPD had assembled a network of militant cadres at Daimler. According to a police report from early November, these included Eugen Wirsching, fitter; Otto Braune, fitter; August Ziegler, fitter; Oskar Foerster, machine technician; Karl Straub, lathe-turner; Karl Grosshans, fitter; and Franz Grimm, day laborer.[2] One of the prominent Stuttgart radicals, Fritz Rueck, reported that when the USPD turned its efforts to building an organization in the Stuttgart factories during the early autumn of 1918, it found a number of eager volunteers at Daimler. They met to discuss politics in a room next to a workers' tavern in Untertuerkheim. Rueck, who often spoke with the group, noted the attentiveness of the Daimler workers in these discussions. On the other hand, he alleged, it was difficult to find people at Bosch "who had an understanding of political questions."[3]

By mid-October, the budding political unrest at Daimler merited the attention of the army general staff in Berlin. Police officials in Wuerttemberg indicated that the latest efforts of the independent social democrats in the area were beginning to bear fruit. "The movement [is] serious. Leaflets have been distributed [at] the Daimler plant, signed by the international Spartacist group. . . . In the event of mobilizing Stuttgart troops, reliability is doubtful."[4]

The revolutionary movement in Stuttgart quickly recognized the fertility of the Daimler work force for its organizing efforts and paid special attention to its work in the Untertuerkheim plant in late October. The first mass action in Stuttgart took place at the end of the month, when several thousand marched through the city, after hearing reports from USPD Reichstag deputies about the political situation in Berlin. Following the resignation of General Ludendorff, a group of militants led by Fritz Rueck visited Daimler to talk to several hundred workers in the cafeteria during the night shift. It was this meeting that allegedly elected the first workers' council in Wuerttemberg, although this is disputed.[5] According to the SPD politician Wilhelm Keil, the workers put Rueck at their head, and along with a few soldiers who were present, followed the "Russian model" of creating a council.[6]

In the next several days, preparations began among the USPD and Spartacist militants for a demonstration strike in conjunction with the mass actions which were supposed to occur throughout Germany. The strike was set for November 4, which (according to the mistaken militants in Stuttgart at least) was supposed to be the day for the uprising in Berlin. At a meeting of USPD organizers from the Stuttgart factories on the afternoon of November 3, the Daimler workers expressed strong misgivings about the planned strike. As one of the participants put it: "There was, however, no turning back. . . . With a packet of handbills and leaflets, the factory representatives went out to mobilize the colleagues for the following morning."[7]

On the gloomy morning of November 4, excitement and confusion reigned in the Untertuerkheim factory as the men and women arrived for work. The workers aligned with the USPD and the Spartacists passed out the leaflets announcing the mass action to the arriving workers. Quickly, Salm and Schifferdecker convened an emergency session of the workers' committee. Since only one of the elected representatives was known to be a supporter of the radical independents, the overwhelming majority of the committee followed the lead of the two chairmen and rejected participation in the day-long action. According to a police report, "The representatives of the independents, however, threatened Salm and Schifferdecker with violence and with disconnecting the machinery. At the assurance of the independents that it would be a peaceful demonstration for the conclusion of an armistice and peace, the workers' committee finally declared itself in agreement with a day-long demonstration strike." Meanwhile, the independents had shut down the plant, switching off engines and power supplies. Word soon reached the Interior Ministry in Stuttgart that 12,000 workers were off the job at Daimler, but that not all were still on the scene.[8]

A leader of the militants, Rueck, later told a different account. Early on the morning of November 4, a worker from Daimler had gone off to fetch him, appealing that "it would be good if you could be at the plant at 9:00, at the beginning of the breakfast pause." Arriving at a side gate, Rueck was greeted by a USPD cadre, who told him that the whole factory was in an uproar. "Our leaflets have been distributed, but in the meeting of the factory representatives . . . the Social Democrats and trade unionists came out sharply against a strike. Several of the departments have shut down, and the Social Democrats are now unsure of themselves. Perhaps you could go onto the palisade and say a few words—half of the factory can hear you from there."

Several workers helped Rueck to climb the palisade. From there he saw "head next to head in the factory buildings pressed against the window." Raising his voice so that he could be heard, he declared "what all already felt"—that the war could not go on any longer, that a fundamental change in German society must be brought about. The comrades should all make the strike and demonstration a success and stop work. The doors of the factory buildings swung open, and a mass of workers began to assemble, several thousand strong. Quickly, the Social Democrats on the workers' committee gave up their opposition, and several majority Social Democrats joined the vanguard of the demonstration as it began to exit the Daimler factory and head toward Wangen, across the river on the route to downtown Stuttgart. Three workers unfurled red flags and hoisted aloft a sign, "Nieder mit dem Krieg, hoch die Republik!"[9] A Daimler clerk, Sophie Dohring, marched in the front ranks, and many women workers participated in the demonstration. The sight of the Daimler workers impressed the soldiers in the Berg barracks, but it was all on the wrong day. Berlin had not risen on the fourth. The demonstrators dispersed without incident after Interior Minister Koehler received several spokespersons for the group. Thus began the revolution in Wuerttemberg, not with a bang but an error.

In the wake of the one-day strike, the radical factions seemed initially confused and disorganized. Their credibility had suffered, to be sure, for the rest of Germany had not revolted on November 4. Blos, later the SPD's President of Wuerttemberg, dismissed the demonstrators of November 4 as "a few thousand workers . . . [mainly] from the Daimler factory."[10] The DMV characterized the participants as "immature youths, the curious, and passers-by." On November 5, at a meeting of trade unionists and representatives from the SPD and USPD at Daimler, all parties agreed to work against the disruption of the plant by "irresponsible and unknown" elements. This marked an admission of error by at least several of the USPD organizers at the plant.[11] Social Democrats in the factory attacked the alleged duplicity and adventurism of the radical opposition, and seemed to briefly improve their position on the shop-floor. In the name of the workers' committee, Salm and Schifferdecker told the work force to resist the entreaties of unauthorized agitators, who were still trying to stir up trouble.

Nevertheless, the shadowy Stuttgart workers' council, based at Daimler, dispatched a letter to the regional officers of the *Stellvertretendes Generalkommando,* informing the generals of a number of "decisions" which the council had made. "The members of the workers' council are immune," the generals were told, "from interference by the factory owners, and from arrests and forced induction into the military." The military should immediately lift its new ban against Rueck and instead cooperate with the council's efforts by providing helpers and supplies of paper.[12]

Sensing that the radicals in the workers' council were isolated from the masses of area factory workers, the government in Stuttgart precipitated the next wave of unrest by locking up the radicals Rueck and Thalheimer on treason charges. In addition, the government issued warrants for 16 members of the Stuttgart workers' and soldiers' council formed earlier at Daimler "because of the preparation of revolutionary leaflets."[13] A police roster of the sixteen indicates that the average age of those arrested was slightly over 37 years. Of the fifteen about whom information was provided, seven were skilled metal or machine workers, one was a skilled woodworker, one a skilled handworker, three were unskilled laborers, and the other three included a typesetter, a fabric cutter, and a shoemaker. The police reported the marital status of ten: seven were married and three single. All, of course, lived in the area, and most were apparently Swabian by birth.[14]

Minister Koehler had informed the party heads prior to ordering the arrests; even the SPD found the move "understandable." Quickly, on the morning of November 8, demonstrations broke out at Daimler, which trade unionists soon joined. The wave of protest was so strong that Vorhoelzer, the head of the Metalworkers' Union in Stuttgart, telephoned the SPD leader Keil between 9 and 10 A.M. and warned that if the prisoners were not set free immediately, the trade union leaders would lose all influence with the workers, with unforeseeable consequences. Meanwhile, a delegation of Daimler workers led by Salm and Schifferdecker was en route to the ministry of the interior to plead for the release of the political prisoners. It was typical of the tactical considerations of the majority SPD workers' leadership at Daimler that it initially eschewed calling for mass street demonstrations to back its demand.

Before reaching the ministry, the delegation stopped at the trade union house to meet with Keil, the chief of the regional SPD. A large number of party and trade union officials had already gathered there. Plans for a mass protest for the next day, November 9, were readied, and the leaders of the USPD were invited to a session to be held that afternoon. The Daimler delegation, which a number of leading party and union functionaries had joined, proceeded to the Interior Ministry. They informed Minister Koehler of their plans for the demonstration. Although not in the least pleased, Koehler was powerless to stop their plans.[15]

The afternoon meeting between the trade unions, SPD, and USPD—the first session between the factions of the workers' movement since the split in Wuerttemberg—was tense and lengthy, but the sides agreed to call for a joint demonstration the next day. They agreed on a joint leaflet, which became the revolution's manifesto in Wuerttemberg.

"The old Germany is no more. A new Germany exists," it proclaimed. The parties and unions issued nine demands, which were to serve as the immediate political agenda for November 1918 in Stuttgart. These included: (1) the introduction of a republic; (2) a general, direct, and secret suffrage with proportional representation; (3) abolition of the upper house of the legislature and of all privileges of wealth and birth; (4) new elections; (5) the speedy conclusion of a peace agreement, with disarmament and dissolution of the standing army; (6) the immediate lifting of the state of siege and of censorship; (7) the release of all persons held for political grounds or for reasons of military discipline; (8) the lifting of the Auxiliary Service Law, along with the carrying out of the unions' programs for the transitional economy; in addition, the implementation of the socialist programs of the political parties and the unions; and (9) the settling of war debts through a financial policy based on taxing war profits and property.[16] The leaflet, bearing the endorsement of unions, SPD, and USPD, was distributed early on the morning of November 9 at Daimler in Untertuerkheim and at the other workplaces in Stuttgart.

Saturday, November 9, was another cloudy day in Stuttgart. At Daimler-Untertuerkheim, groups of demonstrators began to gather shortly after dawn. Not a policeman was to be seen anywhere. *Vertrauensmaenner* from the trade unions and the political parties organized the demonstrators into orderly ranks. By mid-morning, tens of thousands of demonstrators were pouring into downtown Stuttgart. A radical paper reported: "The vanguard of the revolution, the Daimler workers, pressed into the waiting city from Untertuerkheim in impressive ranks. At the head marched sailors and drivers. In the front rank, next to the red flag of freedom, marched four Turkish soldiers. The workers carried placards: 'Down with the war! Up with the socialist republic!' and red flags waved above the flaming hearts and minds of the masses."[17]

As the throngs marched into the *Schlossplatz* downtown, the speakers began to deliver their messages from three platforms erected around the surrounding plazas. In accord with the arrangement between the two socialist parties, a speaker from each addressed the demonstrators. Keil of the SPD

Ernst Berge.

Alfred von Kaulla.

In the Daimler foundry, ca. 1914. At the right, a worker readies a mold, while another purifies the forming sand. To the left, a cast-cleaner begins to dislodge sand and impurities from the surface of a cast, while a skilled worker looks on.

Smiths in the Daimler forge, c. 1910. Note the large presses in the background.

A Daimler department, 1903: skilled fitters.

A skilled turner cuts a crankshaft on a lathe in Untertuerkheim, c. 1904.

Fitters adjusting and assembling parts of axles, 1912.

Skilled fitters assembling chassis, 1912.

Woodworkers carving and joining sections of automobile bodies in Untertuerkheim, 1906.

Upholsterers stuff and sew the seats for a Mercedes, 1914.

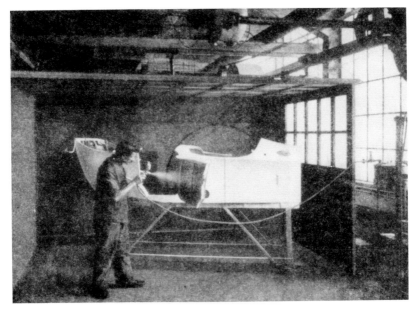

A simple labor-saving device, c. 1914: a compressed-air paint gun.

A master (in his black suit) looks on as painters apply a coat to the undercarriage, c. 1906.

The assembly hall for autos in Untertuerkheim, 1906: skilled fitters.

Touch-up work after the final assembly, c. 1912.

The assembly hall for airplane motors in Untertuerkheim, 1915 or 1916. Note the women working on the second floor.

WILLE und **TAT**

Wille und Tat haben die Geschichte
unserer Werke geschrieben.
Tradition und Qualität begründen
unseren Weltruf.

MERCEDES-BENZ

The *Uebermensch* and the Mercedes Star: an ad from the *Voelkischer Beobachter* on the occasion of the 1934 party rally in Nuremberg.

In the wake of widespread unrest in its factories, demonstrated by a work stoppage in Untertuerkheim and the balloting for the councils of trust, an ad from the *Voelkischer Beobachter* from May 1, 1935. On the same day, an official harangued the assembled Mannheim workforce: "Danke fuer Ihre Undankbarkeit!" ("Thanks for your ungratefulness!")

On the third anniversary of Hitler's Chancellorship: an ad from the January 30, 1936 issue of the *Voelkischer Beobachter*.

Hitler leaving the Landsberg Prison, 1924. According to the new official company work on its Nazi past, Jakob Werlin's children now deny that their father was the man who picked up Hitler at the prison and drove him home.

Mercedes enthusiast Hitler returns to Landsberg ten years later.

A symbol of the Third Reich. The Mercedes Star on Land, at Sea, and in the Air: Hitler with the chiefs of the armed forces in a company propaganda college.

A symbol of the Third Reich, I. Having just been named Chancellor, Hitler leaves President Hindenberg on January 30, 1933.

A meeting at the annual auto fair in Berlin: Goebbels (in light-colored coat), Hitler, Jakob Werlin (in SS uniform).

Left to right: Hitler, Goebbels (partially hidden), Goering, and Wilhelm Kissel.

Goering and Hitler chat at an automobile exhibition as Jakob Werlin (here in civilian clothes) looks on.

Happy foreign workers from the Sindelfingen factory enjoy their free time singing folk songs, or at least that is what this company photo would have us believe . . .

Gurjakin
Semen
geb.08.03.26
Ljudimowe
Wohnung:
Ludwigsfelde

L 62617
/13

Ausweis Nr. ...1..26.55....

1. berechtigt zum Betreten des Werkes 10

ausgestellt am:

13.06.44

Ausgabestelle:

2. Ausweis ist Werkeigentum, er darf an keinen Werkfremden ausgehändigt werden. Verlust muß **sofort** dem Leiter der Werksicherheit gemeldet werden.
3. Beim Ausscheiden muß der Ausweis an d. Leiter d. Werksicherheit über das Lohn- bzw. Personalbüro zurückgegeben werd.
4. Verstöße gegen Ziffr. 2 u. 3 sowie Unterlassen der Verlustmeldung werden nach der BO vorbehaltlich strafrechtlicher Verfolgung geahndet.
5. Inhaber muß d. Ausweis an d. Kontrollstellen **unaufgefordert** vorzeigen u. muß ihn während d. Arbeit stets b. sich führen.

1/0396

Two views of an ID card of a forced laborer deported from the Soviet Union to the Daimler-Benz Genshangen factory.

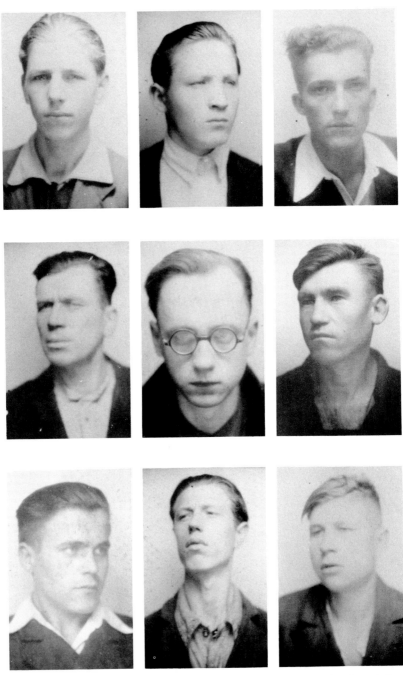

Photos of anonymous laborers from the Soviet Union who were deported to the Daimler-Benz Genshangen factory.

declared: "We want to shake off the yoke of class domination and make known how Europe and above all the German people can return to peace and good fortune after this war with its sea of blood and tears."[18]

The first test of strength between reformists and radicals under the new conditions after the revolution occurred on November 14. On that day, factory elections were held to choose the Stuttgart workers' council. In nearly all Stuttgart factories, slates run by majority Social Democrats and the trade unions swamped the radicals. In all, more than two-thirds of the elected delegates stood in the SPD's and trade unions' camps.[19]

The situation was different, however, at Daimler in Untertuerkheim, the largest of the Stuttgart plants. There, the slates of the majority Social Democrats and the independent radicals ran neck-and-neck, with the SPD squeaking through with a narrow victory in the final popular vote total. Nevertheless, each side sent 15 delegates to the workers' council. The SPD sent its big guns at Daimler, Salm and Schifferdecker, to the *Rat*. Salm received the most votes of any candidate—5,513—but an Independent Social Democrat, Wirsching, a metal fitter, was a close second, with 5,347 votes. In addition, the Daimler workers sent a number of leading Spartacist militants in the Stuttgart area to the workers' council. Among them were Thalheimer, Unfried, and Hoernle, who received their first (and only) positions in a postrevolutionary governmental institution. Although none of the three worked at Daimler, the work force nevertheless sent them to represent it on the council.[20]

The elections to the *Arbeiterrat* of November 14 marked an important milestone in the history of the workers' movement at Daimler. The radical opposition, which had not even contested the elections to the plant's workers' committee two months earlier, was now about as strong as the Social Democratic/trade union leadership which had dominated the workers' representation since the first organizing drive in late 1905. The small Christian and Hirsch-Duncker fractions had not even had time to put together slates for the council elections, and they received no votes.

Having scored an unexpectedly strong showing in the ballot, the loose confederation of radicals pressed their oppositional campaign. They began a drive to force a no-confidence vote in the sitting workers' committee at the plant. On November 20, 1918, Berge wrote Kaulla that "the extreme tendency is drilling ever further everywhere and one must be ready for new surprises."[21] Within days, the Daimler chief expressed his pleasure that the radicals' campaign had "produced a very strong opponent"—the trade union leaders—"who according to my conviction are best suited to take up the fight" against the radicals.[22] Berge's optimism was short-lived: the economic disorganization of demobilization served to win the radical faction more adherents in the closing weeks of 1918.

DEMOBILIZATION AND REFORM IN UNTERTUERKHEIM

When the armistice silenced the guns and grounded the airplanes on November 11, Daimler was left atop a mountain of military contracts. Orders for 8,879 airplane motors were on hand, probably worth more than 145 million marks. Contracts for 46 airplanes and uncounted thousands of spare parts were also on the books.[23] In addition to its enormous business volume on behalf of military aviation, Daimler's growing efforts to supply land forces with motorized weapons, especially the anti-aircraft guns and tanks developed with Krupp, had provided tens of millions of marks of lucrative contracts and guarantees.

With the end of the war, it was inevitable that the huge contracts which Daimler had from the military would soon be annulled. It was clear to the owners of the company that many of the 20,000 employed in Untertuerkheim and Sindelfingen would have to be released. Some workers left of their own accord in the days after the armistice to return to their homes and families, especially those from other parts of the country. On November 12, the day after the conclusion of the armistice, 384 workers left their jobs in Untertuerkheim. The work force melted away slowly in the next weeks, reaching 11,460 on December 5. Its high-point had been 15,238 on October 16, 1918; it totaled 15,063 on armistice day.[24] Daimler's direction noted privately on November 23 that the workers' committee supported its efforts to get workers to leave and had worked effectively to "keep the exodus going." The firm still hoped to avoid mass layoffs.[25]

Meanwhile, the highest councils of the unions and the industry sought to work out agreements to guide the economic transition to peacetime. What shape should the postwar economy take? How would the nation demobilize and which social relations within German industry would mark the social landscape?

The epoch-making Stinnes-Legien pact, signed on November 15, 1918, built the framework for the postwar era of industrial relations, and, as one historian has written, helped "determine the course of revolutionary events and prevented an economic and social collapse from following the political."[26] The chair of the general committee of the free trade unions, Carl Legien, obtained official recognition from industry for the unions and the right to organize. Factory committees and collective bargaining agreements were henceforth to mark industrial relations in the factories while the eight-hour day was to become general in German industry. Capital and labor set up a deliberative unit containing representatives of both to "by-pass the state bureaucracy and the Reichstag in the organization of demobilization and the transitional economy."[27] As some of the wartime controls were being dismantled, economic and social power was in effect turned over to organized industrial and union groups which acted collectively together for the purposes of "crisis management" under conditions of defeat and revolution. This mixed authority was to serve as the model for, in the words of the pact, a "general solution of all economic, social and legal questions touching on industrial life under the equitable expression of all interests."[28]

In southwestern Germany, the Wuerttemberg Association of Metal Industrialists and the DMV (along with the other trade unions in the industry) ratified on the same day the compromises which this "political calculus" had fashioned. They agreed to the general guidelines for the transition period in order to preserve the "urgently necessary calm and order in the factories." These stated that the work hours could be set according to the requirements of the branches within the industry but could not amount to more than 48 hours in the week. Despite the shortening of the working hours which this entailed, wage rates were to remain at their present levels; the resulting short-fall was to be made good so that workers' earnings were not diminished. "Joint steps" were to be taken by the employers so that "at least ⅔ of the funds given out would be replaced by the Reich."

The question of layoffs, which was especially critical for the bloated factories of the metal and machine-building industry, received special attention from the negotiators. In general, "the dismissal of workers is to be avoided as long as possible," a maxim which was silly under the circumstances but reflected the trade unions' interest in protecting jobs. "Where they could not be avoided" (which was practically everywhere), one week's notice was necessary. The guidelines drafted by employers and unions specified the kinds of workers who would lose their jobs: foreigners, single workers who were not independent of their parents or guardians, those who had been commissioned under the Auxiliary Service Law, those who had previously been in agriculture or domestic service, those from the nonmetal trades who were again offered employment in their earlier industries, and women "who were first taken into the metal industry during the war." Any further layoffs required "the understanding of the workers' committees."[29]

At the same time, places had to be made in the factories for all those returning from the armed services who had been employed there at the outbreak of the war. If possible, they were to be given back their earlier jobs, with the same wages as all the rest. Crippled veterans were also to be given their positions and paid like the others, regardless of the disability benefits they might receive.

At the same meetings, the DMV assured the employers that it did not support the "unauthorized" move at Daimler and other factories to win a "one-time cost of living payment." This reflected the confusion within the organization as the country passed through the *Wende* of 1918, for a number of the highest union officials had been involved earlier in pressing for this demand at Daimler.

The work of the trade unionists at Daimler and at other big firms in the Stuttgart area made clear that they would indeed "go along with industry out of the fear that Russian conditions could happen in Germany."[30] The participants in these Stuttgart talks were guided by the spirit of November 1918. As formulated in a communiqué from the national organization of German Metal Industrialists, the hallmarks of this new spirit for management included "the recognition of trade unions [and] . . . the reaching of labor contracts."[31] For unions, the order of the day was constructive engagement and agreements with industries and firms, rather than strikes, demonstrations, and disorder. For Daimler, the times demanded that "ways and means be found to bring along the work force and to keep from driving it into the streets." Indeed, according to Berge, the prospects for pacifying the work force seemed promising.[32]

By December 2, 1918, the lists for the people to be dismissed by Daimler had been drawn up and began to be implemented. The cutbacks were across the board, although skilled machine and handworkers remained in proportionally greater numbers. Women and unskilled day laborers were especially targeted. All but a handful of the nearly 2,700 women left the Daimler work force, with large blocs leaving daily in early December. On December 6 and 7 alone, 2,049 were given their walking papers, 759 of them women. Many unskilled day laborers were released, as were skilled fitters. According to a Daimler memo, Schifferdecker of the workers' committee "has resigned himself to [the dismissals]." The workers' committee later explained that its main goal was to protect those workers who had to "support their families . . . and therefore are dependent on their earnings."[33] Daimler's daily reports from the period lists them as having "left . . . gone home or back into earlier business."[34]

The government of Wuerttemberg was interested in expediting the dismissals, for it wanted above all to "make the current burden for the industry bearable, so that industry is kept trim for action."[35] By mid-December, DMG found it difficult to proceed with dismissals while maintaining order at the factory. A letter from Berge mentions the rank and file's growing dissatisfaction with the sitting workers' committee and the difficulties with the dismissal of superfluous workers in the same breath.[36] Indeed, a growing number of dissatisfied workers labeled the workers' committee "mercenaries of capital" for their cooperation in facilitating the dismissals.[37]

During the period from November 12 to December 21, in which 6,145 persons were dismissed, only 287 were hired, presumably men returning from the front for the most part. The rationale for the dismissals was therefore not to make room for the returning heroes but rather to liquidate labor-power which had become superfluous in the new situation. The law of the market held sway in Untertuerkheim during the first weeks of the "social republic."

There was another important factor at work in determining who was laid off—the political beliefs of the workers. As Berge wrote in December, "With the exodus from the factory, the retention of the solid elements is [the goal] being worked toward as much as possible, but despite this, there are still enough turbulent spirits in the factory and the control over them is so difficult, because the boundary between the Independent Social Democrats and the Spartacists is not entirely clear." [38]

For the women going back home or now out of a job, there was assistance from neither Daimler nor the trade unions. Indeed, the only help available was the sort frequently offered by Catholic agencies, which taught sewing, mending, and cooking classes for "girls seeking service positions." [39] There were also reports of homeless female workers at large on the streets. The national authorities in Berlin noted that "a large number of the women working in the factories producing for the war effort are currently homeless, unemployed, and without shelter." [40] They expressed concern that they would become a reserve army of the unemployed, available for prostitution.

Indeed, there were very few alternatives open for the thousands of women released by Daimler. Even marriage was a questionable prospect, since the carnage between the armies "left a surplus of three million women" in Germany, as one politician noted. [41] The experience of the Daimler women workers during the initial weeks of German democracy indicates that the social and economic gains offered working women at the outset (next to the historic political advance of the suffrage) were meager.

The war years had seen long work days, up to six or even seven days each week. Men and women often worked more than 60 hours a week in service of the war effort. After the war, working hours were frequently adjusted, and were often drastically shortened to save jobs for male employees.

From November 12 to December 2, the 44-hour week reigned at Daimler, with workers on the job eight hours a day from Monday to Friday and four hours on Saturdays. With a large work force and few orders, and with inadequate supplies of coal at hand, management cut the work week to 30 hours as of December 3, initially divided among a six-day work week which was reduced to five as of late February 1919. From mid-April onward, "normal working hours" were restored, initially 44 hours a week but 46 hours after the collective bargaining agreement for the industry went into effect on June 10. [42] This translated into a work day which began at 8:00 A.M. and ended at 5:20 P.M., with an hour's break beginning at noon. On

147

Saturdays, a short shift began at 8:00 A.M. and ended at 12:30 P.M. A five-day work schedule prevailed only in the smith so that the furnaces which consumed scarce fuels were stoked only five days each week.[43] This schedule and the 46-hour week were the rule at Daimler until the industrialists in the south German metal industry displayed their muscle in 1922 by forcing through a 48-hour week, despite a protracted strike.[44]

Payment of workers' wages under these circumstances of shortened work weeks presented problems for unions and corporations in late 1918 and 1919. Trade unions and industrial organizations in Stuttgart initially petitioned the Berlin authorities in November to cover two-thirds of the lost wages for the workers, with the firms covering the remaining third. Having received no answer from Berlin, the employers' organizations and unions turned to the provisional government in Wuerttemberg for relief. Under a formula agreed to by all parties in the talks at the end of November, the workers had to endure 10 percent of the loss of wages themselves, with the state making up two-thirds of the remaining shortfall and the industry covering the remaining third.[45] Thus, one of the first fruits of the revolution for the industrial work force at Daimler and at other factories in Stuttgart was a decline of 1.5–2.0 percent in their wages.

This arrangement lasted until January 27, 1919, when a new formula providing a measure of relief for Daimler and other firms went into effect. According to the new regulations, the company still had to pay the workers for the limited amount of labor actually performed. The supplementary remuneration would now, however, come from Stuttgart's unemployment funds for the most part: 70 percent of the earnings for time worked were subtracted from the welfare rate for an unemployed worker in Stuttgart, according to his marital and familial situation. The worker received the remaining 30 percent, which was disbursed from community funds through Daimler. If this wage package did not amount to 90 percent of the earnings for a 55 ½ hour week prior to November 15, the firm had to make up this difference out of its own money until February 15.[46] These complex provisions shifted more of the burden for supporting workers in military industries during demobilization to public authorities and gave firms like Daimler assistance in adjusting to the new situation. They also tied the ultimate earnings of workers to the level of public support provided to the unemployed.

Both the "normal" and shortened work weeks were maintained only by utilizing a wide variety of fuels in place of coal which was very scarce. Charcoal, brown coal (lignite), tar oil, leather waste, and old cloth were used when available. An average of 28 tons of fuels were used daily to produce steam for the smith and the other workshops at the plant. An additional 20 tons of coke and other energy sources were needed to fire the annealing ovens in the metal hardening department, smith, and foundry. Despite the attempts to find alternative energy sources, the workshops were plagued by occasional disruptions of energy supplies. For example, the steam necessary to power the hydraulic hammers in the smith was frequently inadequate.

Similarly, the shortage of electricity was acute. Daimler contracted with the city electric works in Muenster (Bad Cannstatt) to supply its needs. Of the 2,900 kilowatts required daily, the city could supply only 1,100 itself. The firm had to help with the production of electrical current by delivering tar oil to the generating plant, receiving the current produced with it in return. Engines which had been produced to drive heavy artillery vehicles were also brought into operation in the plant to take up some of the slack. For these energy needs, another 39 tons of tar oil and 35 tons of other fuels were required each week. In addition to the solid fuels and electricity, 5000 cubic meters of natural gas were required for the toolmaking and metal hardening departments, copper forge, foundry, and repair shops. The city gas works could not supply Daimler with sufficient quantities of natural gas, causing problems in the workshops.[47]

During 1919, the division of labor within the corporation was developed further with the relocation of many woodworkers and handworkers to the Sindelfingen factory. This process had begun with the opening of this facility for the production of airplanes in 1915. In the months after the armistice, the firm employed 130 woodworkers at the facilities to produce wooden furniture for bedrooms, living rooms, and dining rooms. A speculator bought up the lot and shipped it to Switzerland, reaping a large profit in the process. The head of the wood department, Haag, was subsequently sacked.

By late 1919, Sindelfingen was the Daimler installation responsible for the production of auto bodies. Skilled metal workers who could no longer be used were sent back to Untertuerkheim; more skilled workers, upholsterers, painters and lacquerers were sent to Sindelfingen. In general, skilled woodworkers were in short supply in 1919 in Wuerttemberg, especially those who were needed to build the wooden car bodies, but the scarcity of available housing to rent in Sindelfingen increased the difficulty in attracting workers. To alleviate this, DMG helped to erect 50 single family houses and turned several of the cafeterias which had served the huge wartime work force into housing.[48]

The utilization of Sindelfingen as an auto body plant by and large completed the removal of the independent handworking and woodworking trades from Untertuerkheim. Groups of woodworkers remained at Untertuerkheim, but generally only those such as the model builders who worked closely with the metalworkers in the foundry. Groups of skilled metal workers remained at Sindelfingen, but their task was to assist in the production of car bodies.

The workers at the Untertuerkheim and Sindelfingen plants did not immediately cease building military machinery with the end of the war. Between November 10 and December 15, 1918, amidst revolution and demobilization, 302 airplane engines were finished and delivered.[49] Most of these seem to have already been in the final stages of construction by the termination of hostilities. Negotiators from Daimler and the War Ministry met in Berlin in December and January. In the decisive talks in January, DMG was represented by an official, Arthur Loewenstein.

The parties reached a series of agreements liquidating many but apparently not all of the firm's monetary claims about it wartime role. One of these awarded DMG 4,895,000 marks for the 302 airplane motors delivered between November 10 and December 15, 1918.[50] A major agreement in December called for the payment by the Reich of 75 million marks on a number of the firm's outstanding claims. The company used the money to pay off outstanding debts to Stuttgart banks which had helped finance DMG's wartime expansion and to fund its day-to-day operations. Indeed, the 75 million marks helped to stave off a merger with three other motor companies, including Opel (and apparently Benz), which was being considered to improve the firm's postwar prospects.

In addition, Daimler pressed for a final financial settlement with the War Ministry for the annulment of the military contracts, but the unsettled Daimler Affair made progress on this front impossible before it was disposed of once and for all. Nevertheless, the prospects for putting the scandal to rest for good seemed reasonably bright to Berge in January 1919, for the War Ministry had offered "to be of help and to lead the interests of DMG to good end."[51]

In the aftermath of the armistice, much of Daimler's effort was devoted to the destruction of airplane motors, submarine engines, half-finished materiel, and parts, often under the supervision of allied military officers. Work soon commenced on automobiles—on the models being built in 1914.[52] To facilitate the resumption of civilian production, the firm reacquired half-finished vehicles which it had earlier sold to the government. At first, there were few orders on hand, but the persistent inflation soon helped to generate more orders, for commodities such as automobiles became attractive investments as the currency declined in value. Nevertheless, it is necessary to put Daimler's production of 621 automobiles in 1919 and 1,616 in 1920 into perspective: in 1916, Henry Ford had already sold 785,000 Model-T's.[53]

THE "UNITED PROLETARIAT" AND THE WORKERS' MOVEMENT

The radicalization of the Daimler work force proceeded apace. On December 13, 1918, the USPD/Spartacist factions scored a stunning success: the work force voted no confidence in the sitting workers' committee by a 3,715 to 3,354 tally.[54] Elections for a new committee were scheduled for the end of January 1919.

In the interim, the Stuttgart radicals, again spearheaded by their Daimler contingents, took their campaign for a government based on the workers' and soldiers' councils into the streets. Demonstrations, led by USPD and Spartacist militants, erupted early on January 9, with thousands of Daimler workers again marching across the Neckar into downtown Stuttgart. According to one report, the Spartacists at DMG shut down the machinery and the plant at 9:00 A.M. and mobilized a column of workers for the march into Stuttgart. In the process, fistfights broke out in several factory departments. A number of windows were broken at the plant.[55] Thousands joined the march, but the strife between workers' factions proved to be too much for others, who just went home. A Daimler official alleged that the government had promised the company military assistance to contain the demonstration, but that none had been forthcoming. The fact that some of the workers were armed dissuaded the firm from undertaking its own counter-measures.[56]

A potential tragedy was apparently avoided in east Stuttgart on January 9. The demonstrators from Daimler changed the course of their march to circumvent the Berg barracks, where Captain Holz's troops were reportedly waiting "to receive the Daimler workers with machine guns and hand grenades."[57]

These "January protests" in Stuttgart were not a putsch attempt; rather, they were intended as a show of solidarity with the Berlin demonstrators and to protest the dispatching of Wuerttemberg troops to Berlin. Armed clashes erupted at several points around Stuttgart on January 9 and 10, resulting in a number of dead and wounded; but they were sporadic and often provoked by nervous security forces. For example, the first casualties occurred when troops fired at bourgeois counter-demonstrators at the Rotebuehlkaserne, having mistaken them for attacking Spartacist columns. Less than 36 hours later, the demonstrations had been quashed, and the provisional government, which had fled to the fortified new train station downtown, was again master of the situation.

In the wake of the January days, the Social Democratic-led government rounded up the leaders of the Spartacists in Stuttgart and held them for five months. The internments soon contributed to a slow-motion replay of the unrest which had followed the incarceration of many of the same radicals the previous November.

Three weeks later, in late January, the elections for the new Daimler workers' committee were held. The USPD and Spartacists received 32 seats on the body; the SPD and the trade unions won 27 seats.[58] For the first time at Daimler, the Social Democratic labor movement was reduced to a minority, if still quite powerful, faction. Men describing themselves as revolutionary socialists, such as Groetzinger and Grosshans, were now among the leading spokespersons for the Daimler workers' committee; men like Salm and Schifferdecker, who had guided the committee through years of difficult negotiations and often grudging cooperation with the Daimler management and the German military, had lost their first elections.

Within days, the new chairman, Groetzinger, drafted a letter to the firm which challenged the agreement under which the workers had borne 10 percent of the shortfall in wages. The chairman, on behalf of the new majority, asked the firm to make up this shortfall because the "rise in the prices of foodstuffs and other necessities continues and the deterioration in workers' income cannot be borne." In addition, the committee pointed out that the new "normal" working hours totaled only 48 hours weekly, as opposed to a minimum of 55 ½ hours during the war, necessitating an immediate increase of at least 15% in the firm's piece-rates.[59]

The significance of these new problems should be carefully noted. The committee implicitly criticized the earlier agreement between unions, industry, and *Land,* and declared that the workers had borne enough sacrifices during the war and the postwar economic mobilization. The committee's brief was a reminder of the deterioration of the living conditions of the work force during the war, when their standard of living was met by working long overtime hours in service of the war effort. Now, the new workers' representatives insisted that it was only right that their living standards be pegged to the new shortened work week, even if that meant hiking the piece-rates by 15 percent.

That the new committee championed these reform measures shows up the limitations of the traditional characterization of the division in the labor movement as involving "reformists" and "revolutionaries". At Daimler, it was the USPD/Spartacist factions which pressed for reforms and improvements in wages and working conditions at the plant, in contrast to the willingness of the SPD and many trade unionists to be accommodating to management in the aftermath of the November revolution. Indeed, the post-November division in Daimler's shop-floor politics can be better described as being one between reformists and defenders of the new status quo. It was hard-headed reformism which drew the masses behind Daimler's Independent Social Democrats and Spartacists as much as the political allure of the militant socialist parties in early 1919. Or rather, both were widely perceived as being closely connected: radical socialist politics meant political revolution *and* the transformation of the factory regime.

Surprisingly, the firm was slow to recognize the decisive shift in opinion among its work force. On December 7, less than a week before the no-confidence vote, Berge reported that the radicals' recent activity was linked to "a feeling that their existence was more and more threatened, which corresponds to the facts."[60] After the ballot, the management in Untertuerkheim grew pessimistic. Berge had refused to have anything to do with the Stuttgart *Arbeiterrat*, apparently because of a pledge of support he had given the workers' committee.[61] He soon noted that the new workers' committee would most likely be more radical than the one voted out. "The long war has so exhausted all strata of the population that the Spartacists gain more ground with the mentally inferior [sic]. If it goes any further, we will not make it through without a civil war."[62]

The election results were no accident, and almost every event over the next 18 months proved that the radicalization of the Daimler work force had been thoroughgoing. Indeed, within weeks, a new militant strike movement had been born at Daimler, a movement which would pose one of the most serious threats to the authorities in Wuerttemberg in the postwar era.

The movement was born out of working-class frustrations with the course of events in Germany and Stuttgart in late 1918 and early 1919. Here, much more than local frustrations were decisive. The uprisings and ensuing repression in Berlin and Munich, the imprisonment of the radical leaders in Stuttgart in January 1919, the murders of Rosa Luxemburg and Karl Liebknecht, the failure of the socialists to win majorities in either the national or state assemblies, the slow pace of reform, the persistent shortages of food supplies—all contributed to the growing dissatisfaction in the factories and working class communities along the Neckar. Thus, in the immediate aftermath of the war and revolution, the radical movement at Daimler and in the greater Stuttgart area increasingly professed a national identity, ranging well beyond Swabian regionalism.

On Monday, February 25, many of the Daimler workers staged a wildcat strike at 10:30 A.M. and gathered for a mass meeting. Three of the most prominent independents at the plant, including Groetzinger, who had just become chairman of the factory council, addressed the work force about recent events in Wuerttemberg, including the arrest and forced deportation from Wuerttemberg of two German Communists, Levi and Schulz, on the previous Friday, and the continued internment of the radical leaders rounded up in the wake of the January disturbances in Stuttgart. The independents sponsored a resolution which the mass meeting adopted. This document marked the beginning of the Movement of the United Proletariat:

> The lessons of recent times force us to the realization that the workers of all political tendencies must stand united and [in] closed [ranks] against the reaction if the work force is not to be deceived about the fruits of the revolution. In the next days, workers' assemblies are to be called in the whole industrial area of Stuttgart in order to bring about the unity of the workers on a revolutionary basis. These assemblies are to be held without the participation of the leaders. The workers of DMG demand the immediate release of the political prisoners and protest the expulsion of Levi and Schulz. The workers demand the immediate lifting of the state of siege.[63]

In addition, the assemblies demanded new elections for the workers' and soldiers' councils.[64]

The mass meeting selected a six-member committee, consisting of three Social Democrats and the three from the USPD/KPD grouping to prepare further actions to unify the workers "from below." According to the historian Manfred Scheck, "this was the germ-cell of the 'action committee of the united proletariat,' which was formed in the following days."[65]

The next day's *Sozialdemokrat,* the organ of the Stuttgart USPD, greeted the news: "Bravo Daimler workers! You have already repeatedly been among the foremost for the rights of the proletariat. March again this time boldly and united to the new struggles!"[66]

Quickly, other factories in the area followed suit, ratifying the demands of the Daimler work force and selecting committees with equal numbers of Social Democrats and radicals to unify the proletariat from below, without the interference of leaders. Already on February 25, the work forces of the smaller Werner and Pfleiderer factory in Stuttgart and of the state-owned repair work shops chose action committees with two SPD members and two independents.[67] It should be noted, however, that the radicals' insistence on the exclusion of "leaders" from the "unification" process did not overly handicap their efforts, for most Spartacist and many USPD leaders were in prison in the wake of the January demonstrations. Thus, the movement was not a campaign of the Leninist vanguard in the Stuttgart area, but espoused a brand of proletarian radicalism in a mass movement unencumbered by the domination of a cadre of leaders. As one of the movement's leaflets proclaimed, "Not through theoretical discussions, not through resolutions and not through the affirmation of socialist ideas will the proletariat achieve strong unity. That's only possible in the incandescence of the class struggle.

The general strike is the first action."[68] Days before the start of the general strike, the action committee emphasized that the decision to strike should come from the "masses of workers," not from the leaders.[69]

The government of Wuerttemberg responded quickly to the launching of the campaign at Daimler. Two days earlier, it had reinforced the ban on outdoor public assemblies and street demonstrations, after learning that plans were afoot for a general strike allegedly to protest the murder of Kurt Eisner and the putsch in Bavaria.[70] It distributed a statement on February 26 denouncing the Spartacists, who "have murdered peaceful miners in the Ruhr [and] have locked 600 miners in the shaft to let them starve," although these charges were false. It urged the workers to "Follow your leaders, who have fought for decades in the service of the people."[71]

Nevertheless, the movement picked up support during March in the industrial regions of Stuttgart. Action committees and unification committees were chosen in most large Stuttgart factories. The head of the security forces, Hahn, alleged: "In the factories, the sheer terror of the radicals reigned. Every moderate opinion was suppressed with fists, hammers, metal rods, etc."[72] The factory committees sent representatives to a strike committee which in turn chose a nine-member action committee to coordinate the movement in the whole area, made up of three Communists, three Independent Social Democrats, and three SPD members. On March 21, it presented the government with its demands in the form of an ultimatum.[73] The government was not about to capitulate to the demands of the radicals, so a confrontation loomed.

In the last week of March, the movement at Daimler and the other plants took the next step. The work force, by an overwhelming 4,625 to 1,931 margin, authorized the calling of a general strike. From the size of the vote, it is clear that many workers who supported the Social Democrats voted for the strike.[74] Large majorities at Bosch and at the Fortuna and Normawerken in Bad Cannstatt were also in favor of the general strike, with less overwhelming pluralities at other plants. Daimler-Sindelfingen, for example, approved the general strike by a mere 1,045 to 925 margin.

The political conflict in the industrial region of Stuttgart escalated decisively on March 31, as thousands of workers failed to report for work. The general strike was on. Monday, the first day of the action, was surprisingly calm. The action committee moved about the area, frequently changing its location, and tried to monitor events with a network of messengers on foot and bicycles.[75] Strikers staged a number of demonstrations, mainly without incident, although attempts were made to shut down the city street cars in Bad Cannstatt. The government again withdrew to the heavily guarded confines of the new train station and declared a state of siege for Stuttgart and the surrounding towns on Monday evening. Hahn's security forces prowled the working-class districts of eastern Stuttgart, searching houses and looking for weapons.[76]

The paralysis of the city became nearly total the next day. The street car drivers began a job action to force the city government to give them a three-mark bonus. That morning, representatives of the organizations of "artisans, salespersons, . . . doctors, pharmacists, lawyers, architects and artists" called for a "defensive strike" and issued their own demands under the slogan "Order, Security and the Possibility of Work." The "defensive strike," according to its promulgators, was an "unlimited acknowledgement of the people's state and a demonstration of trust for the government which fully and totally fulfills these demands."[77] The *Buergerstreik* completed the virtual shutting down of Stuttgart, as even bakeries and dairies stopped production and deliveries.[78]

Violent armed clashes erupted across eastern, working-class Stuttgart on the second day of the strike. An armed group of around 30 men opened fire on a security patrol in Bad Cannstatt. A crowd subsequently sacked a doctor's house in the immediate area from which someone had fired at the insurgents, according to the rumors in any case. Shots were fired at an armored car, and a hand grenade was hurled at it as it drove past the Daimler factory from Untertuerkheim to Bad Cannstatt. A fire fight erupted as it arrived in Bad Cannstatt, and five strikers were shot. Other clashes were reported in both communities, and militants seized a quantity of arms and ammunition in Untertuerkheim the same day.

The best documented incident on the strike's second day, an event which the bourgeois *Schwaebischer Merkur* called "the cannibalistic Ostheim case," occurred across the Neckar from Untertuerkheim in Stuttgart-Ostheim, where many workers from Daimler lived.[79] A security patrol of eight men attracted a crowd as it moved through the workers' district near Ostendplatz around 10:00 in the morning. As the crowd grew more menacing, the patrol broke ranks and fled, seeking refuge in a nearby house. They nearly succeeded in escaping, but their flight had been seen by a streetcar driver, Gustav Buerkle. According to witnesses, Buerkle pointed out the house and called out "They're in there!" A small group of men, made up of two other street car drivers, Adolf Gsell and the 18-year-old Artur Palm; a foundry worker, Friedrich Schilling; a cement worker, Albert Reichert; and led by "a man about 22 years of age with dark hair and mustache who wore an artillery cap and probably a field gray uniform," tried to force their way into the house. As the members of the patrol again tried to escape, a shot rang out. A soldier fell to the sidewalk, mortally wounded in the eye. According to a witness, a man wearing a seaman's uniform went over to the body and kicked it a few times. Several others allegedly joined in pummelling the body. Afterward, the corpse was dragged away and laid across a bench in a nearby square.[80]

At least 19 men were charged with "treason, especially rebellion" in connection with the incident. Among the witnesses who came forward and gave evidence against them in the subsequent days were the soldiers who escaped, a butcher, two bakers, a salesman, a train conductor, and the 13-year-old son of a policeman. In addition, several of the defendants gave statements implicating their fellows in the attack. According to the police interrogation of the defendants, only two indicated affiliation with any political group: the street car driver Buerkle: "I'm a member of the majority SPD but let myself be taken into the Communist Party," and the cement worker Reichert: "I'm a member of the USPD and have not participated in Spartacus."[81]

On Wednesday, the security situation for the government on the outskirts of the Daimler works threatened to get out of hand. According to the *Schwaebische Tagwacht*, a crowd forced its way into an artillery storage hall in Untertuerkheim and allegedly carried off weapons and ammunition, including machine guns. The security forces arrived too late, but recovered a large amount of materiel which had been left outside the facility. Early the next morning, the security forces surprised a group of 120 armed workers, allegedly Spartacists, who were spending the night at the Hirsch tavern in Untertuerkheim. No shots were exchanged, and about 60 were apprehended. As a result of the successful security operation, the government was able to claim later that day that "Untertuerkheim and Wangen [which lies directly across the Neckar] are firmly in the hands of government troops."[82]

Despite the government's claims, sharp clashes erupted on Thursday around Wangen and Gaisburg, where 400 armed men, with eight or 10 machine guns, had erected crude fortifications. Several salvoes from the government's guns set them fleeing, and troops subsequently searched Wangen for weapons.

By the end of the week, the strike was beginning to buckle. At least 17 persons had been killed in Stuttgart in the violence related to the strike, including two members of the security forces. Sweeps by the security forces had prevented the strikers from consolidating or holding any fixed area or neighborhood for any substantial length of time, for the firepower of the radicals was no match for Hahn's troops. The revolutionaries displayed a general reluctance to shoot it out with the security forces.

Daimler's management announced on Sunday that the plant would re-open the next day, although the work force was holding out for the release of the radical prisoners and the lifting of the state of siege.[83] Nevertheless, according to the press, Tuesday morning presented a "normal picture" in and around Stuttgart.

The strike had important consequences for all of the main parties in the dispute: the government of Wuerttemberg, and the parties and organizations of the working class. The government, led by Social Democrats, won, and beat back the most serious challenge to its authority in the postwar era. The SPD, however, had been battered by its success. In the subsequent months, its authority and prestige fell to a low ebb in the Stuttgart factories, a decline confirmed dramatically by the elections to the Betriebsrat in March 1920. The effectiveness of the raids and tactics of Hahn's men in routing the strikers was difficult for many Social Democrats to identify with, particularly for those in the working-class communities which had been the scene of clashes or searches. In the wake of the strike, however, the SPD representatives in the Stuttgart factories pressed for more economic and social reforms, including the vigorous carrying forward of the work of the socialization committee.[84] Such demands came to naught.

For the labor movement, the strike was a dismal failure and a defeat. Moreover, it helped to shatter the myth of the mass strike which had proved so resilient on the German left. A powerful strike, with wide support in the factories of greater Stuttgart, had not been able to move either the SPD or the government to accede to the strikers' demands. The drive for the political unity of the working class suffered a setback; the labor movement remained hobbled by the split between "reformist" and "revolutionary" camps. At Daimler and elsewhere, the split was doubly debilitating: the labor movement on the shop floor and inside the factory moved increasingly to the pace set by the USPD and Spartacist factions, while at the level of regional politics, the voice of labor was the soft chorus of the Wuerttemberg SPD and trade unions.

Within weeks, tensions between the factory committees and management flared anew at the largest factories in the Stuttgart area. The correspondence between top managers at Daimler indicates that they feared another walkout in the last two weeks of April, but one failed to materialize.[85] Indeed, in the wake of the strike, the rank and file seemed to grow wary of militant mass action. In the following months, the threat of strike action at Daimler and elsewhere receded. A police report noted that "repeatedly, the votes in Daimler . . . have yielded decisive majorities for the rejection of a strike." The authorities attributed the reluctance to strike to a "[fear] of the loss of wages, and the [lack] of slogans with drawing-power [zugkraeftigen Parole]."[86]

Cleavages and tensions within the radical wing of the workers movement had also contributed to the development of the situation. "The opposition between KPD and USP[D] is becoming sharper daily," the police reported of the situation at Daimler and in the other large Stuttgart factories. The Communist Party believed that the USPD "is not energetic enough" and "fears that if it comes to power with the USP, it will be betrayed by the latter, just as the USP believes itself to have been betrayed by the majority socialists." The Independent Social Democrats, for their part, were suspicious of the "all too great youth and immaturity of [the Communists'] leaders." At the same time, the police noted a flood of anti-Semitic leaflets in all of the big Stuttgart factories. In these months, the new political anti-Semitism was making its first appearance at Daimler and elsewhere, vilifying Jews as the masterminds of red revolution. "The leaflets against the Jews are described as the concoction of the government, which wants to make the communists mistrustful against their own leaders."[87]

The police also asserted that the pressures resulting from rising prices for food and other necessities had moderated. They noted with satisfaction the easing of tension "in the largest industrial work forces, especially at Daimler." On the day of mourning for the dead Luxemburg and Liebknecht, July 21, the security forces reported work stoppages in the larger factories, but took solace from the fact that militant demonstrations had not erupted in Stuttgart.[88]

If police intelligence was correct that the lull in mass strike action reflected a calmer mood among Stuttgart workers, there is no evidence that the rank and file grew disaffected from their radical leadership. In the next indication of support for the various faction of the workers movement, the Betriebsrat election of March 1920, the overwhelming majority's preference for the candidates and programs of the USPD and KPD—who put up separate slates—was stronger than ever before (see chapter 6.).

Yet to understand the dynamic of workers' politics in the wake of the November revolution, it is important to remember that, by and large, the radicals at Daimler did not eschew the pursuit of the traditional trade union goals of improved wages and working conditions in the hope that final deliverance from capitalism was at hand. As the general strike was ending, the governing body of the workers' committee at Daimler dispatched a blunt note to the Daimler directors requesting increased compensation for the continuing rise in living costs. "Because of the extraordinarily high prices of foodstuffs, which have seen a substantial increase since last fall, the work force sees it necessary to demand a cost of living payment from the firm." According to the workers' committee, this payment should be 650 marks for persons over 20 years of age and 500 marks for the younger workers. An additional 50 marks should be earmarked for each child. The first cash installment should be distributed on May 3. "We'd like an answer or negotiations with the workers' committee today, because the work force has tumultuously demanded this."[89]

Little did the negotiators from the workers' committee realize that inflation, entrenched since 1916, would continue to erode labor's standard of living for another 4 ½ years, no matter what relief payments they might be able to obtain from Daimler or from the regional and national authorities. Although the earnings of organized workers kept pace better than those of civil servants and white collar workers, clearly this was not enough in the aftermath of a revolution from which workers expected so much.[90]

The best that the workers' committee could achieve, however, was the submission of the matter to the Stuttgart arbitration committee, which agreed with the firm that DMG "was not able to give in to the claims of the work force."[91]

The work force responded to this setback with new tactics on the shop-floor. Groups of workers who were crucial to the functioning of the whole factory—the electricians, the boiler stokers, and those who serviced and operated the hydraulic pumps and compressors—staged short wildcat strikes after the lunch break on May 6—only days after the signing of the landmark collective bargaining agreement for the south German metal industry—to press the campaign for more money. As Berge noted, "While earlier the tactic of the workers was to rise against us in a closed mass, the individual departments are now coming [out] for themselves and demanding immediate wage improvements under the threat of strikes."[92] This pattern had apparently begun shortly after the new committee took office, when workers in the smith staged a mass meeting to demand increased wages in their department.[93] The firm, Berge claimed, "is not able to settle or to negotiate every wage claim immediately."

Daimler in turn summoned four leading members of the workers' committee and threatened to close the factory if the disruptions in the service departments continued. "There really is no other way left, since the behavior of these people can partly be understood only as provocation." The stoppages ended soon afterward, although, in management's eyes, the general situation at the factory remained unsettled.[94]

Yet the defeat of the Movement of the United Proletariat and the more limited departmental actions which ensued in the following months at Daimler indicate that the authorities had succeeded in temporarily isolating and containing the radical movement. Although it would eventually recover during 1920, the powerful challenges of early 1919 had been foiled.

GRUPPENFABRIKATION: TOWARD THE REORGANIZATION OF PRODUCTION

As strife flared repeatedly in early 1919, the company's management was far from paralyzed. With the wartime experience of mass production fresh in the minds of Daimler's directors, they began a radical reorganization of the company's production processes. It stopped far short of Ford's revolution in

America a decade and a half earlier, yet the emerging new arrangement at Daimler nonetheless marked a clear break with the previous organization of the workplace and set the stage for the thoroughgoing industrial transformation of the late 1920s and 1930s. Moreover, in the context of labor's new militancy, which was well entrenched in many Daimler departments, the company's reorganization of parts of the labor processes was fraught with political overtones.

The enormous scale of military production had created strains in the prevailing organization of industrial production. The growth of the factory greatly increased the distances over which components had to be moved during production. The expanse of the plant meant that additional labor and resources had to be engaged in order to move parts from one workshop to another—which often meant moving them from one building to another. It became clear to the Daimler management that something had to be done to tackle the growing costs and effort needed to haul pieces around. "The disadvantage of transport fell so heavily on the scales that the usual advantages of this organization were more than outweighed," Richard Lang, Daimler's chief engineer, asserted in 1919.[95]

At the same time, the supervision of the multiple labor processes involved in turning out parts became more difficult as larger batches of components shifted from one department to the next. For example, parts for carburetors, transmissions, and engines all went through the same machine departments, although they differed greatly from one another, as did the cutting and assembly operations involved in producing them. The problem was compounded as all of the different pieces were collected in the assembly workshops for assembly by the fitters. Supervision was possible in the workshops at Daimler "only with great difficulty, when it is not impossible," Lang observed.

DMG had recognized the need for a radical reorganization of the plant during the war, with the fast-paced serial production of airplane engines, but since it could not have been carried out without severely disrupting military production, the settlement of the matter was postponed until after the conflict. The reorganization began sometime in early 1919. As Lang described the new factory organization:

> The [new] ordering of production which we describe as group production *[Gruppenfabrikation]* begins with the placing together in one group of a certain number of parts belonging together (e.g. all the parts of the carburetor, water pump, linkage, transmission) to carry out the whole fabrication in a production group. Such a production group is constituted from all kinds of machines and encompasses fitters and other hand workers besides machine workers. It is self-contained and independent from other work departments.[96]

This new organization of the factory greatly shortened the distances over which parts had to be transported. "Only the rough pieces come in from storage," Lang observed. The supervision of the work was also "incomparatively better," for engineer, master, and workers were concerned with a single part which they could know thoroughly without needing elaborate construction drawings. All could now better understand and oversee the various production processes involved in turning out the components. Management hoped that any one within the group could now suggest small cost-saving improvements in the machinery or work procedures. The result would be a "far-reaching knowledge of the special equipment and tools, the improvement and cheapening of the individual labor processes, the raising of the personal achievement and, with this, the worker's earnings, and the improvement of the design and building of the components themselves."[97]

DMG's chief engineer recognized that the new system had special disadvantages. It required more space, machinery, and trained supervisory personnel. Neither Lang nor anyone else in Daimler's direction mentioned that the war had provided the company with important benefits in just these areas. The plant had more than doubled in size, and hundreds of new machines had been acquired. Although the evidence here is sketchy, DMG clearly had added more supervisors during the war to oversee the nearly 15,000 workers in Untertuerkheim.[98]

In a most enlightening fashion, Lang later described how group production altered the manufacture of engine crankcases in Untertuerkheim. Before and during the war, the halves of the crankcases had "wandered" between seven workshops, first into the milling or planing department, then over to the drills, then to the fitters to be screwed together, next to the lathe machines to bore out the reservoirs, then to the drills again to make the passageways for the circulating oil, then into another lathe shop for another set of cuts, and finally back to the drilling workshop. Under the new group organization, the milling machines, drills, and lathes, as well as the assembly station for fitters, were brought together into a single area. At the same time, the personnel could now easily check each part at every stage to make sure that the cutting and assembly procedures had been executed properly. If alterations were necessary to bring it up to the specifications, the crankcase did not have to leave the department for touch-up work to be done.[99]

The new arrangement made a powerful impression. For the factory investigator Hellpach, his visit to a new Daimler group was the "winningest surprise I have ever experienced in a factory." The facilities were impressive, and "the engine housing grew before our eyes." With little effort, one could spot the beginning and end of the production process in the department, as well as "the line of development in the finishing of the motor housing."[100]

The wonder of group production was not without its dark side, and this drawback affected neither engineer nor direction directly. After a time, Lang and Hellpach noted that the greater uniformity within the jobs could adversely affect the workers and even cause them to fell alienated and bored. In Lang's view, this threat of monotony was superseded by the "new feeling of responsibility" which grew up in workers who never lost sight of the components on which they were working.

For one production analyst, the new Daimler organization recalled older organizations of the workplace. The novelty lay "in the transformation of an operation organized along the lines of serial production into the group production form, historically an older form." The Daimler engineer compared it to the basic principle guiding a "mechanical workshop with perhaps 10–20 workers, ... on the border between hand-worker shop and factory."[101]

This resemblance, however, was merely formal. Daimler's group production was no reversion to a less modern, more primitive organization. Rather, it was the sweeping restructuring of the factory, which broke down the traditional Daimler departments in which turners had worked with other turners, fitters with other fitters, etc. In the new form, the objects being produced took priority over the groups of like workers and labor processes which had always been grouped together. Schematically, the production of components proceeded spatially in proximate lines, and it is clear in retrospect that the postwar reorganization brought Daimler-Untertuerkheim to the threshold of assembly-line production.[102]

Whether intentionally or not, the reorganization of the plant into productive units broke down the old communities of workers in the Daimler workshops. Ever since the plant's opening, skilled turners and fitters and trained millers had worked together and even staged job actions with one another, with few direct connections with other workshops. It is worth noting that this reorganization—expressly carried out for economic reasons —was effected as workers resorted to the tactic of small-scale actions in the departments. As one of Lang's later collaborators observed, group production tended to "atomize" the work force and led to a more specialized and stricter division of labor within the factory.[103] The impact of uprooting the factory workshops on the workers' movement was probably contradictory: while shattering older units of solidarity, group production created new possibilities for workers' solidarity.

THE FIRST COLLECTIVE BARGAINING AGREEMENT

While labor and management clashed at Daimler, representatives from unions and management covering much of southwestern Germany reached agreement on a collective bargaining agreement in Heidelberg. The agreement, bearing the signatures of negotiators from the Metalworkers Union (DMV), the Christian and Hirsh-Duncker unions, and the Association of Wuerttemberg Metal Industrialists, regulated wages and working conditions for tens of thousands of employees in southwestern Germany. It marks one of the most significant milestones in the development of industrial relations following the revolution.

The negotiations in Heidelberg were "exceptionally difficult,"[104] especially those concerning the length of the work week. The DMV continued to insist on the 46-hour week, and prevailed. The result of the talks was the Heidelberg Agreement, a settlement which formed the basis for the separate regional agreements. The contract for Daimler and the rest of Wuerttemberg was hammered out in ensuing discussions in Stuttgart.

The result was a far-reaching codification of industrial practices at Daimler and other works in the region. The biggest advance over the prewar situation was the shortening of the work week, which was fixed at 46 hours, not including the daily pauses for breakfast, vespers, and lunch. In most other areas, the agreement ratified the already prevailing practices. Wages were to be paid weekly, with management's statistical reckoning for the week accompanying payment. Overtime work was to be avoided wherever possible; where it could not be, it would be rewarded with 25 percent in extra wages for the time worked. Workers were entitled to a three-day paid vacation after one year of employment, six days after three years, and a maximum eight days after six years.[105]

The contract also confirmed the role of the workers' committees in the functioning of the factories. It provided for the resolution of disputes concerning contract provisions through the arbitration committees which had been originally set up by the Auxiliary Service Law and confirmed by the Stinnes-Legien pact.

A key feature of the accord was the confirmation of the piece-rate system. To be sure, the procedures for setting rates and recording the work performed were strictly delineated in paragraphs 11–17. Nevertheless, with the agreement the DMV gave up its fundamental rejection of piece-work, which had been incorporated in its battle-cry "Piece-work in murder-work!" The union explained this change by contending that this old motto "no longer held unconditionally with today's technology." Whereas even a few months before, following the November upheavals, the workers had generally rejected the piece-rate system, the union held that it was now universally permissible. At the end of 1919, only a single contract in the industry, covering 37 employees, forbade piece-rates.[106]

The agreement between labor and capital was an index of the relative strengths of the contracting parties at the time it was being hammered out. The standing of each, however, was a complicated combination of a number of factors. For one, the condition of the labor market was important, and here the general oversupply of labor worked against the labor organizations. Another factor was the organized power of the metal workers, most importantly in the DMV. The strength of the employers' organizations tended to offset the power of labor in the negotiations. Labor's position, to be sure, masked internal divisions; nevertheless, it was able, for the time being, to force recognition of the 46-hour week.

On the political level, the parties were also fairly evenly matched. The federal and state governments, both still led by Social Democrats, were committed to the gradual socialization of parts of the economy. According to the predominant view of social democratic politicians in the *Land,* however, the most critical social need was the restoration of the health of industry. In practice, the national and state governments prized the achievement of pacts within German industry which neither enfeebled industry nor denied labor's aspirations for a humane regime within the factories.

The pact in the metal industry is an indication that these goals still could be met fairly easily in the spring of 1919. However, the facility with which the agreement was reached was the result of a political, social, and economic conjuncture which would become no better for labor in subsequent months and years.

The radical workers' committee at Daimler had no basic objections to the agreement. It obtained several amendations in the classification of employees for the payment of wages, and also changes in the wage-rates for certain workers.[107] In talks with DMG officials, the workers' committee held that the reckoning of the length of service for the purpose of allocating vacation time should include the time spent in military service or working under military command at other factories. The minor points which the workers' committee raised demonstrates that both the SPD and the radical factions accepted the agreement as a positive step in regulating wages and working conditions at the firm.[108] To be sure, many in the radical camp held out hope for a more far-reaching transformation of the factory regime, but no one was interested in actually obstructing the present agreement.

Indeed, in the subsequent months most strife at Daimler concerning the agreement centered around wage rates (see table 5.1). The firm estimated that the wage provisions of the new contract would cost it nearly 1.6 million marks in the first year alone.[109] It warned the workers' committee that the current operating losses were so large that they could not be borne for long. It urged workers and clerks "in their own interest" to work intensely so that the current difficulties—caused by "poor productivity and high costs"— could be surmounted.[110]

Yet as prices continued to rise through the rest of 1919 and into 1920, new upward adjustments of wages were necessary. While the parties worked these out, an interim payment was disbursed to the Daimler work force in January 1920. Married male workers received 80 marks, while women and single men were given 60 marks. This agreement continued the pattern at Daimler: whether worked out by the "moderate" SPD representatives or the "radical" USPD/Spartacists committeemen, agreements on layoffs and wages discriminated against women. Not only had the female presence in the plant been abruptly curtailed in the weeks after the war, but also those few who remained had to settle for wage and cost-of-living awards which were always below that of their male counterparts.

The 1919 model of the workers' committee interpreted its mandate to protect the interests of the workforce in ways which were more far-reaching than the Daimler direction would have preferred. In November, the commit- tee announced that the workforce would no longer work on those contracts destined for the export market—apparently mainly autos—which were being sold at prices below cost. This practice, the committee alleged, "ap- pears [to] severely endanger the further operation of the works of the Daimler-Motoren-Gesellschaft [vitally] necessary for the interest of the workforce." This business practice was "further undermining the financial productivity of the firm."[111]

The Wuerttemberg Minister of Labor, Leipart, intervened quickly in the

---

TABLE 5.1

Wage Goals at DMG According to 1919 Pact

	Marks Per Hour
Skilled Workers over 25 yrs. of age	2.62
Skilled Workers 22–25 yrs. of age	2.25
Machine Workers (Angelernte) 25 +	2.25
Machine Workers (Angelernte) 22–25	2.00
Day Laborers (unskilled) 25 +	1.76
Day Laborers (unskilled) 22–25	1.54
Women over 20 yrs. of age	1.10

Source: AGM DBAG DMG 37 Kollektivabkommen fuer die Metall-Industrie. Berechnung der Mehr-kosten.

dispute. "In light of the facts, I cannot take issue with the decision of the workforce to avoid further work on the contracts which do not cover costs and which therefore undermine the financial productivity of the firm." Because of DMG's overriding importance for the economy, its continued operations "must be secured with all means;" therefore, the Minister ordered that all of the firm's contract prices be adjusted to meet costs.[112]

Daimler soon annulled several of its contracts and offered the parties new ones "corresponding to the conditions prevailing in the current market."[113] Even a pro-business publication was led to marvel how Daimler and other firms "which defend themselves against the workers' committees . . . with passionate intensity, understand how to make these . . . institutions useful for themselves when it suits . . . their business purposes." According to this view, the perhaps unintentional connivance of the Daimler direction with the workers' committee had the effect of furthering the false view which connected "higher prices for the industry and higher wages for the worker." It also served to undermine the sanctity of contracts, not only between consumers and sellers, but also between labor and management.[114] Perhaps only a cynical observer would note that the workers' committee and the Daimler direction negotiated a 60 to 80 mark bonus for the labor force in the following weeks.

WAGES, 1919–1920

The piecework system at DMG survived the revolution and the first year of the republic, despite the traditional hostility of workers and their organizations to it. In February 1919, for example, Daimler smiths demanded the immediate abolition of piecework. At about the same time, workers' representatives were objecting to it in principle and in practice, claiming that it contradicted the principles of the revolution and had led to abuses of the workforce and to a poisoning of the atmosphere at the plant. Yet within a matter of months, labor had dropped most of its objections, agreeing to the incorporation of a section regulating the piecework system into the Heidelberg Agreement of 1919. By early 1920, piecework was more entrenched than ever at Daimler. There were 355 more pieceworkers in April 1920 than in the previous May, and their percentage of the total work force had grown to 47.2 %, from 44.9 % eleven months earlier. Among skilled workers, the share working for piece-wages increased from 53.2 percent to 56.7 percent over the same period. What had happened?

In its annual report for 1919, the Metalworkers' Union held that the introduction of new technology had helped to make piece-rates less objectionable to workers. However, little innovative technology was introduced at Daimler or in the rest of the industry in the early months of 1919, so this explanation is unsatisfactory. The movement of wages at Daimler in 1919 and early 1920 helps explain why the piece-rate system became less contentious in the first year of the republic. In March 1919, the earnings of skilled workers were roughly equal, whether they were paid by the piece or by the hour. Two months later, the skilled piece-rate workers received on average 5.4 percent more than those paid by the hour. By the spring of 1920, their advantage had increased a bit more, to 6.4 percent.

For Daimler's contingent of trained and machine workers, those who worked by the piece benefitted even more. The differential between piece-workers and the hourly workers increased by almost 10 percent from the spring of 1919 to April 1920.

There were other grounds for retaining and even expanding the piece-work system at Daimler in 1919 and 1920. For one, with the resumption of production in 1919 (after the months of transition which had seen much effort expended on dismantling materiel which had been built for the war effort), it was clear that the piecework system would flourish. In addition, it gave management more control over the workers. If the worker were paid according to the work he actually performed, he would be less likely to chat (*schwaetzen*), to agitate among his fellows, or to disrupt the production process, at least if he were a classic *Homo economicus*.[115]

The earnings of the two most important categories of workers—skilled and trained machine workers—converged during 1919 and 1920. At the beginning of 1919, skilled workers paid by the piece received almost 17 percent more money than those with less *Berufsausbildung*. A year later, the difference had sunk to 12 percent, and ebbed toward 10 percent during 1920. Among the workers paid by the hour, skilled workers received roughly one-fifth more wages than their less skilled colleagues in 1919 and 1920.

The highest paid workers overall were those laboring in the foundry, including the skilled woodworkers whose efforts were part of the production process there. These formed the aristocracy of the Daimler work force during the revolutionary period.[116] Certain groups of lathe-turners also did well, but only if they were paid by the hour. Other machine workers— millers and lathe-turners—lagged behind the average earnings, as did the workers employed in the large toolmaking department at the plant.

Among the unskilled, the more than 1,000 male day-laborers in Unter-tuerkheim fared comparatively well. From March 1919 to April 1920, their wages increased by 76%, the highest rate of increase for any category of DMG workers.[117]

Women, however, did poorly at Daimler. Most of those who escaped the mass dismissals in late in 1918 were not around to see the summer of 1919 at the Untertuerkheim plant. Their wages were low, and downright paltry in comparison to their fellow employees in the departments in which they worked: less than two-thirds of those unskilled males, slightly more than half of those of male machine workers, and often not much more than 40 percent of the highest paid skilled workers. A few of these same female workers had performed the same jobs as machine workers during the war, also for low pay.

THE REVOLUTION AT DAIMLER

What does the experience of the Daimler-Motoren-Gesellschaft suggest about the German revolution and its aftermath? For one, it does not appear that the radicalism at Daimler was generated and borne by those who Karl Heinz Roth called the "mass workers."[118] They were the unskilled employees who were not part of the traditional labor movement, organized at Daimler by the DMV and DHV, and the Social Democrats. The militants and spokespersons of the radical factions at Daimler were the same types of workers who headed the traditional "reformist" camp: male, skilled, with perhaps a slightly higher probability of being paid by the piece. Paradoxically, the transitional period of demobilization at Daimler tended to reinforce the position of such workers by removing women and unskilled and "semi-skilled" workers, even as it undermined industrial-political stability. The gradual eclipse of the traditional workers' leadership at Daimler can be attributed, to a large extent, to the fact that most of the changes which they wanted to effect in the factory regime were already in place by the last year of the war, and the bulk of the workforce was not satisfied. To be sure, the boundaries between political groupings at times tended to be vague, particularly between the USPD and Spartacists, but also between the SPD and the more radical workers, as the balloting for the general strike authorization in March 1919 showed. The radicalism of the postrevolutionary period combined dogged, practical work for the improvement of wages and working conditions within the factory with a militant politics for the socialist transformation of Germany society.

The Movement of the United Proletariat, culminating in the general strike, was the most remarkable expression of this unity of form and substance. Rooted in the factories of greater Stuttgart, the movement made explicitly political demands, borne out of mounting disappointment with the course of events in the postrevolutionary period. Yet it remained isolated, even within Wuerttemberg, and cracked in the face of Hahn's troops and the government's steadfastness. Its collapse did not uproot the popular movement at Daimler; rather, the committee and its network of 150 *Vertrauensleute* spread through every Daimler department, pressed forward with its efforts, among them supporting the collective bargaining agreement worked out in the spring of 1919, bargaining incessantly for wage adjustments in the face of rising prices, monitoring the firm's contracts, or agitating on behalf of Soviet Russia.

From February 1919 onward, the militance within the Daimler factory worked increasingly on two levels. For one, the workers' committee labored long and hard to portray a united front to the direction and the outside authorities. With this attitude, they followed in the footsteps of the traditional labor movement in the metal and machine industries, seeking to reinforce the solidarity of all the occupational branches in the factory over fractional departmental identities. At the same time, the workers' committee took advantage of the diversity of this unique factory which housed most of the occupations of the metal and machine-building industries, as well as many wood- and handworkers. Individual departments were increasingly the scene of protests and work stoppages, beginning with the workers in the smith in February and the plant maintenance workers in late April. Yet, the firm's retreat to the peripheries of the German industrial economy with the end of the war eliminated the mass market for its goods, which had been provided by the military's purchases of tens of thousands of engines and vehicles. With the end of the war economy, the alternative of American-style "Fordism" was now wholly missing for Mercedes. The return of the *status quo ante bellum* heralded a life and death struggle for survival at Daimler, and soon set the stage for a new, more extreme toughness in arranging affairs with the workforce.

The inability of the labor movement at Daimler to reconcile its drive for practical reform with its desire for fundamental social change and to appeal successfully for support in the broader political community would become clear in 1920.

6

THE END OF THE
REVOLUTIONARY ERA
IN UNTERTUERKHEIM

N 1919, Germany became a republic. Throughout 1919, the National
Assembly meeting in Weimar drafted the constitution of the new republic, chose Friedrich Ebert, one-time saddler and leader of the SPD, as the
first president, concluded an unpopular peace with the victorious Allies
which cost the nation dearly, and sought to secure the industrial regime of
labor-management arbitration and cooperation known as the *Arbeitsgemeinschaft* while rejecting the socialization of big business. New surges of
the inflation which had begun early in the war punished the German economy during the revolution of 1918–19 and in the winter of 1919–20,
eroding living standards and destabilizing the processes of state-building.

Nevertheless, rebellion repeatedly welled up from below in 1919 and
1920. Amid thousands of deaths, government soldiers and *Freikorps* units
crushed left-wing insurrections in Berlin, Munich, Braunschweig, Magde-
burg, Dresden, Leipzig, and Stuttgart. Neither Communists, independent
socialists, nor Social Democrats could capture the energies of the workers in
the factories of greater Stuttgart. Indeed, the movements of radicalized
workers in the Stuttgart area in 1919–20 emanated, by all accounts, from
the four largest factories in the region, although proletarian unrest was by
no means confined to them. The four—the Daimler-Motoren-Gesellschaft
in Untertuerkheim, the Bosch factories in Stuttgart and Feuerbach, and the
Maschinenfabrik Esslingen—were also the largest employers of metalwork-

ers and machine-builders in the region. During the national mobilization for military production, the huge armies of workers which they had amassed dwarfed the size of other firms in the Stuttgart area.[1] During the November revolution, the January actions of 1919, and the Movement of the United Proletariat in March and April 1919, the workers from these plants— especially those from Daimler, who had been dubbed the "vanguard of the revolution" by the last Interior Minister in old Wuerttemberg—played a key role, leading the militant challenges to the authorities.

During this period, the considerable power of the Daimler workers grew from the way their rank-and-file attempts to restructure the relations of authority within their factory connected with the radical political movements of the revolutionary period. That "socialism" had sweeping ramifications for the factory regime and that it ultimately derived its legitimacy after November 1918 from the goal of the labor movement to fight to restructure working conditions were tenets which united many radical workers, no matter whether they supported the Social Democratic, Communist, or independent socialist organizations. It is therefore not surprising that Daimler's management sometimes found the boundaries between workers' groups during the revolution diffuse and unclear. This chapter will begin by portraying the shop floor struggles which sustained and energized the workers' movement at the largest of the factories in Wuerttemberg.

1920: WORKING TO A NEW TEMPO

The Daimler plant in late 1919 and 1920 was a unique collection of a dozen workshops in which nearly 9,000 people, nearly all of them males, labored to turn out a variety of engines, chassis, and motor vehicles. As a result of wartime expansion, it was beset by enormous plant overcapacity and continued to be plagued by the lack of a mass market for automobiles in Germany. Of the total work force in 1920, the owners classified "more than half" as nonproductive, meaning that they were engaged as engineers, clerks, maintenance staff, builders of machines and tools for plant use, chauffeurs, firemen, and electricians.[2] Foremost among the productive laborers were the members of the metal and machine-building trades and skilled woodworkers and upholsterers.

In many departments and in the "groups" which were being designed by the plant's engineers in 1919–20, workers toiled at banks of machines imported from America or of German-make. In others, such as the foundry, workers used their skills by performing hand work, assisted by tools or machines. The ranks of skilled workers were supplemented by the "trained" but technically nonskilled machine-workers—millers, grinders, planers, drillers—and the unskilled day-laborers.

Theoretically, the work rules promulgated during the prewar years remained unchanged until 1920. Power followed ownership, and the directors and shareholders at DMG still owned the tools and machines, raw materials, buildings, and space. Before the war, the large Metalworkers' Union began working with Daimler's managers and owners to temper arbitrary power and create working conditions which were considered reasonably good compared with other factories in Wuerttemberg. However, the situation at the Daimler factory had changed dramatically in the interim. Both at Daimler and in the nation as a whole, the labor movement had achieved a position of influence which the business community recognized with the war-time Auxiliary Service Law of December 1916, the Stinnes-Legien pact of November 1918, and the collective bargaining agreement of May 1919. In addition, in the elections to the workers' committee in January 1919, the militant candidates fielded by the Independent Social Democrats and the Communists in Untertuerkheim had gained the majority and routed the traditional Social Democratic leadership of the workers, a measure of the radicalization in progress at Daimler.

The radicals' position of strength was confirmed by the election for the Betriebsrat in March 1920. The choice of the new factory councils across Germany in the spring of 1920 marked the consolidation of what the postwar revolutionary period had accomplished in the realm of intra-factory industrial relations. The new factory councils were the direct descendants of the committees legally established by the *Hilfdienstgesetz* of 1916. As such, they heralded the defeat of the revolutionary councils which had been touted as the germ-cells of the socialist republic by the radical men and women of 1918–1919. Designed to give workers an institutionalized voice in the management of industrial affairs, the factory councils marked a milestone in the course of the reformist German labor movement.[3] Social Democrats saw them as supplanting the radical demand for the revolutionary hegemony of the workers within the spheres of economic production and the state, and as opening the era of the *Arbeitsgemeinschaft,* the regulated, if not entirely peaceful, coexistence of capital and labor.

The ascendant radical groupings within the Daimler work force disputed this reformist vision as they campaigned for the vote in March 1920. For them—the Communists and Independent Social Democrats in particular—factory councils were to be used as the advanced bases for a new revolutionary onslaught. The company itself opposed the new law on the factory councils, but decided, in its own words, "to fulfill it loyally."[4]

Late in the winter of 1920, DMG began to organize the election procedure. According to the provisions in article 15 of the new law, the Betriebs-rat at Daimler would consist of 24 members—19 workers and five clerks. These were to be drawn from two constituent bodies—the workers' council, with its 22 members, and the clerks' council, with 11 members. Three supplementary members would be elected to the workers' council and six to the clerks' council. All employees over 18 years of age were allowed to vote, and those who were at least 24 years old and who had been employed at DMG for at least six months with at least three years overall employment were eligible for election. The firm vehemently protested the provision that gave young workers the vote. "The law-giver therefore accepts that [he] who as a thirteen year old boy stuck a rose in the buttonhole of his departing father in August 1914 could have acquired a sufficient sureness of political judgment in the last five years of golden freedom in order to participate equally alongside the old factory veterans."[5] Even so, 700 employees were too young to qualify.

Once the firm, in accordance with the new law, announced the election on March 4, the workers' organizations had until March 11 to nominate their slates. Four lists competed for the workers' votes, and two for the clerks'. List one was the slate entered by the Communists, list two by the Social Democrats, and list three by Christian trade unionists, members of the Hirsch-Duncker organizations, and other non-socialist groups. There was a fourth list, submitted on the eve of the deadline, which was that of the Independent Social Democrats.

The Communists submitted 24 names for their slate, which was identified by a drawing of a red-colored factory building. By far the most youthful faction, their average age was 31.6 years. Only three were over 40 years of age, of whom the oldest was 47. Eleven were between 25 and 29. The Communists also had been the most recently hired. They had been on the job an average of only two and one-half years, having been hired, for the most part, during the massive expansion of DMG in 1917–18. Despite the firm's persistent claims that radicals at Daimler were outside agitators and not Swabians, 20 of the 24 Communists (83%) had been born in Wuerttem-berg. One each was from Saxony and Thuringia, another from Prussia, and the fourth from Austria.[6]

The Social Democrats submitted 43 candidates for the Betriebsrat vote. The list was symbolized by a blue flower. The average age was 38.4 years. Only 6 (13.6%) were under 30 years of age. Most were between 33 and 43 years. The Social Democratic candidates had been at Daimler for an average of six years. Nearly 77 percent had been born in Wuerttemberg and another 11 percent in Bavaria.

The small Christian and Hirsch-Duncker unions at Daimler fielded a third list with 44 candidates. This was the most elderly grouping (42.5 years on average) and nominated the oldest candidate, a 65 year old man. Indeed, three of their candidates were over 60, and another ten were between 50 and 59 years of age. Only six (13.6%) of the non-socialists were under 30. On average, they had been employed at Daimler for seven and one-half years, making them the group with the most service at the firm. They were also, by and large, another group of native Wuerttembergers, with 79 percent hailing from the *Land*.

As exemplified in a surviving leaflet, the non-socialist propaganda urged the work force to resist using the Betriebsrat for "party-political purposes." "For us, it is good to build up the battered economy and to achieve practical, present-oriented work in the social sense. We reject . . . the choosing of so-called revolutionary factory councils." The slogan adopted by the allied Christian and Hirsch-Duncker candidates proclaimed: "Against the . . . sole rule of profit. For equality, the common good, and sound social progress."[7]

The last list, with 46 candidates, was submitted by the independent socialists. This grouping was the second oldest collectively (38.8 years), although none of its candidates was over than 49. Two thirds of its nominees were between 33 and 42. The average length of employment was 4.4 years, behind only the Communists. As with the other lists, these men came chiefly from Wuerttemberg (78%).

One of the USPD list's electoral leaflets charged that the reform-minded supporters of the Weimar Republic's *Arbeitsgemeinschaft* wished to "lull the work force in order to convert it into a willing tool of the capitalists." The new arrangements for regular consultation between capital and labor were meant "to narcotize the masses." Instead, the new factory councils "should serve as organs of struggle." To achieve this, the candidates urged the employees to select "men and women who will fight resolutely for the rights of the work force," and to spurn the "traitors" in their midst. "When you go to the vote-urn, think back on the sufferings of the war, think of the victims of the revolution, . . . think of the tax-law with which you are now burdened, and *do not forget the deeds* of men like Salm and Schifferdecker during the war, who are now presented to you as the candidates of the *Arbeitsgemeinschaften*."[8]

Two slates, one of Social Democrats, the other of radicals, contested the election to the clerks' council. The firm compiled no information on the age of the candidates, allegedly because of its deference to the sensitivities of the large number of women on the lists. There was little difference between the lengths of service and places of birth of the nominees of the slates: 5.9 and 5.4 years respectively, and overwhelmingly from Wuerttemberg.

In the superheated atmosphere following the Kapp putsch and the defeat of the "Red Army" of the Ruhr, which sparked a violent demonstration at Daimler on March 19 (see below), the election turnout on March 25 was impressive. Almost 95% of the workers and 86% of the clerks cast ballots. The results (shown in table 6.1) were a sweeping victory for the left. The independent socialists, with a majority of the ballots, scored 12 of the seats, while the Communists won five. The Social Democrats received four mandates, and the nonsocialists a single seat.[9] Thus, the revolutionary socialists won a solid majority of the workers' council, controlling 17 of the 22 seats. The firm saw the results as a victory for the "herd" mentality of the workers.

For the next five months, the Daimler factory council was headed by a loose confederation of independent socialists led by the two chairpersons, Groetzinger and Goennenwein. Both were skilled workers and members of the USPD. Little is known about them. Goennenwein was a 42-year-old fitter who hailed from Gottlieb Daimler's hometown, Schorndorf. He became an assistant master at a small factory before coming to Daimler during the war. Originally an adherent of the right wing of the SPD, he became a leftist during 1919, and was considered a supporter of armed socialist revolution at the time he headed the factory council in the summer of 1920. He lived in Hedelfingen, a village a kilometer south of the factory, and headed the local USPD club there in 1919 and the KPD's local organization in late 1920.[10]

In early August, solely on its own initiative, the Betriebsrat authorized the formation of a "political workers' council," which was to prepare the Daim-

TABLE 6.1
The Betriebsrat Election, March 1920

List	# on List	% from Wuertt.	Average Age	% Under 30 Yrs.	Time at DMG
KPD	24	83	31.6 yrs.	45.8	2.5 yrs.
SPD	43	77	38.4	13.6	6.0
Non-socialist	44	79	42.3	13.6	7.5
USPD	46	78	38.8	13.0	4.4

Workers' List	Votes	% of Total	# of Seats
KPD	1,573	23.6	5
SPD	1,341	20.1	4
Non-socialist	293	4.4	1
USPD	3,445	51.8	12

Sources: AGM DBAG DMG 168 Fuer die Betriebsratswahl, and *Daimler Werksnachrichten*, June 3, 1920, pp. 21–28.

ler workers for the proletarian revolution and the new era of rule by the institutions of the working class. A fiercely contested election put six independent socialists and ten Communists on the new council, which was to attend the factory council's meetings with the Daimler direction.[11]

This sharp radicalization of the work force, reflected in the constitution of the workers' representation and in the claims of the "political workers' council," was also registered in relations between labor and management on the shop floor. Accounts of the conflicts within the factory were published by both Daimler and the Wuerttemberg government in late 1920.[12] They reveal a powerful challenge to the relations between labor and management which had prevailed earlier in the plant. As the owners of the plant put it, "Every order was fought and circumvented, work on personal private projects and outright theft took a ruinous toll, the authority of the master, the engineer, and the firm's direction was challenged and rendered ineffective through open force of a kind that finally made the further operation of the factory impossible."[13]

The challenge to the work relations prevailing within the production process took a wide variety of forms, including the significantly increased power of the elected representatives of the workers on the Betriebrat and of the more radical shop stewards of the trade unions inside the factory. In addition, workers and their representatives pressed forward with direct action on the shop floor, slowing the pace of work, attempting to set hourly and piecework wage rates, regulating output, refusing overtime, challenging —sometimes violently—factory supervision, demanding a say in the choice of plant supervisors, and pressing for a closed union shop.

The Betriebsrat elected on March 25, 1920 soon took up residence in a suite of five offices in the plant provided by the firm, equipped with typewriters, a telephone and even secretaries. The typical *mise-en-scene* included "thick tobacco smoke hanging above a visitor, agitational sheets of the usual kind strewn about on the tables, around which a number of idle council members stood, permanently politicizing."[14]

No matter what the political persuasion, the talk of the workers there often turned to socialism. This seemed to have especially appalled the plant direction, for it indicated to them that the members of the Betriebsrat were more interested in the "program of their party" than in "concrete joint work with the leadership of the firm."[15] For its part, the factory council later responded that the "direction of DMG, whose sales and technical ability [are] not up to the mark, appear to have no idea at all of the politics and world view of the workers, or else it would know that all of the socialist parties want to replace the present capitalist disorder with a socialist order."[16]

From March to August 1920, Daimler had to live with a militant factory council supported by 75 percent of the rank-and-file. The Betriebsrat, through its smaller operating committees, played a crucial role in the life of the plant during the spring and summer of 1920, regularly meeting with the firm's directors and operating the various funds for relief payments to injured and ill workers. Daimler's management watched and waited.

The plant direction viewed the council's role in disbursing relief payments as a direct threat to the operation of the factory, for it assured the "sole domination of the leftist parties" in the "economic and personal lives of the individual workers." The Betriebsrat waged an "unscrupulous political Terror" against the workers, riding roughshod over the rank and file "with force and threats."[17] The council countered these charges by pointing out that the Daimler workers had chosen it by a secret ballot, and that all of its actions were the result of majority decisions involving not only the council but also mass meetings of the rank and file.[18] Indeed, as the Wuerttemberg government later noted, the rank and file in the plant was on occasion more militant than the Betriebsrat itself and disregarded its moderating efforts, as when the government tried to introduce a new tax on wages in August 1920.[19]

Workers often tried to slow down the pace of work in the departments of the factory. One worker, who began his employment in 1917 and left in August 1920, reported that he was often told by his fellow workers to either work more slowly or to leave Daimler. A trade unionist, for example, told the workers in his department to work more slowly. When one worker refused, the steward demanded that he be sacked immediately. A member of the Betriebsrat from the foundry prevented a piece-worker there from doing his customary 77 pieces of work a week, a total considered too high. These moves were often made to try to force up piece-rates. In the machine shop, two workers' representatives required the piece workers to submit the rates offered to them by management for inspection. The workers then refused the work if their representatives had not approved the rate. Management charged that 30 percent of the work in the department was rejected regularly because of this practice, and that it was part of a systematic attempt to set piece-rates above the official guidelines.[20]

In the department which adjusted and fine-tuned the Daimler motors, a shop steward had instituted a system "with the help of the like-minded" whereby all the piece-rate wage cards from his department passed through his hands before being delivered to the master for processing. According to the firm's owners, this worker representative regularly altered the wage cards. Times logged for work on a certain motor which seemed too brief to him were simply changed. A declaration which he induced the workers in his department to sign read,

All piece-rate wage cards for finished motors must pass through the hands of the workers' committee. It will then pass them further on. This is in the interest of each individual worker, and it becomes obligatory by the signing [of this] to comply strictly with this, since only through it can [our] unity be maintained. The department will take notice of the contravention of its interests.[21]

In another department, a union militant looked at the piece-rate wage cards in his department to control the wages of the employees. If someone earned more than the departmental average, he was frequently subjected to insults, according to a corporation report. The firm charged that the aim of such procedures was to achieve an increase in the rate.

Among the welders, pieceworkers consistently refused the rates proffered by the plant managers during the spring and summer of 1920. The officials were compelled to raise the rates "if the work should be carried out at all." Even then, up to 50 percent more time was expended on the job than earlier, DMG claimed. On one occasion, a leader of the welders went so far as to shut down the department, denounce the scheduled piece-rates before the assembled personnel, and "raise the rates on his account, despite the objection of the manager." In the Daimler foundry, the workers themselves simply began to set their own rates, which, not surprisingly, were invariably higher than management's.[22]

In general, this kind of struggle was "carried through similarly in a large portion of the workshops and carried out by members of the factory council and shop stewards." Few of the workers' representatives were recognized as such by the firm's officials, and "the greater majority of their activity was carried out without the permission of the superiors during work time."[23] In other words, the employees had attained considerable power within many workshops in the factory, and sometimes even took the initiative in setting piece-rates themselves. Daimler officials charged that the Betriebsrat used "this expanded network" of ad hoc representatives and militants to prevent wages from "attaining a certain level" so that it could then demand higher wages. Indeed, against the premises of corporate orthodoxy, the Daimler workers believed that their incomes should be improved by struggling for higher wages rather than by increasing the intensity and productivity of their labor.[24]

Overtime had long been a sore point with the work force, as we have repeatedly seen. During the slump in the sales of motor vehicles in the spring and summer of 1920, there was very little occasion for management to request overtime work. Nevertheless, the company reported that on an occasion when it asked an unskilled laborer to perform an hour's overtime, a member of the factory council forced him to turn it down.[25] Similarly, although the times saw little in the way of new technology introduced into the production process at Daimler, the company reported that its introduction of each new work method was hampered by the Betriebsrat in violation of the legislation creating the factory councils "to cooperate in the introduction of new work methods."[26]

Several of the demands raised by workers provoked the scorn of management. A "trouble-maker" in the machine shop for turning metal parts demanded that the pieceworkers there be granted certain time periods for chores such as studying the firm's proposed piece-rates (about a half hour) and completing piece-rate wage cards (a quarter hour).[27] Others thought that masters and supervisory officials should be more circumspect in their dealings with the workers. One employee complained to a shop steward that the master in his department timed his performance on the job by means of a stopwatch, that universally hated tool for measuring the efficiency of factory workers. According to the firm's report, the shop steward announced, "The next time, immediately report it; then we shut this place down."[28] The entry of an engineering official into the foundry—the place of work for an especially truculent group of employees—provoked a near riot on January 17, 1920. The workers surrounded the official, and a former who would later be elected to the Betriebsrat demanded an explanation as to why he had suddenly appeared there. The assembled workers then allegedly forced him to leave their department by throwing him down the stairs, tearing his collar and suit in the process.[29]

Management's attempts to keep the employees on the job at all times were similarly unsuccessful. The master who told one rank-and-file militant to stay at his job instead of agitating received the direct reply: "Don't you realize we're in a revolutionary period?"[30] The master in the mechanical department who tried to maintain order by having workers write down the times of their comings and goings was directly countermanded by the chairman of the Betriebsrat.[31]

A segment of the work force claimed the right to use the tools in the Untertuerkheim facility to make things which they and their families needed. The company scornfully labeled this practice "socialization."[32] One engineering official alleged that 50 percent of the work day in the department to which he was assigned was devoted to such activity, certainly an outrageous exaggeration in view of the firm's production statistics for the year.

The Betriebsrat, for its part, ridiculed the company's charges. It denied that thievery and unauthorized work [Pfuscharbeit] were especially widespread, and noted that both it and the workers themselves had tried to stop such infractions by reporting large thefts—by company officials—immediately.[33]

These reports indicate that the traditional structures of authority at the Daimler factory—if we can use "traditional" to describe the factory regime in effect from 1903 to 1918—were being directly challenged in 1920, and that the employees' representatives and even the workers themselves were making a powerful bid to exercise more control over the conditions of their work within the various departments. Some Daimler workers may have been ready for a new stage of the struggle: the company reported finding firearms at the factory in August 1920.

Repeatedly during the first eight months of 1920, employee organizations and work force mobilized for political action. There seem to have been four separate occasions which moved the Daimler workers to action in 1920: the repression of the rebellion by the Ruhr workers in the wake of the Kapp Putsch, the assault by the Poles on the Soviet Republic, price increases for food and other staples, and the new income tax on workers' wages passed by the Reichstag in the summer of 1920. By all accounts, large sections of the Daimler work force participated in all four campaigns.

In March, the workers undertook a campaign in solidarity with the insurrection in the Ruhr which broke out following the attempt by right-wing army officers in Berlin led by General Walther von Luettwitz to install Wolfgang Kapp as leader of a "national" Germany. Although the putsch collapsed so quickly in the face of united opposition from labor in Berlin that the general strike did not spread to the Stuttgart area, armed detachments of revolutionary workers gathered in the Ruhr and clashed with army troops. The Reichswehr, which had refused to move against the putschists, dispatched strong units to crush the powerful movement in Germany's industrial heartland.[34] On March 19, word spread through the Daimler plant that a train on the factory grounds was being loaded for the transport of supplies to the Reichswehr units moving into the Ruhr. Soon, a crowd of workers streamed to the station and tried to prevent the departure of the supply train by tearing up the tracks leading out of the station. Despite the vigorous and violent protest, the supply train eventually did depart. This was the only such solidarity action in southwest Germany.[35] According to the firm, only a "small part" of the employees had remained on the job during the demonstration. The newly elected Betriebsrat, however, demanded that no worker be paid for the time while the demonstration was transpiring, not even those who stayed behind. It claimed that the solidarity of the work force demanded that on such occasions, not a single worker should remain behind in the factory. It was the duty of management to support the solidarity of the workers.[36]

The solidarity issue was also raised six weeks later, when the Betriebsrat called an assembly during working hours related to the upcoming demonstration by Communists and Independent Social Democrats in support of the Soviet Revolution. A number of workers stayed away from the assembly, apparently remaining on the job. The Betriebsrat demanded, presumably unsuccessfully, that these workers forfeit their wages for this period and instead donate them to the firm's general relief fund, the usual procedure for paying fines incurred through violations of the work rules.[37]

The Betriebsrat carefully organized the subsequent march in support of the revolutionary regime in Russia. On May 20, in defiance of the expressed wishes of the Daimler direction, the following leaflet was distributed to the employees:

> Proclamation: The Betriebsrat has taken notice of today's demonstration on behalf of Soviet Russia, to take place at 4:00 this afternoon at the *Schlossplatz* in Stuttgart, and therefore has decided that today, Thursday the 20th, closing time is one hour earlier, 2:55 P.M. We ask all workers to take note of this.[38]

The demonstration took place without incident.

Another action was staged, this time in the factory, in solidarity with the Soviets over the summer. A reputed emissary of the Soviet Republic appeared at the factory and gave a political speech during working hours in the canteen. "Numerous workers" left the workshops to attend, and were admitted to the canteen area in violation of the rules by using a pass prepared by communist militants at the plant under the arrangement of the Betriebsrat. According to the breathless account of the horrified plant directors, the legate allegedly told the assembled workers to learn from the mistakes of the Soviets and make shorter work of their own bourgeois by sending all of them "to the wall" after the revolution.[39]

The agitation at Daimler on behalf of Lenin's Russia climaxed several days later. On August 3, thousands of workers streamed out of the factory departments to the vicinity of the main warehouse, where three new motor vehicles were being loaded onto a train, apparently destined for the German army. Rumors had swept the plant that they were actually destined for Poland to assist the campaign against Soviet Russia being undertaken by the regime there. The workers, equipped with welding torches, unloaded the vehicles and destroyed the frames, inflicting damages estimated at several hundred thousand marks. In the process, one worker lost a foot. The enraged management charged that the chairman of the Betriebsrat was at the factory at the time but had refused to intervene, claiming he had taken a vacation day. Corporation officials quoted the council's vice chairman as telling the demonstrating workers, "Of course I can't tell you to actually destroy them," the implication being that such sabotage was exactly what he had in mind. Afterward, workers sold photos of the destroyed vehicles in the workshops for one mark apiece. The company later charged that "such acts of violence corresponded to the conceptions of the majority of the Betriebsrat."[40]

As the result of the action, the firm sacked two workers, Roesch and Merk, who worked in the shop which had supplied the welding torches for the demolition. As news of the dismissals spread, thousands gathered at the offices of the Daimler directors. The crowd soon forced its way into the administrative suites and demanded the reinstatement of the fired employees immediately. The chief director of the Untertuerkheim facility, Ernst Berge, personally withdrew the notices of dismissal, and the demonstrators subsequently dispersed. According to the accounts of the management officials present, several workers had brought tools with them, and brandished them menacingly during the uproar.[41]

Workers soon mobilized against the inflation which incessantly taxed their incomes. The period from early 1920 to early 1921 was marked by a temporary slackening of inflationary pressures and a "relative stability" of the value of the German currency. But between December 1919 and February 1920, food prices in the urban areas of Wuerttemberg had risen 45 percent. Again, in the wake of the first election to the Reichstag on June 6, the prices of dairy products jumped 50 percent. High prices pressed hard on the living standards of the Daimler workers in 1920, as on those of all workers in the Stuttgart area. While rumors spread that speculators and hoarders were responsible for the inflationary spiral, the Daimler workforce played an important role in the campaign against high prices and shortages in the late spring and summer of 1920.[42] The Betriebsrat marshalled its forces for a massive show of strength in the June 22 demonstration in downtown Stuttgart. The circular it distributed to employees prior to the march describes the choreography for the Daimler formations:

> After the conclusion of work at 3:25 the colleagues will form themselves according to workshops and departments into a column, six across, inside the factory under the leadership of the Betriebsrat and the shop stewards, whose task it will be to get all of this done quickly. The front of the column will face the Gaisburg exit of the factory.[43]

Over 100,000 workers from the Stuttgart area assembled on the *Schlossplatz* on June 22. The municipal drivers shut down the city's streetcars in a gesture of solidarity. In addition to the demands for relief from high food prices and shortages, the demonstration's organizers put forth the demands for the distribution of weapons to the workers to preclude another right-wing putsch attempt and for the erection of a workers' republic.[44] In the wake of the protest, 164 Daimler clerks signed a letter to the clerks' council

protesting the way workers, including their leaders, had labeled nonpartici-
pants *Tropfen* [sic] and *Pfui*.[45] They also denounced the coercion which they
complained had been employed to get them to attend.

THE LOCKOUT OF 1920 & ITS CONSEQUENCES

As the movement against high prices was cresting in Wuerttemberg, the
Reichstag's vote for a 10 percent tax on wages introduced a new source of
disaffection and agitation among the working class. The tax, the fruit of the
finance reforms of Reich Finance Minister Matthias Erzberger in 1919–
1920, had enjoyed the support in principle of most of the SPD and USPD
deputies in the Reichstag, even though there had been no income tax before
the war. Initially, the Communists and other leftists took the lead in foment-
ing a new wave of anti-tax agitation, although the trade unions were also
clearly upset. In late June, the Wuerttemberg trade unions sent the Reich's
Finance Ministry a telegram rejecting the new tax, particularly in light of the
already crushing burden of high prices for food and other necessities. Nevertheless, they rejected "ill-considered individual actions," fearing the heightened possibility of a right-wing putsch and the damage to the interests of the
laboring class that might result from a wave of proletarian unrest at the
time.[46]

In early August, the Communists organized a moderately successful pa-
rade in downtown Stuttgart to protest the new tax. Around 10,000 people
turned out and heard the KPD speakers demand "the annulment of war
debts, the confiscation of large estates, immediate consolidation of the *Betriebsraete*, control of the production and distribution of the necessities by
the representatives of the workers, disarming of the bourgeoisie and the
white guards, arming of the proletariat."[47] The Communist tactic combined
the fight against the new tax with the struggle for new "revolutionary"
councils in the factories to intensify the political fight there.

Under the terms of the new tax law, which was approved by the Reichstag on March 29, 1920, "The employer must withhold [10%] of the wage
. . . and affix and validate a tax stamp on the tax card of the worker." The
tax was intended to go into effect for the work week of July 1, 1920, but
Reichstag and Reichsrat did not agree on the wording of the law until July
15. No attempt was made to collect the tax until August.[48] The government
of Wuerttemberg contended that the movement against the tax "or against
its magnitude" was chiefly confined to the four great factories in the Stuttgart area—Daimler, the two Bosch plants, and the Maschinenfabrik Esslingen—and "to single factories in the *Land*.[49] This was clear after delegations
from these four plants visited the Finance Ministry in the days after the law

went into effect. They described it as an "exception law" [Ausnahmegesetz] directed solely against the workers and clerks.

In early August, Daimler put out a circular informing its employees that the firm would begin to deduct the tax from their wages after August 1. The news stirred up considerable unrest among the employees. Despite this, the Betriebsrat privately assured the firm that, subject to negotiations, it would accept the tax if the authorities ever made the company legally culpable for failing to collect it. On August 5, negotiations began in Stuttgart between representatives of municipal and state agencies, members of the factory councils from Untertuerkheim and Sindelfingen, and a lawyer from Daimler. A representative from the Unterteurkheim work force declared that workers could not part with another pfennig of their income in light of the hard economic times. The workers, he claimed, wanted the law altered and not executed in its present form. The Betriebsrat, he added, felt it incumbent to make this request, for it feared that serious trouble would break out if the tax went into effect.[50]

The lawyer Doeser, on behalf of the firm, informed the officials that Daimler was currently considering shortening the work week from 46 to 32 hours a week. Such a move would deprive workers of 30 percent of their income. In addition, the current plight of the firm, Doeser asserted, would not permit them to raise wages in the foreseeable future.

The spokespersons for the governmental agencies in attendance responded that it was clearly not in their power to reject or alter a national law. Pressed by the Daimler lawyer to reply, the Wuerttemberg Finance Minister volunteered that all he could do was to send on their protests to Berlin by telegram.[51]

Talks between the Daimler Betriebsrat and three directors of the firm continued at Untertuerkheim. Council members told them that they would cooperate with the enforcement of the tax and would use their influence to try to still the opposition to it. They would even personally intervene to halt any demonstrations.[52]

On the first pay day of the month, August 6, Daimler deducted the tax from its employees' salaries. The response was tumultuous. Crowds of workers demanded to have the deductions repaid immediately. Management, "under the force of circumstances," relented and refunded the money.[53] The workers even quickly thwarted Daimler's effort to deduct the work-times lost as a result of the disruption from their wages.[54]

Similar scenes took place at the Bosch factories and in the Maschinenfabrik Esslingen. Under strong pressure from the workers at Diamler and the other firms, the trade unions called for a protest against the tax in Stuttgart on Monday, August 9. In their mobilizing pamphlets, the unions asserted that "factory shrinkages and layoffs are appearing daily. In light of the ever more gripping economic privation, the 10 percent tax is an economic catastrophe for the working class. . . . [It] is an exception law directed against the working people."[55]

Monday's action came off peacefully, with a delegation visiting Wuerttemberg's President von Schubert. The President said he was powerless to do anything but send a telegram to Berlin forwarding their concerns.

The government in Berlin responded to the unrest in Wuerttemberg by dispatching Reich Finance Minister Moesle to Stuttgart on August 13 to meet with employers and workers about the tax. The minister expressed his surprise at the resistance in Stuttgart, for the tax was being accepted regularly elsewhere in Germany. The tax was not weighted against the poor and the workers, he insisted. On the contrary, the upper income brackets would pay more. There could be no question of postponing or abolishing the tax, which was desperately needed to stave off the rapidly approaching bankruptcy of the federal government. Indeed, the states and local communities would each receive a third of the money raised, according to Moesle's representation. The alternative was total fiscal anarchy.

The employers at the meeting with the minister responded that they could no longer bear the brunt of the efforts to carry through with the withholding of the tax. The workers' spokespersons repeated that the crisis of short work weeks and diminished earnings along with soaring prices precluded the workers' assent to payment of the tax. The Finance Minister warned that under no circumstance would the law be waived or changed. To back up his resoluteness, the Berlin government published a notice in the *Staats-Anzeiger fuer Wuerttemberg* three days later, declaring that "the national government is determined to meet, with all of its power, any attempt to illegally refuse the tax payment and to protect those employers and officials obliged to carry out the law."[56]

Another attempt was made subsequently to come to an understanding on the tax question at Daimler. The primary spokesperson for the Betriebsrat, Goennenwein, asserted that the storm of protest could not have been averted and should have been foreseen. "I repeat, we as Betriebsrat have done the utmost, but were unable to bring the law to execution. We could no longer prevent the anger of the masses from making itself felt."[57]

Sekler, one of Daimler's directors, responded that "the law cannot be carried through. . . . It would lead again to violence as on last Friday. . . . We have to report this to our [employers'] organization and to the financial authorities."[58]

There is evidence that a plan for an interim compromise was floated on August 18, under which only 5 percent would be deducted from wages, effective immediately. By this time, the positions of the sides had hardened to the point that anything short of a confrontation seemed unlikely.[59]

The state government also met on the 18th and again the next day to figure out its next move. Talks with both employers and unions were put off pending regional meetings of the Free Trade Unions, to be held on August 22 and 23. At the union's sullen sessions, the delegates adopted a resolution amid sharp attacks demanding that the "unbearable tax" be abolished. To this end, the conference called for a national referendum to decide the fate of this new "unsocial" burden. At the same time, however, they warned against "partial actions" which could only split the anti-tax movement and lead to its defeat.[60]

The resolution passed at the union parley made it clear to the government that an understanding on the tax issue was now probably out of reach. State officials now readied their plans for enforcing the law, meeting on August 23 and 25 with officials from the four problem-factories. A later government report contended that "there was no doubt that when the workers had [finally] recognized beyond a doubt the tax deduction under the pressure of governmental action, the whole matter for the government would be settled, and the armed forces might would be withdrawn from the factories."[61]

With plans to force a final solution of the tax controversy now afoot in the ministries downtown, one last effort was made to effect an understanding with the workers' representatives. Individual meetings at the firms which were centers of resistance failed to produce a breakthrough. The session at Daimler, held on the morning of August 23, was unproductive, but yielded a telling discussion of the state of mind of a large part of the work force. Goennenwein, speaking on behalf of the Betriebsrat, repeated that the council had tried, to no avail, to influence the workers on this matter. Additional discussion would now be pointless. Further, the workers were no longer in the hands of the leaders. It was impossible to squeeze the tax out of their desperately strapped wages. He thought that the workers generally sensed that the state needed taxes, but they also knew who in Germany had the wealth. They had been "squeezed like a lemon" for too long. The taxes, they felt, singled them out at a very difficult economic juncture. If the law were changed to make it more fair, and if prices were reduced 50 percent, then the workers would pay the tax. If the regime tried to use force to make the workers pay, there would certainly be a general strike.

Another member of the Daimler Betriebsrat told the government officials that the workers there now saw the impossibility of continuing to live in a "capitalist system." "An end must be put to the misery of the proletariat under this system—to the need, hunger, and poverty—by struggling to destroy the state. Nothing could be granted for the needs of this state. This state must disappear as quickly as possible, and the whole capitalist society must be radically changed." After this rhetorical *tour de force,* Daimler's Berge asked the council members if violence would accompany another attempt to collect the tax. Goennenwein replied that nothing had changed since they had last discussed the matter on August 18. The negotiations broke off.[62]

On the night of August 25, large police forces directed by the chief of the security forces, Paul Hahn, at the behest of the Wuerttemberg government began occupying Daimler and both Bosch facilities. Similarly, the authorities in Esslingen moved into the big machine factory there. Within hours, the centers of the tax resistance movement had been seized. The state government, which had already discussed the measures to be taken with the firms' owners, sent them a letter stating that the police were being sent "to prevent violence."

> The government deems it necessary that you close your factory from this day on until the threat to managers and clerks and to the company and its facilities in carrying through the tax deduction is quashed. The protection of your factory will be taken over by the police force.[63]

At the same time, the government posted placards around all of the occupied facilities, informing the workers that "the managers of the factories, in agreement with the government, have closed their factories from Thursday until the threat to those managers and clerks carrying through the tax deduction is ended. The protection of the factory facilities has been taken over by the police. Attempts to enter the works will be repelled by force."[64]

Workers who turned up as usual to go to work on August 25 met instead closed factories occupied by heavily armed police, with signs at the gates warning "Stop! Who goes further will be shot dead!"[65] In addition, the Daimler-Motoren-Gesellschaft had posted an official notice:

> Explanation to our employees:
>
> Our employees have, through the threat of force, prevented the carrying out of the legal tax deduction and forced the repayment of a sum of taxes which had been withheld. The exertions of representatives of the government to induce our employees to change their disposition have remained without success. Because of this, the Wuerttemberg government has ordered us to close the factory. In addition, our workers have destroyed three automobiles ready for delivery, and, when the factory managers ordered the dismissal of two of the participating workers, they have forced the withdrawal of these dismissals through the threat of violence. Because of the illegal actions of our employees, the further orderly operation of our factory has become impossible. The factory has been placed under police protection by order of the state government and will remain idle until further notice. With this, our employees are notified of their dismis-

sals, effective immediately. The wages and payments due, as well as the dismissal papers, will be sent through the post.

—DMG[66]

Thus, with the connivance of state and local authorities, Daimler locked out more than 9,000 employees—7,776 industrial workers, 1,048 clerks, and 345 apprentices.[67] Ostensibly, the police action and lockout had been planned only to break the protracted resistance of the workers to the new tax.

The workers at the four plants immediately proclaimed a general strike, and were soon joined by municipal streetcar drivers, the electrical workers in Bietigheim, and the employees of the Eisenmann factory. It was hoped that the action would eventually embrace all "from mid-wives to grave-diggers."[68] Picket lines thrown up around the Daimler factory kept even plant officials from entering the facility. One hundred workers seized the nearby railway station, but retreated in the face of the inevitable police assault.[69]

The factory councils of the closed plants sought to exclude the trade unions from leading "such a large movement." An "action committee" formed by the councils issued four demands of the striking employees: the immediate withdrawal of troops and police from the occupied factories, the reopening of the works for all concerned, reimbursement for lost wages, and the resumption of negotiations with the government regarding the new tax.[70]

The governmental authorities and the employers' associations refused to meet with the "action committee." Instead, on September 1, with the strike eight days old and crumbling, they offered to negotiate with all of the trade unions, including the small Christian and liberal Hirsch-Duncker groupings. The "action committee" relented and turned the affair over to the "economic organizations" for a salvage operation. Talks between the employers, the unions, and the authorities got underway immediately.[71]

Before the parties could reach a compromise agreement, the negotiations were rocked by a bombshell. On September 2, the Daimler-Motoren-Gesellschaft announced that it was withdrawing from the talks and from membership in the employers' Association of Wuerttemberg Metal Industrialists, which had been the contracting party with the trade unions in the landmark 1919 collective bargaining agreement. Furthermore, the company announced it would keep the factory shut until it could change the "working conditions" in its facilities. As the firm later expressed it: "DMG had no time. In the course of two months, there were six revolts in the plant; the conditions had become such that the masters wanted to lay down their posts. . . . It was rejected to take back the work force and then again to dismiss a large part [of it]."[72] The firm wished to fire thousands of employees and to reopen with a compact labor force which would work 46 hours a week. As DMG Director Lang explained it, "The firm wants to have law and order [Ruhe und Ordnung]. Therefore, the workforce should be able to achieve a sufficient wage, but this is only possible with a 46-hour work time." With a shorter work week, "the sense of responsibility of the individual workers would suffer."[73] No compromise was possible as far as Daimler's directors were concerned. "The facility in Untertuerkheim will either be reopened under conditions which the board of directors can justify, or it will remain closed."[74]

■

Thus, Daimler seized the opportunity presented by the government of Wuerttemberg's strong measures to enforce the tax law into the *Land* to recast the working conditions and the balance of power in its Untertuerkheim facilities. In mid-1920, a company study of the operations at Untertuerkheim had concluded that "a fundamental restructuring must be carried through with all means and without delay." Among the areas targeted were the "unusually" large numbers of unproductive and productive workers and clerks at the plant who achieved "extraordinarily meager productivity." In addition, the "old-fashioned . . . machinery and factory organization" and the insufficient utilization of machine work in the production process were scored by the study. The employment of "more and better machine work and of less [skilled] hand work" was necessary in order to improve Daimler's performance. "The highly developed, obedient machines" were "preferable to the whims of the hand worker." The overvaluation of skilled hand work at DMG had led to the current situation in which "the whole factory is stuffed" with parts and sections of motors and vehicles "that cannot be delivered." In other words, "much is done, but little is ever finished."[75]

The solution to Daimler's problems lay in adherence to a fundamental maxim in tune with the times: "With far fewer personnel, produce more; save and save, but in the right places." Two measures should be carried out immediately. All means should be used to reduce the number of employees, including, if necessary, the payment of large sums of money to induce them to leave more or less voluntarily. "This would perhaps be less drastic" than firing them.

The other necessity was the immediate limitation of production so that would be offering only two or three types of cars. "The old system, that the customer should educate the manufacturer, should be broken; the opposite must be done, if one wants to really and continually earn money." The firm should not produce for merely any clientele, but only for the "noblest."

Indeed, there were enough of these latter types to purchase a "sufficient number" of Mercedes cars to keep Daimler profitable.

The advantage of offering only two or three types of cars was "cheaper, more precise, and more continuous production." The author of the firm's study foresaw the more profitable employment of labor-power, with lower piece-rates but in the end a better paid and more satisfied work force. Labor-time would be saved in the production of the necessary parts, and new techniques to lower production costs could be worked out. The report concluded that Daimler found itself in a serious situation, and needed unity and cooperation within the firm to solve its problems. "The tempo of the execution [of these proposals] must not be listless, because it means that a large, indeed a very large task must be performed. Through perseverence and love of the challenge at hand, it will certainly be crowned with success."[76]

The firm's direction justified its recasting of working conditions and the balance of power in its factory in part by highlighting the turmoil which it claimed had disrupted the harmony of the plant. Nevertheless, DMG contended that the major factor which led it to take the radical action of dismissing thousands of workers was the sharp deterioration of its export market during the summer of 1920 and the firm's resulting financial crisis. It is not possible to test the company's claim, but it should be noted that 1920 was not a crisis year for German exports in the main. Although the value of the mark had actually risen in the spring of 1920, Germany "continued and would for some time continue to enjoy an export advantage because of the relative low value of her currency compared to those of her chief competitors."[77] The state government and, of course, the factions of labor greeted Daimler's claims of a crisis caused by a collapse of its exports with some skepticism.

Discussions between the owners and the Betriebsrat on measures to alleviate the alleged financial emergency, including layoffs, began in July. As early as July 9, Director Dr. Sekler had informed the Betriebsrat that the cash-flow situation of the firm was deteriorating.[78] In the middle of August, the firm began to grapple with the economic conditions in a serious way. In 1907, it had been able to lay off half of its work force with nary a second thought to the employees' reaction; this time it confronted a militant, powerful workforce with legally entrenched organizations and rights.

On August 12, Berge, the business manager, described the extent of the problem to the Betriebsrat. "Our debts here have increased to 64 million marks." Added to unpaid taxes and a considerable bank debt, the total debt, "according to a rounded estimate" had reached 172 million marks, by his account. "We must make sacrifices, so that the rest can work further."[79]

The domestic market for Daimler motor vehicles had all but collapsed, and exports had fallen because "we stand in a very sharp competition with the Entente countries, chiefly with the United States." Survival meant taking certain steps, as "painful" as they might be.[80]

Berge then outlined two proposals for the Betriebsrat's consideration: "Either the working time is reduced to four days with the reduction of the work force by 2,360 workers, or the working-time [is] reduced to three days . . . with the work-force reduced by 1,470 men."[81]

Without accepting or rejecting either option, the chairman of the Betriebsrat responded by asking if supplementary support would be paid to those working a shortened week as was done in other factories. Berge responded curtly, "I also understand that workers cannot make ends meet with such wages, and that therefore a supplementary support payment is introduced. We introduce short work weeks because we have no money. I ask you to understand, we cannot introduce a short work week in order to pay at the same time the hours that are cut out." To raise money, the firm also wanted to "get rid of" its works at Sindelfingen, as well as the smaller plant in Berlin-Marienfelde, and had conducted negotiations with an American firm which had not, however, submitted an acceptable offer.[82]

Clearly distrustful, the Betriebsrat indicated that it wished to undertake an examination of the financial situation at DMG. When Berge hesitated, because "we have no time to lose," the council demanded a week to properly study the finances and to deliberate on its own recommendations. Reluctantly, Berge agreed to give them several days: "Next week must decide, or else I must say to you that we shut down." A member of the Betriebsrat complained, "We can see that this firm is not in the condition to lead the workers out of this situation. This time must be used to keep the workers above water. We must orient our production to the east . . . to Russia. Has the firm yet entered an agreement with a Russian trading firm?" The business manager replied impatiently, "We need money. I would not want to know what happens if we stood there on a pay day with empty hands."[83]

The parties resumed negotiations two days later. The chairman of the Betriebsrat asked the firm's directors to explain why their business manager had stated earlier that orders for a full year had been received and were on hand, and that cutbacks and layoffs would not be necessary. Director Sekler responded that there were currently 114 orders worth 65.5 million marks on the books. The economic climate, he added, had worsened since the Kapp putsch five months earlier, and was now "weakening . . . from day to day." Both sides explored ways to limit the crisis, such as beginning to produce other products like typewriters or watches, without success. Finally, the chairman of the Betriebsrat placed the council's new demands before management. If there were to be layoffs, there would also have to be supplemental payments "to hold the workers above water," just as was the case in "all the industry of greater Stuttgart." Those cut back two days (40%) should receive a 30 percent remuneration; three days (60%), a 50 percent payment. "If the firm cannot guarantee this, it must seek the ways and means, possibly with the Ministry of Labor."[84]

The directors turned this down. Director Lang thought that the workers' hardship had been exaggerated. "From a worker I have heard," he continued,

> that it is his opinion that 80% of those in his department can sit out a half year without being abandoned to need and without becoming a burden to the community. A large portion of the workers come from rural communities and own plots of land. In the small communities workers can easily find another job. . . . The younger people should consider choosing another occupation or try to find work on the other side of the border.[85]

Why could the council not agree immediately to the cutbacks? he asked. "I am convinced that the gentlemen do not have doubts because of personal mistrust. It lies in the difficulty they would find themselves in with the work force."[86]

The spokesperson for the Betriebsrat responded: "Director Lang's interpretation is correct. If we went to the workers and clerks and said, so-and-so many workers will be laid off, and so-and-so many will be released, it would cause a storm. The workers are excited. We agree that mistrust dominates a part of the work force."[87] Searching for a compromise, the Betriebsrat suggested that the whole matter be referred to the Stuttgart Arbitration Council and the Wuerttemberg Ministry of Labor. The directors ended the meeting by agreeing to call these intermediaries into the dispute.

Daimler submitted its case for layoffs and cutbacks to the Arbitration Council on August 17. In a succinct precis of the firm's economic situation, Daimler's management declared that the steps were necessary on two grounds: "one, the financial situation of the corporation and two, the fall in the sales of our products." The firm's total debt was put at 161 million marks.[88]

The battery of statistics submitted to buttress the firm's case indicated that the total expenditures for June amounted to 52,005,721 marks, while 1,679,307 marks were paid to workers in wages and 1,284,000 marks to clerks in salaries. Thus, wages and salaries represented less than 6 percent of costs in June. Even if an estimate of the wage bill is measured against the considerably lower costs for July, the percentage is still under 10 percent, a rate lower than in the last stable prewar years.[89]

The Arbitration Council met with representatives of both sides on August 17 for more than four hours. It decided that the firm must fulfill section 74 of the Factory Council Law, which held that employers must hold negotiations with the Betriebsrat whenever large numbers of employees faced lay-offs in order to agree on the scope of redundancies and on measures to mitigate the hardships which the laid-off workers would encounter. Although the deepening crisis was already apparent in July according to the firm's own testimony, news of its severity had only been presented to the Betriebsrat for the first time on August 12 "because the majority of the directors had been on vacation."[90] Therefore, the Arbitration Council judged that the firm must present the factory council with both a definite set of measures to accomplish the shrinkages and the economic data with which the factory council could test the firm's economic plight. New negotiations would then begin on August 21.

Responding quickly to the arbitrators' decision, the firm requested that the Arbitration Council itself examine the books, "since the Betriebsrat would give nothing, even after the examination of our records as to their rightness . . . in order to give away nothing of its confrontational opinion." The Arbitration Council soon agreed to begin an audit under the auspices of the Wuerttemberg Ministry of Labor.[91]

The directors of Daimler and the Betriebsrat held a lengthy negotiating session on August 18. At it, the factory council seemed to hold the initiative. It gained the firm's agreement to provide the documents for an extensive scrutiny of the firm's financial condition, to be completed by October 1, six weeks hence. At the same time, the two sides clashed on the question of whether there were workers at Daimler who did not really need their employment. The directors held to their belief that there were employees— even if only five or ten!—who would accept a furlough voluntarily. Director Lang, who had said a few days earlier that he knew a worker who believed there were employees who did not need their jobs, now held that "I can say positively to you, that people who could make out quite well without employment in the factory are known to me."[92] The chairman of the Betriebsrat disputed this, citing the work of the Demobilization Committee after the war which sought to make room in industry for returning soldiers without ousting from a job anyone who truly needed one. Those who did not need work had already been weeded out, he contended.

The separate audits by the Labor Ministry and the Betriebsrat went on during the next week. At the same time, the resistance of the Stuttgart-area workers to the new income tax was hardening, while the provincial regime prepared its tough enforcement measures. While the Daimler-Motoren-Gesellschaft was being wracked by this dual crisis, the spectacular scandal of the last year of the war, which had seen the firm placed under military supervision and the suspension of its top director in March 1918, catapulted onto the front pages of many of the nation's newspapers again. The findings of the special investigatory commission impaneled by the Prussian War

Ministry, which had apparently been made in 1919 but never released,[93] were leaked to the newspaper of the white-collar workers' union, *Der freie Angestellte*.[94] The revelations, which dominated the front pages of *Vorwaerts* and the Social Democratic press in Wuerttemberg during the week of August 23, severely damaged the credibility of the Daimler-Motoren-Gesellschaft, just as the initial revelations had 29 months earlier.

The scandal was even worse than had been believed, according to the unreleased ministry report. Instead of Daimler's having amassed 25.2 million marks profit on its stock-capital of 8 million marks between 1914 and 1917, the sum which was widely believed and which had scandalized much of German public opinion and provoked cries of outrage in the Reichstag in the late winter and spring of 1918, the investigatory commission of the Prussian War Ministry placed the firm's actual earnings in the neighborhood of 95–110 million marks. Most of the profits had been concealed by Daimler's unique brand of bookkeeping, which the German Association of Bookkeepers had described in 1916 as "indistinct designations and arbitrary numbers: that is the Daimler balance."[95] For one, the firm had listed its considerable property holdings as expenditures.

The so-called Daimler Scandal continued to contribute to the poisoning of the relations between employers and employees after the war. The widespread belief that the firm's owners had made enormous profits during the war, had fraudulently covered them up, and had even gone so far as to fabricate statistics in the hope of obtaining higher prices for its military wares created the impression in a workforce struggling to make ends meet that their bosses would go to every extreme to fleece them. As *Vorwaerts* put it on the eve of the lock-out, "DMG means *Die Machen Geld* (They make money) . . . by plundering the German people."[96]

■

The government's occupation and forced closings of the four Stuttgart-area factories gave the owners of the Daimler-Motoren-Gesellschaft the opportunity to decide the question of the proposed layoffs and shrinkage of the work force and to settle the score with its employees and the Betriebsrat. In the aftermath of the general strike at the end of August, negotiations had begun between the trade unions, the Association of Wuerttemberg Metal Industrialists, and the provincial government. Once the unions were forced to admit the utter necessity of the income tax on September 1, the way was open to an eventual settlement which would lift the government's occupation of the factories and allow work to resume.

At this point, Daimler acted swiftly. On September 2, the day before the other parties announced a final agreement, it withdrew from the employers' organization and from the negotiations. Its new position was voiced by the business manager Berge, now back from his vacation, at a meeting called on September 4 by the Wuerttemberg Ministry of Labor. "The DMG cannot possibly enter the [final] agreement of September 3. It has legally closed. . . . The facility in Untertuerkheim will either be reopened under conditions which the board of directors can justify, or it will remain closed."[97] The firm had no money and no contracts, and "for that the dictatorship and terrorism of the saboteurs in Untertuerkheim was responsible," director Sekler added.[98] Indeed, the theme of a factory crippled by terrorism became the dominant one in Daimler's campaign to justify its legally questionable use of the government's occupation of its premises for its own purposes. The factory would open again only on the terms of the directors, Berge declared. "A co-determination right [Mitbestimmungsrecht] for the work force in the reopening of the factory has been ruled out; the factory will be opened and every single worker asked whether he accepted the conditions of the firm or not."[99]

The firm's strategy to circumvent its legal responsibility to consult with the Betriebsrat regarding the layoffs was to insist that it had closed, and no longer had either employees or Betriebsrat, and thus no legal obligations. This drastic move had been prompted by the failure of "all attempts to reach a betterment of relations through peaceful means" which had foundered on the determined resistance of the factory council and the violent behavior of the employees. "Here stood two world views against one another. . . . Because of the inability to carry through the curative measures, only the means of closing the works was finally left." The firm claimed it was the Betriebsrat which had violated the law by failing to cooperate with the economic retrenchment which the firm had deemed necessary.[100] Thus, after six months in which the tide had been running against the left, with both the defeat of the revolutionary Red Army of the Ruhr and and the massive losses for the reformist SPD in the recent June Reichstag elections, and with the arguments among the factions of labor at a peak, Daimler chose the moment it thought it could prevail to unleash its counteroffensive.

The Wuerttemberg government, a centrist one with a Social Democrat in the Labor ministry which enjoyed the tolerance of the SPD benches, found this stance distasteful and unjust, but was powerless to take any action against the company. "The government regrets the situation. . . . It lacks the means to move the firm to another position."[101] The state's earlier assurance to the workers, that "in what concerns the re-hiring of the released and striking workers, the government will not let this question be mixed up with the planned shrinkages of the works," was quickly forgotten.[102] Later, a memorandum from the federal Labor Ministry shed light on the authorities' reasoning, or rationalizations: "What we seem to have here is not a dismissal of all employees but instead a simple reduction in the size of the work force."

Nonetheless, the government refused to end its occupation of the Unter-tuerkheim plant, despite the firm's use of its measures designed to enforce compliance with the tax for its own wholly arbitrary purposes. An official asserted that "a withdrawal of the police troops would endanger not only the resumption of work soon, but would also not lie in the interest of the work force."[103]

Serious talks finally began under the auspices of the Arbitration Council on September 10. The owners were in the driver's seat. Director Sekler announced that "3000–4000 workers, chosen according to social [crite-ria], will find employment at 46 hours a week."[104] A work week of this length was necessary to guarantee "law and order," since short hours caused dissatisfaction. The representatives of the Betriebsrat and the trade union who were present feebly rejoined that the firm had decided to "kill" 5,000 workers.

After the parties were dismissed, the Arbitration Council drafted a pro-posal for the reopening of the plant. The work week would total 40 hours. A council of seven workers—four from the Betriebsrat, two from the Metal-workers Union (DMV), and one chosen jointly by the tiny Christian and liberal organizations—would be set up to work with the owners in hiring a new work force. The workers would enjoy all of "their old rights." The earlier collective bargaining agreements in the metal industry would govern working conditions. The firm would pledge to add new shifts later "as soon as the conditions permit." The council gave the parties until noon the next day to accept or to turn down the proposals.[105]

For its part, management demanded a number of revisions in the draft. For example, it insisted on the incorporation of the principle of a 46-hour week, although it consented to a 40-hour week under "present conditions." It eliminated any reference to adding shifts in the future. Still seeking to reduce the presence of the earlier Betriebsrat, it agreed to the composition of the new worker representation on the condition that it could choose among alternate and substitute members of the factory council to fill the four seats alloted to members of the previous Betriebsrat. It also forbade that any of the union's representatives be drawn from the Betriebsrat. Finally, it de-manded the reopening of negotiations on wages. In the end, all of its points were incorporated by the Arbitration Council.

Both sides approved the final agreement on September 13. An identical one between the clerks and the firm was closed the following day. Within days, the commissions of workers and clerks began operation. The firm set the size of the work force and laid out the guidelines for the rehiring of employees. These guidelines, designed to "oust" the "terrorists and sabo-teurs" (i.e., the militant workers), stated, (1) those who were not dependent on work in the factory should not be rehired; (2) those who lived outside the area from Plochingen in the east to Waiblingen in the north to Feuerbach in the west (i.e., the Stuttgart metropolitan area) should not be rehired unless they were crippled war veterans or irreplaceable "special workers"; (3) the unmarried workers, unless they had "special obligations," would also be low on the scale of desired workers; (4) the level of skill would be taken into consideration; and, (5) seniority should be weighed in favor of the workers, especially for those who had already served at Daimler before the war. All were ranked according to these social criteria on a scale of one (optimal) to six (undesirable). "Those with the largest numbers were destined not to be recalled."[106] As the firm explained it to one of the workers who was fired, "We had to limit the area of our work force (which encompassed almost all of Wuerttemberg before the shutdown) to the area Plochingen-Waiblingen-Zuffenhausen-Fellbach-Leonberg. The workers who came from further out could not be taken back. Nor could those who had support from an agricultural enterprise or who were unmarried."[107]

The commissions exercised a sharply circumscribed prerogative, and finally decided to withdraw from the process. "We leave it to the firm's prerogative to lead this action . . . to its conclusion." Despite the withdrawal of the workers' commissions from the process, the firm pronounced its behavior in the choice of its new work force to have been in accord with the September 13 agreement and with section 74 of the Factory Council Law. On Friday, September 24, the factory resumed operations with 3,270 workers and 585 clerks, compared with the 7,776 and 1,048 respectively on the eve of the shutdown. About 57.5 percent of the workers had lost their jobs, along with 44 percent of the clerks.[108]

Daimler's streamlining of its work force—its attempt to re-create its solid, reliable core, its *Stammarbeiterschaft*—took an inordinate toll on workers under 25 (see table 6.2). More than 91 percent of them were slashed from the firm's payroll; barely 115 remained at the Untertuerkheim works. Almost half of the workers older than 25 were made redundant. Nevertheless, the 3,000 older workers who were recalled constituted a remarkable 96 percent of Daimler's new and improved industrial army.

The mix of skilled and unskilled employees in the New Model work force was to an even greater degree than before weighted toward the skilled sector (see table 6.3). The percentage of the skilled in the Daimler ranks grew by more than seven percent in the aftermath of the lockout, to 58.6 percent. The proportions of machine workers and unskilled day laborers both declined, to 29 percent and 12.2 percent respectively. In addition, the handful of women who had survived the mass dismissal of female laborers in November 1918 was completely eliminated; all 59 of them were fired.

The piece-wage system was even more firmly entrenched in the wake of the summer's confrontation in Untertuerkheim (see table 6.4). More than half of all the workers in the departments (50.8%) worked for piece-rates in September 1920; among skilled workers the proportion surpassed 60 percent. There was a small decline in the piece-rate among the machine workers, yet more than half of them remained *Akkordarbeiter*.

Most wages in the reopened plant showed gains over the period before the lockout, yet these were uneven and not universal (see table 6.5). Skilled workers and machine workers—whether on hourly or piece-rates—received the largest hikes of between four and six percent over what they made seven months earlier. On the other hand, the wage-rates for the unskilled day laborers stagnated or even declined. For example, the rates paid to the older day laborers increased by less than one percent, while those of the coterie of 44 young laborers under 18 years of age fell by nine percent.

Thus, in the new age at Daimler, the emphasis was clearly on age and

TABLE 6.2
Daimler Workers Older & Younger than Age 25, 1920

	Over Age 25	Under Age 25
Before Lockout		
Skilled Workers	3,092	570
Piece-rate	1,739	339
Hourly Wage	1,353	231
Machine Workers	1,935	384
Piece-rate	1,101	231
Hourly Wage	834	153
Unskilled Workers	839	343
Women Workers	48	11
TOTAL	5,914	1,308
%	81.9	18.1
After Lockout		
Skilled workers	1,810	35
Piece-rate	1,095	17
Hourly Wage	715	18
Machine Workers	892	23
Piece-rate	475	12
Hourly Wage	417	11
Unskilled Workers	328	57
Women Workers	0	0
TOTAL	3,030	115
%	96.3	3.7

skill. The firm's rationale was a complex conjuncture of the economic and the political. Hard times and a growing debt demanded, at least according to the owners, a contraction of the workforce along with the retention of those older, reliable skilled workers who were seen to be indispensable to the production process at DMG and to the firm's future. At the same time, managers viewed the reestablishment of their control over all aspects of the firm's industrial life to be absolutely essential. This goal demanded the destruction of worker power on the shop floor and the expulsion of those elements deemed most disruptive. Daimler even justified its sacking of 142

TABLE 6.3
Daimler Workers According to Main Categories, 1920

	Before Lockout April 1920	After Lockout September 1920
Skilled Workers	3,662 (50.7%)	1,845 (58.7%)
Piece-rates	2,078	1,112
Hourly Wage	1,584	733
Machine Workers	2,319 (32.1%)	915 (29.1%)
Piece-rates	1,332	487
Hourly Wage	987	428
Unskilled Workers	1,182 (16.4%)	385 (12.2%)
Women Workers	59 (0.8%)	0 (0.0%)
TOTAL	7,222	3,145

TABLE 6.4
Method of Payment at DMG, 1920

	Before Lockout (%)	After Lockout (%)
Skilled Workers		
Piece-rates	56.7	60.3
Hourly Wage	43.3	39.7
Machine Workers		
Piece-rates	57.4	53.2
Hourly Wage	42.6	46.8
Unskilled Workers		
Hourly Wage	100.0	100.0
Women Workers		
Hourly Wage	100.0	0.0

disabled war veterans as part of its mopping-up operation. "Those injured in the war participated in the front ranks of the outrages," it claimed. "If the employees had not indulged in sabotage and terror, if they had not insensibly refused the tax . . . then the closing and occupation [of the plant] would not have been necessary." Daimler attacked the disabled veterans for having also made unspecified "frivolous and unacceptable demands" which delayed the return to work.[109]

Both economic and political rationales had served to return an older, more skilled, less "disabled," more "reliable" rank and file in September 1920. Daimler had "cleared the factory of Communists," and independent socialists.[110]

In the first weeks after the factory resumed operation, the corporation held elections for a new factory council. The SPD-oriented slate of the Free Trade Unions won 2,037 votes and 12 seats, while Christians and liberals each received a seat for their 325 and 177 votes, respectively. More than 700 reinstated workers abstained, for no USPD or KPD slate had contested the election. The regional factory inspectors asserted at the time that "the re-shaping of the relations inside the factory has been expressed in the new elections," a questionable assessment given the absence of the radical left from the process.[111]

The quick collapse of the radical workers' movement at Daimler seems perplexing at first. Most of what had been won since the war and the revolution in the tumult on the shop floor as far as a greatly increased say in the operation of the plant is concerned was eliminated by one quick, solid blow. Two factors are critical, however, in understanding the radicals' summer defeat. For one, the employer offensive embraced all of the large workplaces in the greater Stuttgart metal industry. Daimler, Bosch, and the Maschinenfabrik Esslingen acted in unison in late August and remained

TABLE 6.5
Wages at Daimler, 1920 (Pfennigs per hour)

	Before Lockout		After Lockout	
	Piece	Hourly	Piece	Hourly
Skilled Workers	347.2	326.1	361.4	344.4
Machine Workers	309.7	271.2	327.3	285.9
Unskilled Workers	0.0	234.4	0.0	236.5
Women Workers	0.0	149.0	0.0	0.0
Supplemental Payment as percent of rate	60.0	60.0	66.0	66.0

obstinately united during the critical days before the trade unions began their damage control effort on September 1. Perhaps most important to the quick defeat of the workers, however, was the intervention of the government in Wuerttemberg. For the first time, the radical movement of the factories directly confronted the power of the state at the plant gates. In the fray, the local institutions of the factory rank and file were ultimately no match for the steadfastness and armed force of the government. Two years earlier, in June 1918, Daimler workers had pulled back in the face of the looming confrontation with the army authorities. Now, by pressing the campaign against the new tax and then forcibly resisting its imposition, the radical movement crossed the threshhold—almost unknowingly, it seems—from its industrial disputes with owners to a direct challenge of the authority of state institutions. The authorities pounced and prevailed, especially at DMG, opening the way for the corporate foragers to quickly mop up.

The impact of the dismissals on those workers who were let go is difficult to assess adequately. In Eugen May's memoir of his life as a worker in southwestern Germany, he records his experiences toiling in a quarry near Stuttgart in late 1920. "Almost all of my colleagues at the quarry, who without exception were unemployed metalworkers from Daimler, suffered more or less under a psychological depression, and were upset with their fate, which had seen them thrown out of their vocation." May noted that these workers responded with "bitter voices" to his own good humor and "optimism."[112]

The lockout and project to sanitize the work force politically in the late summer of 1920 marks the end of the revolutionary period as far as the 9,000 employees of the Daimler-Motoren-Gesellschaft are concerned. As Daimler reported on November 16, 1920, the lock-out had benefitted the firm: Work now proceeded "with more law and order and with more seriousness."[113] Despite the apparatus of labor relations in the Weimar Republic, the new order which prevailed after September 1920 was an attempt to expand Daimler's corporate prerogative. True, the Betriebsrat continued to exist and, after 1922, sent two representatives to the board of trustees, but it is hard to portray the new period as marking a radical difference from the situation in which the workers' committee had operated before the war. The new factory work rules, which were promulgated shortly after the reopening of the works in September 1920 and which had to be accepted in writing by all employees as a condition of employment at the plant,[114] were virtually a reiteration of the earlier rules from 1909. They delineated clearly the prerogatives of the direction regarding hiring and firing, discipline, and the setting of piece rates in the manner of the *status quo ante bellum*—but with one exception: the workers had now lost the right to use the factory elevators.[115]

The police occupation and the lockout over the tax question precipitated the crushing defeat of the radical workers' movement in the greater Stuttgart area. The German Metalworkers' Union (DMV) later reported that the employers utilized the agreement ending the lockout to exclude every "unloved" worker, including many worker representatives. Its year-end report lamented: "It had been a very bitter lesson which the Wuerttemberg working class could have been spared if they had not let themselves be driven by senseless and irresponsible elements because of the tax issue."[116] The highpoint of workers' power in the factories had passed; the unions and councils were forced to fight doggedly to retain the gains made as far as working hours and wage rates were concerned. The radical wing of the workers' movement, although electorally strong in Stuttgart through the end of the Weimar Republic, ceased to be able to inspire militant struggle on the shop floor, and instead ossified into another contender in the sectarian world of the German left.

■

By early 1922, the employers in the southwestern metal and machine-building industries moved over to the offensive. Indeed, the decline of the workers' movement at Daimler in the early 1920s corresponded to the waning of the power of the Metalworkers' Union. The great strike of south German metalworkers in the spring of 1922 again showed that Daimler's bosses, this time in league with the industrialists of Baden, Wuerttemberg, and Bavaria, could remain firm in the face of its workforce, and defeat the union in Untertuerkheim and Sindelfingen.

The issue was the length of the work week, which had been set at 46 hours by the historic Heidelberg agreement in April 1919. The employers were generally unhappy with this concession to the workers, and soon moved to rescind it.[117] Complaining that the work week was too short and was crippling the hyperinflating German economy, the organization of metal industrialists announced it would revoke the provision in the contract mandating the 46 hour week. At the same time, the industrialists offered more vacation days and the improved regulation of piece-rates as concessions to the workers. The employers wanted to win an extra two hours of labor per week and maintained they were merely acting to enforce the eight hour work day. Heavy industry backed them, and one of its leading representatives, Paul Reusch of the Gutehoffnungshuette, urged them on.[118]

The Metalworkers' Union rejected the employers' plans. To back its decision, it submitted the matter to the rank and file in a referendum on February 13. In a result which hardly could have been surprising, 94,322 of 104,318 participating workers rejected the lengthening of the work week.[119]

The Wuerttemberg metal industrialists appealed to the Arbitration Committee in Stuttgart, which approved the lengthening of the work week and offered the workers a smaller than expected supplementary cost of living payment. The DMV protested, and 80 percent of the workforce likewise rejected the new guidelines. An effort by the SPD Labor Ministry in Wuerttemberg to mediate was rejected by the employers, who instead insisted that the terms of the settlement proposed by the Arbitration Committee in Stuttgart be made binding.[120]

On March 9, the DMV functionaries in south Germany moved to shore up resistance and to set a strike deadline in the factories it represented. In Wuerttemberg, 40,000 workers walked off the job on March 16 and 17. The small Christian and liberal unions supported the strike.[121]

The strike did not begin at Daimler in Untertuerkheim until March 22. The firm's direction publicly claimed that a majority of its workers had actually voted in favor of accepting the Arbitration Committee's proposed settlement, and thus it announced on Tuesday, March 21, that the new daily work hours for the 48 hour week would go into effect the next day.

As Wednesday dawned on the Neckar, large contingents of pickets gathered at Daimler, blocking entrances to the plant grounds. The firm claimed that many of the pickets did not work at the factory. The throngs of union pickets directed the workers to a mass meeting on the Canstatter Wasen, where union officials addressed the Daimler workers. According to a report prepared by the firm, only 300 of its workers actually reported for work in their workshops on Wednesday.

By early April, 64,000 were on strike or had been locked out in the southwest, with another 48,000 in Bavaria. Despite mediation efforts by Reich Minister of Labor Brauns and Stuttgart's Mayor Lautenschlager, the strike dragged on.[122] The industrialists' appeals to the workers and to public opinion, carried in the local press, blasted the demagoguery and the limited understanding of economics of the union officials.

For its part, the DMV saw the industrialists' insistence on lengthening the work day as the first move in a drive to rescind the eight hour day. Although the industrialists' demands did not seem to exceed the eight hour day from Monday through Saturday, the union's conception of the work week had usually included a work-free Saturday afternoon. In the union's view, the employers were attacking the reforms which had been won after the end of the war. Since nearly all of the business community considered the eight hour day itself to be a grave impediment to economic recovery, the DMV felt it urgent to prevent the employers' counteroffensive from gathering momentum.

May Day, a Monday that year, infused the strike movement with new life and enthusiasm. Stuttgart's streetcar drivers stayed away from work in sympathy, as columns of workers and family members converged on the central market. Social Democrats, independent socialists, and Communists addressed the gathering, which had a festive air. The strikers made plans for a hike and picnic on Tuesday, May 9, to be accompanied by proletarian music groups.

On May 2, strikers staged large demonstrations at Bosch and in front of the offices of the employers' association in Stuttgart. At the same time, Daimler launched an offensive to break the strike, reported later by the police to have become more turbulent. On Wednesday, May 3, the corporation sent each of its workers a form, asking them to express their opinion whether their strike should continue or end. At the same time, Daimler offered an hourly bonus to anyone who would return to the job. On Thursday, the company reported that 1,200 workers had agreed to return to work. At the same time, it alleged in a newspaper advertisement that the union had launched a "terrorist campaign" against the Daimler workers, by demanding that each turn in the Daimler form in order to receive further strike payments. Since Daimler claimed it wanted only "to make possible the free expression of opinions," it counseled its employees merely to submit a note which pledged to meet all of Daimler's conditions about wages and hours.[123] Later, it claimed that 1,600 workers and clerks had expressed their willingness to go back to work.[124]

Early Monday morning, May 8, police, pickets, and an unknown number of workers wanting to go back to work descended on Untertuerkheim. Roaming strikers blocked entrances and clashed with police trying to reopen access to the plant. A factory official was allegedly beaten, and a number of others injured when the crowd backed them into the factory fence. On the streets around Daimler, bands of strikers slashed the tires of the cars of employees reporting for work. Others trying to enter the complex were manhandled, and several policemen may have been injured. The strikers escorted 200 war invalids into the plant in a column. During the confrontation, the police took a number of strikers into custody. One bourgeois paper termed the actions of the Daimler workers "a full-scale maneuver for the formation of a red army in Wuerttemberg."[125]

The Daimler management responded quickly to the escalating clashes at its gates. It announced that it was closing the factory for six weeks because of the "open violence of the communist masses."[126]

In the following week, four factories in Bad Canstatt—Norma, the Fortuna works, Werner & Pfleiderer, and Hesser—announced they were closing their factories for six weeks in solidarity with Daimler's action. Local DVP officials simultaneously demanded strong state action against the Metalworkers' Union. Meanwhile, both the Stuttgart daily, which supported the industrialists, and the DMV's newspaper warned that the strike was benefitting the Communists, who were using it to radicalize the workers.[127]

With industry idled more than two months, and the militants in the two camps—the Daimler-Motoren-Gesellschaft and the Communists—increasingly setting the pace of the dispute, many trade unionists and industrialists felt that the efforts to negotiate a settlement should be revived. Representatives of capital and labor began a new round of talks before the Arbitration Committee on Monday, May 22.[128]

By Wednesday, an agreement between the parties was reached. Quite simply, the employers won. The 48-hour week became a reality, albeit with a face-saving device. According to the agreement, the 48th hour of the work week would accrue an overtime bonus until it could be transcribed into the factories' work rules. At that time, the overtime bonus would fall away.[129]

Weary of the long strike, the metalworkers voted overwhelmingly to accept the proposed resolution of the conflict. Nevertheless, more than a quarter of the strikers wanted to continue the walkout. In addition, 20,000 workers—more than the number who had voted to accept the settlement—abstained. The Communists in the labor movement quickly branded the settlement a clear defeat for the union. When Daimler and a handful of smaller firms began to dismiss those believed to be troublemakers in the aftermath of the battle, strife persisted in the factories. According to the union, Daimler was the "most reckless" with its vengeance dismissals.[130] Additional talks were required to settle the matter at DMG. Yet, the negotiations could not save 17 of the strikers at Daimler in Untertuerkheim. In Sindelfingen, despite continuation of the strike until mid-June, Daimler dismissed 70 workers. Meanwhile, three workers at Bosch and three at the Maschinenfabrik Esslingen left "voluntarily," under the pressure of their bosses.[131]

Within weeks of the bitter end of the dispute, trouble flared once again. The assassination of Walter Rathenau in June 1922 sent a wave of revulsion through many Germans, including Daimler workers, and was the occasion for more protest. When trade unionists and spokespersons of the KPD, USPD, and SPD called for a general strike and public assemblies on June 28 against the "reaction," thousands of Daimler workers joined in.[132] A second round on July 4, which saw 58 percent of the work force walk off the job, led to clashes between workers and police at the prison on the *Urbansstrasse* in Stuttgart. Hundreds of demonstrators tried to break into the prison, where the pickets arrested at Daimler on May 8 and elsewhere were apparently still being held. In the fighting, one gendarme was seriously injured.[133]

In all, the government prosecuted 64 of the workers and their supporters, including an unknown number from DMG. A court sentenced 58 of them to prison sentences in 1923.[134]

During the strike, the Stuttgart police had noted the pervasive disappointment and bitterness among the workers in the metal and machine-building industries at being forced to surrender one of the biggest industrial achievements from the revolution. In its wake, the area factory councils rebuked the local union leadership: two-thirds voted "no confidence."[135] Communist influence in the local metal workers union increased in the following months, but brought no new strategies for resisting the employers' ineluctable pressure to eliminate the industrial results of the "demagoguery" of 1918–1919.

The escalating economic and political crises of 1923 and subsequent reorganization left labor at Daimler with less influence then it had enjoyed since the beginning of World War I. Although the task is complicated by the almost complete lack of documentation from the months of hyperinflation in 1923, there are several points which can be made. For one, the year was one of growing distress, with indexed wages keeping a step behind the spectacular depreciation of the currency, although by one account wages lost less of their value as the year progressed. In the metalworking and machine-building industries in Wuerttemberg, frequent negotiations set wage-rates weekly, on the basis of the exchange rate of the U.S. dollar during the previous three days, especially after the collective bargaining agreement expired in April. Daimler issued its own notes which a number of shops in Untertuerkheim may have honored to cover food prices.[136] Then, the weeks at the end of 1923 and the beginning of 1924 were a time of painful dislocation, as wages and prices were adjusted to the new Reichsmark.[137]

Hyperinflation spawned a political crisis in Wuerttemberg, as in the rest of Germany. In 1923, Communist support grew quickly, so that in early 1924 the KPD polled majorities for the first time in most Stuttgart factories.[138] Although the state government declared a state of emergency in the autumn of 1923, the local press contained few reports of disturbances, and these were usually related to the appearance of armed Nazi bands. In Untertuerkheim, a mass meeting of Daimler workers on October 26, 1923, demanded strong government action against hoarders to secure the food supply and against National Socialist bands, along with the suspension of the state of emergency and the release of workers who had been picked up in preemptive raids.[139] But this was not much more than a ritual; probably no one except the security forces was listening.

STABILIZATION AND RATIONALIZATION

In the wake of the crisis of 1923, Daimler's directors flung another challenge at the Social Democratic and Communist representatives of the work force. A nationalist group, calling itself the "workers of the fatherland" [*vaterlaendische Arbeiter*], began a campaign to conquer the factory council in early 1924. Their cadres attacked the "functionaries" of the "international" unions for repeatedly "betraying" the workers since the world war. The DMV dismissed the nationalist as a new "yellow" group who were supported and financed by Daimler's "swastika directors." The election resulted in a rout of the nationalists, who received 165 of 3,360 votes, and no representation in the Betriebsrat. The DMV's slate of Social Democratic and Communist trade unionists won 15 of 17 seats, with the liberals and Christians each capturing one place in the council. Despite the nationalists' dismal showing, DMG—dubbed the "German-nationalist swastika company [deutschnationale Hackenkreuzgesellschaft]" by the Metalworkers' Union—had apparently been willing to assist a group which wanted to replace the traditional free, liberal, and christian unions in the factory council.[140]

Daimler's more radical stance did not end with the tough line it took against its "undisciplined" work force between 1920 and 1924. According to a report by the public prosecutor in Munich, DMG joined a select group of German companies: it donated money to the National Socialist German Workers' Party in the early 1920s.[141] What the corporation hoped to gain from its support for the National Socialists at a time when they had not yet established themselves on the national political scene is wholly unclear, but the significance of its donation would become more apparent a decade later.

The company's more hostile attitude toward the DMV carried over into its wage policy. Workers' wages at Daimler sank well below the levels at other factories in the metalworking and machine-building industries in Stuttgart by the spring of 1925 (see table 6.6).

TABLE 6.6
Average Hourly Wages at Major Factories in Stuttgart, 1925 (Pfennigs per hour)

(P = piece-rate workers; H = hourly-rate workers)

	Skilled		Trained		Unskilled		Women	
	P	H	P	H	P	H	P	H
Daimler	94.5	90.5	81	75	71	62	52	46
Bosch	106.5	95	92	72	74	68	64	52
Eisemann	105	93	90	71.1	–	63	55	49
Fein	105	102	86.6	–	–	64	58	50
Fortuna	98	93	84.5	72	–	64	58	48
Terrot	98	90	83	75	–	–	–	–
Werner & Pfleiderer	98	95	85	77	71	64	–	–

Source: AGM DBAG DMG 37 Durchschnittsverdienste am 20.5.1925

Daimler's tougher attitude toward its work force was not the only obvious feature of the post-inflation era. The currency stabilization set the stage for a host of epoch-making changes in Untertuerkheim. Since 1920, the Deutsche Bank had moved heavily into the board of trustees and pressed for the merger of the beleaguered German automobile manufacturers plagued by massive overcapacity into a streamlined, rationalized I.G. Auto. As the historian of the Deutsche Bank recorded, "the German auto industry needed a fundamental rehabilitation" in the face of mounting losses. "[Deutsche Bank director Emil Georg von] Stauss and other bankers had it in their minds to create a German auto trust."[142]

Only Daimler and Benz were immediately open to the bank's overtures. At the behest of the bankers Jahr and Stauss, the "community of interest Daimler-Benz" came into being on May 1, 1924. Yet the plight of the Daimler company worsened dramatically during late 1925. The company's deathbed struggle had seemingly begun. Massive layoffs rocked Untertuerkheim, and half of the work force was dismissed.[143] In the context of one of the worst crises to shake Daimler, the company's official who tended its ties with the Reichswehr, director Friedrich Muff, literally begged Kurt von Schleicher and the army for a spectacular bailout to save his corporation. Muff wrote at the behest of the board of trustees, which by now was filled with officials of the Deutsche Bank, and "as a former member of the general staff." "The question, whether our company can hold its head over water for a few more weeks if no miracle occurs, probably must be answered with a 'no.'" Muff reminded Schleicher of Daimler's spectacular service as a leading military producer during the war, and asserted that the continued existence of Mercedes was critical in light of the "national defense and the (in the near or far future) national tasks." Assistance to Daimler was in the national interest, at least according to Daimler.

"We do no want the money we need without giving something in return. I can imagine the preservation of our factories—by which I mean not only the buildings and machine parks but also the core of technicians and workers—through the purchase of products—automobiles and trucks, certainly on a large scale," Muff wrote. Thus, the bailout could take the form of advance payment for military orders. At the same time, DMG's representative pleaded for large contracts for airplane motors so that the company could resume production of these items, still coveted by the military brass.[144]

The army's answer is not available, but military contracts would be forthcoming within two years.[145] The Deutsche Bank and the failing company in Stuttgart proceeded with their own merger plans in the following months. Daimler and Benz, whose governing boards were intertwined from 1924 to 1926, sealed their merger in the summer of 1926 after overcoming a host of technical problems. They settled on a team headed by Benz's

Wilhelm Kissel, a clever, tough-minded engineer and businessman from the Rheinpfalz who had been at the company since 1904 and among the inner circle there since 1914.[146]

The new Daimler-Benz commanded a stock-capital of 36 million RM, which was soon raised to 50.36 million, making it the second largest motor vehicle company in Germany (second only to family-owned Opel). In the first two years of its existence, it required heavily financial infusions in the form of massive loans from the Deutsche Bank. By September 1926, the company's bank debts reached 35 million RM.[147]

The new Daimler-Benz Aktien-Gesellschaft possessed a large, mainly idle, productive apparatus. Daimler's large factory in Untertuerkheim—the headquarters for the new company—along with the auto body factory in Sindelfingen and the smaller facility in Berlin-Marienfelde were now joined by the two Benz works at Mannheim and Gaggenau. Heavily indebted, with only a small fraction of its capacity in use, Daimler-Benz faced a long, tough battle to make its operations profitable in a nation in which mass motorization had, up to that point, hardly taken root. The first step was the reorganization and rationalization of the company's facilities, a process begun hurriedly during the last year before the 1926 merger and taken amidst the "great wave of the rationalization movement" in the auto industry between 1925 and 1928.[148]

In the first two years of the new company's existence, Daimler-Benz instituted an industrial rationalization program which was in large part accomplished by late 1927.[149] In Untertuerkheim this meant the extension of the organizational scheme introduced by Lang in 1919, *Gruppenfabrikation*. The point of this new organization was to limit the time lost by moving the materials and parts from workplace to workplace. Assembly line production it assuredly was not, for the factory produced only 20 of its cheapest, 8/ 38 six-cylinder models and two of its huge compressor models per day. Daimler-Benz and its fans claimed that the company's "pursuit of quality work" meant that the countless parts in its vehicles had to be repeatedly checked and inspected during the production process, and this ruled out mass assembly lines. Nevertheless, since the merger the new company had procured many special machines, some of American make, which simplified and accelerated many of the labor processes and allowed the firm to employ cheaper, unskilled labor.

Daimler-Benz's rationalization program went furthest at the auto body plant in Sindelfingen, where it had gotten underway in earnest in 1925 even before the official merger during a long dispute with the work force. At the beginning of December 1924, workers at the plant struck in a pay dispute. On December 4, Daimler locked out its employees, and kept its facilities closed to them until March 1925. The masters and apprentices remained on the job, while the firm subcontracted orders for the production of auto bodies to other companies, for example, the Glaeser firm in Leipzig. At the same time, Daimler constructed the first moving assembly line in building number two. It was not until the next year, following the merger with Benz, that production fully got underway with the new assembly line.[150]

Thus, in the wake of the lockout and the difficult merger process of 1925–1926, the company extensively reorganized a large part of the production processes in Sindelfingen according to the new work organization which had been introduced into the American automobile industry during the previous two decades. The precondition was probably the company's decision to build only a limited number of standard auto bodies. As the centerpiece of the facility, it installed an assembly line. The belt moved only 3 1/2 meters an hour but permitted the fashioning and assembling of an auto body for the 8/38 horsepower model in ten hours.[151]

How did the introduction of the assembly line affect the work of employees at Sindelfingen? It should be remembered that the facility employed mostly skilled non-metalworkers—woodworkers, painters, upholsterers, and glassworkers—but also skilled fitters and mechanics. The transition at Sindelfingen changed the composition of the workforce. While formerly all lacquerers were skilled workers, only a third were skilled in the new workplace, where mostly nonskilled, cheaper workers used compressed air guns to quickly apply paints and lacquers to the wooden and metal car bodies. In the machine shops for woodworking and in the final body assembly departments, the composition of the workforce was evenly divided between skilled, trained, and unskilled workers.[152]

Everywhere in the facility, the Daimler-Benz managers strengthened the hold of the piece-rate system. Among the workforce it was the exceptional worker who was paid by the hour. Thus, almost every worker received a wage reckoned according to what he produced or performed. Incentives were built into the system. In a report which was sharply criticized by at least a section of the labor movement, the national factory inspectors noted that average wages in the plant increased by about 15 percent in the aftermath of the changeover. It should be noted, however, that there were initially more overtime hours in the newly organized plant. Among those who did not work on the assembly line itself but on the woodworking machines or in the upholstery shop, for example, the factory inspectors registered a wage increase by only about 30 percent of the employees. On the other hand, the workers on the body assembly line saw their wages increase by only about 5 percent.[153]

The reorganization of the Sindelfingen factory and of most of the jobs in it led to a small exodus from the plant. About 3.7 percent of the total work force quit their jobs or were laid off each month. Many of these could not adequately perform their new jobs or simply could not adjust, and had to be let go. Significantly, the factory hired fewer workers in the year after the plant reorganization—only 3.3 percent per month. By the second half of 1928, Daimler-Benz had sacked 200 workers. Taken together, the universal institution of piece-rates, a wage inherently tied to performance, and the small, steady decline in the work force marked a halting step in the direction of what has come to be termed Fordism. According to Gramsci's analysis, which was suggested by the development of the Ford automobile factories in the U.S., Fordism is "an ultra-modern form of production and of working methods, . . . [which] derive[s] from the necessity to achieve the organization of a planned economy." "Force"—the destruction of effective trade union power—and "persuasion"—higher wages, social benefits, and propaganda —are usually required to bring about this modernization. Here, "hegemony," that is, the ability of the dominant social class to organize society, is "born in the factory and requires for its exercise only a minute quantity of professional political and ideological intermediaries."[154] With trade unions living on at Mercedes until 1933, and with wages near or below the average for industry in the area, nothing approximating this kind of industrial regime would come to Daimler-Benz until perhaps the National Socialist military buildup of the mid- and late 1930s. During the late 1920s, Daimler-Benz was able to meet its production requirements by employing fewer workers, most of whom were working more over the pay period, including overtime as reflected in their increased wages. Over the same timespan, the average length of the workweek was scaled back by 11 percent, from 54 to 52, then to 48 hours. By all accounts, the work on Daimler-Benz's auto bodies proceeded at a faster pace.

The work force may have benefitted monetarily from the more intense pace, but the accident rate mounted after the reorganization. In the year after the changeover one of every ten workers suffered an industrial accident, and 5.1 percent of these were classified as "serious" accidents. Although the details are not available, the accident rate on the assembly line was probably quite high, because at the same time that of the most dangerous department for workers, the woodworking machine shop, declined sharply by about 23 percent. The Communists complained that many more workers became ill because of the "hectic work" which now ruled the daily regimen. Despite these setbacks, labor—even its radical wing—in the auto industry contended that working people would ultimately benefit from the rationalization of the industry. At a meeting of workers' representatives in 1930, conferees believed that industrial change promised higher wages and the increased consumption of new types of goods. "The revolutionary automobile will serve the cause of the revolutionary workers."[155]

Whatever the future promise, workers' grievances in the post-rationalization period concentrated on the repeated "arbitrary" cuts in the piece-rates and on unfair treatment by departmental masters. As a result of new piece-rates, the average hourly earnings of a group of employees had been slashed from RM 1.35 to RM .80. For the plant's workers, this was "unbearable." The masters were allegedly guilty of arbitrarily dismissing workers and of rudely treating their charges. Although the labor court reversed the firm's dismissal of a protesting young worker as having been without reason, such action could not stem the tide at Sindelfingen, which was pressing hard against the unions.[156]

The rationalization of the Daimler-Benz factory in Sindelfingen in 1925–1927, an immediate result of the merger and the crisis which forced it, left its mark on the workforce. In its wake, workers worked longer, harder, and earned a bit more money. The company was the beneficiary of more work from fewer hands. Many more were lower-paid trained workers, and the role of skilled workers in the production of Mercedes auto bodies was effectively reduced. Chief engineer Lang was able to report to the board of directors in 1928 that the firm had successfully cut its costs. The reason was the redesign of components and the "effective utilization of new machines," which permitted the employment of "unskilled workers with lower wage rates . . . in place of skilled workers . . . for a whole line of jobs."[157]

The rationalization movement in Untertuerkheim and Sindelfingen—it is less well-documented at other Daimler-Benz factories—quickly, if only briefly, turned the firm's financial situation around. At the shareholders' meeting of the Deutsche Bank in 1927, the bank official Wasserman reported that Daimler-Benz's bank debts had been reduced by three-fourths since the merger only a year before, although the available data do not bear this out.

TABLE 6.7
Daimler-Benz's Economic Performance, 1926–1928 (in thousands of marks)

	Share-capital	Long-term Debts	Short-term Debts	Machines, Tools	Profits—Reingewinne
1926	36,360	2,810	40,345	8,686	121
1927	50,360	21,161	26,567	12,082	384
1928	50,360	21,273	38,512	16,157	13

Source: Richard Adelt, Die Krise in der deutschen Personenautomobil-Industrie (Dissertation, Muenchen, 1931), pp. 5–6.

(see table 6.7). The Deutsche Bank had succeeded in preserving "an economically irreplaceable corporation."[158] After two years of hard work since the merger process had begun in earnest, the Daimler-Benz complex "has arrived again in navigable waters." Despite heavy new debts assumed by financing the purchases of machinery for the rationalization, a new, tentative confidence made the rounds at the headquarters in Stuttgart.[159]

7

CRISIS AND NEW ORDER, 1929–1945: NATIONAL SOCIALISM AND A MODEL COMPANY

A DECADE after the end of World War I and the revolution, capital and labor at Daimler had reached an important juncture in their joint history. The merger with Benz, the rationalization measures subsequently effected in the network of factories, and the infusion of loans from the Deutsche Bank had put the business on a surer footing by 1928 than it had enjoyed since the end of World War I. The protracted struggle with labor had left the workers and their organizations contained and on the defensive. Trade union membership in the important Untertuerkheim factory had declined. Even if the DMV still spoke for the largest group of Daimler-Benz workers, the labor movement was ever more hobbled by the cleft between Social Democrats and Communists, which grew more acerbic in the wake of the Comintern's shift in 1928 to an uncompromising policy against "social fascists," especially in the ranks of labor. But both for management and for workers of all political persuasions, a debilitating economic shock was only just around the corner.

Although Daimler-Benz made better use of its productive capacity than any other major German auto company in the last pre-depression year, 30 percent of its capacity lay idle. Its brief shift to profitability was tenuous. Car prices were low, and Daimler-Benz offered a range of full-sized and luxury models, but the company had reached the limits of its markets. Auto taxes were high, and exports had begun to fall. Within months, the waves of the depression began to crash onto the company. Its business collapsed during the next four years. The crisis wiped out the progress which had been made in the wake of the merger. In June 1931, the chairman of the board of trustees, Stauss, lamented that the company's rationalization measures would have produced a profit in 1930 if business had not declined so precipitously.[1] The bitter reality, however, was a loss of 15.5 million marks. The orthodox conservatism of the Center Party Chancellor Heinrich Bruening, put into effect through presidential edicts under Article 48 of the Weimar Constitution, did not relieve the growing economic distress, as the depression turned into a cataclysm for Germany.

At this juncture Daimler-Benz chose to introduce its first genuinely mid-sized car. In 1931, the company brought a new, smaller model, the 170, into production. The swing-axled vehicle, described by an auto chronicler as "the most important new appearance of the model year 1932," came onto the market at the depression's nadir. Despite its 4,400 mark selling price, the 170 could not dent the stark crisis afflicting the corporation and the industry. In the first nine months of 1932, Daimler-Benz sold a dismal 32,343 cars, compared with 48,949 during the same months of 1931.[2]

Given the company's track record as an armaments concern, it should not be surprising that Daimler-Benz again looked to the German military for assistance as the crisis deepened. By 1931, Daimler-Benz was at work on the construction of two test-model tanks.[3] At about the same time, Mercedes sold large numbers of trucks to the Soviet Union in a bid to shore up slumping sales. In the summer of 1931, Kissel announced to officials gathered at the Deutsche Bank in Berlin that the company had lined up sales of equipment to the Soviets worth 4.8 million marks.[4] Thus, what few new business opportunities the company had as the new decade dawned came from the industrializing Soviet Union, which was hectically proceeding with Stalin's Five Year Plan.

Despite everything, sales fell to 43 percent of the 1928 level by 1932. Complaining bitterly of the "economic and political depression," the company laid off almost half of the work force.[5] In mid-1930, for example, the company laid off 325 workers in Untertuerkheim, with 325 more scheduled to be sacked shortly thereafter. Each received 30 marks severance pay, much less than a week's average wages.

With each successive quarter, the situation worsened. By the autumn of 1932, Daimler-Benz's work force had dwindled to 5,700, not much more than a third of the pre-depression total. The whole mechanical department at Mannheim, for example, was idled, and the machine park integrated into the Untertuerkheim facility. A plant closing of this order was a devastating blow for Mercedes, one which could be repaired only by an inconceivable boom.

Massive wage cuts in the form of lower piece-rates were frequent. As the Communist newspaper at Daimler-Benz in the early 1930s, *Der rote Mercedes,* complained, the workers in 1930 "simply received their piece-rate cards, [and] on them, 10, 15, even 20 percent of the piece-rate which had been paid until then were missing."[6] The slide in workers' earnings accelerated in 1931 and 1932. In January 1931, Daimler-Benz cut wages for piece-workers in Untertuerkheim by 5 percent, and for hourly workers by 5 percent. November saw an additional across-the-board cut of 5 pfennigs per hour. To begin 1932, the company enacted yet another 5 pfennig per hour wage cut.[7] Workers' earnings suffered similarly at other Daimler-Benz factories.

It is not possible to construct a full portrait of workers' politics at Daimler-Benz between 1930 and 1933. What is known is that the factory councils were sharply divided between representatives of the free trade union DMV and the Communist RGO, and that a certain degree of apathy existed among the work force. In 1930, at least, the DMV faction presided over the majority in Stuttgart, but was hampered by internal dissension. The Communists won some success by vigorously denouncing the mounting toll of layoffs and wage-cuts. In Sindelfingen and Mannheim, the councils were almost evenly split between Communists and Social Democrats, and the bickering was intense.[8]

In December 1931, the Bruening government, with the support of the SPD, enacted an emergency decree which contained wage reduction provisions and circumvented Weimar's usual bargaining procedures. The company's subsequent announcement of layoffs and wage-cuts for the Sindelfingen factory provoked mass meetings and tumultuous scenes in the closing days of 1931. The attempt to assemble a strike committee from all factions—led by Communists—broke apart on the bitter discord between SPD and KPD. By the early days of 1932, it had collapsed. The Social Democrats complained of the "broad, unbridgeable division" within the Daimler-Benz work force. The leadership of both groupings pleaded for unity, but neither was willing to unite with the other.[9] During 1932, Daimler-Benz strove to expel "the most well-known agitators" from the plant. In late December, it fired the "ringleaders of the Communists."[10] Thus, the political situation within the Mercedes work force starkly illuminated the bitter strife within the labor movement which hobbled the German left as the depression hit rock-bottom. It was a chasm within the working class which could be bridged from neither side.

National Socialist groupings gained a foothold in the factories after 1930, particularly among clerks. In 1931, a third of the clerks' representatives at Daimler-Benz were Nazis. A small cell of the National Socialist Factory Organization (NSBO) was apparently founded in Untertuerkheim in late 1931. The relative handful of NSBO organizers spoke for few workers in

Untertuerkheim; the opportunities provided them by the paralysis of labor were left largely unexploited. Nevertheless, for serious Social Democratic and Communist workers, the period was one of depression, powerlessness, and increasing demobilization. When Chancellor von Papen deposed the SPD-led government of Prussia on July 20, 1932, throngs of workers gathered in their redoubts in Stuttgart and Wuerttemberg to protest. As an unemployed Daimler-Benz worker observed: "They waited for the order [to arm themselves and fight], but no order came. . . . At this point, the political and trade union parts of the workers' movement had already arrived ideologically at zero. The Nazis had already seized the offensive, and their agitation showed an impact on the work force." On January 30, 1933, the hammer-and-sickle flags and the banners of the anti-Nazi Iron Front, with its insignia of three parallel arrows, disappeared overnight from the working class neighborhoods in east Stuttgart and around Daimler-Benz, to be replaced by swastikas, often hurriedly sewn over the old revolutionary emblems.[11]

THE MERCEDES REICH

Leading managers of Daimler-Benz lent valuable assistance to the National Socialists before Hitler became Chancellor in 1933. The corporation even claimed that it was responsible for "helping to motorize the movement."[12] The incomplete record shows that at least one official of Daimler-Benz illegally provided vehicles for the NSDAP election campaigns, although it is unclear whether this ever directly involved a decision of the corporate chairman or the board of directors.[13] Similarly, what may have motivated the Nazi supporters at Daimler-Benz cannot be ascertained.

Daimler-Benz's activist chairman of the board of trustees, the "political banker" Stauss, led an initiative by "big business"[14] and the Deutsche Volkspartei (DVP), the party headed by the imaginative Foreign Minister Gustav Stresemann until his death in 1929, to work with Hitler and the National Socialist Reichstag delegation in October 1930. His admiration for Hitler and his "close ties" to the National Socialists led a number of Jewish customers to close their accounts with the Deutsche Bank in 1931. Stauss also apparently raised and passed on funds to Goering in 1931. The banker temporarily cooled to the NSDAP following a press attack on him in the summer of 1932, and he subsequently supported the von Papen government.[15] Stauss, fond of estate life, was temperamentally suited to Papen's plans for a dictatorship of barons and businessmen. Nevertheless, Stauss became a vice-chairman of the Nazi Reichstag in 1934. He was later described as having "run over" to the NSDAP "because of the economic situation."[16]

In early 1931, Daimler-Benz began to place conspicuous display advertisements in the movement's newspaper, the *Voelkischer Beobachter*. In 1931, nine ads appeared; in 1932, 18, even though the paper was banned for a spell in mid-November.[17] In comparison, the company did not advertise at all in the Nazi organ in 1930. The ads may have been part of an arrangement for lending or giving vehicles to Hitler and the NSDAP: given the crisis and acute cash shortage, Daimler-Benz had little money to shower on right-wingers of any kind in 1931–1932. At the same time, Mercedes drastically curtailed its advertising in the SPD's *Vorwaerts*.

Although the company's ties to the NSDAP were never officially discussed at the meetings of the directors or the trustees, a clear pattern of support had emerged by 1932. As Jakob Werlin, the director of the company's Munich office, wrote Kissel in May 1932 after a discussion with Hitler: "Naturally I did not leave unmentioned that we have always shown the greatest obligingness to the party and in several cases [even] led . . ." Other companies may have been motivated "more from fear than from love of the fatherland, while we have consistently cherished the tie with the NSDAP for years in anticipation of the future development . . ." Daimler-Benz's chairman Kissel responded, "We have no occasion to diminish the attention which we have until now afforded Herr Hitler and his friends; he will be able to rely on us in the future, as in the past."[18] Needless to say, the company's assistance did not mean that National Socialism was a creation of Mercedes-Benz or of any other group of industrialists, or that German big business paid the bills of the NSDAP, but instead gives us reason to question the conclusions of a recent study that "The executives of some of the biggest corporations, such as the Mannesmann steel firm and the Daimler-Benz automotive works, conspicuously abstained from any political activities."[19]

The new National Socialist government in Berlin brought quick relief, and a spectacular turnaround was achieved at Daimler-Benz. By 1934, business had more than doubled, and better yet for the *Herren* of Daimler-Benz and the Deutsche Bank, the company had achieved a "pleasant increase in profits."[20] Very early on, the corporation was clear that the improvement in its fortunes was "the glorious result of the actions of the new government" rather than the cyclical upturn which business correspondents had already noted in late 1932 and which the corporation felt in January 1933.[21] Table 7.1 shows the dimensions of this extraordinary expansion, which, far more than being only an economic recovery, marked Daimler-Benz's rise to world industrial power. The grand Mercedes Reich was built with the Hitler regime's massive military buildup.

Daimler-Benz accomplished its recovery and rapid expansion without any major concession to the National Socialist government. Several "non-Aryan" trustees left the board of trustees in 1933–1934. The most visible change was the addition of the chief of the firm's Munich office, Jakob Werlin, to the board of directors. Werlin, already an associate director of the company, was a personal friend of Hitler's whose ties with the Fuehrer dated back to the months before the November 1923 putsch, when Hitler ordered a large Benz automobile, apparently to transport him to the Reich capital in the event of a successful completion of the March on Berlin. When Hitler left the Landsberg penitentiary in December 1924, Werlin allegedly picked him up at the gates of the prison and drove him away. Benz and the NSDAP had also shared quarters in Munich, which brought Werlin into daily contact

TABLE 7.1
The Daimler-Benz Aktien-Gesellschaft, 1926–1944

Year	Workers	Capital (RM in mills.)	Production (RM in mills.)	Military % of Production	Capacity % in Use
1926	7,500	36.36	68	8	30
1927	18,124	50.36	121.4	10	60
1928	16,733	50.36	130.8	10	58
1929	14,281	50.36	130.4	12	50
1930	9,786	50.36	98.8	15	35
1931	9,334	43.62	68.8	17	23
1932	9,148	43.62	65.0	19	26
1933	14,312	26.17	100.9	26	60
1934	22,975	26.17	146.8	35	86
1935	26,697	26.17	226.1	38	95
1936	32,164	26.17	295.1	43	90
1937	40,361	26.17	367.6	47	85
1938	46,713	26.17	396.2	51	97
1939	42,979	39.15	438.4	65	95
1940	46,248	50.2	(539)	76	92
1941	54,851	75.2	?	79	98
1942	62,886	90.3	844	85	98
1943	64,497	120.3	951	91	100
1944	63,663	120.3		93	100

Sources: 1. Historische Datensammlung 1886–1980; after 1932, provided by AGM DBAG. 2. Historische Datensammlung 1886–1980. 3. Historische Datensammlung 1886–1980; 1940 estimate from *Leistungsbericht* . . . ; 1942 & 1943 from O.M.G.U.S., *Ermittlungen gegen die Deutsche Bank;* 4–5. Hamburger Stiftung fuer Sozialgeschichte des 20. Jahrhunderts (HSG) *Das Daimler-Benz Buch,* p. 333.

with the Nazi entourage. Throughout the Third Reich, Hitler and Werlin remained personal and business friends, with the Fuehrer even personally penning happy birthday notes to Werlin during the last weeks before the launching of Operation Barbarossa. According to American intelligence documents obtained under the Freedom of Information Act, Werlin "personally administered" Hitler's package of Daimler-Benz stocks which the Nazi leader held in the firm.[22]

As one of the five directors of Daimler-Benz, the company entrusted Werlin with the task of maintaining its good ties with the new regime, whose leading men were already enthusiastic fans of Mercedes vehicles. According to a company document, Werlin's duties included the "care of business ties with Reich, state, and local authorities, as well as the NSDAP, whose organizations and formations [are] in close contact with Untertuerkheim." Werlin's work apparently included giving Nazis officials Mercedes cars as gifts or at substantially reduced prices.[23]

Two programs of the new regime contributed above all else to the breathtaking growth of the Mercedes Reich. The first, following on the heels of the new Chancellor's appearance at the Berlin automobile show in February, was the elimination of the heavy taxes on automobiles on April 10, 1933, which provided a boost to the German vehicular industry. The new law read: "Personal motorcycles and motor vehicles, and general omnibuses driven by internal combustion engines, which come into operation for the first time after March 31, 1933, are freed from tax."[24] The law demonstrated the commitment of the Hitler regime to the motorization of Germany. Hitler's wish to consolidate the regime and his plans for achieving a revision of the Versailles system—eventually through armed force, if necessary—underlay his fervent support for the construction of motor vehicles and for the cult (widespread among auto enthusiasts) of Daimler-Benz. Soon, a massive road-building program was underway, providing jobs for thousands of the unemployed and, later, roadways for the Third Reich's motorized armed forces.[25]

Auto and truck producers like Daimler-Benz deeply appreciated the regime's moves on their behalf. The National Association of the Automobile Industry, in which Daimler-Benz's Kissel was a prominent director, enthusiastically solicited donations in June 1933 for the NSDAP from its members through the *Adolf-Hitler Spende der deutschen Wirtschaft,* a fund which eventually raised 700 million marks for the coffers of the Nazi party.[26]

The second development, undoubtedly more decisive for the company's fate over the next 12 years, was the launching of the Hitlerian military buildup. Simply put, Daimler-Benz bore a large part of the responsibility for motorizing the German army and creating the Luftwaffe. New factories were built, and old ones were expanded. By the fall of 1933, Daimler-Benz had received a new commission from the army for armored vehicles and tanks, along with Krupp, MAN, Rheinmetall, and Henschel.[27] The company also gained a big contract from the army for 3,000 heavy trucks, part of the "motorization of the army."[28]

The factory complex at Berlin-Marienfelde, which had been idle through the depression, was brought back into operation for the production of armored vehicles at the end of 1933 and later greatly expanded to enable it to mass-produce airplane motors. In November 1933, Jakob Werlin informed the corporation that Hitler had personally told him that "we can expect to be supported [at the Marienfelde factory] especially energetically by the Reichswehr." Daimler-Benz later contended that "far-reaching guarantees were made to our director . . . to the effect that the operation of the works in Marienfelde would be provided with sufficient business with army contracts from the War Ministry for the next years."[29]

The leader of Daimler-Benz's first large-scale effort on behalf of Hitler's military buildup was Wolfgang von Hentig, a man related by marriage to the armaments industrialist Paul Rohde. Hentig quickly turned a neat profit for Daimler-Benz. As he wrote Stauss in a confidential note in 1934, "The sum of RM 1,870,000 approved for taking up production in Marienfelde was already almost earned in 1934." The company apparently felt it prudent to hide half of this handsome profit in its earnings report. Ever helpful, the regime also provided credits for new construction and for the procurement of machinery, although the firm had close ties to the Deutsche Bank and its financial resources.[30]

The critical role which military contracts came to play in the life of the firm was underscored in 1937 when the Reich designated the heart of Daimler-Benz—the Untertuerkheim and Sindelfingen facilities—"armaments factories," thus assuring that they would continue to receive special treatment and play a critical role in the event of any mobilization for war.[31]

It was the modern factory for airplane motors built at Genshagen in the 1930s, however, which best showed up the commitment which the Nazi regime and Daimler-Benz made to each other in the Third Reich. Daimler's role as the most important producer of airplane engines in the history of German aviation secured the successor firm a leading part in the buildup of the Luftwaffe. By the fall of 1935, a year before the beginning of the Four Year Plan, firm and regime had agreed on the construction of a large, new state-of-the-art factory for the mass production of airplane motors to be located in the Teltow area south of Berlin.[32]

Work on the new facility, including the railroad tracks and a train station needed to connect it with the rest of the Reich, began in early 1936 at Genshagen. The Air Ministry bore most of the construction costs for the installation. Its remote location was dictated by "military considerations":

the wish to keep the new installation relatively hidden in the rolling countryside which was partly covered by woods.[33]

The new unit was called the Daimler-Benz Motoren-Gesellschaft m.b.H., and employed workers from all regions of Germany, as well as many from what had been Austria and the Sudetenland of Czechoslovakia. The plant grew quickly, and had 10,000 workers by 1941. It produced thousands of airplane engines before the attack on Poland, and many received their first in-combat test with the Condor Legion in the Spanish Civil War.

THE WORKERS IN THE NEW ORDER AT DAIMLER-BENZ

The National Socialist regime swept away the trade unions and the ensemble of institutions—factory councils, associations, and arbitration committees—which had shaped the industrial order since the First World War. On the wreckage, it constructed a new system of labor relations based on the factory community *[Betriebsgemeinschaft]* whose coordinates were—to borrow the title of a recent work which explores the levels of domination in German fascism—fear, reward, discipline, and order.[34] The most important piece of social legislation, the Law for the Order of National Labor decreed on January 20, 1934, served as the charter for the new factory order. In the wake of the declared "abolition" of class conflict, it carried over the *Fuehrer* principle into German industry in a manner which bore an unmistakable resemblance to the cherished corporate notion of *Herr im Hause*.[35]

The landmark legislation contained at least seven major sections detailing the responsibilities and duties of the factory leader and the new organizational creations of the Nazis, the councils of trust and the trustees of labor. According to this charter of labor, "the leader of the plant, as opposed to the followers, has decision-making power in all matters pertaining to the plant as they are regulated by this law." Who was to lay down the law in the factories was clear in the commentary on the law: "In his decisions on social matters the leader of the plant is in principle unhampered by any rights of co-determination on the part of his followers."[36]

The new councils of trusts, to be set up in plants with more than 20 employees from lists of National Socialists and endorsed by the workers in a ballot, were a far cry from the old factory councils. As one observer put it, "in contrast to the Betriebsrat law of 1920 which stated that the works council should 'represent the special interest of the employees as against those of the employer,' the main duty of the members of the [councils of trust] is to 'deepen the mutual confidence that must exist within the works community.' "[37] According to the text of the law, the councils of trust were "to advise on all measures for the improvement of labor performance, for the shaping and execution of working conditions, especially factory order."[38]

The trustees of labor, officials responsible to the Economics Ministry, looked after the "maintenance of the peace in the factories." They could intervene in industrial affairs to try to solve problems, preferably in such a way "that the class struggle would not flare up because of brutal economic repression."[39] In all, there are only a few examples of the activities of the councils of trust or the trustees of labor at Daimler-Benz, and neither can be described as particularly interventionist.

There can be no more dramatic proof of this than the coolness with which Kissel summarily dismissed the entire council of trust at the Untertuerkheim factory in early 1937. Citing factional conflicts among the members, the Daimler-Benz chairman alleged that "comradely and exemplary cooperation" had become impossible among the members, and "in the end, this is known among the work force." Kissel informed the regional trustee of labor that he would not allow any of the old members to sit on the new version of the council. The purge and the new appointments he had made, Kissel reported, were "accepted by the work force without any unrest."[40]

The setting of wages also had nothing directly to do with the councils of trust. Workers' wages had fallen sharply at Daimler-Benz during the depression, and remained at their low levels during the first years of the Third Reich. Hourly rates for skilled workers in the Untertuerkheim factory actually fell by 4 percent in 1933 and 1934 before recovering a bit by mid-decade (see table 7.2). At the same time, trained machine workers and day laborers suffered smaller losses in their hourly wages. The machine workers in particular closed the pay gap with their skilled compatriots: while the hourly averages for skilled workers in Untertuerkheim had not yet reached their 1929 levels in 1940, trained workers earned 6 percent more than they had in 1929.

While wages slowly recovered from their lows of 1932–1934, the big new contracts from the government's rearmament programs came rolling in and put the corporation under pressure to produce more efficiently. More and more conveyor belts and assembly lines began moving the large lots of components through the production and assembly processes more quickly. The exact timetable is difficult to flesh out, but by the mid- and late 1930s, moving belts and assembly lines were central features of the factories in Untertuerkheim, Mannheim, and Sindelfingen, and almost certainly the others as well. The corporation's investments in new machines, usually special machines of German and American manufacture, increased at a rapid pace through the 1930s.[41]

In the context of rapid expansion and rationalization in the late 1930s, Daimler-Benz launched a pioneering attack on the wage system which had existed since the nineteenth century, with its categories (skilled, trained, and unskilled) founded on the level of skill and ability. The full-scale assault which a company official claimed would replace payment by "ability *[Koennen]*" with payment by "performance *[Leistung]*" began in 1938 at the Mannheim factory and spread to other plants during the war.[42] In the pseudo-scientific words of a DAF theoretical tract which appeared simultaneously, "The point is to get away from the wage as payment for a commodity, namely labor, and to realize the wage as the recognition for performance."[43] In the context of repression and disenfranchisement, this marked a watershed in the unmaking of the German working class.

Daimler-Benz's new wage system grouped the jobs in the corporation's labor processes in eight "wage groups." (See table 7.3.) Wage group D, for example, included many jobs which were performed by skilled and trained machine workers. The choice of machine tools, the setting up of the machines, and the final turning operations were rated "B" jobs, while the cutting operations—grinding, drilling, milling, and most turning—were "C," "D," and "E" jobs. In the assembling and testing departments, most were "D" jobs, with each operation paid at a relatively low rate of remuneration.[44] The range of the skilled fitter was rapidly shrinking. With the precise catalogue of labor processes, fixed across a wide spectrum of wage-rates, the ability of the worker was supposed to count for little at Daimler-Benz on payday. And just in time, too—with the demands of the years 1938–1941 about to hike the need for labor-power even further. As the corporation boasted in 1941, "with the new wage system, the time of internal wage conflicts and dealings *[Aushandeleien]* is now past for the factory."[45]

The wage group system which replaced "payment by skills with remuneration by 'value of the job' " spread through the metal and machine-building industries in 1942 and 1943. Siemens, for example, switched to the new system in 1943. It is not possible to assess its impact on Daimler-Benz's performance, but Fritz Sauckel, the commissioner general for labor deployment, waxed enthusiastic in September 1942 about what had been attained thus far with it in the war industries: "increases in efficiency that . . . usually amounted to around 20 percent, but often much more."[46]

The new wage system was founded in the context of the specific relations of authority which existed in Daimler-Benz's factories and which probably mirrored those prevailing in other large manufacturing companies. The new factory regulations which Daimler-Benz promulgated in 1937 explicitly spelled out the Mercedes/National Socialist order. There were, of course, only two participants in the "factory community": the "factory leader" and the "followers." The "followers" were bound to whichever tasks leadership had set, and could be moved around the factory from job to job. Overtime was mandatory, as was work on weekends or on the night shift. Even the daily working hours could be extended if the leadership decided that more work had to be done on the shift.[47]

The grievance procedure in the factories was regulated by the "spirit of factory . . . comradeship." If an individual "follower" had a complaint or grievance, he or she was permitted to bring it to the attention of a National Socialist functionary, a member of the council of trust, or the "factory leader."[48]

A worker who wanted to leave had to give management up to two weeks' notification (or even longer) of his or her intention to quit. If the "factory leader" had a bone to pick with a "follower," however, the procedure was quite different, and the firing was immediate. The infractions to be dealt with summarily included "national treachery, proven through malevolent

TABLE 7.2
Wages and Working Hours at Daimler-Benz, 1929–1937, 1940

Year	Workers	Weekly Hours		Hourly Wages (Pf.)	Weekly Wages (RM)	Yearly Wages (RM)
1929	3,656	44.5	Skilled	124.6	55.85	2,904
			Trained	109.3	49.00	2,548
			Unskilled	82.8	37.12	1,930
1930	3,125	43.0	Skilled	125.5	53.96	2,805
			Trained	111.3	47.85	2,488
			Unskilled	82.3	35.38	1,839
1931	2,871	40.3	Skilled	118.0	47.79	2,485
			Trained	104.2	42.20	2,194
			Unskilled	77.0	31.18	1,621
1932	2,580	38.05	Skilled	106.8	40.66	2,114
			Trained	94.8	36.10	1,877
			Unskilled	71.5	27.22	1,415
1933	3,528	47.5	Skilled	104.1	49.79	2,589
			Trained	93.4	44.67	2,322
			Unskilled	72.2	34.53	1,795

Sources: Staatsarchiv Ludwigsburg E 258 II Bue 578 Bl 478 DBAG to Wuertt. Stat. Landesamt, Sept. 25, 1935 for 1929–35; AGM DBAG Kissel XIII, 1 Kissel to Werlin, Feb. 9, 1938 for 1936–37: these

talk and acts against *Volk* and the state, acts and insults against comrades and . . . against the factory order," along with drunkenness and the betrayal of factory and business secrets.[49]

All of those employed at Daimler-Benz worked longer hours under National Socialism. By the end of the 1930s, the length of the working week totaled 54 hours, exceeding the 48 hours of the last pre-depression years. In late 1940, the work week reached 60 hours.[50] Lower wage rates, lower price-rates, stricter discipline, longer hours, many more jobs—these were the fruits of National Socialism for the workers of Daimler-Benz.

The firm's own records show that the mass production for military orders and the policies followed vis-à-vis its workers paid off handsomely. Between 1932 and 1940, Daimler-Benz's total production grew by 830 percent. At

TABLE 7.2
Continued

Year	Workers	Weekly Hours		Hourly Wages (Pf.)	Weekly Wages (RM)	Yearly Wages (RM)
1934	6,058	49.00	Skilled	102.6	50.27	2,614
			Trained	93.5	45.81	2,382
			Unskilled	73.3	25.91	1,867
1935	6,990	49.40	Skilled	104.2	51.75	2,691
			Trained	95.8	47.58	2,474
			Unskilled	74.4	36.95	1,921
1936		49.4	Skilled	106	52.38	2,724
			Trained	94.8	46.84	2,436
			Unskilled	79.9	39.46	2,052
1937		49.4	Skilled	111.1	54.92	2,856
			Trained	100.0	49.38	2,568
			Unskilled	83.0	41.08	2,136
1940	8,275	54.0 (60.0 after 9/1)	Skilled	124	66.96	3,608
			Trained	118	63.72	3,433
			Unskilled	93	50.22	2,706

totals are apparently averages for the whole company (calculated from monthly averages); *Leistungs-bericht* . . . , p. 134 for 1940 (calculated from hourly averages).

TABLE 7.3
I. Daimler-Benz's Wage Groups, 1941

Wage Group A: Skilled work requiring extraordinary handworking abilities, as well as a self-sufficient disposition and unusually responsible leadership qualities.

Wage Group B: Highly skilled work in individual production jobs, requiring self-sufficiency as well as facility with drawings and designs.

Wage Group C: High-grade skilled work in individual or serial production, requiring precision and the performance of a wide range of operations.

Wage Group D: Normal skilled work in the trades. Normal skilled work in serial production. Work of the trained or machine trades *(Anlernberufe),* which are equivalent to a part of a skilled trade. General work in the workshop requiring circumspection, individual initiative and special trust.

Wage Group E: Difficult and more independent work of the trained trades and the workshops. Included are dirty, dangerous, and unhealthy jobs.

Wage Group F: Work in the trained trades and workshops requiring functional training.

Wage Group G: Simple jobs requiring a certain dexterity or physical exertion.

Wage Group H: Simple jobs which can be done after directions are given.

II. Level of Piece-Wages for Male Workers According to Wage Group

Group A = 112%
Group B = 100%
Group C = 94%
Group D = 88%
Group E = 83%
Group F = 76%
Group G = 72%
Group H = 69%

Source: AGM DBAG Kissel XIII, 2 Kurze Denkschrift ueber die Einfuehrung der Entlohnung nach Taetigkeitsgruppen in der Flugzeugindustrie. Anlage 4 Daimler-Benz AG, Lohngruppen nach Taetig-keitsbewertung; Anlage 3 Abstufung der fuer die einzelnen Taetigkeitsgruppen angesetzten Loehne in % . . .

the same time, its work force grew by about 500 percent, and the wages and salaries of its work force by 643 percent (see table 7.4). Thus, the average remuneration per employee rose by 129.8 percent, although it is not possible to reckon how the increase was distributed among groups of workers and clerks. It is essential, however, to note that the work week was perhaps 42 percent longer than in 1932. Starkly put, National Socialism saw the increased exploitation of the work force at Daimler-Benz. It is doubtful whether the 30 percent increase in wages and salaries during the 1930s compensated for more than a portion of the longer working hours, the "piece-rate exploitation," and the new prerogatives of management, which workers were now more likely to experience in a more direct, unmediated way in the aftermath of the destruction of the labor movement and the socialist parties.

Yet increased exploitation was not the only experience of National Socialism for the work force at Daimler-Benz. Mercedes was a Nazi "model factory," and that meant that the firm maintained visible social programs for its workforce. There were lunchtime concerts, lectures, and films; there was a works orchestra, as well as other music ensembles and choirs; there were sports clubs and hiking groups. All were designed to produce, in Daimler-Benz's words, "the securing of social peace, maintenance of efficiency and improved productivity, and the maintenance of the joy of working."[51]

The firm's initiatives included frequent mandatory lectures on "racial political questions" for the Daimler-Benz's young male and female workers,

TABLE 7.4
Daimler-Benz's Performance, 1932–1940: The Company's Report

	Workers	Wages & Salaries	Production
1932	100	100	100
1933	137.6	148.3	153.8
1934	229.1	224.6	226.2
1935	289.6	314.1	347.9
1936	339.2	393.2	454.0
1937	441.9	533.5	614.1
1938	485.5	598.4	710.8
1939	516.9	649.9	819.0
1940	495.7	643.6	830.9

Source: AGM DBAG Goldene Fahne, *Arbeits- und Entwicklungsbericht 1941/42*, vol. 56. These statistics were provided to the German Labor Front.

or concerts by formations of the Wehrmacht "to demonstrate the inner ties with the soldiers of our glorious Wehrmacht."[52] Once a year, the regime celebrated labor day, and Daimler-Benz joined in the pagaentry. On a typical holiday, April 30, 1940, Wilhelm Kissel delivered a speech before dignitaries from the firm and NSDAP, which was carried to every part of the factory by loudspeakers, while afterward the factory orchestra performed a concert."[53]

TABLE 7.5
The Daimler-Benz Empire, 1942–1945

Factories (in 1944)	Total Workers	Foreign Workers
Untertuerkheim (engines for airplanes and warships, R & D)	10,285	4,603
Sindelfingen (truck bodies, V-2 tail)	4,702	1,483
Berlin-Marienfelde 40 (tanks)	4,966	2,526
Berlin-Marienfelde 90 (airplane motors)	2,669	1,080
Mannheim (heavy trucks)	3,657	cc 1,231
Gaggenau (heavy trucks)	3,177	601
Koenigsberg (tank repair)	323	175
Genshagen (airplane engines)	11,233	cc 6,593
Kolmar (airplane motor parts)	1,558	146

cc—There are records of concentration camp inmates or Jewish slaves at these plants. Because of the incomplete evidence, no plant can be excluded as definitely not having employed slave labor.
* 1943
There were also 10,668 clerks, engineers, technicians, and supervisors employed at DBAG in 1944.

NAZIS, INDUSTRY, AND LABOR: ACCOMMODATION OR OPPOSITION?

A historian has recently written that "between the extremes of political-militant resistance against the Nazi regime, on the one hand, and approval of the regime, on the other, a wide spectrum of behavior patterns existed." [54] Even "resistance," as a catch-all category for activity entailing differing degrees of risk-taking and with widely varying motives and aims, should be revised, perhaps along the line of a recent attempt to distinguish between "opposition *[Dissens]*" and "resistance *[Widerstand]*." [55]

TABLE 7.5
Continued

Factories (in 1944)	Total Workers	Foreign Workers
Rzeszow Reichshof (airplane motor parts)	3,999 *	3,681 *
Neupaka (airplane motor parts)	4,214	4,107
Flugmotorenwerke Ost-mark (airplane engines)	17,396	cc 10,489
"Werlinbau" in Minsk (repair of trucks and tanks)	?	cc ?

There were dozens of smaller facilities and works for which figures cannot be compiled.

TOTALS	81,059	36,147 (44.6%, *not* including camp inmates or POW's)

Sources: AGM DBAG DBAG 31; B.I.O.S., "Report on visit to Daimler-Benz"; Zentrale Stelle der Landesjustizverwaltungen (Film 4, et al.); total for Ostmark is from Beiratsbericht (1.1–31.3.1944, ergaenzende Angaben, B.) TOTALS are numbers in AGM DBAG for whole concern + figures for Ostmark.

Nevertheless, the available sources limit the kinds of questions we can pose and answer here. Did the workers and the directors at Daimler-Benz resist the Nazis? The directors certainly did not.

With one exception, the directors and trustees of Daimler-Benz never opposed the National Socialist regime. This fact is not difficult to understand. In the words of one historian, "There was nothing socialist about Hitler's economics. . . . The repeated and famous declarations of the Nazi intention to socialize people rather than factories meant that far-reaching programmes of state control over the economy were unnecessary."[56] Daimler-Benz, *Herr im Hause* once more after decades of intrusions by socialists, trade unionists, and their Republic, was one of the most important makers of National Socialist power, and benefitted enormously from the regime's tax policies and arms buildup. In this context, the old debate about the primacy of economics or politics is ill-suited to advance our understanding of Daimler-Benz's role in National Socialist Germany. The interests of firm and regime generally coincided, with beneficial results for both parties. Daimler-Benz produced masses of engines and vehicles for profit and was rid of the labor movement; the regime founded the resurgence of German military power on the firm's quality industrial designs and products. One exception is the case of the Daimler-Benz trustee Hermann Koehler, leader of the Wuerttemberische Vereinsbank before 1918 and director of the Stuttgart branch of the Deutsche Bank. In 1943, while on a train, he told an acquaintance that in the wake of Stalingrad the military situation was hopeless, and that Germany should try to make peace with its enemies before it was too late. He was overheard and reported to the Gestapo, which picked him up in Stuttgart and spirited him off to Berlin, where the People's Court quickly tried and convicted him. On November 8, 1943, he was executed.[57]

The company itself was a personal favorite of the *Fuehrer,* who generally rode in Mercedes cars, as did the rest of his entourage. Nazi swastika and Mercedes star were virtually intertwined, and not only in the company's vulgar advertisements in Nazi organs. In one memorable shot in Leni Riefenstahl's classic rendering of the photo-opportunity known as the Nuernberg rally of 1934, *Triumph of the Will,* the Mercedes star on Hitler's car blazes more radiantly than any swastika in sight. (Hitler himself presented the filmmaker with her own Mercedes which he obtained from the firm for halfprice.) In shambles and on the brink of failure in the early 1930s, the firm's rise to industrial greatness between 1933 and 1945—beyond mere "recovery" from the depression—was linked to the practice and delusory "success" of National Socialism. Daimler-Benz was the armaments firm without equal in Nazi Germany. Airplane motors and spare parts, tanks and armored vehicles, heavy trucks, later even a major tail section of the V-2 rocket, aviation research and development—no other motor company did so much for the Third Reich. To be sure, the firm gained quite a bit from Hitler's triumphs—not only production contracts but also cheap foreign workers and concentration camp inmates, and booty from firms like Peugot, the Polish Brczeski-Auto in Posen, and—whether an arrogant boast or not —the ability to use the secret police to bring a stubborn shareholder into line.[58] There may have been problems at times with the factions in the regime and other companies, but neither Daimler-Benz nor any of its leading personnel were ever moved to want another kind of political system.

It is not clear how fully Daimler-Benz's leadership was informed about the every detail of the regime's intentions in the late 1930s, but there is no doubt that the top directors knew the Reich was about to embark on fateful policies, and that their efforts were critically important to the regime's plans. During the summer of 1938, Goering secretly briefed the chiefs of Daimler-Benz, BMW, and other big companies building the Luftwaffe about the challenges which lay ahead:

> Now we are fully embarked on the way to mobilization-capacity and we will not be able to deviate from this mobilization capacity for years. . .
> Therefore, I would like to make a heartfelt request of you. Consider yourselves as the industry which has to build up the Luftwaffe and which is bound up with the Luftwaffe to the end. Do understand that every personal interest has to take second place. What does your factory mean in relation to the nation? . . .
> Gentlemen, I have . . . to praise, recognize, and thank. . . . The airplane industry is in the know. Among the airplane motor industry, clarity is also generally the rule. It will be the task of Mercedes to build as many of [the] 601 [motors] as possible.[59]

In this context, Kissel's boast to his fellow directors eight months later appears in a different light. "Our cross-country vehicles have performed excellently in the occupation of the Sudetenland and in the advance into Czechoslovakia [Tschechei]. Consequently, more such vehicles shall be ordered." Production was now at a peak: "The factories are fully occupied with army and state orders."[60] Never did Mercedes's dedication to the military preparations waiver, and now it had begun to pay off for the regime as well.

Inevitably, the situation of the company's workers differed from that of those at the top. In general times, the Nazi regime considered the working class—or das Arbeitertum, to use the Nazi term—the chief cause for anxiety and alarm in their "people's community." It was "the single threatening collective entity seen by a regime which otherwise only identified specifically constructed groups (Jews, priests, free masons) as dangerous."[61] Most of the active opposition came from the underground organizations of the political parties of the working class, and the Gestapo arrested tens of thousands between 1933 and 1945. Nevertheless, the resistance was individualized, and rarely, if ever, coalesced into mass actions. The working class did not massively and frontally attack the Hitler regime; a few workers even seemed to enjoy the spectacle of it all.

It is a daunting task to track and analyze opposition and worker resistance. Most of the documentation—e.g. the SS and Gestapo records—has been lost, and the rest is unavailable, either in the German Democratic Republic or in closed company archives in the west. A very sketchy— perhaps only suggestive record of worker resistance in the Daimler-Benz firm —can now be assembled from, e.g., materials from the company archives, the so-called Sopade reports from Germany collected by the SPD in exile, works by East German historians which emphasize the important role played by Communists in the attempts to spread opposition to the Hitler regime, and miscellaneous references and memoirs. This work will present the evidence as best as it can and will suggest avenues for evaluation and analysis.

In the first days of the Nazi regime, a mood of resignation prevailed among workers at the Daimler-Benz factory in Stuttgart. When the NSBO called a factory assembly shortly after the new government took power, the company allowed it to hold the session inside the factory, reversing its earlier policy that workers' meetings had to be held outside of company property. "The workers just listened. There was no great approval. But they all stood up, not only as the Deutschland-Lied was sung, but also during the Horst-Wessel song. I was surely the only one who left the assembly on this afternoon. [I found that] the factory gates were locked shut. . . . No one had the courage to leave the factory out of protest against the Horst-Wessel song."[62] The locked gates showed the firm's cooperation with the Nazi meeting.

Surprisingly, discouragement did not mean defection to the Nazi camp. A spectacular display of the judgment which Daimler-Benz workers passed on the new Hitler regime came with the elections to the factory councils in the late winter of 1933. At the Sindelfingen factory, 11 of the 12 seats went to Social Democrats and Communists, while the Nazis won only one seat. The DMV received 588 votes, the Communists 432, and the Nazis 162. At the Mannheim factory, the Daimler-Benz workers elected four Socialists and one Communist, while only one representative of the NSBO squeaked through.[63]

The regime destroyed the trade unions on May 2, 1933, and deprived the workers of their leadership. The move had already been prepared: between March 11 and April 4, 1933, sixty Communists and Social Democrats from Untertuerkheim and Luginsland were arrested and held in a nearby riding hall. The new authorities dissolved or smashed a score of organizations and clubs in these communities in the spring of 1933.[64] There was no mass protest in the face of the paroxysm of terror and repression which shook Germany in the spring of 1933. Soon, the directors of Daimler-Benz no longer needed to take heed of its workers' wishes, at least as long as so many in the area were unemployed. There is evidence that the company undertook at least several reprisals against politically suspect workers in 1933. One of the firm's letters informing an employee of his dismissal from October 1933 reads, "Because of subversive activities *[Wegen staatsfeindlicher Umtriebe]* we are immediately firing you."[65]

Economic conditions at Daimler-Benz quickly improved, and jobs were created. There were, however, a few bumps along the road to world power during the furious buildup, especially between 1935 and 1939. The SPD's secret correspondence reported that the company wanted to lay off 1,500 workers in Stuttgart in the fall of 1935, apparently because of problems in financing the government's military programs. A year later the weekly working hours were temporarily shortened to 38 hours a week, because of shortages of raw materials.[66] In 1937, the SPD's correspondent reported that the Mercedes operation in Stuttgart was riddled with "contradictions" which were disrupting production at the plant, particularly shortages of steel and aluminum which frequently led to workers being sent home. On the other hand, in departments where no shortages reigned, twelve-hour shifts with only a half-hour lunch break were the rule.[67]

Wages in departments employing scarce skilled and machine workers were sometimes forced upward. At Berlin-Marienfelde, a new army contract in 1935 for the production of large six-wheel transport trucks had been accompanied by wage hikes of 4 pfennigs an hour for groups of machine workers.[68] By 1936, wages began to rise rapidly.

The first sign of widespread disaffection among the workers at Daimler appeared in early 1935. A report on a job action at the Untertuerkheim factory affords a rare glimpse of intra-factory conflict during the mid-1930s. On April 5, 1935, 60 fitters on an assembly line stopped work for at least 30 minutes after having been paid less than usual when a shortage of mud guards for vehicles delayed the production line. According to the council of trust's secret investigation of the incident at the plant, there was no demonstration or "passive resistance," and work resumed after management met the workers' demand to be compensated for the loss of wages caused by the parts shortage. A few days later, workers distributed leaflets near the factory complaining of the "wage robbery" which had been prevented only by the concerted action of the Daimler-Benz workers.[69] In the subsequent ballot on the Nazi slate for the council of trust, one quarter of the workers cast invalid ballots and another quarter altered their ballots before casting them.[70] The factory's council of trust immediately informed the political police of events.[71] It cannot be determined whether the incident had any subsequent disciplinary consequences.

The elections for the factory "councils of trust" also provoked a resounding display of no confidence in the factory and national regimes in other plants. In Mannheim on April 12, an overwhelming majority of the workers —950 of 1,475 voting—cast invalid votes in the elections for the council of trust. As a result, the Nazi candidates who headed the list were not elected. Subsequently, the regional trustee of labor declared the election invalid and appointed the council himself.[72] At the company's labor day festivities on May 1, a leading Nazi sharply attacked the Daimler-Benz workers, reminding them all that they had benefitted from the regime's policy. "Thanks for your ungratefulness [Undankbarkeit]. . . . Those who reject National Socialism should pack their bags and go to Russia!"[73]

Between 1935 and 1937, the age-old strife over the piece-rates and the way they were set provoked a handful of noteworthy clashes in the Daimler-Benz imperium. A worker in Untertuerkheim noted: "The piece-rate exploitation [Akkordschinderei] was unbelievable. And he who turned to a calculating official because [of the way the wages had been computed] . . . risked dismissal. The Gestapo sent him off to the Black Forest, where he had to build the West Wall."[74] The SPD correspondent in Stuttgart noted in 1936 that there had been "spontaneous" job actions in the large factories there because of the lowering of piece-rates, the "brutality" of the masters and poor hygienic conditions. Subsequently, management had sometimes even gone "half-way" to meet their workers' complaints. Yet job actions remained isolated. "So we could ascertain that in defensive reactions in individual departments at Daimler-Benz and Bosch . . . the workers in other departments in these factories had no idea that something like a strike had occurred."[75]

There were at least two strikes in the Mannheim factory between 1935 and early 1937, although the exact dates can no longer be determined. In 1935, workers upset with the disciplining and insulting of a comrade by a company official struck in a department there after a party official was unable or unwilling to intervene on their behalf. After a three-hour work stoppage, the factory's management agreed to apologize for the actions of its official. In 1937, an exile paper appearing in Paris reported that the cast cleaners in the foundry at the Mannheim plant had struck for 4½ hours after management slashed their piece-rates by 10 percent. The strike failed, and it is unknown how the strikers were subsequently disciplined.[76]

Such job actions, along with all the military work going on at Daimler-Benz, offer one reason why the firm beefed up security in its factories in

1936. In Untertuerkheim, for example, Daimler-Benz introduced a strict new system whereby each employee had to present a company photo-ID card to gain admission to the factory complex. Workers who forgot to bring their ID cards with them were sent home.[77] The company also appointed special liaison officials to coordinate Daimler-Benz's work with the political police.[78] In addition, factories across Germany expanded their police units and gave them dark, Nazi-style uniforms.

The chief agency for policing the work force and preserving the "joy of working," however, was the NSDAP and its formations, especially the German Labor Front (DAF). DAF claimed universal mass membership at Daimler-Benz. Yet after seven years of National Socialism, 1,818 workers and clerks in Untertuerkheim belonged to the party, 17.4 percent of the total. The clerks, among whom were many technicians engaged in state-funded engine research and development, may have been a bit more liable to be attracted to National Socialism than were the workers.[79]

Regarding the firm's directors, if the associate directors are included in the total, two-thirds of the firm's top managers were members of the NSDAP. Yet among the firm's top council, there were notable exceptions. The director Wilhelm Haspel, who would take over the direction in 1942, was not a member, presumably because his wife was half-Jewish. Although some at Daimler-Benz today contend that a number of Nazi directors may have secretly harbored doubts about their creed, no one can determine the depths of their faith in Hitlerian delusions. Indeed, such considerations are largely irrelevant. Membership in the SS and NSDAP mattered, and was a sign that the men who joined—for whatever reasons—had cast their lot with National Socialism.

Only a handful of sources report on wartime resistance, and most of these come from the German Democratic Republic. They indicate surprisingly persistent activity by small groups of workers, especially at the big works in Berlin-Marienfelde. A postwar newspaper report asserted that "in Marienfelde a fascist terror existed, which hardly could have been found in another factory in Berlin."[80] Despite the conditions at the factory (or perhaps because of them) small groups in the Berlin area repeatedly built up contacts with workers at the production complex. During the first weeks of the war, a group of youths with contacts at Daimler-Benz distributed leaflets, proclaiming "only the overthrow of Hitler and his band of war-mongers will bring peace." The ringleader was executed.[81] For the period from the attack on Poland until the attempt to assassinate Hitler in July 1944, there were at least six oppositional groups operating among workers at Daimler-Benz in Berlin-Marienfelde before being rooted out. One of these, the so-called *Kampfbund* assembled by the Communists Prenzlau and Jacob, organized discussions and illegal weapons training. As a result, the regime executed at least five Daimler-Benz workers, while a minimum of two others died while being held.[82]

Stuttgart-Untertuerkheim also saw a little wartime resistance activity.[83] Although incidents of sabotage and resistance there cannot be easily traced or corroborated, the company considered the general situation among its work force unsettled and difficult in the fall of 1939 and again in the spring of 1941. It therefore withdrew its attempt to get hold of Italian workers for its plants in Untertuerkheim and Sindelfingen after the German authorities gave the Italian government assurances concerning the provision of food supplies to Italian workers. "With certainty," Daimler-Benz informed the German officials, "a disturbance of the factory order [Arbeitsruhe]" would result if the Italians came to Mercedes-Benz.[84] In the spring of 1942, the secret police complained of high absenteeism at Mercedes in Gaggenau and at least raised the possibility that it might reflect low worker morale.[85]

Later, one of the best known proletarian groups in the Stuttgart area, the Schlotterbeck family which was betrayed by a police informer, tortured, and executed in late 1944, lived in Luginsland, the colony founded by Daimler workers, and members of the family had worked at Mercedes at various times during the preceding two decades.[86]

Even more inaccessible to research are the relations between German and foreign workers in Daimler-Benz's factories during the war. The walls of Nazi apartheid separated native and foreign workers. There are a handful of reports of German workers aiding inmates, for example, by bringing emaciated female prisoners pieces of bread, but it is impossible to ascertain the scale of such assistance, or whether it expressed solidarity or merely sympathy with their plight.[87]

On the basis of the scattered remaining evidence, it is not possible to characterize the workforce at Daimler-Benz as "integrated" into the Third Reich. At the same time, the intermittent job actions and the existence of knots of resisters, even during World War II, do not necessarily bespeak any united anti-Nazi front among the workers. Rather, they show that the National Socialists faced considerable obstacles in realizing their policies at Daimler-Benz, and suggest that the regime may have been correct when it considered the working class to have been the Achilles heel of the *Volksgemeinschaft*.[88]

GENSHAGEN: MOTORS AND WAR CRIMES

The Mercedes empire reached mammoth dimensions during World War II (table 7.5). Its main facilities included large works in Stuttgart, Sindelfingen,

Mannheim, Gaggenau, Berlin-Marienfelde, Genshagen, Koenigsberg, later in Kolmar (Alsace), Rzeszow/Reichsof (Poland), and Neupaka (Czechoslovakia). Daimler-Benz also took over the huge Flugmotorenwerke Ostmark in Wiener Neudorf (Austria) in the fall of 1941. Chairman Kissel assessed the company's good fortune as "one of the greatest—no, the greatest success— that our firm has ever had."[89] Daimler also ran Avia in Prague, Manfred Weiss in Budapest, Fiat in Turin, and uncounted repair facilities and workshops, especially on the eastern front deep inside the USSR.[90] The Mercedes armaments network embraced major firms such as the Austrian Steyr-Daimler-Puch, Henschel, and the Niedersaechsische Motorenwerke. Daimler-Benz produced tanks, trucks, engines for warships, parts for the V-2, and especially enormous lots of airplane engines during the war. In its facilities, research went on to design better engines and tanks, and perhaps even, according to the vague and uncorroborated report of a former employee, on a plan for a truck to gas human beings.[91]

The firm and its leading personnel were center-stage in the "self-management" groups within the Ministry of Weapons and Ammunition which sought to coordinate and to increase war production after 1942. Daimler-Benz directors and managers sat on the main committees for airplanes, tanks, and naval undersea weaponry, along with their numerous subdivisions and rings, which coordinated production and directed industrial cooperation across a wide range of company and bureaucratic boundaries.[92] Perhaps most important was the Daimler-Benz-Ring, Special Committee T-2, which supervised the Mercedes aviation colossus in Speer's armaments ministry and which was headed by the company's post-1942 chairman, Wilhelm Haspel. In general, the point was to rationalize profit-making war production in German industries.

In addition, Hitler appointed director Werlin to be *Generalinspektor fuer das Kraftfahrwesen* on January 16, 1942. "The general inspector is answerable immediately to me. He receives directives only from me." His task seems to have been to maintain the Reich's vast fleets of vehicles—tanks, trucks, and cars—which the military and the German state operated in occupied Europe. Werlin immediately ordered the construction of three large works in Minsk, Riga, and Dnjepropetrowsk. Daimler-Benz was responsible for the large facility in Minsk, where it was aided by large numbers of Soviet prisoners of war and Jews from the Minsk ghetto.[93]

Through Werlin, Daimler-Benz had access to the innermost circles of the Third Reich. According to one intelligence report, Werlin "is always at the *Berghof* in Berchtesgaden and thus sees things from the inside." Werlin also traveled widely in occupied Europe and regulated the company's massive cash reserves in Swiss bank accounts. "[Werlin] mentioned that the money which Daimler-Benz has in Switzerland amounts to 240 million [Swiss] francs," one intelligence source noted. Among his contacts there was Eduard Schuelte, the man who passed on—from an as yet unknown source—news of the Holocaust to Allied intelligence in Switzerland.[94]

On a massive scale, Daimler-Benz threw tens of thousands of men and women, including foreign workers and concentration camp inmates, into the battle to produce engines for the German air force, as the Luftwaffe took to the air between 1939 and 1941 to wage extensive aerial campaigns over Poland, western Europe, England, and the Soviet Union. Daimler-Benz airplane engines powered a large share of the Luftwaffe's fighters and bombers. The company's factory at Genshagen for producing airplane engines, headed by Mercedes director and National Socialist Karl C. Mueller, was critical to the war effort.[95] The plant built more than 34,000 airplane motors during its years of operation, 1936–1945. The Allies themselves considered it one of the most important German factories for the mass production of aircraft engines and the largest of the Daimler-Benz production facilities.[96]

On the eve of the influx of foreign labor, more than four-fifths of the employees were males, almost half of whom were skilled workers. A sizeable contingent of women, more than 12 percent of the total work force, labored as machine or unskilled employees. Other women performed tasks in the clerical departments. From a variety of sources, it is possible to obtain a sense of the productive life of the facility. In a report intended for authorities in the German Labor Front (DAF), the firm boasted in 1940 of the "rational labor process" at Genshagen. Assembly line work, particularly in the assembly of engines, was the rule.[97] A few years later, slaves also found a rational division of labor in the production process, especially with the numerous assembly lines at the plant. Strikingly, the factory was chock full of thousands of the most modern metal-working machines. Most were new special machines for milling, grinding, and polishing metal parts and engine components. In addition, a large complement of lathes was on hand for the precision cutting operations of the skilled turners.[98]

According to factory officials, wages at Genshagen were high during the last prewar years, due to the shortage of workers which was partly the result of the factory's remote location, and partly the result of the general shortage of skilled metal workers caused by the military buildup. Nevertheless, the wages reported by the company were significantly lower than those at Daimler-Benz in Stuttgart a decade earlier. Women earned only 70 percent of what males earned for comparable work, while skilled workers generally made 12–15 percent more than the average earnings of trained machine workers. Similarly, unskilled laborers received about one-seventh less than the machine workers.[99]

A large contingent of youths, many of whom were male apprentices, were also on hand. Almost none of the 311 girls and young women under 21 years of age was an apprentice. Youths under 21 received an average of 27 to 45 pfennigs per hour for their work, only 25–40 percent of what males earned.

The Nazi presence at Genshagen was large and obtrusive. There, 150 functionaries formed the party's organization at Daimler-Benz/Genshagen in 1940, dispensing charity to the ill and propaganda about racial matters and history, often accompanied with movies. The workers may have found little time to concentrate on the lessons which party and company officials strove to impart, for they worked six days a week, nine to nine and one-half hours a day. Women, who were supposed to have a "weaker constitution," labored an hour less per day. After the outbreak of the war, Sunday work became increasingly widespread.[100]

Although hundreds of French POWs were already employed before Operation Barbarossa, the composition of the work force in Genshagen changed radically in 1941–1942.[101] The breakdown of the Blitzkrieg on the Russian steppes in late 1941, with the heavy losses in planes, vehicles, and tanks suffered by the Germans, and the subsequent economic mobilization for a total war of lengthy duration brought an influx of forced laborers from occupied Europe. On March 21, 1942, Hitler ordered his new commissioner for Labor Mobilization, the Nazi functionary Fritz Sauckel, to mobilize "all available labor-power, including recruited workers and prisoners of war." Soon, in thousands of towns, villages, and farms across Europe, German troops and occupation authorities began enlisting, inducing, and kidnapping millions of men, women, and children to work in German businesses and on German farms. By 1944, 2.4 million were working on the land and another 4.7 million in industry—a total of 7,126,000 persons, one of every five workers employed in the German economy.[102]

Tens of thousands of foreign workers came to the Daimler-Benz empire. There is some evidence that the dimensions of Daimler-Benz's utilization of foreign labor were greater in 1942 than that by other big armament firms. While 24 percent of the employees at 22 large German arms companies were foreign workers and prisoners on Sept. 1, 1942, 32.9 percent at the Mercedes-Benz concern were foreign workers and 4.3 percent were prisoners of war.[103]

In 1942, their numbers at Genshagen surpassed 6,000, nearly half of all the persons there. Of these, 2,781 were Russians. The nationalities of all the *Fremdarbeiter* are impossible to ascertain, but it can safely be assumed that most were probably from Poland and the Soviet Union. In addition, there were large contingents of French and Soviet POW's, more than 16 percent of the total by 1943.[104]

Besides Germans, forced laborers, and POW's, Daimler-Benz also employed concentration camp inmates from Sachsenhausen and Ravensbrueck at Genshagen. According to the commander of the Sachsenhausen concentration camp at Oranienburg, Anton Kaindl, Daimler-Benz requested and received 1,000 inmates for its Genshagen operations. All of them were apparently women. These slaves were part of some 15,000 camp inmates at Sachsenhausen which German firms applied for, usually through the responsible camp official, an SS-*Untersturmfeuhrer* named Rehn. Siemens, Heinkel, and Damag were among at least thirteen other firms receiving the Sachsenhausen slaves.[105]

Because of Daimler-Benz's use of inmates in its Genshagen factory, U.S. military authorities would consider bringing charges after the war against Max Wolf, one of the company's managers, under the Allied Control Council's Law No. 10, which ordered the "punishment of persons guilty of war crimes, crimes against peace and against humanity." Wolf's name appears on a list of 72 "leading industrialists, financiers, and economic figures in Nazi Germany" suspected of crimes against humanity in connection with the German war effort. Wolf's and Daimler-Benz's offense was that "Daimler employed Sachsenhausen conc. camp labor,"[106] only a portion of the company's wartime culpability from the use of such labor-power.

Daimler-Benz also used Jewish women from the concentration camp at Ravensbrueck in its Genshagen operation.[107] The detailed account of one of these, Eva Fejer from Hungary, is on file at the Wiener Library. Her experience at Daimler-Benz began in November 1944, several months after the German concentration camp system had been clogged with the Jews being deported from Hungary as part of the Final Solution. Hitler himself had given permission in the spring of 1944 for the use of Jewish-Hungarian slaves by the Fighter Planes Staff, which was coordinating the relocation of aircraft factories in gigantic underground bunkers, and which was thus in dire need of labor power to meet its production goals. About half of the available workers were women.[108]

Some time after Fejer arrived at Ravensbrueck, camp authorities summoned the prisoners for an inspection by a director of Daimler-Benz. The frightened and depressed Fejer, who knew German, served as translator for the officials on this occasion. The group selected 60 Jewish women for work at Daimler-Benz. The 17-year old Fejer testified that she had convinced the smartly dressed firm official (he was wearing a leather jacket) to include her in the work detail by telling him that she had recently worked in a machine factory—in the bicycle department of the Manfred Weiss works. The Daimler-Benz representative was impressed, and took her along.[109]

After receiving a medical examination, the women were loaded into open trucks for the trip to Genshagen. En route, the convoy drove through Berlin, which, after an aerial bombardment a short time earlier, was ringed with flames. "The burning Berlin gave us new courage; we said to ourselves that the war could not last too long," she recalled.

The sixty Jewish prisoners joined 1,000 women from Poland, the Ukraine and other parts of the Soviet Union, as well as 20 other Jews at Daimler-Benz/Genshagen. They lived in air-raid bunkers and in the factory itself. To be sure, conditions were better than at Ravensbrueck. The factory and air-raid shelters were heated, and there was even a wash-room with hot water. The women slept in bunk-beds on sacks of straw, and there was only one blanket for every two persons. Female SS-troopers guarded the workers. The SS at Daimler was not as brutal as at Ravensbrueck; the women at the plant were beaten only when they failed to obey orders.

The daily routine centered, of course, around work in the factory. The work-day was exacting. The inmates were awakened between 5:00 and 5:30 A.M. and were able to drink a kind of coffee around 6:00. At 6:30, the authorities called the roll in the factory. Fejer and her fellow prisoners worked from 7:00 to 7:00 during the first two weeks of every month, with an hour long pause at noon and a fifteen minute break at 4:00 P.M. During the third week, the work day lasted until 9:00 P.M., during the fourth week until 11:00 P.M. At 7:30 P.M., the women received a half hour break and ate their evening soup. Twice, usually at the end of the month, the workers had to toil the whole night long until noon of the following day.

The women worked in three main divisions on assembly lines building components for the Daimler-Benz airplane engines and assembling the complete motors. A few Germans were sprinkled through the plant, presumably as supervisory workmen [Einrichter]. Each main division of the complex was dominated by the assembly line, which could be worked by the concentration camp inmates. U.S. intelligence confirmed this near the end of the war, noting that "production [is] organized on a conveyor belt system with [a] high degree of labor specialization." Materials and components flowed through the plant from north to the assembly hall at the southern end of the plant.[110]

During the First World War, the assembly of Daimler's airplane motors had required hundreds, even thousands, of skilled fitters. A quarter century of industrial and technical change had radically altered the production processes at Daimler. The move from skilled metalworkers to concentration camp inmates for fitting together the components of Daimler-Benz motors is symbolic of the changes in the labor process in the German motor building industry during a half-century which was marked in production technology by the accomplishments of men like Taylor and Ford. The widely touted "German precision labor" at Daimler-Benz had become an advertising gambit; untrained women—industrial slaves—could assemble the Mercedes-Benz airplane engines.

According to the surviving account of the young Hungarian, most German workers—with the exception of a few young ones who had been "spoiled by the Hitler youth"—went out of their way to be nice to the Jewish women, even bringing them extra rations. Many seemed to be opponents of the Hitler regime. One such foreman, a man who whistled opera melodies on the job, frequently sang a heartening anti-Nazi rhyme while working next to Fejer.[111]

Fejer and the group of women inmates working at Daimler-Benz in Genshagen were moved back to Sachsenhausen in March 1945, apparently to be gassed. They survived when the camp's gas chamber failed to function while she and her colleagues were locked inside.[112]

A small group of SS members, who were being punished for transgressions they had committed in the service, provided an unusual complement of those working at Genshagen. Their superiors even punished them in front of the mainly foreign-born work force, who invariably regarded the degradation of the SS troops as entertainment. A Daimler-Benz official, Werner Romstedt, complained about this practice, apparently fearing that the foreign workers and prisoners of war would lose respect for the SS troops. As his report noted, the foreign workers and POW's "stand inside the fence and watch the thing with smiles." This elicited sharp protests from top SS officials, who issued instructions that no German soldier be punished in front of foreigners. As the furious SS General Gottlob Berger wrote, "The English have ruled the world for 300 years; never has a foreigner been allowed to watch the punishment of English soldiers."[113]

The removal of the big factories in the airplane motor industry to fortified bunkers, caves, or quarries got underway in the face of the Allied bombing blitz of 1944. The Fighter Staff ordered the dispersal of 27 main airplane plants to 729 small plants. Many Daimler-Benz works were subsequently relocated, and a chain of concentration camps attached to Natzweiler—Mannheim-Sandhofen, Wesserling-Urbis, A 10, Neckarelz—filled with prisoners in Baden and Wuerttemberg.[114]

The biggest of the operations, supervised by the SS, was the removal of most of the Genshagen facility to a large gypsum quarry near Neckarelz. The big subterranean factory, code-named Goldfisch, was to produce the major engine components, such as crankshafts, cylinder heads, and connecting rods for shipment to Genshagen, where the final assembly of the engines continued.[115] Thousands of foreign workers and concentration camp inmates under the leadership of Director Mueller performed the difficult and dangerous excavation and moving operations, and many died.

Operation Goldfisch was plagued by a myriad of problems, among them being the poor productivity of the concentration camp inmates. Finally, in March 1945, Daimler-Benz and Director Mueller, disgusted by these sick and starving "do-nothings" [Faulenzer], offered to pay the SS 10,000 marks

for the removal *[Abtransportierung]* of their concentration camp inmates.[116]
The Goldfisch operation and much of the Daimler-Benz empire had ground
to a halt.

RZESZOW (REICHSHOF) & VIENNA: FOLLOWING THE FLAG

As economic mobilization for a lengthy war got underway in the second half
of 1941, the German regime gave Daimler-Benz two important facilities for
producing airplane motors. One was in the Generalgouvernement (GG) at
Rzeszow (Reichshof) in Galicia, about 130 kilometers east of Krakow, while
the other lay on the outskirts of Vienna.

With its takeover of the Rzeszow operation, Daimler-Benz joined the
plundering of occupied Poland in a big way. Rzeszow lay in an area which
the National Socialists intended to "re-Germanize" after the war. Between
1939 and 1941, the streets were given German names, and governor Hans
Frank ordered the city renamed "Reichshof," its name during the Habsburg
monarchy. After director Haspel inspected the facilities, the board of directors greeted the company's success in acquiring the new factory, which was
"well-furnished . . . [with] a useful core work-force."[117]

Throughout Galicia in 1942, labor became scarce and difficult to obtain,
especially after Sauckel, the regime's official for organizing the forced labor
programs, increased the pressure to ship Polish workers to factories in the
west. Thus, even as the extermination of the area's large Jewish population
got underway in earnest, a labor shortage threatened to cripple war production in the Generalgouvernement.[118]

By the summer of 1942, Daimler-Benz requested Jewish forced laborers
for its Reichshof factory, but initially none were available. In mid-July, the
German authorities invited the factory's officials to "participate in the next
combing-out action in the neighboring Debica region."[119] A few days later,
a company official left Reichshof with three or four trucks and drove to
Debica, where 5,000 Jews from the town's ghetto had been herded together
by the SS to be deported to Belzec. The official later described it as "a real
market for human beings," for a number of other corporations were also on
the scene seeking slaves. As the Daimler-Benz manager later recalled:

> I sought out the Jews according to their physical condition. I generally
> chose the younger men, for I thought that they would be physically and
> mentally suited to our work on the machines. . . . The Jews were supposed
> to be employed in separate work places, but were not supposed to be
> given difficult manual labor. . . . Inevitably, I separated [the workers] from

their families. Shattering scenes transpired. . . . The Jews had their belongings with them. The SS men were equipped with wooden batons and struck the Jews.[120]

As the Daimler-Benz official watched, the deportation of the inhabitants of the Debica ghetto to Belzec got underway.

After several additional "combing out actions" in the regions near Przemysl and Debica in late July and early August in which about 100,000 persons from the surrounding area were deported to Belzec and killed, Daimler-Benz/Reichshof built up its work force to 390 Jewish forced laborers.[121] Thus, when these forced laborers arrived at their new jobs at the Reichshof factory without belongings, they had just been separated from their families and friends for good during raids which were part of the "final solution" in the GG.

The company had hurriedly erected its own camp for them, "so that," in the words of the factory's construction report, "100 Jews are housed in a 30-man barracks." Two brick ovens warmed each barracks, while the nearly 400 men shared two portable toilets. Two barbed wire barriers enclosed the perimeter of the barracks,[122] and SS troops and plant security "guarded" the camp.[123] Daimler-Benz's Jews were isolated from the two ghettos in Rzeszow, one for other workers, the other for elderly men, women, and children.

The Jews worked and lived apart from the others at the factory. The corporation placed nearly all of them in "productive work and in productive departments," indicating that they performed the tasks of skilled and trained (machine) workers. About 100 worked in the assembly halls, while another group worked on the special machines. They received nothing for their efforts. As the company's guidelines specified, "The Jews receive 80 percent of the wages paid to Polish workers. . . . The wages are to be handed over to the police."[124] At the same time, there were about 300–400 German workers at Daimler-Benz/Reichshof, as well as more than 3000 Poles.[125]

The Jews were subject to outrages at the hands of company officials and SS guards. Daimler-Benz's leader of the labor office at the factory, Helmut Lafferenz, killed three brothers in September 1942 after they apparently hesitated to obey a work command. Lafferenz played a sadistic game with the three, shooting and then murdering the brothers in front of a group of Jewish slaves.[126] There were other murders—at least five others—by company officials or SS men at the Reichshof factory, often preceded by torture sessions. Some of these had apparently been precipitated by escape attempts.[127] Others were sadistic episodes perpetrated by zealots at Daimler-Benz.[128]

The killings of Jewish slaves by company personnel in occupied Poland were the product of a uniquely ugly racism. At the same time, they marked the low point in the brutal deterioration of the business's increasingly instrumental attitude toward those working in its factories, a downward spiral which had begun a quarter century before, but which now assumed an entirely different quality with the influx of Jews and inmates into its facilities.

By mid-November, the number of Jews had reached 500. There is reason to believe that the Nazi authorities had intended to deport them to Belzec around November 18, 1942, but this did not happen.[129] The authorities apparently spared most or all of Daimler-Benz's Jewish slaves in 1943 when the National Socialists liquidated the Rzeszow ghettos. Some of the firm's German employees from Untertuerkheim watched as the ghetto residents were herded directly past the factory gates to the train station and witnessed mass killings as the SS murdered up to 500 persons during the nightmarish march to the train and deportation. The only other thing which can be said with any certainty about Daimler-Benz's use of Jewish forced laborers at Reichshof is that they numbered 334 in the summer of 1943 at the beginning of the factory's last year of operation, and that any Jews remaining in the Reichshof area were supposed to be killed when the Soviet offensive in the summer of 1944 which burst into Galicia forced the evacuation of the area factories before stalling east of the town. Some, however, survived the war.[130]

For the Poles, wages were low, and living and working conditions were harsh. The officer supervising the local armaments factories, including Flugmotorenwerke Reichshof, lamented the general situation in the area in early 1943: "A single man needs 800 zlotny monthly for a barely adequate life, and a married man with children [needs] 1200 zlotny, while the highest wage [in the area] amounts to only 320 zlotny."[131] Although the Poles were not work slaves, an undetermined number died at the hands of the authorities in Reichshof.[132]

The ranking Daimler-Benz man on the scene, Werner Romstedt, who had been the DAF's and Himmler's candidate to take over leadership of the concern in Stuttgart, won the attention of the top German officials in the GG for the company's accomplishments. "In labor discipline and in our method of leading men, particularly in handling the foreign workers [fremdvoelkischer Belegschaftskraefte], we set the pace in the whole GG," a company official boasted.[133] In addition, Romstedt alleged that there had never been a single case of sabotage at the plant, a claim which the existence of a vigorous resistance movement among Poles at the plant casts into doubt.[134]

Hans Frank, the governor of this region of occupied Poland and one of the chief architects of the extermination of the Polish Jews,[135] visited Daimler-Benz/Reichshof in early 1944 and allegedly described it as *"the* model factory" in the GG.[136]

Daimler-Benz's production of airplane motors and parts in Reichshof totaled 14 million marks in 1942, 19 million in 1943, and more than 10 million in the first half of 1944. In light of the rock-bottom wage-costs, the Mercedes factory in the GG may have turned a profit for the company.[137]

Four months later, the Soviets drove into the region. Romstedt and Daimler-Benz evacuated the factory on July 26, 1944.[138] The personnel manager at Reichshof, Rahmig, moved on to Kolmar in Alsace and then to the east German city of Kamenz, where the Kolmar factory was relocated in the closing months of 1944 as the Americans swept across France. It is possible that parts of the Reichshof factory also wound up in Kamenz, although no proof of this is available.

Daimler-Benz's makeshift operation at Kamenz also employed concentration camp inmates, apparently from Gross-Rosen and Flossenbuerg.[139] In the early months of 1945, SS doctors allegedly murdered an estimated 60 or 70 prisoners in Kamenz who were too ill or too weak to work by injecting them with poison. After the war, a report noted that Rahmig as well as the factory doctor Neste had been summarily tried for crimes against the inmates working in Kamenz and shipped off to the Soviet Union.[140]

The second, even larger jewel fell into Daimler-Benz's grasp in late 1941, inducing the company's chairman to hail one of the great events in the corporation's history. This was the Flugmotorenwerke Ostmark with facilities near Vienna and in Bruenn, which the regime transferred from Junkers to Daimler-Benz. According to the plans of the Daimler-Benz directors, the factories would produce 1,000 Mercedes airplane motors a month, with deliveries scheduled to begin in early 1943. Although the company and the Air Ministry threw millions of marks into the project, the scarcity of skilled workers and the poor performance of the thousands of prisoners of war, Czech and Croatian workers brought in to build up and work in the plants disrupted Daimler-Benz's efforts to bring the complex on line.[141] Goering's growing anger with the situation at the Flugmotorenwerke Ostmark—he called it a "pigsty" during a January 1943 inspection—led to the dismissal of officials and to the exodus of several Mercedes executives from the board running the project.[142]

The new chief, Meindl, had run the Steyr production facilities at the Mauthausen concentration camp, and his task was to get the production lines rolling as quickly as possible. He put his experience at Steyr/Mauthausen to use; in late July 1943, he requested a thousand slaves from the SS for the construction work and another thousand who could be used in metalworking operations. The first 201 concentration camp inmates arrived in early August, and the barracks in which the construction workers had lived itself became a concentration camp.[143] This camp at Wiener Neustadt contained between 1,700 and 3,000 inmates until it was evacuated in March 1945.[144] Many of these prisoners worked at the Flugmotorenwerke Ostmark, while others toiled in neighboring factories. Inmates from the camp at Wien-Schwechat also helped build the Daimler-Benz airplane motors on the outskirts of Vienna.[145] Although Meindl's leadership tended to limit the influence of the directors in Untertuerkheim, Daimler-Benz remained responsible for production, and the factory was one of the most critical in the corporation's airplane motor complex, or "ring," as it was termed.[146]

STUTTGART-UNTERTUERKHEIM

The Daimler-Benz factory in Stuttgart-Untertuerkheim, backbone for the provisioning of the German air force in the First World War, again played an important role in supplying the German war machine. It was a center for the research and development of airplane motors for bombers and fighters; more than a third of its employees worked in R & D. Trucks, automobiles, motors for coastal patrol boats, a few airplane motors, and spare parts for these and for Dornier planes were also produced in Untertuerkheim. U.S. intelligence described the facility as a collection of assembly lines and machine parks, with a foundry for light metals and a small forge.[147]

The plant maintained a workforce of 13,000 to 15,000 persons during World War II. The composition of the Daimler-Benz workforce changed markedly in the conflict. During 1941, the first foreign workers began to arrive. By early 1942, there were 1,400 at Daimler-Benz in Stuttgart, out of a total of 14,000 workers. In addition, 1,670 German women worked at the plant in January 1942, approximately the same share as in 1940. Several hundred persons listed as prisoners of war also moved into the plant, but the total apparently never exceeded 500.[148]

The biggest change in the work force in Untertuerkheim occurred in 1942 and 1943, with the importation of nearly 4,000 additional foreign workers, the largest contingents coming from the occupied areas of the Soviet Union.[149] The labor shortage hit hard, and Daimler-Benz pleaded for more workers (300 in June 1941, then 560 in September).[150] Finally, chairman Kissel dispatched a request for an aide to arrange for a share of the new reservoir of labor-power which had recently opened up in the east: "I was very interested about your report on the Leningrad refugees. . . . [Tell me] how I can arrange it so that our company and above all the Untertuerkheim factory can receive as many as possible." Apparently, he succeeded. A month later, Kissel sought another infusion of "Russian civilian workers."[151]

By the end of 1942, the number of foreign workers increased by 2,598, while 853 fewer Germans worked in Untertuerkheim than at the beginning of that year. By the summer of 1944, 1,200 of the foreigners were Soviet women. The scale of foreign labor, nearly always imported by force or even kidnapped,[152] in the production process at Daimler-Benz in Stuttgart was even greater than the statistics generated by the company (32.6 percent for 1944 and early 1945) show. If the nearly 5,000 working on the research and the development of new motors are excluded, the percentage of *Fremdarbeiter* producing motors and spare parts probably greatly exceeded 50 percent from 1943 to early 1945.

The number of German women at Daimler-Benz in Untertuerkheim increased by only 460 by August 1944, to 2,130. Hitler himself instructed industry to refrain from the full-scale introduction of women into the factories. As a secret account prepared for Chairman Kissel of the instructions laid down by Hitler and General Schell declared, "The Fuehrer has decided that the German woman should not come to the fore in the labor process as up until now."[153] Thus, neither the numbers of women working at the plant during World War II nor their share in the total work force ever reached the levels of the First World War, and are a striking indication of the degree to which one of the Reich's resources—women—remained confined to the family front during the "total" war. "The nazi regime consistently attached a peculiar importance to family, domesticity and child-bearing. . . . [T]he removal of women from political life and the attempts to restrict employment were an integral part of the general attack on liberalism, and in the eyes of the ideologues the raising of the birth-rate had an important place in the strategy for the racial superiority of the German people."[154] In addition, keeping women in the home was also intended to prevent the kind of social unrest which led to the revolution of November 9, 1918, and the "stab in the back" of conservative and Nazi legends.

The working hours in the Stuttgart factory were 11 hours on weekdays, eight hours on Saturdays, and four hours on Sundays. Only 15 percent toiled on Sundays. The night shift was practically nonexistent in Untertuerkheim, with a mere 5 percent working during the evening or at night.[155] This was also a marked departure from the situation prevailing there during the First World War, when night shifts were an important feature of factory life.

Though detailed statistics on absenteeism among workers are lacking, the U.S. intelligence fixed the figure after the war at a "fairly constant" 15 percent. This was twice the rate of World War I. Due to the lack of available sources, it is not possible to generalize with certainty about the frequency of absenteeism among foreign workers, but the reports of industry officials indicate that German workers missed work much more frequently than did foreign workers.[156] If this was also true at Daimler-Benz in Stuttgart, then the absentee-rate for Germans may have on average surpassed the peaks from World War I registered in July 1918 during the influenza outbreaks which came on the heels of the dispute between workers and army in June 1918.

Daimler-Benz's foreign workers were housed in 70 facilities around the Stuttgart area. Many of these were barracks complexes. Up to 1,200 mainly Russian laborers lived in the 13 barracks "Im Kies" in Stuttgart-Hedelfingen. About 500 Russians slept in a barracks complex in the *Gengenerstrasse* in Wangen. Daimler-Benz spent more than a million marks to build housing for 1,350 guest workers in the Rosensteinpark, the wooded *Buerger* promenade in Stuttgart between the railway station and the Neckar River. The school in Fellbach became a barracks for the foreign workers brought into Germany to work at Daimler-Benz.[157] Even the Music Hall in Untertuerkheim, where the Daimler workers' movement had held many a mass meeting for social justice during the three decades of its existence, became a barracks for a group of Soviet women.[158] Seventy-eight French workers were crowded into quarters in Luginsland, the colony built by Daimler workers in the 1910s and 1920s.

More than 230 employees looked after the foreign workers and the barracks in which they lived. These included cooks, cleaning personnel, fumigators, and two doctors. In the almost four years that foreign workers were at Daimler-Benz, the firm paid these personnel 2.9 million marks, much more than it paid the thousands of men and women deported from the occupied regions of Europe.

There was another group of workers, invisible in the company's documents, who also "serviced" Daimler-Benz's foreign workers—women forced into prostitution. The government's documents are clear: all German companies employing foreign laborers in Germany were directed by the regime to open brothels in or near the laborers' barracks. The Nazis had, of course, cracked down hard on prostitution in the 1930s, attacking it as "asocial" and a degradation of German womanhood. According to Nazi guidelines, women from each of the eastern national contingents or gypsies were to be pressed into prostitution by the German corporations operating the bordellos for the barracks. The goal of this officially sanctioned prostitution was to prevent "the endangering of German blood" through sexual contacts between the German and east European populations. Although it is not clear how the official orders were translated into practice at Daimler-Benz's facilities, there is no evidence of widespread corporate defiance of this or of any other regulation pertaining to foreign labor inside Germany during World War II. What is clear is that for at least some of the foreign women brought to Germany, the exploitation to which they were subjected reached astonishing extremes: virtual work-slaves for German industry, they were now forced to be sex-slaves for their countrymen. Thus, for the industrial firms of wartime Nazi Germany, women of the "subhuman races" became members of a "subhuman gender." In Nazi racial and sexual apartheid, their class and their race created an extraordinarily unique and acute experience.[159]

The firm's foreign workers in Stuttgart were supposed to receive a payment of one mark per day. The head of Daimler-Benz's department for foreigners in Untertuerkheim later estimated that an average of 3,390 foreigners were employed between 1941 and 1944, and that to clothe, feed, house, and watch them, the firm spent about 9.6 million marks from mid-1941 to May 1945. Thus, a reasonable estimate is that Daimler-Benz spent approximately 710 marks a year per person in employing foreign workers during World War II at Untertuerkheim. During the same years, the firm probably paid one of its workers 2,500–3,000 marks annually in wages, with hundreds of additional marks in social benefits. Whatever the productivity of the foreign workers (and there is reason to believe that it was good), the men and women deported from occupied Europe were a good bargain for Daimler-Benz's operations in Untertuerkheim, perhaps even better than the thousands of women used during the labor-power shortage from 1914–1918.

One out of every three foreign workers came from the Soviet Union. More than 1,600 hailed from France, and other large contingents were from occupied Czechoslovakia, Holland, Italy, Armenia, Poland, and Belgium. The youngest worker was 12 years old, the oldest 68.

Little can be said with certainty about the lives of these Daimler-Benz workers. A company official later asserted that 50 of its French workers housed at a barracks in Sillenbuch were provided each day with 200 grams of meat, 100 grams of cereal, 50 grams of lard, and 50 grams of bread, with coffee in the mornings. Daimler-Benz's foreign workers also had the opportunity to turn their attention to propaganda books, newspapers, and movies in their spare time. Because of the dearth of available evidence, one can only imagine how dreary the lives of these men and women were while working at the Third Reich's military giant in Untertuerkheim.

Likewise, little is known about the firm's police, or about the Gestapo and DAF personnel who controlled and disciplined Daimler-Benz's foreign workers. A firm official in Untertuerkheim claimed after the war that the beating of these workers had been strictly forbidden. Nevertheless, the subsequent leader of the trade union IG Metall in Untertuerkheim reported after the war that Daimler-Benz treated foreign workers "brusquely" and beat them.[160]

The employment of seven million forced laborers from occupied Europe in the German economy during World War II seems unimaginable without the entire range of labor policies pursued under the Nazis—repression and rationalization—which were part of a strategy (not overwhelmingly successful) to "unmake" the German working class and to draw working people into a racist "social contract" founded on the plundering of Europe and the destruction of eastern peoples and the Jews. The forced exploitation of millions of Europeans by German firms and their existence within the Reich in an apartheid of strictly policed barracks and ghettos meant that the National Socialist racial hierarchy of masters and subhumans became a universal feature of daily life. This strictly enforced racial separation became central to the everyday experience of the German working class from 1941 to 1945 and to the workers of the Daimler-Benz factories in Stuttgart-Untertuerkheim, Sindelfingen, Mannheim, Berlin-Marienfelde, Genshagen and elsewhere. In the words of a historian:

> Competition over domination formed the material practice of the Third Reich. As de Tocqueville put it, 'a despot easily forgives his subjects for not loving him, provided they do not love each other.' The latter—love, trust, solidarity—indeed were in short supply among the Germans, and solidarity with the dominated became treason. Equality for all Germans in a new *Volksgemeinschaft;* freedom as participation in domination; egotism in the interest of the 'common good'—these were the ideological essentials of the Nazi state, which did not require that everyone become a Nazi as long as the National Socialist leadership could convince Germans of the benefits of racist rule.[161]

Judged in this light, the production facilities of the Daimler-Benz A.G. in Germany and occupied Europe richly deserved the honored gold flags as "model factories *[Musterbetriebe]*" which the DAF solemnly and ceremoniously bestowed on them many times during the Third Reich.*

WARTIME TESTS: THE BOMBING AND THE BATTLE OF THE MERCEDES SUCCESSION

The air war intruded into Daimler-Benz's main works on four occasions. The British Royal Air Force attacked the plant for the first time on the night of November 26/27, 1943. Thirty-eight bombs fell on the factory, destroying an estimated 18 percent of the built-up area, and 3.2 percent of the plant's machinery. Production was hardly disturbed. Similarly ineffective were the RAF's raids on February 20/21 and March 1/2, 1944. A total of 25 bombs hit the plant, doing little significant damage.[162]

---

* In June 1988, forty-three years after the Allies liberated the last of its forced laborers, Daimler-Benz informed the Red Cross that it would distribute DM 20 million to survivors. Daimler-Benz's announcement marked a change in corporate policy: in January 1987, the firm had informed an aging former concentration camp inmate that "no individual compensation" would be paid to him or to other survivors (letter in possession of author).

The Americans had better luck. The 8th Air Force's raid by 193 B-17 Flying Fortresses on September 5, 1944, devastated wide areas of the factory, completely destroying 41 percent of the built-up area in Untertuerkheim, and killed 68 people. The bombs put many machines out of action—12.7 percent of the plant's machinery was destroyed outright and another 43 percent suffered significant damage, but it must be remembered that much of the factory's plant had already been dispersed to 14 small locations in Wuerttemberg.[163]

Hardest hit, however, were the facilities in which the research and development departments—working on designs for revolutionary long-range bombers which would hit American cities, by some accounts—were headquartered.[164] Many of these areas received numerous direct hits, and work came to a halt for six full weeks. The devastation of Daimler-Benz's R & D departments meant that the firm's updated DB 603 L engine could not be brought into mass production before the war ended, although by the late summer of 1944, the Reich's position was already hopeless.[165]

In light of the evidence, it seems unassailable to contend that Daimler-Benz maintained a decisive level of control over its own affairs during National Socialism. The chairman of the company until 1942, Wilhelm Kissel, commanded wide respect in both business and party circles. By any measure, Kissel was an esteemed businessman, having guided the company, along with the Deutsche Bank's Stauss, to the pinacle of industrial power in the new order. He contributed prominently to a National Socialist artists' group. He sat on the board which supervised German radio's external propaganda broadcasts. He rubbed elbows with top directors from Krupp, I.G. Farben, and the Vereinigte Stahlwerke on the industrial association's Tax Committee, and, later, the Colonial Committee, dreaming their fantastic dreams of planning "to cover the future needs of the German colonies" in the heady late summer months of 1941.[166]

At the same time, Kissel championed the new order in his own corporation. An official of the DAF assessed Kissel's contribution to National Socialism in glowing terms:

> Kissel set himself the goal of developing a single National Socialist model business out of Daimler-Benz. The company was on the best way to this goal. Through the five gold flags and 25 achievement diplomas were not only the social achievements of the company recognized, but even more the economic accomplishments and with them the achievements of the corporation in the political interests of the people's community.[167]

In the summer of 1942, Kissel died. His death set the stage for a bitter clash over Daimler-Benz's choice to head the firm, but Daimler-Benz—with the help of allies at the very apex of Nazi power—prevailed in an illuminating display of the balance of power within a key sector of the German economy.

Daimler-Benz's boards of trustees and directors chose one of their own, Wilhelm Haspel, who managed Daimler-Benz's relations with the Luftwaffe, as Kissel's successor. Although Haspel's performance in this capacity was praised by friend and foe alike, he had never joined the party or any of its associated organizations. Furthermore, his wife, Greta Schwab, was half-Jewish, a fact which infuriated party and DAF officials.[168]

Using as intermediaries Jakob Werlin, the Fuehrer's personal friend, and Stauss, the banker who chaired the board of trustees and who was well-connected with numerous Nazi luminaries, the Daimler-Benz board of directors received the personal blessings of a number of top Nazis for the new arrangement, which included the retention of board member Carl Werner, the Mannheim factory's leading officer, whose wife was Jewish. Werner had distinguished himself by aiding the NSDAP before 1933 by illegally providing motor vehicles for its election campaigns, although he himself was not a party member.[169] For reasons which had more to do with the need to shore up the industrial front than gratitude for past service, Hitler and Goering approved of the changes.[170]

The prospect of racially "tainted," and thus, according to DAF logic, unreliable businessmen running Daimler-Benz was more than an influential group of ultras in the DAF and SS could stand. At the end of August, leading officials from these organizations, including Dickwach, protested the new personnel arrangement, and enlisted the assistance of SS-chief Heinrich Himmler in a campaign to overturn the decision at Daimler-Benz. As SS-officer Gottlob Berger asserted in a letter to Himmler: "For the DAF, it is a battle of decisive importance, because here will be shown whether the DAF and thus the party has something to say in such personnel matters or whether they can be arranged according to old procedures of the board of directors, regardless of how it is oriented to the Third Reich."[171]

Himmler was quickly convinced. He wrote director Werlin that he personally considered the presence of Haspel, Werner, and a third firm official, Hoppe—also with a Jewish wife—"an affront to the National Socialist state." He announced that he would intervene with Goering and Hitler "if this arrangement is not immediately changed."[172]

Neither Dickwachn nor Himmler charged that Haspel or the others had actually done anything at Daimler-Benz to injure or impede the Reich's war effort. Their complaints were racist and ideological. Haspel's "Jewish relation" [juedische Versippung] made him unsuitable to lead this National Socialist "model business." What was at stake was no less than the faith and confidence of the rank-and-file Nazis at the firm, who marched behind Daimler-Benz's *Fuehrer* in the struggle to realize "the National Socialist idea of work."

"For a National Socialist model factory, the point is not merely the unobjectionable functioning of the objective world *[Sachwelt]* or the realization of partial ideals," but the complete realization of the Nazi factory model with its leadership principle, the DAF's Dickwach wrote. Charging that Daimler-Benz's board of directors was, in the wake of Kissel's death, "nothing other than a democratic institution," the DAF official demanded that the "leadership principle of National Socialism" be resurrected at Daimler-Benz. The directors' decision must be rescinded.[173]

Two weeks after their campaign surfaced, and with no real chance of converting Hitler or Goering to their side, Haspel's detractors apparently changed their tactics. They now took up the cry for the creation of dual-power at the firm. They demanded that a devout Nazi director at Daimler-Benz, Romstedt, be made "leader" of Daimler-Benz, with the tainted Haspel being allowed to continue to handle business affairs. Romstedt, the SS alleged, was Kissel's own choice as successor, but he had not been able to arrange the orderly transfer of power before his death. DAF and the SS credited Romstedt with playing a critical role in spreading the National Socialist spirit at Daimler-Benz. He was their candidate to consolidate and expand their influence in the post-Kissel era, even if they grudgingly accepted that Haspel would have to play a key role in guiding the firm. "If Dr. Haspel refrains from leadership matters *[Menschen-Fuehrungsfragen]*, then there is nothing to object to if he, as a member of the board of directors, takes over the economic post" at the side of the factory leader.

The DAF men took the opportunity to complain about Daimler-Benz's general lack of cooperation with their mega-bureaucracy since Kissel's death and sought to place the current dispute within that context. "Dr. Kissel had given his whole effort to work with the party and DAF;" now the board of directors, especially Jakob Werlin, who headed another Nazi formation, the motor transport agency, frequently obstructed their work. DAF now feared that all of its work at Daimler-Benz was "being wiped out with one stroke."[174]

The camps in the clash over the leadership of Daimler-Benz in the summer of 1942 were clearly demarcated. On the one side were the DAF officials and the radicals in the party; on the other were those working with other Nazi organizations and the German military, and, apparently, nearly all Daimler-Benz officials. It must be emphasized that at no time did the controversy revolve around Haspel's loyalty to either Hitler or National Socialism. Indeed, Hitler himself, always a Daimler-Benz fan, sided early on with the recommendations of Speer and Goering that Haspel be permitted to assume the helm at Daimler-Benz despite his marriage to a "half-Jew." Although

Hans Huschke, and not Romstedt, eventually become nominal "factory leader," the direction of the firm was left to Haspel and his colleagues on the board of directors. (Subsequently, Romstedt was entrusted with the Reichshof factory, demonstrating the importance of that facility for Mercedes-Benz.) Haspel later claimed that Romstedt behaved responsibly and acted "like anything but a party comrade" in his service for the company at Untertuerkheim.[175]

There is evidence, however, that the SS kept the firm, Werlin, and perhaps other directors under close surveillance after the affair, perhaps because Himmler had failed to sustain his position that Haspel and the others must go.[176] Nevertheless, there is no evidence that Daimler-Benz encountered any difficulties in obtaining concentration camp inmates for its works from the SS. In the partial documentation that survives, there are records of shipments of slaves into the Mercedes empire during 1944 from Auschwitz, Natzweiler, Sachsenhausen, and Ravensbrueck.[177]

Haspel, who himself wanted to loose the secret police on a difficult business colleague, continued to be harrassed by the Gestapo. Exasperated by the treatment he received, he offered to give up his position in the key General Committee on the production of motors, which coordinated this vital sector of the war economy. In late 1944, he and his colleague Werner faced induction into the armed forces because of their wives' racially "tainted" status, but the personal intervention of Speer and Hitler spared them once again. Hitler, in his conversation with Speer on November 4, 1944, stipulated that "Dr. Haspel and Dr. Werner should remain in their positions until the end of the war and that in no way should disadvantages develop for them because of their Jewish relations."[178]

The Haspel affair shows the extent to which a key segment of the *Wirtschaft* retained controls of its own affairs during World War II. The SS recognized this in the dispute with Daimler-Benz, and complained that a larger issue had been irreversibly decided. An SS official asserted that "heavy industry has won," even if "the *Fuehrer* continues to talk to the German nation about the Jews."[179]

The Daimler-Benz affair in the late summer of 1942 highlighted the critical importance of war production over almost everything (the murder of the Jews being an exception), coordinated by Speer's armaments ministry at the cost of other Nazi institutions, in this case the German Labor Front and the SS. The system of committees and rings coordinating war production was an effective regulative instrument guided by hundreds of businessmen and experts. "Outside" influences—in this case, the DAF and SS—were increasingly pushed back and kept away from the military-industrial complex.[180] Daimler-Benz could remain master in its own house, even if the house had been largely built by National Socialist military spending.

■

The Allies occupied the workplaces of the Mercedes firm in April and May 1945. The company had hurriedly deposited its German moneys in Stuttgart in the closing phase of the war. Committees of anti-fascist workers—Social Democrats, Communists, and independent Socialists, 85 percent of whom were skilled workers over 40 years of age—sprang up amidst the ruins of the factories in greater Stuttgart. But power lay with the occupation troops. The Americans, who had seized the factories in Untertuerkheim and Mannheim, used the Mercedes network of factories and workshops to repair their tanks, trucks, and jeeps, and to produce three-ton trucks and smaller vehicles. In addition, Daimler-Benz soon erected a large new repair shop in Waiblingen near Stuttgart for the Americans.[181] Mercedes was no longer the marshaller of foreign workers and concentration camp slaves, no longer the pillar of the Hitlerian war machine. The new line in Untertuerkheim soon found expression in a company document submitted to the American occupation authorities: "The firm has always followed the tendency not to enter a war production program but to concentrate on automobile production."[182]

The Nazi "model company" had become—almost without missing a beat—a valuable servant of the American military. For Daimler-Benz, a kind of political-economic miracle had begun.

CONCLUSIONS

I N early April 1938, on the occasion of the plebiscite on the annexation of Austria, Chairman Kissel sent a broadside to his colleagues in German industry in support of Hitler and the achievements of National Socialism. It was an extraordinarily self-confident performance. His appeal amounted to a rendering of the history of his company and his industry. "Remember the time when your factories were filled with discord and conflict, when your work forces were disrupted by Marxist theories and principles, when power and intelligence were wasted in an all-consuming conflict, and work was viewed as an evil to be avoided, when mistrust and agitation, frictions, lack of discipline and resistance were the order of the day, and an inner division made people unhappy and unfree," the Daimler-Benz chairman began his resumé. "Think about how the works and factories suffered from the lack of work, how the [factory] halls and rooms became ever more desolate, how the machines lay idle, the sales volume declined and businesses collapsed. Chaos was on the doorstep. No business executive will forget the time in which the disruption by the parties and the doings of the trade unions made impossible the unity and concentration of forces in the factories."

Now, everything had been transformed. A new *Werksgemeinschaft* had been forged, while Germany's workshops were busy in the continuing economic upswing. All this was the work of the *Fuehrer*, Kissel declared, and all Germans "for all times" were obliged to recognize their debt of thanks to him and his accomplishment. All should cast their "Yes!" vote in the plebiscite and thus "express our unsolvable bond with him and with his work!"[1]

Kissel's polemics represented the official line at Daimler-Benz between 1933 and 1945. He certainly erred in casting the work force and labor movement as the disruptive villains in the history of Daimler. At a time when poisonous revisions of the German past are circulating among historians and the public, let us again look back.

After it opened in December 1903, the Stuttgart factory of the Daimler-Motoren-Gesellschaft was a collection of workshops in which large contingents of skilled metal workers and machinists, along with about 150 professional woodworkers, upholsters and painters, produced the components for the Mercedes luxury and sporting cars and assembled the vehicles. It was the most celebrated auto factory in Germany in the years before World War I.

While an industrial and transport revolution was transforming North America, Daimler and the German auto industry went their own special way in the early twentieth century. Confined to the periphery of German society before World War I, Daimler never produced more than 1,500 autos a year in its large factory in Untertuerkheim. Serial or mass production—viewed as vulgarly American—remained out of the question as long as no mass market for autos existed. Unlike the typical prewar German auto factory, which was "a jumble of types, tiny lots which were sent back and forth between departments, interrupted and torn up for acquiring spare parts,"[2] Daimler's plant was essentially rational, if not yet "scientific" in Frederick W. Taylor's sense.

The Ford revolution failed to spark a similar transformation in production methods in Germany. Nevertheless, Daimler sought to improve its position in the German auto industry. Led by the Hamburg businessman Berge and the Stuttgart banker Kaulla, Daimler instituted measures to tighten the central control of the acquisition of materials and labor and of the production processes. The new profile of the central office with its expanded card-filing system, the outfitting office, and the toolmaking department demonstrated the company's commitment to improving its efficiency in the wake of the crisis of 1907–1908 and in the face of competition from other German companies. At the same time, the acquisition of more special machines—above all, milling and grinding machines and revoiving and automatic lathes—set the pace in the attempt to substitute cheaper machine workers for the dearer, skilled labor-power wherever possible. Daimler achieved a measure of success in the decade before the outbreak of the First World War: production almost doubled in Untertuerkheim without any significant increase in the employment of skilled labor.

While Ford had "no use for experience, in the working ranks, anyway,"[3]

Daimler's skilled workers retained their dominant position in the production processes before the war. Drawn from the small Swabian villages near the Neckar between Plochingen and Ludwigsburg, many of them settled in the working class neighborhoods of Unter- and Obertuerkheim, Wangen, Ostheim, Gaisburg, and Bad Cannstatt. Daimler workers were diligent members of the German Metalworkers' Union, the largest trade union in the Kaiserreich. In the struggles of the prewar era, they broke new ground and attained modest improvements in working conditions: shorter working hours, higher wages, and a grievance procedure for settling disputes over piece-wages. Skilled handworkers and turners, and trained machine workers alike participated in the factory struggles of 1905–1906, 1910, and 1911. Solidarity and optimism about the future were as much features of the workers' movement at Daimler as the practical demands concerning wages and working conditions. Labor strove for the *aufrechten Gang;* it struggled to "stand tall." In all, at a time when German labor was under fire from militant employers in other industries, the union was satisfied with what it had accomplished, and numbered Untertuerkheim as one of the modestly progressive car plants in Germany. By 1914, the moderate trade unionists and Social Democrats Salm and Schifferdecker headed a stable workers' leadership at Daimler.

The First World War drew Daimler for the first time to the center of the imperial military-industrial complex. Daimler sent the German military into the heavens, building almost 20,000 powerful airplane engines as one of the high-priority German factories for the war effort. Mass production, even without a revolution in the production processes, and a duplicitous pricing policy meant enormous, unprecedented profits for the firm and fueled a huge expansion of the facilities, the machine plant, and the work force. Thousands of women workers helped for the first time in the production processes, while more than 5,000 skilled and machine workers returned from the front in the service of Daimler's military aviation project.

Ad hoc contacts between representatives of the company, the trade unions, and the German army (which was very interested in developments at Mercedes) grew more intense between 1915 and 1918. Workers' representatives voiced frequent complaints about wage rates, working hours, and the high-handed practices of management. General von Schaefer's staff and the authorities from the aviation department of the War Ministry in Berlin often accepted the validity of the workers' committees complaints, usually infuriating Berge and his associates in the process. But the triangle at Daimler was a temporary, day-to-day relationship, not a new system of political and industrial relations designed to survive the war.

In the wake of the Daimler scandal in the late winter of 1918, the situation in Untertuerkheim rapidly deteriorated on all fronts. Most portentous was the new sullen, bitter mood of the workers, who pushed aside their moderate leadership for the first time in June 1918 to openly defy the military authorities at Daimler. Even when it seemed that the authorities might strike hard at the upstart Daimler work force, they drew back, accepting the partial legitimacy of its claim for a shortened work week. Influenza and war weariness in the following weeks led workers to stay home in droves, in a kind of partial, informal strike.

When the tiny, radical circles of the Independent Social Democrats and Spartacists turned their attention to agitating among the industrial proletariat of the big Stuttgart factories in the fall of 1918, they found their most receptive audience at Mercedes. Indeed, one of the first revolutionary workers' councils in Germany may have had its home at Daimler in the week before the revolution swept away the newly reformed version of the Kaiserreich.

The social tinder at Daimler and in the Stuttgart area which burst into flames in the autumn of 1918 differed from that fuelling the crisis in northern and central Germany. Although shortages of food and fuel were endemic, Wuerttemberg was not beset by the kind of desperate subsistence crisis which made daily life a painful struggle in many German cities during the last two years of the war. In many a situation report until mid-1918, the Wuerttemberg high command noted the relatively relaxed situation prevailing in the supply and distribution of foodstuffs in the Stuttgart era and duly minimized the potential for civil unrest.

Yet the Daimler workers marched for peace and for socialist republic on November 4, five days before Berlin rose. This "vanguard of the revolution" broke early with its moderate social democratic leadership and gave the radicals one of their few victories in southwest Germany. The radicalization of the workforce proceeded apace even as the masses of unskilled and unorganized laborers, including women, drifted away or were sacked in the last five weeks of 1918. The new representation succeeded in tapping the enthusiasm of the remaining 9,000 or so at Daimler by combining its practical work for a new factory regime with agitation for the national and international triumph of socialism. Thus, the accomplishments of the workers' movement at Daimler included *both* the Movement of the United Proletariat *and* the industry-wide collective bargaining agreement of May 1919.

New relations of authority began to take shape on the shop floor in 1919 and 1920. Led by the overwhelming USPD and KPD majority on the workers' committee and, after March 1920, the factory council, workers challenged the authority of masters and company officials, countermanded the procedures for setting piece-rates, and themselves sought to set the pace of their work. One day they collected the piece-rate cards to make sure no one had tried to "speed up" their department; the next day they marched to demand more money for the unemployed or in support of the Soviet revolution. The situation seemed impossible for the owners, who were now sitting on top of enormous overcapacity in the form of a productive apparatus which had been expanded greatly during Daimler's short wartime interlude of importance. By the summer of 1920, Berge and his colleagues—who now included top men from the Deutsche Bank—were looking for a way to reduce the swollen work force, while at the same time retaining their *Stammarbeiterschaft*, their reliable core of older, generally less militant, skilled workers. If a solution could be found, the company might not only find financial relief, but might also be able to jettison the younger workers who were often behind the turbulent scenes on the shop-floor.

The escalating protests over the new direct wage tax in August 1920 gave the company the pretext to settle its account with its work force. When the government occupied the big factories in greater Stuttgart and the employers locked out their workers on August 25, Daimler pounced. The score Daimler extracted far surpassed anything which other employers in the area had had in mind with the lockout. The axe fell with a vengeance in Untertuerkheim, and 4,500 were sacked. More than 1,800 skilled professionals, 1,400 machine workers, 800 day laborers, and 59 women, along with nearly all those younger than 25 years of age, were now out on the street or reduced to working the city stone-quarry.

Daimler's complete victory wrecked the workers' movement at the factory. Bitter divisions between factions subsequently hobbled labor, which seemed uninterested in re-establishing the broad, militant shop-floor praxis of 1918–1920—or were perhaps unable to do so. It afterwards managed to unite sufficiently in rear-guard actions which sought to stem the employers' counteroffensive to roll back the social and industrial achievements of the Weimar era.

Nevertheless, DMG remained crisis-ridden. A new, bold strategy was clearly needed, for the luxury Mercedes was no ticket to a mass market. Berge and his associates, whose thinking was forged in the prewar years of limited horizons, were part of the problem. Banks, especially the Deutsche Bank, which were now heavily involved in the industry, realized this and, in the wake of the economic disaster of 1923–1924, organized the rationalization of the industry. Although the heady design for a German I.G. Auto miscarried, the two grand auto houses of southwestern Germany, Daimler and Benz, merged in 1925–1926. Only an enormous infusion of bank credit and a tough rationalization program in the new company's works achieved a very modest, and short-lived success in 1927–1928.

Labor at Daimler was unable to deflect the most injurious features of the reorganization. Indeed, the DMV never had a coherent policy on industrial rationalization. Wages were low in comparison with other factories in Stuttgart in 1924–1925, and the general silence on the industrial situation at Daimler-Benz between 1925 and 1929 was broken only by protests over speedups and cuts in piece-rates. Indeed, the almost total lack of archival evidence about the performance of the factory council and the effectiveness of worker representation on the board of trustees between 1922 and 1933 impairs any assessment of the years of comparative "normalcy" at DMG. But—whether because of layoffs of high-paid, highly unionized workers, piece-rate cuts, or apathy—union membership had sunk to less than half of the work force at the DMV's *Hochburg* in Untertuerkheim by the onset of the depression—a powerful indicator that labor felt the effects at Daimler.

The crisis swept away the progress the company had made following the merger and put the divided workers' organizations under a pressure they could not bear for long. Business melted away, while wages were repeatedly slashed and half of the workforce was sacked. Attempts to resist the cutbacks were frustrated by the civil war inside the weakened labor movement. On the other hand, there is no evidence that the National Socialist Factory Organization (NSBO) ever achieved much of a following at Daimler-Benz.

The National Socialists had a certain following among several of Daimler-Benz's leading men. Reportedly, Daimler had already contributed money to the NSDAP before 1923. The chairman of the board of trustees Stauss was a leading fellow traveler who was enraptured by Hitler and became a vice-president of the Reichstag in 1934. Director Werlin credited the company with "motorizing the movement," and in 1942 it came out that director Werner—at the time being questioned by powerful SS circles for having a Jewish wife—had illegally supplied the Nazis with vehicles for their election campaigns. In addition, the company advertised heavily in the *Voelkischer Beobachter,* and delivered valuable resources to the men in the Brown House. As the top man at Mercedes put it more than eight months before Hitler came to power, "He will be able to rely on us in the future, as in the past."

The Daimler-Benz AG did not experience anything which can be termed *Gleichschaltung* in 1933. Several businessmen of German-Jewish descent were forced off the board of trustees. The only major personnel change was the addition of Hitler's old buddy Werlin to the board of directors, but Werlin was already a high official of the company and an associate director. The company was uniquely placed to reap the benefits of National Socialism. Daimler-Benz motorized the new German armed forces and began once again to mass produce airplane motors by 1937. The Mercedes bonanza created new factories, reopened old ones, and piled up contracts and profits which no one in the company could have dared to dream of, even in the first optimistic months after the merger. In this context, it makes little practical sense to exaggerate the independence of the political and the economic spheres in this sector of German society, for Daimler-Benz owed its privileged existence and growing power to the Reich's military build-up. The lust for profit and expansion on the Neckar in Untertuerkheim neatly coincided with the German regime's militarism and its preparations for aggressive war.

The workers faced the Third Reich and their newly emboldened employers alone. The unions, the SPD, and the KPD were gone. *Leistung* was the order of the day in the *Werksgemeinschaft* at Daimler-Benz, and sliding hourly wages and piece-rates in the first years of the regime and, later, the new wage groups based on performance reinforced this. Despite heightened police activity, a number of workers protested on several occasions, although their actions remained small and could be only too easily settled or bought off. Terror and re-education did not secure the integration of the working class into the Third Reich, but certainly administered a decisive strategic defeat to its political projects for emancipation and socialism. After 1936, wages rose rapidly at Daimler-Benz, as the military buildup created a heavy demand for metal workers and machinists. But hours were long, and took their toll on the "strength" which any "joy" from the new social benefits like works concerts, field trips, and guided tours was supposed to create.

With the organization for total war after the autumn of 1941, the iron political-economic logic of occupation and total war took over. Daimler-Benz threw tens of thousands of foreign workers and concentration camp inmates into its battle to produce airplane motors, trucks, tanks, and spare parts. Barracks, camps, and "combing out" missions became integral parts of the Mercedes complex. Its facilities had become collections of labor processes and assembly lines which the brutalized men and women deported from their homes could service. The dialectic which haunted the history of this outfit—the seemingly inescapable economic vulnerability of its enterprises in a land aloof to motorized mass transport, coupled with its constant effort to project power and to accumulate wealth—consumed the thousands of Europeans transported to its facilities. The way out was armaments production, after 1939 under conditions of singular brutality. Genshagen, Rzeszow, "Goldfisch," Vienna, and Minsk became an indellible—and, until today, largely hidden—part of the history of what is today one of western Europe's largest manufacturing companies.

The history which opened with the confident artistry of Swabian machinists and metal workers, and the tough optimism of the labor movement before World War I ended at the demise of Germany in 1945 with huddled foreign inmates assembling motors for no pay. The journey which began when Gottlieb Daimler fired up his first auto in Schorndorf in 1886 wound up sixty years later at the center of the orgy of plunder and depravity known as the Third Reich.

APPENDIXES

APPENDIX 1
Quarters for Foreign Workers at Daimler-Benz, Stuttgart-Untertuerkheim

Name & Location	Number	Nationality
1. Schlachthof Gaisburg	153	French
2. Alte Krone Untertuerkheim	75	Belgian
3. Saengerhalle Ut	242	French
4. Blaues Haus Plochingen	224	French, Serbian
5. Paradies Esslingen	58	Slovenian
6. Ochsen Rotenberg	50	French
7. Antoniushaus Wernau	200	Danish, Czech
8. Bayr. Hof Untertuerkheim	60	Russian
9. Kreispflege Ludwigsburg	116	Slovenians
10. Hirsch Wendlingen	92	French
11. Wilhelmshoehe Kirschheim	65	Czech
12. Fuchsen Kirschheim	102	Czech
13. Schulhaus Fellbach	502	French, Benelux
14. Puppenspiele Sillenbuch	149	French
15. Im Kies Hedelfingen	1,060	Russian
16. Krone Rotenberg	32	Belgian
17. Engelsaal Backnang	136	Russian

APPENDIX 1
Continued

Name & Location	Number	Nationality
18. Adler Wangen	80	French
19. Fleckenried Wangen	400	Russian
20. Traube Sulzgries	50	Czech, Slovak
21. Hirsch Rohracker	60	Czech
22. Krone Denkendorf	86	Dutch
23. Turnhalle Rotenberg	40	French
24. Luginsland Untertuerkheim	78	French
25. Hammer Backnang	40	French
26. Ochsen Deizisau	?	?
27. Krankenlager Sillenbuch	60	"all"
28. Adler Koengen	40	Russian
29. Ochsen Koengen	50	Russian
30. Stern Bietigheim	50	French
31. Post Bietigheim	60	French
32. Gruenwiese Bietigheim	?	Russian
33. Baracke Wannweil	?	French
34. Laemmerbuckel Wiesensteig	?	Russian
35. Goldener Becher Ebingen	63	Russian
36. Buchenwald Ebingen	?	Russian
37. Weissenburg Ebingen	80	French
38. Turnhalle Eislingen	120	Russian
39. Weinberg Eislingen	?	Polish, Dutch
40. Lamm Muehlen	?	Polish
41. Sportclubhaus Tailfingen	40	Dutch, Russian
42. Annestrasse Tailfingen	40	Russian
43. Wiesengrund Koengen	?	Polish, Ital.
44. Zentral-Lustnau	?	French
45. Neckartenzlingen	?	Russian
46. Loewen Wernau	80	Dutch
47. Schetzler Turnhalle	100	Russian
48. Turnhalle Esslingen	150	Russian
49. Rosensteinpark	300	Polish
50. Marienanstalt	12	Danish, French
51. Kirchtal Zuffenhausen	106	Fr. Bel. Dutch
52. Ochsen Struempfelbach	82	Czech
53. Knoch Heilbronn	96	Russian
54. Schule Esslingen	80	Russian
55. Georgihaus Esslingen	86	Russian

* Note: No entries for 59–70

APPENDIX 1
Continued

Name & Location	Number	Nationality
56. Wulle Stuttgart	195	Czech
57. Flaschenhals	140	Armenian
58. Engl. Garten Stuttgart	106	Slovenian
59. Krone Meeterzimmern		
60. Ochsen Wannweil		
61. Gemeinde Wannweil		
62. Tricotwaren Ebingen		
63. Rose Lustnau		
64. Loewe Muehlen		
65. Rose Eislingen		
66. Schwan Metterzimmern		
67. Stuttgarter Hofbraeu		
68. Liederkranz Rotenberg		
69. Adler Deizisau		
70. Barackenlager Wangen		

APPENDIX 2
Nationality, Sex, and Age of Foreign Workers at Daimler-Benz,
Stuttgart-Untertuerkheim

	Total	Male	Female	Ages[1]
Armenian	291	211	80	15–63[2]
Belgian	177	166	11	17–61
Bulgarian	2	2	–	–
Croatian	2	2	–	–
Danish	15	14	1	24–24
Dutch	315	308	7	18–63
Estonian	3	3	–	33–60
French	1,635	1,515	120	17–68
Greek	1	1	–	–
Hungarian	17	16	1	17–52
Italian	419	418	1	20–64
Latvian	2	2	–	60–61
Polish	178	121	57	16–68
"Protektorat"	382	281	101	19–53
Rumanian	6	6	–	20–35
Swiss	5	5	–	–
Serbian	2	2	–	–
Soviet Russian	1,873	1,031	842	12–66
Spanish	6	6	–	26–48
Turkish	1	1	–	–
Yugoslavian	92	85	7	16–48
"Stateless"	137	114	23	15–62
TOTALS	5,566	4,400	1,166	12–68

1.—youngest–oldest
2.—does not include 61 Armenian children

APPENDIX 3
Categories of Foreign Workers at Daimler-Benz Factories in Germany,
1941–1943
(not including concentration camp prisoners or POW's)

Year End	Skilled	Trained	Unskilled	Clerks	Total	(Women)
I. Untertuerkheim						
1941	230	721	147	12	1,110	(29)
1942	451	2,787	389	28	3,655	(566)
1943	457	2,643	699	171	3,970	(672)
II. Genshagen						
1941	822	326	751	0	1,899	(136)
1942	981	1,190	3,794	46	6,011	(1,014)
1943	738	2,933	1,805	66	5,542	(984)
III. Sindelfingen						
1941	117	82	1	4	204	(6)
1942	66	514	244	3	827	(323)
1943	148	1,809	189	13	2,159	(681)
IV. Berlin-Marienfelde						
1941	206	186	329	16	737	(124)
1942	356	724	1,261	40	2,381	(634)
1943	480	919	1,402	53	2,854	(1,166)
V. Mannheim						
1941	12	0	3	1	16	(1)
1942	224	337	132	3	696	(118)
1943	121	446	229	21	817	(164)
VI. Gaggenau						
1941	22	14	5	6	47	(4)
1942	81	520	381	6	927	(199)
1943	99	526	130	5	751[a]	(187)

a. Error in original
Source for Appendixes: AGM DBAG Konrad Zapf, Mercedes-Stern und Fremdarbeiter

NOTES

INTRODUCTION

1. For a discussion of social history and the historiography of German labor, see the introductory essay in my dissertation, "The Workers of Daimler-Unter-tuerkheim: A Study in the History of German Labor," Columbia University, 1987, pp. 1–20.

2. Gerald D. Feldman, "The Origins of the Stinnes-Legien Agreement: A Documentation," *Internationale Wissenschaftliche Korrespondenz zur Geschichte der deutschen Arbeiterbewegung*, 1973, vols. 19/20, p. 45.

3. David F. Crew, *Town in the Ruhr: A Social History of Bochum* (New York: Columbia University Press, 1979), p. 7.

4. H. H. Gerth & C. Wright Mills, *From Max Weber: Essays in Sociology* (New York: Oxford University Press, 1973), p. 138.

1. MERCEDES MYTHOS

1. Whether Daimler or Benz was the inventor who should be credited as the first pioneer of the automobile is disputed, not least of all, at Daimler-Benz, where there is no strict company line on the matter. Allan Nevins sums up the controversy over who really was the "father of the automobile" dispassionately and succinctly:

"1. Daimler completed the first high-speed, four-cycle gasoline engine, more suitable than any other motor at that time for use in motor vehicles.

"2. Benz appears to have made the first tests with a motor vehicle, but these are unauthenticated. Daimler received his patent for a motorcycle five months before Benz's first public tests with his machines; but Benz's authenticated tests are first in point of time.

"3. The tricycle was more like an automobile than was the motorcycle, and apparently operated more frequently and successfully; but Daimler was undoubtedly the first of the two to operate a four-wheeled, gasoline-driven carriage.

"4. Daimler's machines both had two speeds instead of one, and his motor car was undoubtedly superior to Benz's."

"From these facts the reader can form his own judgment." Allan Nevins, *Ford: the Times, the Man, the Company* (New York: Scribners, 1954), pp. 126–27.

2. James Clark Hunt, *The People's Party in Wuerttemberg and Southern Germany, 1890–1914* (Stuttgart: Klett, 1975), pp. 20–21.

3. Odi Burkart, *Die wuerttembergische Automobil- und Zubehoer- Industrie*, Dissertation, Wuerzburg, n.d., p. 77.

4. Erich Preiser, *Die wuerttembergische Wirtschaft als Vorbild. Die Untersuchung der Arbeitsgruppe Ostpreussen—Wuerttemberg*, (Stuttgart: W. Kohlhammer, 1937).

5. In 1914, grains were grown on 42.2% of the region's arable land, vegetables on about 13% and animal feed on 10.5%. Gunther Mai, *Kriegswirtschaft und Arbeiterbewegung in Wuerttemberg 1914–1918*, (Stuttgart: Klett-Cotta, 1983), p. 46; Hunt, *The People's Party in Wuerttemberg*, p. 16.

6. David Blackbourn, *Class, Religion and Local Politics in Wilhelmine Germany. The Centre Party in Wuerttemberg Before 1914* (Wiesbaden: Steiner, 1980), p. 197.

7. In 1907, textiles and clothing employed about 25.2% of the working people of Wuerttemberg; metal and machine-building about 25.5%; and the building trades about 14.3%. Daimler's share of the laboring population in Stuttgart was about 2%. Manfred Scheck, *Zwischen Weltkrieg und Revolution. Zur Geschichte der Arbeiterbewegung in Wuerttemberg 1914–1920* (Cologne: Boehlau), p. 26; Preiser, *Die wuerttembergische Wirtschaft als Vorbild*, p. 95.

8. David F. Crew, *Town in the Ruhr. A Social History of Bochum, 1880–1914* (New York: Columbia University Press, 1979), is the study of such a "new" city.

9. The population of Wuerttemberg grew from 2,169,480 in 1900 to 2,580,235 in 1925. About 56% lived either on the land or in villages with fewer than 2,000 inhabitants. By 1925, the percentage was 46.8%. Both were higher than the national averages of 45% and 35.6% respectively. *Statistisches Jahrbuch fuer das Deutsche Reich*, Berlin, 1920, p. 1; Scheck, *Zwischen Weltkrieg und Revolution*, p. 20.

10. Klaus Megerle, "Regionale Differenzen des Industrialisierungsprozesses: Ueberlegungen am Beispiel Wuerttembergs," in Rainer Fremdling & Richard Tilly, eds., *Industrialisierung und Raum. Studien zur regionalen Differenzierung im Deutschland des 19. Jahrhunderts* (Stuttgart: Klett-Cotta, 1979), pp. 121–

22; Blackbourn, *Class, Religion and Local Politics in Wilhelmine Germany*, p. 142.

11. Hunt, *The People's Party in Wuerttemberg*, p. 21; Blackbourn, *Class, Religion and Local Politics in Wilhelmine Germany*, p. 142.

12. *Chronik der Kgl. Haupt- und Residenzstadt 1912* (Stuttgart: Greiner & Pfeiffer, 1913).

13. Blackbourn, *Class, Religion and Local Politics in Wilhelmine Germany*, pp. 10, 240.

14. Hunt, *The People's Party in Wuerttemberg*, p. 182.

15. Carl Schorske, *German Social Democracy 1905–1917: The Development of the Great Schism* (Cambridge: Harvard University Press, 1955), pp. 130–33.

16. Hunt, *The People's Party in Wuerttemberg*, p. 13.

17. Megerle, "Regionale Differenzen des Industrialisierungsprozesses," p. 123; Klaus Megerle, *Wuerttemberg im Industrialisierungsprozess Deutschlands. Ein Beitrag zur regionalen Differenzierung der Industrialisierung* (Stuttgart: Klett-Cotta, 1982), p. 190. The use of electrical motors to power machinery grew quickly. In 1907, 38.14% of the machines in operation in Wuerttemberg were powered by electricity, while the percentage for the Reich was 29.27%.

18. *Chronik 1912* . . . The birth rates per thousand in the settlements around Daimler in 1906 were: Ostheim 46.2, Untertuerkheim 42.4, Wangen 49.2. For Stuttgart as a whole, it was 29.1. On rents, see below.

19. Fritz Schumann, *Die Arbeiter der Daimler-Motoren-Gesellschaft* (Leipzig: Duncker & Humblot, 1911), p. 146.

20. Thomas Brunne et al., *Arbeiterbewegung Arbeiterkultur. Stuttgart 1890–1933* (Wuertt. Landesmuseum, 1981), is a good portrayal of working class culture in the greater Stuttgart area.

21. Fritz Opel, *Der deutsche Metallarbeiter-Verband waehrend des ersten Weltkrieges und der Revolution* (Hannover: Norddeutsche Verlagsanstalt, 1957), p. 26. It had 61 members.

22. Scheck, *Zwischen Weltkrieg und Revolution*, pp. 29–31.

23. H.C. Graf von Seherr-Thoss, *Die deutsche Automobilindustrie. Eine Dokumentation von 1886 bis heute* (Stuttgart: Deutsche-Verlags-Anstalt, 1974), p. 551; Anita Kugler, *Arbeitsorganisation und Produktionstechnologie der Adam Opel Werke* (Berlin: Wissenschaftszentrum, 1985), p. 110.

24. An exception is the dissertation which Anita Kugler is writing at the Freie Universitaet Berlin.

25. Otto Meibes, *Die deutsche Automobilindustrie. Eine wissenschaftlich gruendliche wie lebendig fesselnde Schilderung der Entwicklung unserer Automobilindustrie mit vielen wertvollen statistischen Angaben* (Berlin: Markwart, 1928), pp. 102–3.

26. For an account of the state of the automobile industry, see Fritz Seidenzahl, *100 Jahre Deutsche Bank 1870–1970* (Frankfurt/Main: Deutsche Bank, 1970), pp. 281–84, especially the speech by the bank director Wassermann to the general convention of the Deutsche Bank in 1927 on its Daimler transactions, and Gerald Feldman, *Iron and Steel in the German Inflation 1916–1923* (Princeton: Princeton University Press, 1977), p. 274. The study by Yuji Nishimuta in

the Japanese-language journal *Shirin* (Sept. 1985) 68(5):767–808, gives a stark assessment of the condition of the industry in 1928 in the tables on p. 786. The production capability of the major producers in 1928 was 261,000 units; actual production totalled 92,000. The corresponding totals for the United States are 9,393,000 and 7,764,000, respectively. I thank the author for translating the tables.

27. Karl-Heinz Ludwig, *Technik und Ingenieure im Dritten Reich,* Duesseldorf: Droste, 1974, pp. 310–14.

28. For the early history of the Daimler-Motoren-Gesellschaft, see any of the hagiographies produced by Daimler-Benz for the 100th anniversary celebration, or Paul Siebertz, *Gottlieb Daimler*. Erhard Fischer, "Gottlieb Daimler, eine Auswahlbibliographie," in the catalogue to the exhibit in Schorndorf, *150 Jahre Gottlieb Daimler* (Schorndorf: Roesler, 1984), pp. 57–62, is a useful bibliography.

29. James M. Laux, *In First Gear. The French Automobile Industry to 1914* (Liverpool: Liverpool University Press, 1976), pp. 15–18, 74; *75 Jahre Motorisierung des Verkehrs. Jubilaeumsbericht der Daimler-Benz Aktiengesellschaft 1886–1961* (Stuttgart: Daimler-Benz, 1961, p. 205); Werner Oswald, *Mercedes-Benz Personenwagen 1886–1984*, 2nd ed. (Stuttgart: Motorbuch, 1985), p. 68.

30. Archiv-Geschichte-Museum, Daimler-Benz Aktiengesellschaft, Daimler-Motoren-Gesellschaft 6 (32) Geschichte der DMG 2.7.1915; *Sueddeutsches Industrieblatt,* May 29, 1914, p. 437; *Zum 25jaehrigen Bestehen der Daimler-Motoren-Gesellschaft,* Stuttgart: Daimler, n.d., p. 39.

31. *Allgemeine Automobil-Zeitung* (Vienna), Dec. 19, 1904, p. 11.

32. AGM DBAG Untertuerkheim 3 (5) Abschrift aus der *Zeitschrift des Vereins deutscher Ingenieure* (April 1905) 14(8):1–6.

33. AGM DBAG DMG 25 Sonderabdruck aus *Zeitschrift des Vereins deutscher Ingenieure,* 1912, p. 981; Anita Kugler, "Von der Werkstatt zum Fliessband," *Geschichte und Gesellschaft,* (1987) 13:313.

34. *Allgemeine Automobil-Zeitung,* Nov. 20, 1910, pp. 28–29. DMG-Marienfelde had produced a 24 hp truck which the army tested in 1904. *Ibid.,* March 31, 1907.

35. Bernd-Felix Schulte, *Die deutsche Armee 1900–1914. Zwischen Beharren und Veraendern,* (Duesseldorf: Droste, 1977), pp. 333–34.

36. AGM DBAG 26 (131) See the brief collection of business summaries from 1900/01–1910.

37. AGM DBAG Werksangehoerige 3.

38. Albrecht Fischer, *Verband Wuerttembergischer Metallindustrieller e.V. 1897 bis 1934,* n.p., n.d., p. 5.

39. See chapters 4–6; e.g. AGM DBAG DMG 37 (1975) Berge to von Kaulla, Dec. 18, 1918, in which Berge refers to his opponents among labor as the "mentally inferior *[geistige Minderwertige]*."

40. AGM DBAG DBAG 2 *Stuttgarter neues Tagblatt,* Nov. 25, 1927.

41. Werner Oswald, *Mercedes-Benz Personenwagen 1886–1984*, pp. 68–69.

42. Wer ist's? Leipzig: Hermann A.L. Degener, 1911, p. 703; Seidenzahl, *100 Jahre Deutsche Bank 1870–1970*, p. 68.

43. Seidenzahl, *100 Jahre Deutsche Bank 1870–1970*, pp. 68, 108.
44. Fritz Stern, *Gold and Iron* (New York: Knopf, 1977), pp. 419–20.
45. Seidenzahl, *100 Jahre Deutsche Bank 1870–1970*, p. 10.
46. Harold James, *The German Slump: Politics and Economics, 1924–1936* (New York: Clarendon Press of Oxford University Press, 1986), p. 143.
47. This correspondence is scattered throughout AGM DBAG, especially DMG and UT.
48. Fischer, *Verband Wuerttembergischer Metallindustrieller*, pp. 4–5, 8–9; Mai, *Kriegswirtschaft und Arbeiterschaft*, p. 144; Gerald D. Feldman, *Vom Weltkrieg zur Weltwirtschaftskrise* (Goettingen: Vandenhoeck & Ruprecht, 1984), p. 52; Juergen Kocka, "Organisierter Kapitalismus oder Staatsmanopolischer Kapitalismus? Begriffliche Vorbermerkungen," in Heinrich August Winkler, ed., *Organisierter Kapitalismus. Voraussetzungen und Anfaenge* (Goettingen: Vandenhoeck & Ruprecht, 1974), pp. 20–23.
49. AGM DBAG DMG 34–36 Satzung der Daimler-Motoren-Gesellschaft, Stuttgart-Untertuerkheim, p. 6.
50. Helge Pross, *Manager und Aktionaere in Deutschland. Untersuchungen zum Verhaeltnis von Eigentum und Verfuegungsmacht* (Frankfurt/Main: Europaeische Verlagsanstalt, 1965), p. 9, for a general view of the process.
51. James, *The German Slump*, p. 143.
52. Office of Military Government for Germany, United States. Finance Division—Financial Investigation Section (O.M.G.U.S.), "Report on the Investigation of the Deutsche Bank," Nov. 1946, p. 75, HSG; *Ermittlungen gegen die Deutsche Bank*, (Noerdlingen: Greno, 1985), p. 88. These lines were written explicitly about the Deutsche Bank's ties with Daimler-Benz and BMW.
53. *Ibid.*, p. 76.
54. AGM DBAG DMG 6 (32). Their connections have been assembled from a variety of sources, including *Wer ist's?;* Seidenzahl, *100 Jahre Deutsche Bank 1870–1970;* O.M.G.U.S., "Report on the Investigation of the Deutsche Bank."
55. Erich Achterberg & Maximilian Mueller-Jabusch, *Lebensbilder deutscher Bankiers aus fuenf Jahrhunderten* (Frankfurt: Knapp, 1963), pp. 255–58; Friedrich Glum, *Zwischen Wissenschaft, Wirtschaft und Politik. Erlebtes und Erdachtes in vier Reichen* (Bonn: Bouvier, 1964), pp. 165, 256, 260, 442; *Ermittlungen gegen die Deutsche Bank*, p. 149; Ernst Willi Hansen, *Reichswehr und Industrie. Ruestungswirtschaftliche Zusammenarbeit und wirtschaftliche Mobilmachungsvorbereitungen 1923–1932* (Boppard: Boldt, 1978), p. 175.
56. Hans Radant, "Zu den Beziehungen zwischen dem Konzern der Deutschen Bank und dem Staatsapparat bei der Vorbereitung und Durchfuehrung des Zweiten Weltkrieges," *Der deutsche Imperialismus*, vol. 2, Berlin: Ruetten & Loening, 1961, p. 16. A decade later, the Deutsche Bank's share remained about the same. AGM DBAG Kissel I, 6 "Aufstellung ueber die angemeldeten Aktien zur Hauptversammlung am 30. Juni 1942," p. 10.
57. AGM DBAG Kissel V, 27 Kissel to Hansa-Lloyd & Goliath-Werke, June 8, 1932. See the essay published after this work was written: Karl Heinz Roth, "Der Weg zum guten Stern des Dritten Reichs," *Das Daimler-Benz Buch* (Noerdlingen: Greno, 1987), pp. 27–389.

2. WORK AND WORKERS

1. Eric J. Hobsbawm, *Labouring Men. Studies in the History of Labour* (London: Weidenfeld & Nicolson, 1964), p. 300.

2. Karl Marx, *Capital*. Vol. I. (New York: International, 1967), p. 178: "We presuppose labour in a form that stamps it as exclusively human. . . . [W]hat distinguishes the worst architect from the best of bees is this, that the architect raises his structure in imagination before he erects it in reality. At the end of every labour-process, we get a result that already existed in the imagination of the labourer at its commencement. He not only effects a change of form in the material on which he works, but also realises a purpose of his own."

3. Schumann, *Die Arbeiter*, p. 34. The phrase is from Hobsbawm, *Labouring Men*, p. 301.

4. In an interview with the author, Friedrich Schimpf, a skilled worker at Daimler in the 1920s, asserted that the workers took great pride when an auto built at the Mercedes plant won a major race. There is no reason to doubt that this had also been the case before the radicalization of the work force after the war.

5. Harry Braverman, *Labor and Monopoly Capital. The Degradation of Work in the Twentieth Century* (New York: Monthly Review, 1974), p. 111; Frederick Winslow Taylor, *The Principles of Scientific Management*, (New York: Norton, 1967), pp. 106–9; Marius Hammer, *Vergleichende Morphologie der Arbeit in der Europaeischen Automobilindustrie. Die Entwicklung zur Automation* (Basel: Kyklos, 1959), p. 6.

6. AGM DBAG. Daimler-Motoren-Gesellschaft Untertuerkheim. Pruefungs-Bericht der Deutschen Treuhand-Gesellschaft Berlin, 1910, Anlage 4.

7. Braverman, *Labor and Monopoly Capital*, pp. 190–91.

8. Schumann, *Die Arbeiter*, p. 24.

9. A number of historians call these types "semi-skilled," but it may be misleading to see them as "semi-anything." James Hinton, *The First Shop Stewards' Movement* (London: Allen & Unwin, 1973), p. 59; Hobsbawm, *Labouring Men*, p. 300.

10. *Verhandlungen des Vereins fuer Sozialpolitik in Nuernberg 1911, 2. Probleme der Arbeiterpsychologie unter besonderer Ruecksichtnahme auf Methode und Ergebnisse der Vereinserhebungen mit einem Bericht von Heinr. Herkner* (Leipzig: Duncker & Humblot, 1911), p. 129.

11. AGM DBAG Protokolle PD 25 Nallinger & P. Daimler to Verwaltungs-Ausschuss DMG, November 3, 1909.

12. Clemens Heiss, "Die Entloehnungsmethoden in der deutschen Metallindustrie," *Schmollers Jahrbuch fuer Gesetzgebung, Verwaltung und Volkswirtschaft im deutschen Reich* (1913), 37(3):1484.

13. See below, chapter 4. Schumann, *Die Arbeiter*, p. 17.

14. *Die Arbeitsverhaeltnisse der Hilfsarbeiter in der Metallindustrie Stuttgarts und Umgebung* (Stuttgart: Schlicke, 1913), pp. 35–36, 48–49.

15. Schumann, *Die Arbeiter*, pp. 41–2, 44. The Daimler apprentices could not draw on their deposited earnings except in the case of a family emergency.

16. Schumann, *Die Arbeiter,* p. 44.

17. *Daimler Werkzeitung,* 1919, No. 1 "Gruppenfabrikation," p. 4. Landes calls this mode of factory organization *Platzarbeit,* but this term appears nowhere in the firm's documents. David Landes, *The Unbound Prometheus, Technological Change and Industrial Development in Western Europe from 1750 to the Present* (Cambridge: Cambridge University Press, 1969), pp. 305–6. A good discussion of the organization of production in metal and machine-building firms is Erwin Meissner, et al., *Technologie des Maschinenbaus,* 7th ed. (Berlin: VEB Verlag Technik, 1973), pp. 36–48.

18. DBAG AGM DMG 4 (26) *Allgemeine Automobil-Zeitung* (Berlin), July 26, 1913, p. 15.

19. *Daimler Werkzeitung,* 1919, No. 1 "Gruppenfabrikation," pp. 4–5. See chapter 5.

20. Hermann Bruns, *Die deutsche Automobil-Industrie mit besonderer Beruecksichtigung der Kleinauto-Industrie bei der Rationalisierung* (Hannover: A. Harbers, 1926), pp. 10–13; Hans Schneider, *Die Entwicklung der deutschen Automobilindustrie nach dem Kriege* (Leipzig: Noske, 1929), pp. 4–5.

21. *Allgemeine Automobil-Zeitung* (Berlin), July 26, 1913, p. 19.

22. AGM DBAG Protokolle PD 10 Aufsichtsrats-Sitzung No. 121, p. 13; Bericht der technischen Direktion an den Aufsichtsrat der Daimler-Motoren-Gesellschaft, p. 7; PD 10 Aufsichtsrats-Sitzung No. 116, December 8, 1908.

23. These are my conclusions from the statistics under "1909" and "1913" in the "Historische Datensammlung 1886–1980," recently compiled by the Daimler-Benz museum. See *Allgemeine Automobil-Zeitung* (Berlin), July 26, 1913, p. 15.

24. Guenter Spur, ed., *Handbuch der Fertigungstechnik.* Vol. 1. Urformen. (Munich: Carl Hanser, 1981), p. 17. F. Schelkle & P. Greiner, *Formen Schmelzen Giessen* (Stuttgart: Holand & Josenhans, 1958), p. 87. Casting remains an exceptionally economical way of shaping metals in the age of mass production.

25. AGM DBAG Protokolle PD 10 Aufsichtsrats-Sitzung der Daimler-Motoren-Gesellschaft, February 5, 1907, p. 2; von Seherr-Thoss, *Die deutsche Automobilindustrie,* p. 47. This work reproduces the plan of the DMG foundry. The Daimler company was a pioneer in using aluminum motor-housings in its vehicles to save weight. In addition, the gear box and central oil pump were made of aluminum. The water pump, driveshaft pins, and housings for the linkage were fashioned from bronze. AGM DBAG Ut 3 (5) Die Fabrikanlage der Daimler-Motoren-Gesellschaft in Stuttgart-Untertuerkheim, 1912, pp. 982(2).

26. "Werkzeichnung-Modell-Abguss," *Damiler Werkzeitung* (1920) No. 14, pp. 225–27.

27. "Voelliger," *Daimler Werkzeitung* (1920) No. 9, p. 153.

28. In 1920, Daimler began a campaign to improve the accuracy of the models constructed in the *Modellschreinerei* and of the pieces cast in the foundry, complaining that raw materials were being wasted by the practice of making parts "fuller"—i.e., with thicker walls. *Daimler Werkzeitung,* 1920, No. 9, p. 157 and No. 14, pp. 225–30.

29. Schumann, *Die Arbeiter* pp. 40–41; von Seherr-Thoss, *Die deutsche*

Automobilindustrie, p. 47. The distinction between formers and casters, mentioned by Schumann, seems to have disappeared by the end of the war. This was already the case elsewhere: in Berlin, "the formers are now at the same time casters. In the morning, they usually take care of the forming; in the afternoon, the casting." Dora Lande, *Arbeits- und Lohnverhaeltnisse in der Berliner Maschinenindustrie zu Beginn des 20. Jahrhunderts,* in *Auslese und Anpassung der Arbeiterschaft in der Elektroindustrie, Buchdruckerei, Feinmechanik und Maschinenindustrie* (Leipzig: Duncker & Humblot, 1910), p. 81. At the Swiss iron and steel plant Georg Fischer, "casters were always formers in the period of the study [1890–1930], and vice versa." Rudolf Vetterli, *Industriearbeit, Arbeiterbewusstsein und gewerkschaftliche Organisation* (Goettingen: Vandenhoeck & Ruprecht, 1981), p. 250. Wolfgang Ruppert, *Geschichte von Arbeit und Industrialisierung in Deutschland* (Munich: C.H. Beck, 1983), p. 81. In 1940, Daimler-Benz began awarding an extra six days of paid vacation annually to the workers on the sandblasting equipment so that they would be sent away for a cure. AGM DBAG Goldene-Fahne. Arbeits- und Entwicklungsbericht (1941/42) 56:41.

30. AGM DBAG Protokolle PD 10 February 15, 1907, p. 2; DMG 11 (11):150; Schumann, *Die Arbeiter,* p. 40; *Allgemeine Automobil-Zeitung* (Berlin), July 26, 1913, p. 17.

31. Schumann, *Die Arbeiter,* pp. 39–40.

32. H. Gnant, *Der Bau- und Maschinenschlosser. Ein Buch fuer Bauschlosser, Maschinenschlosser, Anschlaeger, Schmiede, Mechaniker, Schweisser, Monteure, fuer Werkmeister, Betriebsleiter und namentlich solche, die es werden wollen* (Stuttgart: Dieck & Co., 1925), pp. 251–52.

33. "Plaudereien aus der Gesenkschmiede," *Daimler Werkzeitung,* 1919, No. 10, p. 165. "Gut geschmiedet ist halb gefeilt."

34. AGM DBAG DMG 4 (26) Die Fabrik der Daimler-Motoren-Gesellschaft, p. 982(2).

35. Manfred Rexin, "Willi Bleicher," in Detlef Prinz & Manfred Rexin, *Beispiele fuer aufrechten Gang. Willi Bleicher, Helmut Simon. Im Geiste Carl von Ossietzkys* (Frankfurt/Main: Europaeische Verlagsanstalt, 1979), p. 31.

36. "A good tool is half the work." A. Hegele, *Die Drehbank* (Stuttgart: Franckh'sche Verlagshandlung, 1921), p. 175. For a depiction of eight basic cutting faces, see Max Leuschner, *Fachbuch fuer Metallarbeiter.* Teil 2a. (Hannover: Gebrueder Jaenecke, 1951), p. 84.

37. Otto Hammer, *Vergleichende Morphologie,* p. 6.

38. Schumann, *Die Arbeiter,* p. 38; Lande, *Arbeits- und Lohnverhaeltnisse,* p. 354; Hegele, *Die Drehbank,* p. 181; Meissner, et al., *Technologie,* p. 298.

39. AGM DBAG Ut 3 (5) Abschrift aus der *Zeitschrift des Vereins deutscher Ingenieure,* April 8, 1905, p. 2; DMG 4 (26) Die Fabrik der Daimler-Motoren-Gesellschaft in Stuttgart-Untertuerkheim, p. 982(2).

40. Sixty types are listed in *Statistik des deutschen Reiches 1925,* Vol. 492, 2: Verzeichnis der Berufe und Berufsbenennungen 50, Schlosser.

41. Landes, *The Unbound Prometheus,* p. 305.

42. Schumann, *Die Arbeiter*, p. 37.
43. *Allgemeine Automobil-Zeitung* (Vienna), April 5, 1914, p. 56.
44. AGM DBAG DMG (loose) Bremserei, p. 61.
45. AGM DBAG Protokolle PD 10 Bericht der technischen Direktion an den Aufsichtsrat der Daimler-Motoren-Gesellschaft, n.d., p. 7.
46. K. Jung, "Die Wirtschaftlichkeit der Werkstattarbeit," *Verein deutscher Ingenieure* (1921) 4:94 ff, cited in Otto Fischer, *Die Lohnentwicklung in der Stuttgarter Metallindustrie von 1914 bis 1920*, Diss. Frankfurt/M., 1923, p. 46; Braverman, *Labor and Monopoly Capital*, p. 186.
47. AGM DBAG Ut 3 (5) Werkzeugbau, p. 1.
48. *Allgemeine Automobil-Zeitung*, April 5, 1914, p. 56.
49. AGM DBAG DMG 4 (26) Die Fabrik der Daimler-Motoren-Gesellschaft in Stuttgart-Unterturkheim, p. 982(2); Landes, *The Unbound Prometheus*, p. 313. The centralization of tool distribution and maintenance was a key element in the firm's plans in 1910 to improve the efficiency of its small factory for truck production in Berlin-Marienfelde. See AGM DBAG PD 17 Protokoll No. 1 ueber eine Vorstandssitzung der Daimler-Motoren-Gesellschaft, September 23, 1910, p. 1.
50. *Zum 25jaehrigen Bestehen*, p. 150; AGM DBAG Ut 3 (5) Werkzeugbau, pp. 1–2; Landes, *The Unbound Prometheus*, p. 316.
51. *Zum 25jaehrigen Bestehen*, pp. 146–47.
52. Ernst Valentin, "Spezialmaschinen und Vorrichtungen fuer die Herstellung von Automobilteilen," *Zeitschrift fuer Werkzeugmaschinen und Werkzeuge*, (June 15, 1908), 12(26):1.
53. AGM DBAG Ut 3 (5) Werkzeugbau, p. 1.
54. *Allgemeine Automobil-Zeitung* (Vienna), Nov. 20, 1910, p. 6.
55. Indispensable for understanding the new attitudes of management in the early decades of this century is Taylor's *The Principles of Scientific Management*. To learn how it translated into practice in Germany, see Dieter Groh, "Intensification of Work and Industrial Conflict in Germany, 1896–1914," *Politics and Society* (1978) 8:349–97.
56. I have not found the words "Taylor" or "Taylorism" in any of the firm's documents before 1919. On Taylorism "down the road" at Bosch in 1913, see Heidrun Homburg, "Anfaenge des Taylorsystems in Deutschland vor dem Ersten Weltkrieg," *Geschichte und Gesellschaft*, 1978, p. 179. On Taylorism and the reorganization of work in Germany, see Gunnar Stollberg, *Die Rationalisierungsdebatte 1908–1933. Freie Gewerkschaften zwischen Mitwirkung und Gegenwehr* (Frankfurt/Main: Campus, 1981), pp. 32–42.
57. *Lohn- und Arbeitsverhaeltnisse der massgebendsten Automobil-Fabriken in Deutschland*, (Stuttgart: Schlicke, 1911), p. 21.
58. AGM DBAG Protokolle PD 10 Bericht der technischen Direktion an den Aufsichtsrat der Daimler-Motoren-Gesellschaft, March 21, 1911, p. 6.
59. Ruppert, *Geschichte* p. 92. See also the photographs of Daimler departments in AGM DBAG Fotoarchiv.
60. Schumann, *Die Arbeiter,* p. 35.

61. Lande, *Die Arbeits- und Lohnverhaeltnisse*, p. 328.

62. Quoted in Daimler-Benz A-G, *Das Werk Untertuerkheim*. Stuttgart, 1983, p. 29.

63. See below, chs. 3 and 4.

64. Staatsarchiv Ludwigsburg E 326 19/6 Arbeitsordnung der Daimler-Motoren-Gesellschaft Stuttgart-Untertuerkheim.

65. Schumann, *Die Arbeiter*, p. 35.

66. Julius Deutsch, *Auslese und Anpassung der Arbeiter in den oesterreichischen Siemens-Schuckert-Werken in Wien*, in *Auslese und Anpassung der Arbeiterschaft in der Elektroindustrie, Buchdruckerei, Feinmechanik und Maschinenindustrie* (Leipzig: Duncker & Humblot, 1910), p. 242. Karl Heinz Mommertz, *Bohren, Drehen und Fraesen. Geschichte der Werkzeugmaschinen* (Hamburg: Rowohlt, 1981), pp. 147–49, 194.

67. *Allgemeine Automobil-Zeitung* (Berlin), July 26, 1913, p. 23. See also Mommertz, *Bohren*, pp. 148–52.

68. *Allgemeine Automobil-Zeitung* (Berlin), July 26, 1913, p. 19.

69. Schumann, *Die Arbeiter*, p. 39; *Daimler Werksnachrichten*, July 7, 1920, p. 35; Deutsch, *Auslese und Anpassung*, p. 242; Mommertz, *Bohren*, pp. 129, 147, 195–96; Landes, *The Unbound Prometheus*, pp. 308–09.

70. Deutsch, *Auslese und Anpassung*, p. 243.

71. AGM DBAG Protokolle PD 25 Nallinger & P. Daimler to DMG Verwaltungs-Ausschuss, November 3, 1909; PD 10 Aufsichtsrat-Sitzung, April 15, 1910, p. 8.

72. For example, *Allgemeine Automobil-Zeitung* (Berlin), July 26, 1913, p. 16.

73. AGM DBAG Ut 3 (5) Die Fabrikanlage; *Zum 25jaehrigen Bestehen*, p. 152. The separate auto body department was organized in 1906, although bodies were already being constructed at the factory during its first two years of operation.

74. *Jahresbericht der Gewerbeaufsichtsbeamten und Bergbehoerden fuer das Jahr 1927*. Berlin, 1928, 2(4):72–80. An abridged version appears in Stollberg, *Die Rationalisierungsdebatte 1908–1933*, pp. 167–76.

75. Bernd Flohr, *Arbeiter nach Mass. Die Disziplinierung der Fabrikarbeiterschaft waehrend der Industrialisierung Deutschlands im Spiegel von Arbeitsordnungen* (Frankfurt: Campus, 1981), pp. 18, 169–71. The law is the Gesetz, betreffend Abaenderung der Gewerbeordnung vom 1. Juni 1891, *Reichs-Gesetzblatt* 1891, pp. 278–81.

76. Flohr, *Arbeiter nach Mass*, p. 21.

77. Mayntz, quoted in Flohr, *Arbeiter nach Mass*, pp. 26–7. On discipline in industrial production, see Friedrich Engels, *Von der Autoritaet, Marx-Engels-Werke*, vol. 18 (Berlin: Dietz, 1962), p. 307; and Sidney Pollard, *The Genesis of Modern Management. A Study of the Industrial Revolution in Great Britain* (London: Penguin, 1965).

78. StAL E 326 19/6 Arbeitsordnung, p. 5.

79. *Ibid.*, p. 4.

80. *Ibid.*, pp. 5–6.

81. Overtime figured in many of the workers' protests at Daimler in 1906, 1910–11, 1918–20, and 1928. See chapters 3–6.

82. Lohn- und Arbeitsverhaeltnisse der massgebendsten Automobil-Fabriken in Deutschland, pp. 21–24.

83. Stollberg, Die Rationalisierungsdebatte 1908–1933, pp. 33–35.

84. StAL E 326 19/6 Arbeitsordnung, p. 7.

85. Ibid., pp. 7–9. On the workers' committee, see below.

86. AGM DBAG Protokolle PD 10 Aufsichtsrat-Sitzung, April 24, 1909, p. 5.

87. Lohn- und Arbeitsverhaeltnisse der massgebendsten Automobil-Fabriken, p. 3.

88. See, for example, the Metallarbeiter-Zeitung, Dec. 12, 1903, pp. 393–94. "Akkordarbeit ist Mordarbeit!" ("Piece-work is murder-work!") "With it, every guarantee of the security of even a single set piece-rate is withheld."

89. AGM DBAG Protokolle PD 10 Bericht der technischen Direktion to DMG Aufsichtsrat, March 21, 1911, p. 6.

90. StAL E 326 19/6 Arbeitsordnung, pp. 12–14.

91. Ibid., p. 8. The power to dismiss workers without a notification period dates from January 1911. See chapter 3.

92. Willi Bleicher, quoted in Rexin, "Willi Bleicher," Beispiele fuer aufrechten Gang, pp. 32–33.

93. The company gave Schumann access to its records in Sept. 1909, after Max Weber, who had connections with the firm, pleaded on his behalf. In addition, the regional office of the Metalworkers' Union in Stuttgart helped him with the distribution of the Verein's questionaire, as did the shop stewards at Daimler. The union stewards appealed to the workers at several factory assemblies to cooperate with the study and fill out the questionnaire, but 90% did not. Schumann, Die Arbeiter; Anthony Oberschall, Empirical Social Research in Germany 1848–1914, (Paris/The Hague: Mouton, 1965), pp. 125–31; Max Weber, Gesammelte Aufsaetze zur Soziologie und Sozialpolitik (Tuebingen: Mohr, 1924), p. 1. See the eleven studies published in the Schriften des Verein fuer Socialpolitik, 1910–1912.

94. Weber, Gesammelte Aufsaetze zur Soziologie und Sozialpolitik, p. 1.

95. Max Weber, The Social Interpretation of Reality, J.E.T. Eldridge, ed. (New York: Schocken, 1980), p. 155.

96. David Landes, The Unbound Prometheus, p. 317.

97. Schumann, Die Arbeiter, p. 7.

98. Ibid.

99. Ibid., p. 8.

100. Ibid., p. 9.

101. Marie Bernays, Auslese und Anpassung der Arbeiterschaft der geschlossenen Grossindustrie dargestellt an den Verhaeltnissen der Gladbacher Spinnerei und Weberei A.G. zu Muenchen-Gladbach im Rheinland (Leipzig: Duncker & Humblot, 1910), pp. xvi–xviii.

102. Schumann, Die Arbeiter, pp. 43–62; 79–82.

103. Ibid., p. 62.

104. *Ibid.*, p. 48–56. The records Schumann used no longer exist.

105. Hermann Bruder, *Herzstueck im Schwabenland. Untertuerkheim und Rotenberg. Ein Heimatbuch* (Stuttgart: Buergerverein Untertuerkheim, 1983), p. 423.

106. A West German novel paints a vivid picture of the workers districts in greater Stuttgart before World War I. Manfred Esser, *Ostend-Roman* (Stuttgart: Klett-Cotta, 1983). See the review essay "Rauch ueber dem Osten der grossen Staedte," *Der Spiegel,* Aug. 1, 1983, pp. 123–25.

107. Schumann, *Die Arbeiter,* p. 75.

108. *Ibid.*, p. 85.

109. *Ibid.*, p. 68.

110. *Ibid.*, p. 72.

111. *Ibid.*, p. 88.

112. *Ibid.*, p. 89.

113. *Ibid.*, p. 103.

114. *Ibid.*, p. 104.

115. *Ibid.*, p. 106.

116. *Heimatbuch Untertuerkheim* (Stuttgart: Union Deutsche Verlagsgesellschaft, 1935), pp. 420–421; Brune, et al., *Arbeiterbewegung Arbeiterkultur. Stuttgart 1890–1933,* pp. 33–51.

117. Schumann, *Die Arbeiter,* p. 110.

3. THE WORKERS' MOVEMENT

1. Carl E. Schorske, *German Social Democracy 1905–1917: The Development of the Great Schism* (New York: Harper & Row, 1972); Gerhard A. Ritter, *Die Arbeiterbewegung im Wilhelminischen Reich. Die Sozialdemokratische Partei und die Freien Gewerkschaften 1890–1900* (Berlin-Dahlem: Colloquium, 1959); Guenther Roth, *The Social Democrats in Imperial Germany: A Study in Working Class Isolation and National Integration* (Totowa, N.J.: Bedminster, 1963); Massimo Salvadori, *Karl Kautsky and the Socialist Revolution 1880–1938* (London: NLB, 1979); Peter Nettl, *Rosa Luxemburg* (abridged ed.), (New York: Oxford University Press, 1969); Peter Gay, *The Dilemma of Democratic Socialism: Eduard Bernstein's Challenge to Marx* (New York: Columbia University Press, 1952); G.D. Crothers, *The German Elections of 1907* (New York: Columbia University Press, 1931). For a sensible overview, see Geoff Eley, "Joining Two Histories: The SPD and the German Working Class," *From Unification to Nazism: Reinterpreting the German Past* (London: Allen & Unwin, 1986), p. 171–99.

2. Schorske, *German Social Democracy,* pp. 25, 26, 130–33; 254–55; Manfred Scheck, *Zwischen Weltkrieg und Revolution. Zur Geschichte der Arbeiterbewegung in Wuerttemberg 1914–1920* (Cologne: Boehlau, 1981), pp. 41–51; Joerg Haspel, et al., eds., *Arbeiter. Kultur und Lebensweise im Koenigreich Wuerttemberg* (Tuebingen: Ludwig-Uhland-Institute fuer empirische Kulturwissenschaft, 1979), p. 100; Abraham Ascher, "Imperialists Within German Social Democracy Prior to 1914," *Journal of Central European Affairs* (1961) 20:398.

3. Ritter, *Arbeiterbewegung*, pp. 150–75; Schorske, *German Social Democracy*, pp. 8–16; 88–110; Brune, et al., *Arbeiterbewegung Arbeiterkultur Stuttgart 1890–1933*, pp. 17–23; Fritz Opel, *Der Deutsche Metallarbeiter-Verband waehrend des ersten Weltkrieges und der Revolution* (Hannover: Norddeutsche Verlagsanstalt O. Goedel, 1962), pp. 13–36.

4. Richard J. Evans, "Introduction: The Sociological Interpretation of German Labor History" in Evans, ed., *The German Working Class 1888–1933: The Politics of Everyday Life* (Totowa, N.J.: Barnes & Noble, 1982), p. 19. For a similar description of Social Democratic "popular culture" in Duesseldorf, see Mary Nolan, *Social Democracy and Society: Working-class Radicalism in Duesseldorf, 1890–1920* (Cambridge: Cambridge University Press), pp. 140–41.

5. The phrase is from Vernon Lidtke, *The Alternative Culture: Socialist Labor in Imperial Germany* (New York: Oxford University Press, 1985), e.g., p. 3.

6. These are conclusions from the membership data in *Der Deutsche Metallarbeiter-Verband im Jahre 1906. Jahr- und Handbuch fuer Verbandsmitglieder* (Stuttgart: DMV Verlag, n.d.), pp. 72, 244.

7. *Jahresberichte Gewerbeaufsichtsbeamten im Koenigreich Wuerttemberg fuer 1905* (Stuttgart: Druck der Stuttgarter Vereins-Buchdruckerei, 1906), pp. 93–94.

8. *Metallarbeiter-Zeitung*, March 17, 1906, p. 83. The most important surviving source for the 1906 dispute is the weekly paper of the German Metalworkers' union.

9. *Ibid.*, p. 84.

10. Wilhelm Bremer, a metal former and negotiator in the DMV, died in a streetcar accident in Stuttgart shortly after this session. *Ibid.*, p. 88.

11. *Ibid.*, p. 84.

12. *Ibid.*

13. *Ibid.*

14. *Chronik der Kgl. und Residenzstadt Stuttgart 1906*, edited by the Gemeinderat (Stuttgart: Greiner und Pfeiffer, n.d.), p. 80; *Jahresberichte Gewerbe-Aufsichtsbeamten im Koenigreich Wuerttemberg fuer 1906* (Stuttgart: Druck der Stuttgarter Vereins-Buchdruckerei, 1907), pp. 93–94.

15. *Metallarbeiter-Zeitung*, March 17, 1906, p. 84. The DMV's official report for 1906 gives the figure of 1500 members at Daimler.

16. Walter Nachtmann, "Robert Bosch. Grossindustrieller und Weltbuerger," in Michael Bosch and Wolfgang Niess, eds., *Der Widerstand im deutschen Suedwesten 1933–1945* (Stuttgart: Kohlhammer, 1984), p. 218. For an example of the young Bosch's social democratic tenets (which did not include acceptance of the theory of surplus value), see Theodor Heuss, *Robert Bosch. Leben und Leistung* (Stuttgart: Rainer Wunderlich Verlag Hermann Leins, 1946), pp. 63–64.

17. *Metallarbeiter-Zeitung*, Sept. 8, 1906, Die Mechanische Industrie in Stuttgart und deren Arbeiter, p. 291.

18. *Ibid.* In 1906, wages and working-hours at the most important firms in the metal and machine-building industry in the Stuttgart area were:

Name	# of Workers	Work Day	Work Week	Weekly Turners	Wages H/P # Day Laborers
Bosch	580	8	48	22,60/34,—	20,50/26,70
Daimler	2,200	9	54	20,10/30,90	20,40/—
Eckart	136	9.5	57	26,—/28,20	—/—
Eisemann	128	9	54	24,60/37,40	—/—
Esslingen	150	9.5	57	22,10/27,20	19,—/23,10
Fein	220	9.5	57	25,40/33,10	20,60/—
Fortunawerke	270	9	54	23,50/30,70	18,70/23,40
Terrott	250	9	54	—/36,50	19,50/28,—

Weekly Wages: Hourly Rate/Piece-Rate Workers in Marks

19. *Metallarbeiter-Zeitung*, Sept. 15, 1906, p. 303.

20. Hans Jeurgen Teuteberg, *Geschichte der industrillen Mitbestimmung in Deutschland. Ursprung und Entwicklung ihrer Vorlaeufer im Denken und in der Wirklichkeit des 19. Jahrhunderts* (Tuebingen: Mohr, 1961), pp. 208–09; 520–21. The workers' committtees in Germany gained official recognition through the Auxiliary Service Law of December 1916, and were ceasing to compete with the union movement.

21. The size of the work force fell to 1700. In 1907, the whole Untertuerkheim area used 14% less electricity than in the year before, due to the fact that "the operation of the Daimler work has been sharply curtailed for a long time." *Chronik der Kgl. Haupt- und Residenzstadt Stuttgart 1907*, ed. by the Gemeinderat. Stuttgart: Greiner und Pfeiffer, n.d., p. 71.

22. *Metallarbeiter-Zeitung*, March 2, 1907, p. 72.

23. *Metallarbeiter-Zeitung*, Dec. 28, 1907, p. 418.

24. Staatsarchiv Ludwigsburg E 326 (1) Dem Antrag auf Verurteilung der Firma Daimler, n.d., probably Feb. 1, 1911. On the dockworkers' strike, see *Metallarbeiter-Zeitung*, Aug. 20, 1910; Oct. 8, 1915, p. 321; and Oct. 15, 1910, p. 329. See also Institut fuer Institut fuer Marxismus-Leninismus beim Zentralkomite der SED, *Geschichte der deutschen Arbeiterbewegung*, Bd. 2 (Berlin: Dietz, 1966), pp. 156–57. On the significance of the metal industrialists' threat, see Klaus Saul, *Staat, Industrie, Arbeiterbewegung im Kaiserreich* (Duesseldorf: Bertelsmann, 1974), pp. 114–15.

25. Staatsarchiv Ludwigsburg E 326 (1) No. 14 Bekanntmachung, Sept. 27, 1910.

26. StAL E 326 (1) Dem Antrag.

27. *Metallarbeiter-Zeitung*, Oct. 15, 1910, p. 329.

28. StAL E 326 (1) No. 1 Klage . . . , Jan. 24, 1911; Dem Antrag; *Metallarbeiter Zeitung*, March 4, 1911, p. 70.

29. *Metallarbeiter Zeitung*, Dec. 31, 1910, p. 422.

30. *Chronik der Haupt- und Residenzstadt Stuttgart 1910* (Stuttgart: 1913, p. 43). It is interesting to note that Daimler-Benz reintroduced the week's notification period in 1936, in the context of spreading labor shortages during the

Nazi military build-up, provoking the dissatisfaction of a Social-Democratic commentator in exile. See *Deutschland-Berichte der Sopade*, (1936) 3:1486.

31. *Ibid.;* StAL E 326 (1) Dem Antrag.

32. StAL E 326 (1) No. 6. An unsere Arbeiter, Dec. 30, 1910.

33. StAL E 326 (1) No. 7, An die Arbeiterschaft der Firma Daimler.

34. StAL E 326 (1) No. 19 Gewerbe-Gericht Stuttgart, Oeffentliche Sitzung, Feb. 1, 1911.

35. *Metallarbeiter-Zeitung*, Dec. 31, 1910, p. 422; also StAL E 326 (1) No. 12a Resolution.

36. StAL E 326 (1) The notice to "Schaefer, Masch. Abt.," n.d.

37. StAL E 326 (1) Dem Antrag.

38. StAL E 326 (1) Testimony of Sekler and Lang, Feb. 1, 1911.

39. *Metallarbeiter-Zeitung*, March 4, 1911, p. 70.

40. *Der Deutsche Metallarbeiter-Verband im Jahre 1911* (Stuttgart: Schlicke, 1912), p. 106; *Metallarbeiter-Zeitung*, June 10, 1911, p. 186.

41. Dora Lande, *Arbeits- und Lohnverhaeltnisse in der Berliner Maschinen-industrie zu Beginn des 20. Jahrhunderts* in von Bienkowski, et al., *Auslese und Anpassung der Arbeiterschaft in der Elektroindustrie, Buchdruckerei, Feinmechanik und Maschinen-industrie* (Leipzig: Duncker und Humblot, 1910), p. 331.

42. *Metallarbeiter-Zeitung*, March 4, 1911, p. 70.

43. The pages of the *Schwaebischer Merkur* contain many reports of area residents suffering heat-stroke, including factory workers on the job. The DMV account also mentioned the heat as having contributed to the unrest at the plant.

44. *Metallarbeiter-Zeitung*, August 5, 1911, p. 252; *Jahresberichte der Gewerbe-Aufischtsbeamten im Koenigreich Wuerttemberg.* (Stuttgart: Druck der Stuttgarter Vereins- Buchdruckerei), 1912, p. 19.

45. *Schwaebischer Merkur*, Abendblatt, July 31, 1911, p. 3. This daily stood close to the national liberal Deutsche Partei. Over the years, it published reports which could only have originated with Daimler's direction. For a discussion of the political inclinations of this newspaper, see Otto Groth, *Die politische Presse Wuerttembergs*, Dissertation/Tuebingen, 1913, pp. 87–89 and the forthcoming dissertation by Pierre Lanfranchi, "L'image de l'ennemi dans la presse allemande pendant la premiere guerre mondiale."

46. *Ibid.; Metallarbeiter-Zeitung*, August 12, 1911, p. 258.

47. *Schwaebischer Merkur*, Mittagsblatt, August, 4, 1911, p. 4; *Metallarbeiter-Zeitung*, Aug. 12, 1911, p. 258.

48. *Der Deutsche Metallarbeiter-Verband im Jahre 1911* (Stuttgart: Schlicke, 1912), p. 115; Anhang, p. 116.

49. *Allgemeine Automobil-Zeitung* (Wien), March 3, 1912, p. 18.

50. The rents are compiled from averages in *Chronik der Kgl. Haupt- und Residenzstadt Stuttgart 1905–1911.* See also AGM DBAG *Daimler Werksnachrichten*, March 25, 1920, p. 16.

51. *50 Jahre Gartenstadt Luginsland. Festschrift zum 50jaehrigen Bestehen 1911 bis 1961.* Stuttgart, 1961, p. 6; *Metallarbeiter-Zeitung*, June 10, 1911, p. 186.

52. *50 Jahre Gartenstadt Luginsland,* pp. 6–8.

53. *Ibid.,* p. 8.

54. AGM DBAG Protokolle PD 11 No. 127 Sitzung des Aufsichtrats der Daimler-Motoren-Gesellschaft, Oct. 25, 1912, pp. 3–4; *Daimler Werksnachrichten,* March 25, 1920, p. 20. Daimler's share of 150,000 marks came from the funds of the company's *Arbeiterunterstuetzungskasse.* See Protokolle PD 11, Letter from Berge & Sekler to von Kaulla, June 30, 1914, p. 3.

55. AGM DBAG DMG 5 (29) Gespraech Vischer mit Dr. Schildberger, Oct. 1957.

56. *Daimler Werksnachrichten,* March 25, 1920, p. 20.

57. *50 Jahre Gartenstadt Luginsland,* pp. 12–14.

58. Some of this has been derived from the recollections of Friedrich Schimpf, a retired Betriebsrat member from Daimler-Benz. His family moved into Luginsland with the first group in 1913, and he has lived there ever since. See also *Untertuerkheimer Heimatsbuch,* pp. 420–21.

59. Friedrich Schlotterbeck, *Je dunkler die Nacht. . . . Erinnerungen eines deutschen Arbeiters 1933–1945* (Stuttgart: Gabrielle Walter, 1986), p. 391; *Gartenstadt Luginsland. Gemeinnuetzige Baugenossenschaft e.G.m.b.H. Stuttgart-Untertuerkheim 1911–1936. Festschrift zum 25jaehrigen Bestehen* (Stuttgart: Schoellkopf, Pfund, u. Cie, 1936), p. 3; *Untertuerkheimer Heimatsbuch,* p. 420.

60. *Ibid.,* p. 12.

61. Klaus Saul, *Staat, Industrie, Arbeiterbewegung im Kaiserreich. Zur Innen- und Aussenpolitik des Wilhelminischen Deutschland 1903–1914* (Duesseldorf: Bertelsmann, 1974), pp. 56–57.

4. WORLD WAR I

1. The best resumé of the shape these changes took in southwestern Germany is Gunther Mai, *Kriegswirtschaft und Arbeiterbewegung in Wüerttemberg 1914–1918* (Stuttgart: Klett-Cotta, 1983).

2. Wilhelm Deist, ed., *Militaer und Innenpolitik in Weltkrieg 1914–1918* (Duesseldorf: Droste, 1970), 1:xl.

3. Crown Prince Rupprecht of Bavaria, quoted in Gerald Feldman, *Army, Industry, and Labor in Germany 1914–1918* (Princeton: Princeton University Press, 1966), p. 32.

4. Deist, *Militaer und Innenpolitik in Weltkrieg 1914–1918,* 1:xlii; Feldman, *Army, Industry, and Labor in Germany 1914–1918,* p. 281.

5. The most prominent of the lot was probably Walther Rathenau, heir to German General Electric and organizer in the important raw materials section in the Prussian War Ministry, who looked forward to extending wartime organization, with its committees of businessmen, bureaucrats, and military officers, as the basis of a "new economy." Charles Maier, *Recasting Bourgeois Europe. Stabilization in France, Germany, and Italy in the Decade After World War I* (Princeton: Princeton University Press, 1975), p. 11.

6. Friedrich Zunkel, *Industrie und Staatssozialismus. Der Kampf um die Wirtschaftsordnung in Deutschland 1914–18* (Duesseldorf: Droste, 1974), pp. 9–10.

7. Geoff Eley, "Capitalism and the Wilhelmine State: Industrial Growth and Political Backwardness, 1890–1918," in Eley, *From Unification to Nazism*, pp. 42–58; Juergen Kocka, "Organisierter Kapitalismus oder Staatsmonopolistischer Kapitalismus? Begriffliche Vorbemerkungen," in Heinrich August Winkler, ed., *Organisierter Kapitalismus* (Goettingen: Vandenhoeck & Ruprecht, 1974), pp. 20–23.

8. Feldman, *Army, Industry and Labor in Germany 1914–1918*, p. 521.

9. Deist, ed., *Militaer und Innenpolitik im Weltkrieg 1914–1918*, Bericht des stellv. Generalkommandos des XIII. AK ueber Verlauf und Ergebnis einer Aufklaerungstagung mit Vertretern der organisierten Arbeiterschaft Wuerttembergs, April 25, 1918, 2:937–41.

10. See the discussion of these issues in Ernst Willi Hansen, *Reichswehr und Industrie. Ruestungswirtschaftliche Zusammenarbeit und wirtschaftliche Mobilmachungsvorbereitungen 1923–1932* (Boppard/Rhein: Boldt, 1978), pp. 18–20.

11. AGM DBAG Protokolle PD 25, No. 101 der Verwaltungs-Ausschuss-Sitzung, May 22, 1909, p. 1. In *Allgemeine Automobil-Zeitung* (Vienna), Dec. 3, 1905, p. 40. Berge, noting the close ties in Austria between army and factories, had "no doubt" that intimate contacts would also develop in Germany, "as far as they do not yet exist."

12. AGM DBAG DMG 37 (175).

13. *Die Wiege des Automobils*. Sonderausdruck aus dem 38. Bande der Internationale Industrie-Bibliothek, Berlin: Schroeder, n.d. (1930?).

14. AGM DBAG K. Schnauffer, Die Motorentwicklung in der Daimler-Motoren-Gesellschaft 1907–1918, Teil II, unpublished manuscript, Anlage 63.

15. Reinhard Schiffers and Manfred Koch, eds., *Der Hauptausschuss des deutschen Reichstags 1915–1918*, 4:191–275 (Sitzung 1918). (Duesseldorf: Droste, 1983), p. 2030.

16. HStASt M 77/2 Bd. 10 Denkschriften, p. 46. For an overview of the organization of the war ministries and the air forces, see W. Dieckmann, *Die Behoerdenorganisation in der deutschen Kriegswirtschaft 1914–1918* (Hamburg: Hanseatische Verlagsanstalt, 1937), pp. 28–30, 95–97.

17. Ernst Berge, quoted in *Neues Wiener Tagblatt*, April 11, 1915, p. 29 in AGM DBAG DMG 4 (26).

18. This motor was widely used in German military aircraft in 1914. It powered the army's Gotha-Taube, the LVG and DFW Doppeldecker, the Aviatik-Pfeil and two models of the Albatross Doppeldecker. The navy used it in the Albatross and Friedrichshafen Doppeldecker. Militaergeschichtlichen Forschungsamt, ed., *Militaerluftfahrt bis zum Beginn des Weltkrieges 1914* (Frankfurt/Main: Mittler u. Sohn, 1965), 1:326.

19. AGM DBAG DMG 18 "Abschrift der Fall Daimler," pp. 1–4.

20. AGM DBAG DMG 17 "Produktion neuer Motoren."

21. *Ibid.* See table 4.2.

22. AGM DBAG DMG 81 Letter from DMG to Inspektion der Fliegertruppen, Jan. 15, 1917; Letter from Inspektion to KM Allgemeines Kriegs-Departement, Jan. 22, 1917.

23. AGM DBAG DMG 61 Letter from DMG to Inspektion der Fliegertruppen, June 20, 1917.

24. AGM DBAG Daimler-Motoren-Gesellschaft Stuttgart-Untertuerkheim, Pruefungs-Bericht der Deutschen Treuhand-Gesellschaft, Berlin. 1915, Anlage 3, p. 5; 1916, Anlage 4, pp. 2–4; 1918, Anlage 3, pp. 9–11. The figures for the installation of new machinery in 1918 show a large increase in the acquisition of special machines.

25. AGM DBAG Protokolle PD 11 No. 142 Aufsichtsrat-Sitzung, Sept. 4, 1917, pp. 2–3.

26. There is important, if only partial, documentation of the expansion process in the records. See the "expansion project" from Dec. 5, 1914 for 800,000 marks or the document detailing the 3.7 million expenditure for Untertuerkheim dated June 23, 1915 in AGM DBAG Protokolle PD 11.

27. Daimler-Benz A-G, *Chronik Mercedes-Benz Fahrzeug und Motoren* (Stuttgart, 1973), pp. 114–16; AGM DBAG Untertuerkheim (Ut) 11; Treuhand-Berichte 1915, 1916, 1918.

28. AGM DBAG DMG 17 (83–85).

29. The statistics in AGM DBAG DMG 52 (194), "Bericht ueber den Monat" indicate that the total employment at DMG in Untertuerkheim and Marienfelde fell from 4,231 in July 1914 to 3,189 in August. The firm recovered the loss by October 1914. It is estimated that 135 Daimler workers died in World War I. AGM DBAG DMG 39 Abt. Ausstellungen to Kissel, Nov. 14, 1939.

30. HStASt M 77/2 Bd. 10 Denkschriften. According to an entry on Oct. 23, 1914, workers were reclaimed from the army for labor "1) through ongoing deferment, 2) through leave of absence, 3) through discharge."

31. HStASt M 1/9 Bue 259 Tagebuch-Nr. 662/4.17 AZS 13 Apr. 16, 1917; Odi Burkart *Die wuerttembergische Automobil- und Zubehoer-Industrie*, Dissertation/Wuerzburg, n.d., p. 13, lists, of the 5,958 workers sent to DMG by the military, 3,854 fit for combat (k.v.), 1,402 fit for garrison duty (g.v.), and fully fit for industrial work (a.v.).

32. Burkart, *Die wuerttembergische Automobil- und Zubehoer- Industrie*, pp. 13–14.

33. Hans Wicki, *Das Koenigreich Wuerttemberg im ersten Weltkrieg. Seine wirtschaftliche, soziale, politische und kulturelle Lage* (Bern: Peter Lang, 1984), p. 48.

34. These figures are compiled from the daily totals in AGM DBAG Ut 5. According to Gunther Mai, *Kriegswirtschaft und Arbeiterbewegung in Wuerttemberg 1914–1918* (Stuttgart: Klett-Cotta, 1983), p. 281, this "fluctuation rate" was much higher than at other area firms. The reasons for Daimler's high turnover rate are not clear.

35. HStASt M 1/9 Bue 79 Bl. 57, 60 Aug. 16, 1918 and Sept. 14, 1918.

36. HStASt M 77/1 76 M.A. 30, March 28, 1918.

37. HStASt M 77/1 76 M.A. 43, April 3, 1918.

38. HStASt M 77/1 76 M.A. 76, April 20, 1918, and M.A. 133, May 8, 1918.

39. HStASt M 77/1 76 M.A. 245, July 18, 1918.

40. In the fall of 1916, Daimler's chiefs held that the "acquisition of special machines of American origin cannot be done without," especially because of the "poor productivity, precision and longevity" of those built in Germany. They sought to import seven critically needed models—mainly half-automatic lathes or milling machines which could be worked by unskilled labor—by way of Sweden, but three weeks later, the directors decided against taking the risk. AGM DBAG Protokolle PD 18 Nr. 33 & 34, Nov. 21 and Dec. 13, 1916.

41. HStASt M 77/1 76 See M.A. 45, April 3, 1918; M.A. 51, undated; M.A. 52, April 10, 1918; M.A. 53, 65, 66, 67. On the military supervision and the Daimler Affair, see below.

42. HStASt M 77/1 76 M.A. 76, 77, 78, 79.

43. A feature article in a local newspaper describes how unusual it is for two young female skilled metalworkers in Bad Cannstatt to work in a "male occupation." *Untertuerkheimer Zeitung,* Oct. 31/Nov. 1, 1985, p. 5.

44. Deutscher Metallarbeiter-Verband, *Die Frauenarbeit in der Metallindustrie waehrend des Krieges* (Stuttgart: Schlicke, 1917), pp. 6–7. For a general overview of the employment of women in German industry during the war, see Hans-Joachim Bieber, *Gewerkschaften in Krieg und Revolution,* Band I, (Hamburg: Christians), 1981, pp. 203–210.

45. *Jahresberichte der Gewerbeaufsichtsbeamten des Staates Wuerttemberg fuer 1914 bis 1918,* Stuttgart 1919, p. 7.

46. AGM DBAG Ut 6.

47. Working women whose husbands were no longer at the front no longer needed welfare payments to sustain themselves, thus relieving some of the pressure on state finances, as General Hindenburg wrote Chancellor Bethmann-Hollweg during the war. "There are uncounted thousands of soldiers' wives with no children who only cost the state money. In addition, thousands of women and girls run around doing nothing or following unused occupations. The principle 'He who does not work should not eat' is justified more than ever before in our present situation, also with regard to women." Stephen Bajohr, *Die Haelfte der Fabrik. Geschichte der Frauenarbeit in Deutschland 1914 bis 1945* (Marburg: Verlag Arbeiterbewegung und Gesellschaftswissenschaft, 1979), pp. 105–106.

48. Otto Fischer, *Die Lohnentwicklung in der Stuttgarter Metallindutrie von 1914 bis 1920,* Diss. Frankfurt/M., 1923. Fischer apparently felt that women did not flood the factories to work for the war effort for the same patriotic reasons which drove the men to exert themselves on behalf of the fatherland— women came to work only for the money, while men went to war because they wished to fulfill their duty. In addition, the author was apparently not considering the wage rates he himself provided for these women throughout his study when he wrote of the women workers' "nice money."

49. *Die Frauenarbeit in der Metallindustrie waehrend des Krieges,* p. 7.

50. *Jahresberichte,* p. 22.

51. HStASt M 77/1 76 Oct. 6, 1918.

52. *Jahresberichte*, p. 22.

53. *Ibid.*; Bieber, *Gewerkschaften in Krieg und Revolution*, 1:204.

54. AGM DBAG DMG Ut 6.

55. *Ibid.*, Arbeiterstand im Monat Oktober 1918.

56. HStASt M 1/9 Bue 265 33c DMG to Kriegarbeitsstelle, Dec. 17, 1917.

57. Dr. Marie Elisabeth Lueders, quoted in Fischer, p. 30, followed by the evaluations of executives with whom Fischer consulted.

58. *Jahresberichte*, p. 23.

59. HStASt E 361 226, July 10, 1918.

60. HStASt M 1/9 Bue 265 33c DMG to Kriegsarbeitsstelle, Dec. 17, 1917.

61. Fischer, *Die Lohnentwicklung*, p. 31; *Die Frauenarbeit in der Metallindustrie waehrend des Krieges*, p. 4.

62. HStAS M 1/11 Kriegsarchiv, Band 1092, Jan. 22, 1918, p. 18. Although never excluding them, Christian and Hirsch-Duncker unions were especially unenthusiastic about working women. As the liberals put it in 1916: "The women belongs in the home, in the interests of raising children and of family life." Bieber, *Gewerkschaften in Krieg und Revolution*, 1:208.

63. This is suggested by Erhard Lucas, *Zwei Formen von Radikalismus in der deutschen Arbeiterbewegung* (Frankfurt: Roter Stern), 1976, p. 251.

64. Fischer, *Die Lohnenlwicklung*, p. 30.

65. HStASt M 1/9 Bue 265 33c DMG to Kriegsarbeitsstelle, Dec. 17, 1917.

66. *Die Gleichheit*, March 17, 1916, collected in HStASt M 77/1 60. A survey of wages in the metal and machinery industries contends that the differentials between male and female earnings grew during the war, with women earning generally 49–54% of men's wages between 1916–1918. Gerhard Brey, *Wages in Germany 1871–1945* (Princeton: Princeton University Press, 1960), p. 206. According to Bieber, "in 81.3% of metal factories women received smaller wages for the same work; for three-quarters of them, the difference was 30–50%, for others even 70% or more." Bieber, *Gewerkschaften in Krieg und Revolution*, 1:206.

67. *Jahresberichte*, p. 41. Not only working conditions, but also the burden of family responsibilities took their toll on working women's health. Bajohr has reconstructed a typical women's work day during the war: 4:00—wake up; 6:00—work; noon—lunch break; 13:00 to 18:00—work; 18:00 to 19:30—food shopping, journey home; 19:30 to 20:30—cook, eat, rest; 20:30 to 22:00—housework; 22:00 or perhaps 23:00 until 4:00—sleep. Bajohr, *Die Haelfte der Fabrik*, p. 151.

68. *Die Frauenarbeit in der Metallindustrie*, p. 6.

69. HStASt M 1/9 316a, Dec. 11, 1916.

70. Renate Bridenthal and Claudia Koonz, "Beyond Kinder, Kueche, Kirche: Weimar Women in Politics and Work," in Renate Bridenthal, et al., eds., *When Biology Became Destiny: Women in Weimar and Nazi Germany* (New York: Monthly Review Press, 1984), pp. 45, 47–51.

71. *700-Jahre-Feier der Grossen Kreisstadt Sindelfingen* (Sindelfingen: Roehm, 1964), p. 19.

72. Hermann Weisert, *Geschichte der Stadt Sindelfingen von den Anfaengen bis heute* (Sindelfingen: Roehm, 1975), p. 115. Hans Sonntag, Werk Sindelfingen 1915–1935, unpublished manuscript and photo collection in AGM DBAG, p. 2.

73. AGM DBAG Sindelfingen (Sifi) 1, p. 2.

74. *Ibid.*, p. 9.

75. *Ibid.*, p. 13. In turn, Sindelfingen may have inspired Daimler engineer Richard Lang's reorganization of the Untertuerkheim factory beginning in 1919. See below, ch. 5.

76. HStASt M 77/1 76 Arbeiter-, Maschinen-, u. Materialbestand am 11.4.18 and 7.11.18. HStASt M 77/1 76, M.A. 147, May 24, 1918. According to HStASt M 77/1 76 M.A. 69, the military supervision required that these reports be filled out by the firm twice weekly. Of the 5,616 working at the plant (including 586 clerks) on Nov. 1, 1918, 1,306 were women, 2,841 had been sent from the front by the army, while 1,469 were supplied by the provisions of the Auxiliary Service Law. AGM DBAG Hans Sonntag, Werk Sindelfingen, 1915–1935, p. 9.

77. AGM DBAG DMG Sifi 1, p. 30.

78. Weisert, *Geschichte*, p. 115.

79. *Neues Wiener Tagblatt,* April 11, 1915, p. 29 in AGM DBAG DMG 4 (26).

80. AGM DBAG DMG 17 Berge to PKM, Abt. A.7 L., Feb. 12, 1918. The Daimler board of trustees later expressed its regrets regarding the "capricious action of Herr Berge" but otherwise did not distance itself from any part of DMG's production and pricing policies. Berge, as chief of daily operations and one of the most important figures at Daimler, was clearly empowered to send this letter, and the trustees' regrets were never articulated any further. Protokolle PD No. 143 Aufsichtsrat-Sitzung, March 26, 1918, p. 2. The Daimler Affair has, until now, only been mentioned in the literature. See Feldman, *Army, Industry, and Labor,* pp. 480–81; Mai, *Kriegswirtschaft,* pp. 75–76; Wolfram Wette, "Reichstag and 'Kriegsgewinnlerei' (1916–1918). Die Anfaenge parlamentarischer Ruestungskontrolle in Deutschland," *Militaergeschichtliche Mitteilungen* (1984), 2:43–45.

81. *Ibid.*, p. 2.

82. *Ibid.*

83. AGM DBAG DMG 226, Berge to Weisshaar, Feb. 19, 1918.

84. *Der Hauptausschuss des deutschen Reichstags 1915–1918,* 4:2026.

85. *Ibid.*, pp. 2026–28.

86. *Ibid.*, p. 2026.

87. *Ibid.*, p. 2029.

88. *Ibid.*, p. 2032.

89. AGM DBAG DMG 177/3 Eisernes Buch der DMG; AGM DBAG DMG 17 (82) "Anzeige gegen die Firma Daimler-Motoren-Gesellschaft in Stuttgart-Untertuerkheim wegen uebermaessigen Preiswuchers und versuchten Betrugs," p. 1.

90. AGM DBAG DMG 17 (82) "Anzeige," p. 2.

91. *Ibid.*, p. 2–3.

92. *Ibid.*, p. 4.

93. *Ibid.* The copy from 1921 reads 12,500 marks which has been corrected to read 15,200. According to the context of the paragraph, the latter figure is correct.

94. HStASt M 77/1 76 M.A. 72, April 20, 1918.

95. HStASt M 77/1 76 Bekanntmachung, March 6, 1918.

96. HStASt M 77/1 76 Statement of General Schaefer, March 6, 1918.

97. *Ibid.*

98. HStASt M 77/1 76 Letter from Roth, March 7, 1918.

99. *Ibid.* See *Die Schaubuehne,* March 21, 1918, p. 279.

100. HStASt M 77/1 76 Stellvertretende Generalkommando, Stuttgart, March 8, 1918.

101. HStASt M 77/1 March 7, 1918.

102. AGM DBAG DMG 82 Stadt. Polizeidirektion, March 3, 1918.

103. *Staatsanzeiger fuer Wuerttemberg,* March 14, 1918, Erklaerung. The declaration is reproduced in G. Cordes, ed., *Krieg Revolution Republik* (Ulm: Vaas, 1978), p. 30. See also AGM DBAG DMG 17 (82).

104. *Vorwaerts,* March 9, 1918.

105. *Ibid.* AGM DBAG DMG 18 Der Fall Daimler, pp. 6–7.

106. AGM DBAG DMG 18 Der Fall Daimler, pp. 2–3. This took place at a special meeting of the stockholders in late 1917 and is noted in the financial reports for the year in AGM DBAG.

107. *Ibid.,* p. 22.

108. *Der Hauptausschuss des deutschen Reichstags 1915–1918,* 4:2032–33.

109. *Handel und Industrie. Zeitschrift fuer das gesamte Wirtschaftsleben,* March 16, 1918, p. 154.

110. *Prager Tagblatt,* April 24, 1918 (in DBAG archive).

111. Albrecht Fischer, *Verband Wuerttembergischer Metallindustrieller e.V. 1897 bis 1934.* (Stuttgart, n.d.), p. 5.

112. HStASt 77/1 76 M.A. 72, April 10, 1918.

113. AGM DBAG DMG 17 (81) There were at least four sessions in 1918: March 28, April 8, Oct. 26, and Oct. 30.

114. AGM DBAG DMG 17 (81) March 28, 1918, p. 1.

115. *Ibid.,* p. 5.

116. See below, p. 132.

117. AGM DBAG DMG 17 (81) Am 29.11. mdt. exp. Sch.

118. AGM DBAG DMG 17 (82). Somewhat later, the company sought to explain Wohnlich's motives by presenting its own psychology of clerks: "It is oft observed that clerks who have unimportant posts picture themselves as if their work was decisive and the most important for the whole corporation. This attitude is useful, since it prevents those clerks who have the same job day after day from becoming mentally crippled." When Wohnlich finally received a new task, he was so excited that "he had to perform it several times." When his superior mentioned "something about the Reichstag," the "political fanatic" somehow got the idea that his work was part of an attempt to deceive the Reich. (There is no mention in any of the documents about Wohnlich's political affiliations.) Wohnlich then decided to use his belief in an extortion attempt which

failed. Ultimately, he was a victim of "self-hypnosis" which was so "widespread during the war." This unusual account is from AGM DBAG DMG 86 Wie kam Wohnlich zu seiner Anzeige.

119. On the perception of injustice and the reasons why men and women revolt, see Barrington Moore, *Injustice* (White Plains, NY: Sharpe, 1978), pp. 45–47, 334–336.

120. *Daimler Werksnachrichten,* Oct. 18, 1920. AGM DBAG DMG 18 Notizen zum Bericht, p. 8.

121. *Daimler Werksnachrichten,* Oct. 18, 1920 Beilage.

122. *Ibid.*

123. AGM DBAG DMG 26 (131) Geschaeftsjahr 1914.

124. AGM DBAG DMG 26 (131) Geschaeftsjahr 1915–1918. A document in DMG 86 notes that Berge explained it was necessary to amortize the wideranging investments on factory buildings and machinery immediately during the war because the "possibility of using the new acquisitions after the war could not be [considered] a sure prospect." This unmarked document follows the questioning of the Daimler director Schippert by the Wuertt. Landesgericht, Feb. 25, 1921, in DMG 86.

125. *Bericht der Pruefungskommission des Preuss. Kriegsministeriums in Sachen Daimler-Motoren-Gesellschaft,* Sept. 5, 1919. AGM DBAG DMG 228. According-ing to a letter from Berge to the Staatsanwaltshaft beim Landgericht I in Berlin, dated Nov. 2, 1920, only 100 copies of the report were published. The MdR Keil (SPD) brought an *Anfrage* in the Reichstag in Sept. 1920 urging that the report be made available to authorities investigating DMG's tax payments during the war. DMG 88.

126. AGM DBAG DMG 228 *Bericht der Pruefungskommission,* p. 35.

127. AGM DBAG DMG 82 K. Staatsanwaltschaft Stuttgart, March 14, 1918, p. 1.

128. HStASt M 77/1 76 M.A. 25, March 26, 1918; M.A. 27, March 27, 1918; M.A. 45, April 3, 1918.

129. This account of the military's frustratingly patient acquisition process is based on HStASt M 77/1 76 M.A. 28, 49, 50, 114, 126, 137 (March and April 1918).

130. HStASt M 77/1 76 M.A. 148, May 24, 1918.

131. HStASt M 77/1 76 M.A. 161, May 31, 1918.

132. HStASt M 77/1 76 M.A. 114, April 26, 1918.

133. HStASt M 77/1 76 M.A. 252, July 20, 1918.

134. HStASt M 77/1 76 M.A. 301, Sept. 21, 1918.

135. HStASt M 77/1 76 M.A. 302, n.d.

136. *Handbuch des Vereins Arbeiterpresse* (Berlin: Verein Arbeiterpresse, 1927), pp. 580, 584; Max Schwarz, *MdR. Bibliographisches Handbuch des Reichstage* (Hannover: Verlag fuer Literatur und Zeitgeschehen, 1965), p. 742. Salm was a member of the National Assembly in 1919 and, later, a DMV functionary. He died in the concentration camp Dachau in 1938. Schifferdecker was a member of the Landtag in 1919 and likewise a DMV functionary in the 1920's, but no further information about him is available.

137. HStASt M 630 12 DMV to DMG, May 27, 1915.

138. HStASt M 630 12 DMV (Hosenthien) to Stell. Generalkomm., no date, but between June 9 and June 18, 1915.

139. *Ibid.*

140. HStASt M 630 12 DMG to Stell. Generalkomm., June 3, 1915.

141. *Ibid.*

142. HStASt M 630 12 KW Zentralstelle fuer Gewerbe u. Handel to Stell. Generalkomm., June 18, 1915.

143. HStASt M 630 12 KW Gewerbeinspektor fuer den 1. Bezirk to DMV, August 9, 1915.

144. HStASt M 630 DMV to Gewerbeinspektor des 1. Bezirk, Aug. 12, 1915; HStASt M 630 12 KW Zentralstelle fuer Gewerbe u. Handel to Stell. Generalkomm., Aug. 19, 1915.

145. Mai, *Kriegswirtschaft*, p. 414.

146. HStASt M 1/9 273 Salm & Banhart to DMG, Nov. 16, 1916.

147. HStASt M 1/9 273 DMG to WKM, Nov. 20, 1916.

148. HStASt M 1/9 273 DMG to WKM, Nov. 24, 1916.

149. HStASt M 1/9 273 DMG to WKM Abt. fuer Waffen u. Feldgeraete, Dec. 2, 1916.

150. Juergen Kocka, *Klassengesellschaft im Krieg.* (Goettingen: Vandenhoeck u. Ruprecht, 1978), p. 71.

151. HStASt M 1/9 273.

152. Kocka, *Klassengesellschaft* p. 73.

153. HStASt M 1/9 273 Berge to P. Daimler, Sept. 25, 1916.

154. HStASt M 1/9 273 Berge to Sekler on *Angestellten* agreement of July 4, 1917, July 6, 1917.

155. This account is taken from the "Bericht des Oberkommandos in den Marken an das PKM ueber die Erfahrungen bei der Militarisierung von Betrieben," in Deist, *Militaer und Innenpolitik*, 1:637.

156. *Ibid.*; HSG, Arbeitswissenschaftliches Institut der Deutschen Arbeitsfront, "Die Streiks im ersten Weltkrieg," p. 8. According to this report, the other six were Deutsche Waffen-u. Munitionsfabrik, Berliner Maschinenbau, Borsig, AEG, Argus Motor, and Flug-Verkehr.

157. HStASt M 77/1 76, Nr. 15, Jan. 18, 1918.

158. HStASt M 77/1 76 Berge u. Sekler to Mueller, Feb. 20, 1918.

159. HStASt M 1/9 273 AA to DMG, Jan. 10, 1918.

160. *Ibid.*

161. HStASt M 1/9 273 Weisshaar to Berlin, Jan. 15, 1918.

162. *Ibid.*

163. HStASt M 1/9 273 Inspektion der Fliegertruppen to WKM, Jan. 23, 1918.

164. See the undated document produced after the Feb. 5, 1918 meeting of the *Schlichtungsausschuss*, Schiedspruch.

165. *Ibid.*

166. HStASt M 77/1 76 Nr. 23 AA to DMG, March 22, 1918.

167. HStASt M 77/1 76 AA to DMG, April 10, 1918.

168. HStASt M 77/1 93 Salm & Schifferdecker to DMG, May 23, 1918.
169. *Ibid.;* AGM DBAG Protokolle PD 31 P. Daimler to DMG Verwaltungsausschuss, Sept. 6, 1918.
170. HStASt M 77/1 76 No. 192.
171. HStASt M 77/1 93 von Holzhauser to WKM, June 4, 1918.
172. *Ibid.*
173. HStASt M 77/1 93 This is mentioned in a later letter from Salm to DMG, Aug. 17, 1918.
174. HStASt M 77/1 93 DMV to WKM, June 18, 1918; HStAS 77/1 93 Letter from von Marchtaler, June 16, 1918. R. Leimanis helped decipher this handwritten letter.
175. HStASt M 77/1 93 Issued by *Arbeiterausschuss,* no date.
176. HStASt M 77/1 93 "Geheim!" June 15, 1918; HStAS 77/1 93 Letter from von Marchtaler, June 16, 1918.
177. HStASt M 77/1 93 Militarisierung von Betrieben (General von Schaefer), April 23, 1918.
178. AGM DBAG DMG 31 and HStASt M 77/1 93 Zentralpolizeistelle (Gessler) to Stell. Generalkomm., June 21, 1918.
179. AGM DBAG DMG 31 General von Schaefer, June 1918.
180. HStASt M 77/1 93 AA to WKM, June 21, 1918.
181. HStASt M 77/1 76 Bekanntmachung, June 21, 1918.
182. HStASt M 77/1 76 Holzhauser to WKM, July 27, 1918. The figures which I have used have been collected from the reports in HStASt M 77/1 76.
183. HStASt M 77/1 76.
184. *Ibid.*
185. HStASt M 1/9 273 DMG to WKM Kriegsarbeitsstelle, Sept. 10, 1918; AGM DBAG Protokolle PD 31 P. Daimler to DMG Verwaltungsausschuss, Sept. 6, 1918.
186. HStASt M 1/9 273 Salm to DMG, Sept. 24, 1918.
187. *Ibid.*
188. Sums of 19.5 and 22.5 million marks are also used in the company's letter of October 12, 1918. HStASt M 1/9 273.
189. From the information collected by the military, there is no reason to believe this claim. See in particular the comparison of wages prepared by the *Abteilung fuer Waffen und Feldgeraete* in HStASt M 1/9 273, Oct. 2, 1918.
190. HStASt M 77/1 93 Zentralpolizeistelle Wuertt. to Stell. Generalkomm., Oct. 23, 1918.
191. AGM DBAG DMG 36 (166) Zur Steuer der Wahrheit. Taetigkeitsbericht des Arbeiterausschusses der DMG Untertuerkheim, p. 4.
192. *Ibid.,* p. 5.
193. *Ibid.*
194. *Ibid.*
195. HStASt M 1/9 273 DMG to WKM, Oct. 12, 1918; Fischer, *Verband wuerttembergischer Metallindustrieller E.V. 1897–1934,* p. 17.
196. HStASt M 1/9 273 Telegram from DMG to SS Wumba Berlin, no date, probably Oct. 16, 1918.

197. HStASt M 1/9 273 WKM (Letzgus), Oct. 26, 1918.

198. AGM DBAG DMG 226 DMG to Stell. Generalkomm., Nov. 2, 1918.

199. HStASt M 1/9 273 DMG to WKM Kriegsarbeitsstelle, Oct. 29, 1918.

200. Deist, ed., *Militaer und Innenpolitik*, 2:937–41.

201. The best account of the "Westmeyer group" and political activity in Wuerttemberg during the war is Manfred Scheck, *Zwischen Weltkrieg und Revolution* (Cologne: Boehlau, 1981). Of Westmeyer, the police wrote that his death robbed the radicals of "their most influential and dangerous leader." HStASt E 150 Bue. 2051 (3) 655 Zentralpolizeistelle Wuertt. to Min. des Innern, Feb. 13, 1918.

202. HStASt E 150 Bue. 2051 (2) 470, Polizeidirektion der Stadt Stuttgart to Min. des Innern, April 17, 1917.

203. HStASt E 150 Bue. 2051 (3) 653, Polizeidirektion der Stadt Stuttgart to Min. des Innern, Feb. 4, 1918.

204. HStASt E 150 Bue. 2051 (2) 312, Staedt. Polizeidirektion to Min. des Innern, July 13, 1916; 313, K. Wuertt. Landespolizeizentralstelle Stuttgart, July 21, 1916. It is not possible to verify whether these youths worked at DMG.

205. HStASt E 150 Bue. 2051 (2) 585, Polizeidirektion der Stadt Stuttgart, Aug. 16, 1917; 592, Staedt. Polizeidirektion Stuttgart, Sept. 1, 1917; 593, Sozialistische Jugendbewegung Deutschlands (leaflet).

206. In Duesseldorf, "the new militancy . . . was precipitated by acute food shortages." Mary Nolan, *Social Democracy and Society*, p. 263.

5. RED STAR OVER MERCEDES

1. Arthur Rosenberg, *Die Entstehung der deutschen Republik 1871–1918* (Berlin: Rowohlt, 1930), p. 254.

2. HStAS E 150 Bue. 2051 (3) 798, Polizeidirektion der Stadt Stuttgart to K. Ministerium des Innern, Nov. 5, 1918, pp. 7–8; Eberhard Kolb and Klaus Schoenhoven, *Regionale und lokale Raeteorganisationen in Wuerttemberg* (Duesseldorf: Droste, 1976), p. li.

3. Fritz Rueck, *November 1918. Die Revolution in Wuerttemberg*, 1958, p. 15.

4. HStAS E 150 Bue. 2051 (3) 777, Stellvertretender Generalstab der Armee, Abt. IIIb, Oct. 19, 1918.

5. Manfred Scheck, *Zwischen Weltkrieg und Revolution* (Cologne: Boehlau, 1981), pp. 117–18.

6. Wilhelm Keil, *Erlebnisse eines Sozialdemokraten* (Stuttgart, 1947/48), 2: 37.

7. Rueck, *November 1918*, p. 21.

8. HStAS E 150 Bue. 2051 (3) 798, Nov. 5, 1918, pp. 7–8; and 785, handwritten note, Nov. 4, 1918.

9. Rueck, *November 1918*, p. 22. According to the *Rote Fahne* of November 5, 4,000 workers at Daimler-Sindelfingen staged a wildcat strike and demonstration the afternoon of the same day. HStAS E 135 vorlaeufig Bue 1995. During

1918–1920, nearly all industrial conflicts spread quickly from Untertuerkheim to Sindelfingen. Reflecting on the events of the previous months in January 1919, Berge of DMG wrote, "A strike in Untertuerkheim will steadily have as a consequence the same phenomenon in Sindelfingen." AGM DBAG DMG 26 (131) Letter from Berge to von Kaulla, Jan. 10, 1919.

10. Wilhelm Blos, *Von der Monarchie zum Volksstaat. Zur Geschichte der Revolution in Deutschland, inbesondere in Wuerttemberg,* II (Stuttgart, 1922/23), p. 18.

11. StAL E 150 Bue 2051 (3) 800a, Rundschreiben der Bezirksleitung Stuttgart des DMV gegen wilde Demonstrationen, Nov. 6, 1918; G. Cordes, ed. *Krieg Revolution Republik* (Ulm: Vaas, 1979), p. 76.

12. HStASt E 150 Bue. 2051 (3) Nov. 6, 1918; *Krieg Revolution Republik,* p. 74.

13. Keil, *Erlebnisse,* 2:40–41. Keil wrote that the regime's description of the 16 workers as Spartacist leaders was overblown: "Only a few of these could be described as such." p. 47.

14. StAL E 150 Bue 2051 (3) B1. 807.

15. Keil, *Erlebnisse,* 2: 47.

16. *Krieg Revolution Republik,* p. 80 [*Schwaebische Tagwacht,* Nov. 9, 1918, p. 1]; Keil, *Erlebnisse,* 2: 51. HStAS 135 vorl. 2055 "An das werktaetige Volk Wuerttembergs!"

17. HStAS M E 135 vorlaeufig 1995, *Die rote Fahne,* Nov. 15, 1918, p. 2.

18. Keil, *Erlebnisse,* 2:72.

19. Kolb and Schoenhoven, *Regionale und lokale Raeteorganisation,* p. 18.

20. HStAS M E 135 Bue 83 vorlaeufig 8406, Ergebnis der Wahl zum Arbeiterrat am 14. Nov. 1918.

21. AGM DBAG DMG 6 (37) Berge to von Kaulla, Nov. 20, 1918, p. 2.

22. AGM DBAG DMG 6 (37) Berge to von Kaulla, Nov. 23, 1918, p. 3. For the trade union officials at Daimler and in Germany as a whole, "law, order and hard work went . . . as the first duty of the citizen. The social revolution did not stand on the agenda for them." Heinrich Potthoff, *Gewerkschaften und Politik zwischen Revolution und Inflation* (Duesseldorf: Droste), 1979, p. 30.

23. AGM DBAG DMG 98a Vertrag zwischen dem Reichs- (Militaer-) Fiskus . . . und der Daimler Motoren Gesellschaft in Untertuerkheim, Jan. 11, 1919.

24. These are taken from daily reports in AGM DBAG Ut 11.

25. AGM DBAG DMG 6 (37) Berge to von Kaulla, Nov. 23, 1918, p. 4.

26. Volker Hentschel, *Geschichte der deutschen Sozialpolitik 1880–1980* (Frankfurt/Main: Suhrkamp, 1983), p. 66.

27. Gerald D. Feldman and Irmgard Steinisch, *Industrie und Gewerkschaften 1918–1924. Die ueberforderte Zentralarbeitsgemeinschaft* (Stuttgart: Deutsche Verlags-Anstalt, 1985), p. 22. See Hentschel, *Geschichte,* pp. 67–70.

28. Gerald D. Feldman, "The Origins of the Stinnes-Legien Agreement: A Documentation," *Internationale wissenschaftliche Korrespondenz zur Geschichte der deutschen Arbeiterbewegung,* (1973), 19/20: 83. The Stinnes-Legien pact is in Feldman and Steinisch, *Industrie und Gewerkschaften,* pp. 135–37;

Robert Moeller, "Winners as Losers in the German Inflation: Peasant Protest over the Controlled Economy, 1920–1923," in Gerald D. Feldman et al., *Die Deutsche Inflation. Eine Zwischenbilanz* (Berlin: De Gruyter, 1982), p. 285.

29. AGM DBAG DMG 34 (150/3) Betr: Richtlinien fuer die Uebergangszeit, November 15, 1918.

30. AGM DBAG DMG 35 (150) Auszug aus der Niederschrift ueber die Vorstandssitzung von 26. Okt. 1918.

31. AGM DBAG DMG 35 (150) Rundschreiben No. 85, Nov. 8, 1918.

32. AGM DBAG DMG 37 (175) Berge to von Kaulla, Nov. 26, 1918, p. 3.

33. AGM DBAG DMG 36 (166) *Zur Steuer der Wahrheit. Taetigkeitsbericht des Arbeiterausschusses der D.M.G. Untertuerkeim,* p. 11.

34. AGM DBAG Ut 6.

35. AGM DBAG 37 (175) Berge to von Kaulla, Dec. 6, 1918.

36. AGM DBAG DMG 36 (166) Berge to von Kaulla, Dec. 18, 1918.

37. AGM DBAG DMG 36 (166) *Zur Steuer der Wahrheit,* p. 11.

38. AGM DBAG DMG 36 (166) Berge to von Kaulla, Dec. 23, 1918.

39. HStAS M E 361 Arbeitsministerium Bue 239.

40. HStAS M E 361 Bue 237 Demobilmachungsamt, Dec. 11, 1918.

41. HStAS M 1/9 316 c VI 1b Verhandlungen der verfassungsgegeben Wuertt. Landesversammlung. 13. Sitzung, Stuttgart, 8 Mai, 1919, p. 286.

42. AGM DBAG DMG 17 (83–85) On the agreement, see below.

43. AGM DBAG DMG 37 (175) *Daimler Werksnachrichten* Dec. 3, 1919.

44. See chapter 6.

45. AGM DBAG DMG 37 (175) Die neue Regierungsverfuegung ueber Entlohnung bei Kurzarbeit, Feb. 18, 1919.

46. AGM DBAG DMG 37 (175) Berge to von Kaulla, Nov. 30, 1918.

47. The report on Daimler's energy needs is in *Daimler Werksnachrichten,* Nov. 12, 1919.

48. The information is from an unpublished manuscript and photo collection at DBAG, Hans Sonntag, "Werk Sindelfingen 1915–35." It apparently dates from the late 1930s.

49. AGM DBAG DMG 98a Vertrag zwischen dem Reichs- (Militaer-) Fiskus . . . und der Daimler Motoren Gesellschaft in Untertuerkheim, Jan. 11, 1919.

50. *Ibid.*

51. AGM DBAG DMG 26 (131) Berge to von Kaulla, Jan. 10, 1919.

52. Guenter Werckmeister, "Die DBAG und ihre Ursprungsfirmen 1890–1940," unpublished manuscript, 1940, p. 61.

53. AGM DBAG Statistik.

54. Mai, *Kriegswirtschaft und Arbeiterbewegung 1914–1918* p. 296.

55. AGM DBAG DMG 26 (131) Berge to von Kaulla, Jan. 10, 1919.

56. *Ibid.*

57. Gertrud Kling, *Die Novemberrevolution 1918 und der Kampf um die Verteidigung der Demokratie im Fruehjahr 1919 in Wuerttemberg,* Dissertation, Halle/Saale, 1967, p. 173.

58. AGM DBAG DMG 167 Ergebnis der Arbeiterausschusswahl vom 28. [-30.] 1. 1919.

59. AGM DBAG DMG 37 (175) Letter from AA to DMG, Feb. 11, 1919.

60. AGM DBAG DMG 37 (175) Berge to von Kaulla, Dec. 7, 1918.

61. AGM DBAG DMG 36 (166) Berge to von Kaulla, Dec. 23, 1918; DMG 37 (175) Berge to von Kaulla, Dec. 18, 1918.

62. AGM DBAG 37 (175) Berge to von Kaulla, Dec. 18, 1918.

63. *Schwaebischer Merkur*, February 26, 1919, p. 6.

64. HStAS M E 135 vorl. Bue 2034 "An das klassenbewusste Proletariat!"

65. Scheck, *Zwischen Weltkrieg und Revolution*, p. 212.

66. *Schwaebischer Merkur*, Feb. 26, 1919, p. 6.

67. *Ibid.*

68. HStAS M E 135 vorl. Bue 2117 "Der Generalstreik!"

69. Paul Hahn, *Erinnerungen aus der Revolution in Wuerttemberg. Der rote Hahn, eine Revolutionserscheinung* in *Denkwuerdigkeiten aus der Umwaelzung*, 3. Band. (Stuttgart: Bergers Literarisches Buero und Verlagsanstalt, 1923), p. 75.

70. HStAS M E 135 vorl. Bue. 2037, *Sozialdemokrat*, Feb. 24, 1919 Sonderausdruck.

71. HStAS M E 135 vorl. Bue. 2002, Die Staatsregierung, Feb. 26, 1919.

72. *Darstellungen. Die Kaempfe*, p. 33.

73. Hahn, *Erinnerungen*, p. 75.

74. Kolb and Schoenhoven, *Raeteorganisationen*, p. 330.

75. Hahn, *Erinnerungen*, pp. 75–76.

76. Several of these searches are described in the reports by the security forces in HStAS M E 135 vorl. 2648.

77. *Schwaebischer Merkur*, April 1, 1919, p. 3.

78. HStAS M E 135 vorl. Bue 2006 "An die Frauen und Muetter!"

79. *Schwaebischer Merkur*, April 22, 1919, p. 5.

80. HStAS M E 130a Staatsministerium 35, Staedt. Polizeidirektion Stuttgart, April 4, 1919.

81. *Ibid.*, pp. 27. 29. The police report did not include the suspects' place of employment.

82. *Schwaebische Tagwacht*, April 5, 1919, p. 5.

83. *Schwaebischer Merkur*, April 6 and 7, 1919.

84. HStAS M E 135 vorl. Bue 2648 "Die Betriebsvertraensleute der Sozialdemokratischen Partei Gross-Stuttgarts forden von der Regierung," April 9, 1919.

85. AGM DBAG DMG 37 (175) Telegrams from Berge to von Kaulla, April 22, 23, 24, and 25, 1919.

86. HStAS 150 Bue. 2051 (4) 876, Wuertt. Landespolizeiamt to Ministerium des Innern, July 13, 1919.

87. HStAS E 150 Bue. 2051 (4) 873, Zentralleitung der SK Wuertt. to Ministerium des Innern, July 7, 1919.

88. HStAS E 150 Bue. 2051 (4) 885, Zentralleitung der SK Wuertt. to Ministerium des Innern, July 29, 1919.

89. AGM DBAG DMG 37 (175) Groetzinger to DMG, April 9, 1919.

90. Andreas Kunz, "Verteilungskampf oder Interessenkonsensus? Einkommensentwicklung und Sozialverhalten von Arbeitnehmergruppen in der Inflationszeit 1914 bis 1924," in Feldman, et al., eds., *Die deutsche Inflation*, pp. 367, 370, 380.

91. AGM DBAG DMG 37 (175) Berge to von Kaulla, April 29, 1919.

92. AGM DBAG DMG 37 (175) Berge to von Kaulla, May 6, 1919.

93. AGM DBAG DMG 37 (175) Letter from AA to DMG, Feb. 26, 1919.

94. AGM DBAG DMG 37 (175) Berge to von Kaulla, May 6, 1919.

95. "Gruppenfabrikation," *Daimler Werkzeitung* (1919) No. 1, p. 4; R. Lang and W. Hellpach, *Gruppenfabrikation* (Berlin: Springer, 1922).

96. *Daimler Werkzeitung*, (1919) No. 1, p. 4.

97. *Ibid.* From the available evidence, it is unclear how extensive the reorganization of the plant in 1919 actually was. Daimler's Lang wrote as if it had been a total transformation.

98. See chapter 4.

99. Lang & Hellpach, *Gruppenfabrikation*, p. 3.

100. *Ibid.*, pp. 65–66. The social psychologist Hellpach, who took up the shift to group production at Daimler, was one of the first German professors to lecture on factory psychology at the university of Karlsruhe in 1906–7. There, in 1921, he founded the Institut fuer Sozialpsychologie which made factory problems its area of study. Hellpach brought out his study of group production in 1922. A firm adherent of the "tradition of cultural pessimism, sceptical of progress and critical of capitalism," Hellpach used the Daimler book to press his critique of the factory: he questioned whether it provided the best conditions for modern production. He felt that the factory, with its concentration of workers, brought about "proletarian class consciousness," "social-revolutionary ill-will," and "wage greediness." Daimler's move to group production led him to speculate that it was possible to conceive of alternative organizations of work. Peter Hinrichs, *Um die Seele des Arbeiters* (Cologne: Pahl-Rugenstein, 1981), pp. 170–79.

101. *Ibid.*, p. 1.

102. See Gunnar Stollberg, *Die Rationalisierungsdebatte 1908–1933, Freie Gewerkschaften zwischen Mitwirkung und Gegenwehr* (Frankurt: Campus, 1981), pp. 49–51; and Robert Brady, *The Rationalization Movement in German Industry: A Study in the Evolution of Economic Planning* (New York: Howard Fertig, 1974), pp. 29–30, for a discussion of group and flow production.

103. Lang and Hellpach, *Gruppenfabrikation*, p. 88.

104. *Der Deutscher Metallarbeiter-Verband im Jahre 1919, Jahr- und Handbuch fuer Verbandsmitglieder*. Stuttgart: Schlicke, 1920, p. 266.

105. AGM DBAG DMG 37 (175).

106. *Der Deutsche Metallarbeiter-Verband im Jahre 1919*, p. 58.

107. AGM DBAG DMG 7a Erlaeuterungs-Bestimmungen, Aug. 2, 1919.

108. AGM DBAG DMG 36 Letter from DMG to VWMI Stuttgart, June 30, 1919.

109. AGM DBAG DMG 37 (175) Kollektiv-Abkommen fuer die Metall-Industrie. Berechnung der Mehrkosten.

110. AGM DBAG DMG 36 (167) DMG to AA, June 2, 1919.

111. AGM DBAG DMG 36 (167) Letter from AA to DMG, Nov. 17, 1919, copy.

112. AGM DBAG DMG 36 (167) Wuertt. Arbeitsministerium to DMG, Nov. 17, 1919.

113. *Die Handels-Zeitung des Berliner Tageblatts,* Jan. 13, 1920.

114. *Ibid.* The editorialist also noted that all of the calculations were the firm's own and recalled "the peculiar calculation tricks of Daimler . . . from wartime."

115. Marx thought that the "piece-wage is the form of wages most in harmony with the capitalist mode of production." He also understood its contribution to disciplining a work force: "Since the quality and intensity of the work are here [with the piece-wage system] controlled by the form of the wage itself, superintendence of labour becomes in great part superfluous." Karl Marx, *Capital* (New York: International, 1967), 1: 556.

116. This marks a major change from Schumann's picture of the foundry workers at Daimler in 1908 as being "not necessary" and not really skilled workers. His observation dates from the period before the new foundry was fully operational. Schumann, *Die Arbeiter,* p. 40.

117. Data on wages for the period are in AGM DBAG DMG 37 (175).

118. K. Roth, *Die andere Arbeiterbewegung* (Munich: Trikont, 1975); E. Brockhaus, *Zusammensetzung und Neustrukturierung der Arbeiterklasse vor dem ersten Weltkrieg* (Munich: Trikont, 1975). For an excellent analysis of radicalism among workers in the Ruhr, see Erhard Lucas, *Zwei Formen von Radikalismus in der deutschen Arbeiterbewegung* (Frankfurt/Main: Roter Stern, 1976).

6. THE END OF THE REVOLUTIONARY ERA

1. A military report dated October 28, 1918, provides the following totals for workers at the plants: Daimler-Motoren-Gesellschaft 14,614; Bosch-Stuttgart 5328; Bosch-Feuerbach 4541; Maschinenfabrik Esslingen 3107. HStASt M 77/1 Bue 93, Die kriegswichtigsten Betriebe nach Zonen eingeteilt, Oct. 28, 1918, p. 1.

2. StAL E 392 22 abg. 1 Niederschrift der Besprechung am 14.8. 1920, p. 7.

3. Hentschel, *Geschichte der deutschen Sozialpolitik 1880–1980,* pp. 78–91.

4. *Daimler Werksnachrichten,* June 3, 1920, p. 21.

5. *Ibid.,* p. 22.

6. The information on the lists for the Betriebsrat election is contained in or has been compiled from *Ibid.,* pp. 23–25. The profile of the rank-and-file activists at Daimler emerges from this data.

7. AGM DBAG DMG 167 "Achtung! Achtung! Auf zur Wahl des Betriebsrates."

8. AGM DBAG DMG 167 "Arbeiter! Arbeiterinnen! Zurueck zur Arbeit!" As we have seen, Salm and Schifferdecker, officials of the Metalworkers Union (DMV) and mainstream Social Democrats, were the most prominent figures on

the Workers' Committee at Daimler during the war years. During 1919, both were deputies—Salm in the National Assembly at Weimar, Schifferdecker in the Landtag in Stuttgart. Salm returned to work at Daimler in 1920, and re-entered the workers' committee as head of the SPD slate which received 20% of the vote.

9. AGM DBAG DMG 168 Fuer die Betriebsratswahl.

10. *Handbuch des Vereins Arbeiterpresse*, 4th ed. (Berlin: Verein Arbeiterpresse, 1927), p. 570; AGM DBAG DMG 36 (168) "Die erste Tat."

11. AGM DBAG 36 (168) Zur Wahl "politischer Arbeiterraete."

12. StAL E 326 12/1 "Die Massnahmen der Wuertt. Regierung zur Durchfuehrung des Steuerabzugs," Oct. 15, 1920 and *Daimler Werksnachrichten*, Oct. 18, 1920.

13. *Daimler Werksnachrichten*, October 18, 1920, p. 41.

14. *Ibid.*, p. 42.

15. *Ibid.*, p. 43.

16. AGM DBAG DMG 18 *Ein neuer Daimler-Skandal. Antwort des frueheren Betriebsrates auf die Daimler-Denkschrift* (Stuttgart: Melcher, n.d. [1920], p. 9.

17. *Daimler Werksnachrichten*, October 18, 1920, p. 44.

18. AGM DBAG DMG 18 *Ein neuer Daimler-Skandal*, p. 10, and StAL E 326 12/1, "Die Massnahmen," pp. 76–77.

19. StAL E 326 12/1 "Die Massnahmen," pp. 74, 77.

20. *Daimler Werksnachrichten*, Oct. 18, 1920, p. 45.

21. StAL E 326 12/1 "Die Massnahmen," p. 75 and *Daimler Werksnachrichten*, Oct. 18, 1920, p. 45

22. See StAL E 326 12/1 "Die Massnahmen," pp. 74–77, and *Daimler Werksnachrichten*, Oct. 18, 1920, pp. 44–47.

23. *Daimler Werksnachrichten*, Oct. 18, 1920, p. 46.

24. *Ibid.*, pp. 45–46.

25. StAL E 326 12/1 "Die Massnahmen," p. 75.

26. *Daimler Werksnachrichten*, Oct. 18, 1920, p. 43. See also Hentschel, *Geschichte der deutschen Sozialpolitik 1880–1980*, pp. 78–91.

27. *Daimler Werksnachrichten*, Oct. 18, 1920, p. 45.

28. *Ibid.*, p. 46; see also StAL E 326 121, p. 75.

29. *Daimler Werksnachrichten*, Oct. 18, 1920, p. 47, and StAL E 326 12/1 "Die Massnahmen," p. 76.

30. StAL E 326 12/1 "Die Massnahmen," p. 75. "Wissen Sie nicht, dass wir in der Revolutionszeit sind?"

31. StAL E 326 12/1 "Die Massnahmen," p. 76.

32. *Daimler Werksnachrichten*, Oct. 18, 1920, p. 49.

33. AGM DBAG DMG, *Ein neuer Daimler Skandal*, pp. 11–13. The Betriebsrat charged that thievery and what amounted to embezzlement among company officials were rampant. On one occasion, the council noted, it had collected evidence concerning a certain official of the firm who had stolen 400 meters of copper wire from the administration building to use in the construction of his

villa. Unknown burglars then broke into the Betriebrat's offices and stole the documentation and other evidence. The security guard on duty, whose boss was the alleged thief, was subsequently furloughed and given 5,000 marks severance pay. "Hush money?" the council asked. When a worker reported to management that his master had had a horse collar produced in his department which was then sold privately outside the firm, the worker was transferred to the works at Sindelfingen, which required an hour's extra commute daily in each direction. The master was not dismissed, according to the factory council's report.

34. On the putsch, see Erich Eyck, *A History of the Weimar Republic. From the Collapse of the Empire to Hindenburg's Election*, vol. 1 (New York: Atheneum, 1970), pp. 147–60. For the reaction to the attempted coup in Stuttgart, see the collection of documents assembled by Gunter Cordes in *Krieg Revolution Republik 1918–1920* (Ulm: Vaas, 1978), pp. 158–67, and also Scheck, *Zwischen Weltkrieg und Revolution,* pp. 269–76. On the workers' revolt in the Ruhr, see Erhard Lucas's three-volume work, *Maerzrevolution 1920* (Frankfurt/Main: Verlag Roter Stern), 1973, 1974, 1977.

35. A description of the incident is found in *Die Kaempfe in Sudwestdeutschland 1919–1923. Darstellungen aus den Nachkriegskaempfen deutscher Truppen u. Freikorps* (Berlin: E.S. Mittler und Sohn, 1939), pp. 56–58.

36. *Daimler Werksnachrichten,* Oct. 18, 1920, p. 47.

37. *Ibid.,* p. 47.

38. *Ibid.*

39. *Ibid.*

40. See the accounts in StAL E 392 *Schwaebischer Merkur,* Aug. 4, 1920, and *Schwaebische Tagwacht,* Aug. 5, 1920. See also Karl Weller, *Die Staatsumwaelzung in Wuerttemberg 1918–1920* (Stuttgart, 1930), p. 321.

41. *Daimler Werksnachrichten,* Oct. 18, 1920, p. 50, and StAL E 326 12/1, p. 76.

42. Scheck, *Zwischen Weltkrieg und Republik,* pp. 282–87.

43. *Daimler Werksnachrichten,* Oct. 18, 1920, p. 44.

44. Scheck, *Zwischen Weltkrieg und Revolution,* pp. 284–85.

45. StAL E 326 12/1, p. 74.

46. Scheck, *Zwischen Weltkrieg und Revolution,* pp. 287–89; Harold James, *The German Slump: Politics and Economics 1924–1936* (Oxford: Clarendon Press, 1986), p. 2.

47. Quoted in Scheck, *Zwischen Weltkrieg und Revolution,* p. 288.

48. StAL E 326 12/1, p. 71. AGM DBAG Verband der Wuerttembergischen Industriellen. Rundschreiben 89, July 26, 1920.

49. *Ibid.* For a unique perspective on the opposition to the tax at Daimler, see AGM DBAG DMG 36, Niederschrift der Besprechung am 18.8.1920, pp. 1–4.

50. StAL E 326 12/1, p. 71. For an impassioned expression of this position, see AGM DBAG DMG 36, Niederschrift, pp. 1–4.

51. StAL E 326 12/1, p. 79.

52. *Daimler Werksnachrichten,* Oct. 18, 1920, pp. 50–51.

53. *Ibid.,* p. 50.

54. AGM DBAG DMG 7a, "Betriebs-Anordnung Nr. 1813, August 9, 1920"; "Betriebs-Anordnung Nr. 1814, August 10, 1920."

55. Scheck, *Zwischen Weltkrieg und Revolution,* pp. 288–89.

56. This account is drawn from the government's report on the campaign in StAL E 326 12/1. See also *Der deutsche Metallarbeiter-Verband im Jahre 1920. Jahr- und Handbuch fuer Verbandsmitglieder* (Stuttgart: Schlicke, 1921), pp. 275–83.

57. AGM DBAG DMG 36 Niederschrift, pp. 3–4.

58. *Ibid.,* p. 3.

59. AGM DBAG VWMI Rundschreiben 96, 97, Aug. 18, 1920.

60. Weller, *Die Staatsumwaelzung in Wuerttemberg 1918–1920,* p. 322, and Scheck, *Zwischen Weltkrieg und Revolution,* p. 288.

61. StAL E 326 12/1, p. 81.

62. *Ibid.*

63. StAL E 326 2/11, Letter to the Daimler-Motoren-Gesellschaft from Staatspraesident Hieber, Aug. 25, 1920.

64. StAL E 326 12/1, p. 79.

65. StAL E 392 39, *Schwaebische Tagwacht,* Sept. 10, 1920; and *Metall,* Aug. 8, 1975, B1.2, AGM DBAG DMG 35 (159).

66. AGM DBAG DMG 37 (176) "Erklaerung"; and *Metall,* Aug. 8, 1975, B1.2, AGM DBAG DMG 35 (159).

67. *Daimler Werksnachrichten,* Oct. 18, 1920, p. 55.

68. *Schwaebischer Merkur,* Aug. 27, 1920, p. 4. and Aug. 28, 1920, p. 4.

69. *Ibid.,* August 30, 1930, "Neueste Nachrichten."

70. *Der deutsche Metallarbeiter-Verband im Jahre 1920,* p. 277.

71. *Ibid.,* p. 279.

72. StAL E 392 35/10 Niederschrift ueber die Besprechung bei der Staatsregierung am 4. Sept. 1920, pp. 2–3.

73. StAL 392 40/13 Auszug aus der Niederschrift, 10.9. 1920, pp. 8–9.

74. StAL 392 35/10 p. 4.

75. AGM DBAG DMG 3 (11) Betriebsfragen . . . Zur Sitzung am 14. Juli 1920, dated Aug. 4, 1920, p. 1.

76. *Ibid.,* pp. 3, 7.

77. Gerald D. Feldman, *Iron and Steel in the German Inflation 1916–1923,* (Princeton: Princeton University Press, 1973), p. 161.

78. StAL 392 22 Niederschrift fuer die am 12. August 1920 stattgefundene Besprechung, p. 1.

79. *Ibid.,* p. 2.

80. *Ibid.,* p. 3.

81. *Ibid.*

82. *Ibid.,* p. 4.

83. *Ibid.,* p. 6.

84. StAL 392 22/abg. 1, p. 16.

85. *Ibid.*, p. 18.
86. *Ibid.*
87. *Ibid.*, p. 19.
88. StAL 392 Lang and Sekler to the Arbitration Council, Aug. 17, 1920.
89. *Ibid.*
90. StAL E 392 11/1 Auszug aus der Niederschrift der 171. oeffentlichen Sitzung am . . . 17. August 1920, p. 9.
91. *Ibid.*, p. 10.
92. AGM DBAG DMG 36 Niederschrift der Besprechung am 18.8. 1920, p. 9.
93. See the account of the scandal in chapter 4.
94. StAL E 392 26/6 *Der freie Angestellte*, Aug. 25, 1920, pp. 173–75.
95. StAL E 392 25/1 *Vorwaerts*, August 23, 1920, p. 1; and *Schwaebische Tagwacht*, Aug. 23 and 25, 1920.
96. *Vorwaerts*, Aug. 23, 1920, p. 1.
97. StAL 392 33/10 Niederschrift ueber die Besprechung bei der Staatsregierung am 4. September 1920, pp. 4–5.
98. *Ibid.*, p. 4.
99. *Ibid.*, p. 6.
100. *Daimler Werksnachrichten*, Oct. 18, 1920, p. 49.
101. StAL E 392 34/11 Niederschrift ueber die Besprechung beim Arbeitsministerium, am Dienstag, den 7. September 1920, p. 3.
102. StAL E 326 12/1, "Die Massnahmen," p. 90.
103. StAL E 392 33/10, p. 7.
104. StAL E 392 40/14 Auszug aus der Niederschrift der 192. oeffentlichen Sitzung am . . . 10. September 1920, p. 6.
105. StAL E 392 40/14, pp. 9–12.
106. *Daimler Werksnachrichten*, Oct. 18, 1920, pp. 54–55.
107. AGM DBAG DMG 35 (158) DMG to Franz Walter, Nov. 15, 1920.
18. *Daimler Werksnachrichten*, October, 18, 1920, p. 55.
109. AGM DBAG DMG 35 (158) DMG to Gewerbegericht Stuttgart, n.d.
110. *Jahresbericht der Gewerbeaufsichtsbeamten Wuerttembergs fuer 1920*, Stuttgart, 1921, p. 182.
111. AGM DBAG DMG 36 (168) Fuer die Betriebsratswahl; *Jahresbericht . . . fuer 1920*, p. 29.
112. Eugen May, *Mein Lebenslauf 1857–1920. Die Erzaehlung*, pp. 70–71, in Eugen Rosenstock, *Werkstattaussiedlung: Untersuchungen ueber den Lebensraum des Industriearbeiters* (Berlin: Julius Springer, 1922).
113. AGM DBAG DMG 35 (158) DMG to Firma Bank- und Boersenauskunftei Fritz Kolbe, Nov. 16, 1920.
114. AGM DBAG DMG 7a Betriebs-Anordnung No. 1831, Nov. 1, 1920.
115. StAL E 326 18/5, p. 11.
116. *Der Deutsche Metallarbeiter-Verband im Jahre 1920*, p. 283.
117. *Der Deutsche Metallarbeiter-Verband im Jahre 1921*, Anhang, p. 4.
118. Gerald D. Feldman, *Vom Weltkrieg zur Weltwirtschaftskrise*, p. 179.

119. *Deutsche Metallarbeiter-Zeitung*, March 25, 1922, p. 50; *Schwaebischer Merkur*, March 13, 1922, Abendblatt, p. 1; *Der Deutsche Metallarbeiter-Verband im Jahre 1922*, p. 69.

120. *Deutsche Metallarbeiter-Zeitung*, March 18, 1922, p. 46; *Schwaebischer Merkur*, March 13, 1922, Abendblatt, p. 1; *Der Deutsche Metallarbeiter-Verband im Jahre 1922*, p. 70.

121. *Deutsche Metallarbeiter-Zeitung*, March 25, 1922, p. 50.

122. On April 12, Braun proposed a 47-hour week with one overtime hour per week if needed. Both sides rejected it. Mayor Lautenschlager proposed an immediate resumption of work, in return for a one month delay in implementing the 48th weekly hour. *Schwaebischer Merkur*, April 15, 1922, Morgenblatt, p. 3 and April 28, 1922, Abendblatt, p. 6; *Deutsche Metallarbeiter-Zeitung*, April 29, 1922, p. 74.

123. *Schwaebischer Merkur*, May 5, 1922, Morgenblatt, p. 4.

124. *Schwaebischer Merkur*, May 19, 1922, Abendblatt, p. 5.

125. *Ibid.*, May 10, 1922, Abendblatt, p. 5 and May 11, 1922, Abendblatt, p. 5. The impression is that it was mainly officials of the firm who tried to enter the factory, since workers and clerks would not have owned the cars whose tires were slashed by the strikers.

126. *Deutsche Metallarbeiter-Zeitung*, May 20, 1922, p. 1. A few days later, on official from an unnamed firm received a death threat. If the strike was not quickly settled, the shadowy "Gang of Ten" would kill him. According to a news account, the threatening letter concluded, "we killed thousands in the war: one more or fewer doesn't matter."

127. Although Communists were among the prominent participants in the strike, the national union officials and the Stuttgart *Buerger* were probably more stung by the suprise Communist success in the elections for local union posts. *Schwaebischer Merkur*, March 28, 1922, Morgenblatt, p. 4; May 10, 1922, Abendblatt, p. 5; *Metallarbeiter-Zeitung*, May 20, 1922, p. 85.

128. *Schwaebischer Merkur*, May 20, 1922, Abendblatt, p. 5.

129. *Ibid.*, May 26, 1922, Abendblatt, p. 5.

130. *Der Deutsche Metallarbeiter-Verband im Jahre 1922*, p. 74.

131. Uta Stolle, *Arbeiterpolitik im Betrieb. Frauen und Maenner, Reformisten und Radikale, Fach-und Massenarbeiter bei BASF, Bosch und in Solingen (1900–1933)* (Frankfurt/Main: Campus, 1980), p. 305.

132. AGM DBAG DMG 36 June 28, 1922.

133. AGM DBAG DMG 36, July 5, 1922; *Schwaebischer Merkur*, July 5, 1922, Morgenblatt, p. 6.

134. Bericht des Landespolizeiamtes Stuttgart May 3, 1922, quoted in Uta Stolle, *Arbeiterpolitik im Betrieb*, p. 183.

135. *Ibid.*

136. One side of the note reads, "The Daimler-Motoren- Gesellschaft in Stuttgart-Untertuerkheim and Sindelfingen will pay 50 billion marks . . . against presentation of this coupon." The other side says simply, "Daimlerwagen, Daimlergeld, Wer sie hat, ist gut gestellt."

137. Fischer, *Verband Wuerttembergischer Metallindustrieller e.V. 1897 bis 1934*, p. 52.

138. Thomas Brunne, et al, *Arbeiterbewegung—Arbeiterkultur. Stuttgart 1890–1933* (Stuttgart: Wuertt. Landesmuseum, 1981), p. 81.

139. HStASt E 130 b Staatsministerium Bue. 1083, Kopp & DMG Arbeiterrat to Staatsregierung, Oct. 27, 1923.

140. *Metallarbeiter-Zeitung*, July 19, 1924, p. 94. There is a bit of circumstantial evidence which might support the DMV's charge that the "workers of the fatherland" were a "yellow," employer-supported group. One of their election broadsides, an article from the *Deutsche Werksgemeinschaft*, has been carefully amended at the point where a phrase had been omitted by a typographical error in the original copy. AGM DBAG DMG 36.

141. Georg Franz-Willing, *Die Hitlerbewegung. Der Ursprung 1919–1922* (Berlin: Decker, 1962), p. 193. Willing cites a copy of the document in his own private collection. A DDR history textbook—unfootnoted—charged that Daimler was one of the companies which contributed to the NSDAP in its early years, but there is no evidence to support this in the Daimler-Benz archive. *Deutschland im Zweiten Weltkrieg*, 1, Vorbereitung, Entfesselung und Verlauf des Krieges bis zum 22. Juni 1941 (Cologne: Pahl-Rugenstein, 1974), p. 34.

142. Seidenzahl, *100 Jahre Deutsche Bank 1870–1970*, p. 281. The private archive of the Deutsche Bank refused two requests in 1986 to examine the reports in their possession on Daimler from 1919 and 1923.

143. *Deutsche Metallarbeiter-Zeitung*, August 22, 1925, p. 136 reports the mass layoff of 1,500 workers in Untertuerkheim.

144. Bundesarchiv-Militaerarchiv Freiburg N 42/53 Muff to von Schleicher, Oct. 28, 1925.

145. In 1926, the joint corporate board decided in principle to resume the design and construction of airplane motors, which may have been a violation of the Versailles treaty, and to sell trucks to the Soviet Union. AGM DBAG Protokolle. Vorstandssitzungen 1924–1935. Protokoll der Sitzung des Gesamt-Vorstandes vom 26.2.1926. By 1927, the company was moving ahead with its "tank business *(Panzer-Geschaeft)."* K. Roth, "Der Weg zum guten Stern des Dritten Reiches," *Das Daimler-Benz Buch* (Noerdlingen: Greno), 1987 p. 52.

146. Paul Siebertz, *Karl Benz. Ein Pionier der Verkehrsmotorisierung* (Munich: Lehmanns, 1943), pp. 237, 258–60.

147. Seidenzahl, *100 Jahre Deutsche Bank 1870–1970*, pp. 283–84.

148. Heinz Ludwig, "Die Arbeitslosigkeit in der deutschen Automobilindustrie," in M. Saitzew, ed., *Die Arbeitslosigkeit der Gegenwart* (zweiter Teil) (Munich: Duncker & Humblott, 1932), p. 138. The period of rationalization saw a wave of mergers: besides Daimler & Benz, NAG with Protos, Dux, and Presto; BMW with Dixi, Hansa with Goliath and Hansa-Lloyd, and Horch with Audi, Wanderer, and DKW. The factories of the auto companies were flooded with a wave of automatic and special machines, while the designs for the autos and their components were standardized and simplified, with more aluminum and copper being substituted to lessen costs.

149. AGM DBAG DGAB 2 *Stuttgarter Neues Tagblatt,* Nov. 25, 1927.

150. AGM DBAG Hans Sonntag, "Werk Sindelfingen 1915–1935," p. 15, unpublished manuscript.

151. AGM DBAG DBAG *Hamburger Fremdenblatt,* Nov. 29, 1927.

152. *Jahresberichte der Gewerbeaufsichtsbeamten und Bergbehoerden fuer das Jahr 1927,* 2:72–80 (see also pictures which accompany the inspectors' report); AGM DBAG Sifi 1A (4) *Sueddeutsche Arbeiter-Zeitung,* Nov. 7, 1928.

153. *Jahresberichte der Gewerbeaufsichtsbeamten . . . fuer das Jahr 1927,* 2: 72–80.

154. Antonio Gramsci, *Selections from the Prison Notebooks* (New York: International, 1978), pp. 279, 281, 285.

155. AGM DBAG Sifi 1A (4) *Sueddeutsche Arbeiter-Zeitung,* Nov. 7, 1928 and Aug. 8, 1929; Stollberg, *Die Rationalisierungsdebatte 1908–1933,* p. 90; James, *The German Slump,* p. 199.

156. AGM DBAG Sifi 1A (4) *Sueddeutsche Arbeiter-Zeitung,* Aug. 8, 1929.

157. AGM DBAG Protokolle Vorstandssitzungen 1924–1935. Protokoll der Vorstandssitzung vom 24. Oktober 1928, p. 14.

158. Seidenzahl, *100 Jahre Deutsche Bank 1870–1970,* p. 284.

159. From 1928, the company had a new march, "Unter dem Dreizackstern," composed by Heinz Moench, with lyrics such as "Ob Sizilien oder Polen, Frankreich, Schweiz und Russland/ wo es gilt den Sieg zu holen, ist der Dreizackstern bekannt/ Deutscher Arbeit Ehrenzeichen, fuerchten keine Konkurrenz/ moege nie sein Stern erbleichen/ unser Stolz: Mercedes-Benz! ("Whether Sicily or Poland, France, Switzerland, and Russia, where there's a victory to win, the three-pointed star is known/The badge of honor of German labor fears no competition/Its star will never fade. Our pride: Mercedes-Benz!") The words refer to racing triumphs. AGM DBAG DBAG 108.

7. CRISIS AND NEW ORDER

1. Yuji Nishimuta, in *Shirin* (September 1985) No. 68-5, p. 114 (786); AGM DBAG Protokolle Aufsichtsratssitzungen und verschiedene Sitzungen 1931–1951. Protokoll ueber die Arbeitsausschuss-Sitzung der Daimler-Benz AG am 1. Juni 1931, p. 1; AGM DBAG DBAG 12 *Berliner Boersen Zeitung,* December 17, 1932.

2. Oswald, *Mercedes-Benz Personenwagen 1886–1984,* pp. 240–47; AGM DBAG Kissel I, 3 Protokolle 1930–32, Bericht des Vorstandes fuer das 3. Quartal 1932, Oct. 31, 1932, p. 1. The price is from the advertisement in the *Voelkischer Beobachter,* Nov. 24, 1931.

3. Hansen, *Reichswehr und Industrie,* p. 175.

4. AGM DBAG Kissel I, 3 Protokolle 1930–1932. Protokoll ueber die Arbeitsausschuss-Sitzung der Daimler-Benz Aktiengesellschaft am 21. Juli 1931; Rainer Wohlfeil and Hans Dollinger, *Die deutsche Reichswehr. Bilder Dokumente Texte. Zur Geschichte des Hunderttausend-Mann-Heeres 1919–1933* (Frankfurt/Main: Bernard & Graefe, 1972), pp. 178–79.

5. Daimler-Benz Historische Datensammlung 1886–1980 (1928), (1932).

6. AGM DBAG DMG 159 *Der rote Mercedes,* June 13, 1930, pp. 3, 5. A chief complaint of the Communists was that the DMV officials had consented to all the layoffs and cuts instead of fighting them.

7. StAL E 258 II Bue. 578 Bl 478 DBAG to Wuertt. Statistisches Landesamt, Sept. 25, 1935.

8. DMV Bezirk Stuttgart, *Geschaefts-Bericht ueber das Jahr 1920,* Berlin: Verlagsgesellschaft, n.d. p. 25.

9. James, *The German Slump,* pp. 243, 415; *Sueddeutsche Arbeiter-Zeitung,* Dec. 31, 1931; *Schwaebische Tagwacht,* Jan. 12, 1932; Heinrich August Winkler, *Der Weg in die Katastrophe. Arbeiter und Arbeiterbewegung in der Weimarer Republik 1930 bis 1933* (Bonn: J.H.W. Dietz, 1987), pp. 951–54.

10. AGM DBAG Hans Sonntag, Werk Sindelfingen 1915–1935, p. 18.

11. Prinz and Rexin, eds., *Beispiele fuer aufrechten Gang,* pp. 40–42.

12. AGM DBAG Kissel I, 6 Protokoll der Vorstandssitzung am 29.6.1939, p. 11.

13. Berlin Document Center, Sonderakte 3. Daimler-Benz, Werlin to Himmler, Aug. 27, 1942.

14. Henry Ashby Turner, Jr., *Big Business and the Rise of Hitler* (New York: Oxford University Press, 1985), pp. 142–43.

15. *Ibid.,* pp. 143–44, 321, 464.

16. Friedrich Glum, *Zwischen Wissenschaft, Wirtschaft und Politik. Erlebtes und Erdachtes in vier Reichen* (Bonn: H. Bouvier, 1964), p. 442.

17. There were no ads in the last half of 1930, 9 in 1931 (Jan. 28, Feb. 15/16, March 17, April 17, April 19/20, May 27, June 9, Nov. 24, and Dec. 18). In 1932, display ads appeared on Jan. 1/2, Jan. 27, March 2, April 28, May 3, June 4, June 5/6, June 19/20, July 13, Aug. 6, Aug. 9, Aug. 24, Sept. 1, Sept. 22, Oct. 22, Nov. 16, Dec. 6, and Dec. 20.

18. Confidential material in possession of author, Werlin to Kissel, May 14, 1932 ("Ich habe natuerlich nicht unerwaehnt gelassen, dass wir der Partei jederzeit das groesste Entgegenkommen bewiesen haben und einzelne Faelle angefuehrt" and "waehrend wir schon seit Jahren die Verbindung mit der NSDAP in Erkennung der zukunftigen Entwicklung stets ueberall aus Liebe zur Sache gehegt und gepflegt haetten."); and Kissel to Werlin, May 18, 1932 ("Jedenfalls haven wir keine Veranlassung, in der Aufmerksamkeit, die wir bisher Herrn Hitler und seinen Freunden zugewendet haben, nachzulassen; er wird sich auch . . . ebenso auf uns verlassen koennen, wie in der Vergangenheit.")

19. Turner, *German Big Business and the Rise of Hitler,* p. xxi. After the first draft of this chapter was written, a study of Daimler-Benz's history during National Socialism commissioned by the company appeared near the end of November 1986. See H. Pohl, et al., *Die Daimler-Benz AG in den Jahren 1933 bis 1945* (Wiesbaden: Steiner, 1986). The group which produced the work, the Gesellschaft fuer Unternehmensgeschichte e.V., is supervised by a board of businessmen and scholars which included the chairman of Daimler-Benz at the time, Werner Breitschwerdt. The book's value is vitiated by its avoidance of issues and evidence which tend to reflect unfavorably on the firm's history. For example, Pohl and his colleagues have suppressed the evidence cited here in note

18. Instead of using important documents in their possession, they have cited Turner's sentences approvingly, although Turner never worked at Daimler-Benz or with collections of Daimler-Benz documents in West Germany, North America, and the U.K. In addition, the company-supported work's description of forced labor at Daimler-Benz is extraordinarily understated, in line with the company's official policy at that time of refusing to pay compensation to the survivors of its policy of employing foreign workers, concentration camp inmates, and Jewish slaves in many of its production facilities. See below.

20. AGM DBAG DGAB 11 Rede des Aufsichtrats-Vorsitzender der Daimler-Benz A.G. Herrn Staatsrat Dr. von Stauss in der Generalversammlung vom 2.7. 1935, p. 1.

21. AGM DBAG Geschaeftsbericht der Daimler-Benz AG ueber die Geschaeftsjahre vom 1. Januar 1932 bis 31. Dezember 1932 und vom 1. Januar 1933 bis 31. Dezember 1933, p. 4; James, *The German Slump*, p. 343.

22. Hans Pohl, et al., *Die Daimler Benz AG in den Jahren 1933 bis 1945* (Wiesbaden: Steiner, 1986), pp. 17, 43, 45. Two examples of Hitler's friendly feelings for Werlin: Hitler penned a personal "happy birthday" for him in May, 1941 and later insisted on personally awarding him the Kriegsverdienstkreuz 1. Klasse. Max Domarus, *Hitler, Reden und Proklamationen 1932–1945*, vol. 2 (Wuerzburg: Domarus, 1963), p. 1709; HSG, Nachlass Saur, "Werlin . . . 13/ 15.11.43"; Department of the Army, US Army Intelligence & Security Command, Freedom of Information Privacy Office, Werlin, Jakob: "verwaltet Hitlers Daimler-Aktien"; "Hitler is said to have a large block of shares in this firm." Following his release from Allied imprisonment after the war, Werlin received a post as director of the Mercedes agency in Rosenheim, a Bavarian town 150 miles from Stuttgart. Beverly Rae Kimes, *The Star and the Laurel* (Daimler-Benz, 1986), p. 285.

23. Hans Radant, "Zu den Beziehungen zwischen dem Konzern der Deutschen Bank und dem Staatsapparat bei der Vorbereitung und Durchfuehrung des Zweiten Weltkrieges," in *Der deutsche Imperialismus*, vol. 2, Berlin (East): (Ruetten & Loening, 1961), p. 31. This intelligent essay is invaluable for the history of Daimler-Benz and its role in the military build-up. It utilizes documents from the captured Deutsche Bank collections in the DDR.

24. Willi Jacobi, *Die Massnahmen zur Foerderung des Automobilabsatzes in Deutschland und die bilanzmaessige Auswirkung der Absatzsteigerung*, Dissertation: Frankfurt/Main, 1936, p. 23.

25. Karl-Heinz Ludwig, *Technik und Ingenieure im Dritten Reich* (Duesseldorf: Droste, 1974), pp. 310–314.

26. Dietrich Eichholtz and Wolfgang Schumann, eds., *Anatomie des Krieges. Neue Dokumente ueber die Rolle des deutschen Monopolkapitals bei der Vorbereitung und Durchfuehrung des zweiten Weltkrieges* (Berlin: VEB Deutscher Verlag der Wissenschaften, 1969), p. 114, "Aus dem Rundschreiben des Reichsverbandes der Automobilindustrie an seine Mitglieder vom 12. Juni 1933 ueber die 'Adolf-Hitler-Spende' der deutschen Wirtschaft".

27. Institute fuer Zeitgeschichte NI-1476, October 2, 1933.

28. *Deutschland-Bericht der Sopade 1934–1940* (Sozial-demokratische Partei Deutschlands), vol. 1 (Salzhausen: Petra Nettelbeck, 1980), p. 797.

29. Radant, "Zu den Beziehungen," p. 31; AGM DBAG Kissel I, 4 Protokolle 1933–35, Protokoll der Vorstandssitzung, Jan. 9, 1934, p. 8; Hentig reported about the "privileged calling *[bevorzugte Heranziehung]* of our company, especially our Marienfelde factory." See for example AGM DBAG Kissel I, 4 Protokolle 1933–35, Protokoll der Vorstandssitzung, June 20, 1934, p. 9, for the announcement of a big new Reichswehr contract for Marienfelde.

30. Radant, "Zu den Beziehungen," p. 32. According to AGM DBAG Kissel I, 4 Protokolle 1933–35, Protokoll ueber die Praesidial-Sitzung, Sept. 24, 1935, p. 2, the regime had guaranteed a bank credit of 7.1 million marks for new construction in Marienfelde and in Untertuerkheim.

31. Radant, "Zu den Beziehungen," pp. 32–34.

32. Leistungsbericht der Daimler-Benz Aktiengesellschaft aufgestellt im Arbeitsjahr 1940, Band 19, Daimler-Benz Motoren GMBH, Genshagen (Kreis Teltow), p. 7. The Grossbeeren-Damsdorf railway bounded the facility to the west, and the new Autobahn to the north.

33. *Ibid.*, p. 13.

34. Carola Sachse, et al., *Angst, Belohnung, Zucht und Ordnung. Herrschaftsmechanismen im Nationalsozialismus* (Opladen: Westdeutscher Verlag, 1982).

35. Tilla Siegel, "Wage Policy in Nazi Germany," *Politics and Society* (1985) 1:9; Reinhardt Hanf, *Moeglichkeiten und Grenzen betrieblicher Lohn- und Gehaltspolitik 1933–1939*, Dissertation/Regensburg, 1975, p. 36.

36. Quoted in Siegel, "Wage Policy," p. 9.

37. C.W. Guillebaud, quoted in Hanf, *Moeglichkeiten*, p. 38.

38. Quoted in *Ibid.* They were to have a say in, e.g. scheduling work breaks and setting fines.

39. Timothy W. Mason, "Zur Entstehung des Gesetzes zur Ordnung der nationalen Arbeit, vom 20. Januar 1934: Ein Versuch ueber das Verhaeltnis 'archaischer' und 'moderner' Momente in der neuesten deutschen Geschichte," in H. Mommsen, et al., eds., *Industrielles System und politische Entwicklung in der Weimarer Republik* (Duesseldorf: Droste, 1974), p. 326.

40. AGM DBAG Kissel XIII, 1 Kissel to DAF Abt. Luftfahrt RLM, Berlin, April 6, 1937.

41. There is a mention of an assembly line in Untertuerkheim in 1935, in Sindelfingen in 1927, in Mannheim in 1935. The large investments were discussed regularly at the meeting of the directors and trustees.

42. AGM DBAG Kissel XIII, 2 Dir. Decker-Mannheim: Arbeitsbewertung und Lohnsystem in der Fliessfertigung, Dec. 6, 1941; Kurze Denkschrift, Feb. 1, 1941.

43. HSG, Arbeitswissenschaftliches Institut der Deutschen Arbeitsfront, "Der Akkordlohn. Grundsaetzliches zur Frage der Leistungsbewertung und Leistungsmessung," streng vertraulich, January 1938, p. 4. The quotation is Robert Ley's.

44. AGM DBAG Kissel XIII, 2 Kurze Denkschrift, Arbeitsgang-Verzeichnis, Bl. 2–7.

45. AGM DBAG Kissel XIII, 2 Kurze Denkschrift, p. 5.

46. Siegel, "Wage Policy in Nazi Germany," pp. 21–22.

47. AGM DBAG DBAG 98 Daimler-Benz Aktiengesellschaft, Betriebs-Ordnung 1937, pp. 10–11.

48. *Ibid.*, pp. 21–22.

49. *Ibid.*, p. 8.

50. AGM DBAG DBAG 23 Verwaltungs-Anordnung No. 1271.

51. *Leistungsbericht,* p. 142.

52. AGM DBAG DBAG 23 e.g. March 11 and 25, 1941. For the mandatory attendance of young workers at the racist hate lessons, "all young males who are employed in the factory appear washed for *Jugendbetriebsappel* in clean, blue work uniforms. . . . The females wear BDM [League of German Girls] uniforms." The masters were to insure that all young workers in their departments appeared promptly and in formation at the sessions.

53. AGM DBAG DBAG 23 Bekanntmachung April 27, 1940.

54. Siegel, "Wage Policy," p. 3.

55. Ian Kershaw, "Widerstand ohne Volk?" Dissens und Widerstand im Dritten Reich," in J. Schmaedecke & P. Steinbach, *Widerstand gegen Nationalsozialismus. Die deutsche Gesellschaft und der Widerstand gegen Hitler* (Munich: Piper, 1986), pp. 782–85.

56. James, *The German Slump,* p. 347.

57. Willi Bohn, *"Hochverraeter!"* (Frankfurt/Main: Roederberg, 1984), pp. 146–48.

58. On Riefenstahl's Mercedes, see Pohl, et al., *Die Daimler-Benz AG,* p. 212. On foreign workers and concentration camp inmates, see below. For the looting of a Peugeot works, see, for example, Dietrich Eichholtz & Wolfgang Schumann, eds., *Anatomie des Krieges,* pp. 462–63. The document is a report by a Krupp representative dated October 11, 1944, on his visit to the Peugeot factory in Sochaux. He noted that "all important and modern machines" had already been carried off by Daimler-Benz and Volkswagen. On the looting of French factories in 1944, see Alan S. Milward, *The New Order and the French Economy* (Oxford: Clarendon, 1970), p. 178. On Brzeski-Auto in Posen, see AGM DBAG Kissel I, 6 Protokolle 1938–40, Protokoll der Vorstandssitzung, Dec. 5, 1939, p. 8. On the use of Gestapo against a truculent stockholder, see AGM DBAG Protokolle Vorstandssitzungen 1941–43, Protokoll der Vorstandssitzung, Sept. 9, 1942, pp. 4–5. The new, embattled chairman Haspel told the directors that there "are fundamentally two methods" of silencing the man, Lange, who was apparently raising uncomfortable questions about the company's pre-war policies: "either to offer no further answer or to interest the Gestapo in this affair."

59. Transcript of meeting of July 8, 1938, cited in O.M.G.U.S., *Ermittlungen gegen die Deutsche Bank,* pp. 149–50. The investigators from the U.S. Treasury Department concluded that Goering had told the corporate chiefs that "the war was imminent." I have based my translation on the American investigators' in

HSG, O.M.G.U.S., "Report on the Investigation of the Deutsche Bank," p., 136.

60. AGM DBAG Kissel I, 6 Protokolle 1938–40, Protokoll der Vorstandssitzung, March 24, 1939, pp. 1–2, 6.

61. Timothy W. Mason, "Die Baendigung der Arbeiterklasse im nationalsozialistischen Deutschland," in Carol Sachse, et al., *Angst, Belohnung, Zucht und Ordnung. Herrschaftsmechanismus im Nationalsozialismus* (Opladen: Westdeutscher Verlag, 1982), p. 13. For an example of the use of the term "Arbeitertum", see AGM DBAG DBAG 23 Bekanntmachung, May 11, 1942.

62. *Beispiele fuer aufrechten Gang*, p. 42. In addition to the repression, "the quickness of the political change" was "an important source of the confusion for the opponents of the regime; they made the learning process and the adjustment to the political realities much harder." Mason, "Die Baendigung der Arbeiterklasse," p. 23.

63. Erich Matthias and Hermann Weber, *Widerstand gegen den Nationalsozialismus in Mannheim*, (Mannheim: Quadrant, 1984), p. 80; HSG, *Arbeitertum. Blaetter fuer Theorie und Praxis der nationalsozialistischen Betriebszellen Organisation*, (March 15, 1933), 3(2): 21. Nazi-dominated slates of clerks ran unopposed, and thus were elected.

64. *Herzstueck im Schwabenland*, H. Bruder, ed., p. 368. Among the clubs and associations in Untertuerkheim and Luginsland which were dissolved were the Friends of Nature; the Gymnastic and Sporting Association (with 400 members); football, handball, and bicycling clubs; the Workers' Esperanto Club; the Workers' Free-Thinkers' Club; and the Workers' Samaritan League. The following SPD organizations were smashed: Socialist Workers' Youth Group, the Red Hawks, the Friends of Children, Workers' Relief, and the Reichsbanner. The authorities wrecked the KPD and its organizations: Communist Youth, the Fighting League Against Fascism, the Young Pioneers, Red Support, and International Workers' Aid.

65. Industriegewerkschaft-Metall, "Daimler-Benz—Die Leistung von 160 000 Menschen," March 15, 1986, p. 7.

66. *Deutschland-Berichte*. 2: 1147; 3: 1426; AGM DBAG Kissel III, 2 Kissel to Hentig, Sept. 16, 1936.

67. *Ibid.*, vol. 4, p. 1403.

68. *Ibid.*, vol. 2, p. 325.

69. AGM DBAG Kissel XIII, 1 Aktennotiz 1. Juli 1935.

70. *Deutschland-Berichte*, 2: 546.

71. AGM DBAG Kissel XIII, 1 Aktennotiz 1. Juli 1935.

72. *Deutschland-Berichte*, 2: 545.

73. AGM DBAG Kissel XIII, 1 Rede des Betriebszellenobmanns vor der Belegschaft Daimler-Benz am 1. Mai 1935, p. 4.

74. IG-Metall, "Daimler-Benz," March 15, 1986.

75. *Deutschland-Berichte*, 3:739.

76. *Neue Front,* May 1937, vol 5, no. 6, p. 2. Thanks to Dr. Roland Mueller for this reference.

77. *Deutschland-Berichte*, 3:513.

78. AGM DBAG Kissel VI, 1 Kissel & Haspel to Paul Heim, Dec. 20, 1940.

The note congratulates Heim on his assignment and notes that "you will be active in this capacity in the future as helper *[Hilfsorgan]* to the Gestapo."

79. The data are from AGM DBAG Goldene Fahne. *Einlage zum Leistungsbericht der Daimler-Benz Aktiengesellschaft*, Gefolgschaftszahlen. Werke. Stand am 1. Juli 1940; *Leistungsbericht*, pp. 122, 130; Berlin Document Center Personalakten (see bibliography).

80. *Vorwaerts*, December 31, 1946.

81. *Deutschland im Zweiten Weltkrieg*, vol. 1 (Cologne: Pahl- Rugenstein, 1974), p. 286.

82. "Arbeiter, die 1943 bei der Daimler-Benz AG beschaeftigt waren"; "In Namen des Deutschen Volkes!" (1 H 28/44/ 11 (10 J 631 43); "In Namen des Deutschen Volkes! (Kammergericht 7.0.Js.254.43 "B" (II.11.44)). I thank Dr. Helmuth Bauer for making these documents available. The Volksgerichtshof papers identify the condemned as Daimler-Benz workers.

83. *Ibid.*, 2: 584; 1: 583, 594; 4: 278, 281, 282–83, 559, 565.

84. AGM DBAG Kissel XIII, 1 DBAG to Ruestungs-Inspektion . . . , April 24, 1941.

85. *Meldungen aus dem Reich. Die geheimen Lageberichte des Sicherheitsdienstes der SS 1938–1945*, H. Boberach, ed., Herrsching: Pawlak, 1984, vol 11, p. 4303.

86. Friedrich Schlotterbeck, *Je dunkler die Nacht . . . Erinnerungen eines deutschen Arbeiters 1933–1945* (Stuttgart: Gabriele Walter, 1986), pp. 391–92; Paul Sauer, *Wuerttemberg in der Zeit des Nationalsozialismus* (Ulm: Sueddeutsche Verlagsgesellachaft, 1975), p. 435.

87. Fritz Salm, *Im Schatten des Henkers. Widerstand in Mannheim gegen Faschismus und Krieg*, Frankfurt/Main: Roederberg, 1979, p. 208. According to the author, who cites now unavailable information at the Red Cross center in Arolsen, a Daimler-Benz director, Max Wolf, had women concentration camp prisoners deported to Ravensbrueck after they were found with pieces of bread given to them by Daimler-Benz workers. On Wolf, see below.

88. Wolfgang Zollitsch, *Integration oder Isolation? Die Arbeiterschaft von Grossbetrieben zwischen Weltwirtschaftskrise und Nationalsozialismus (1928–1936)*, Dissertation/Freiburg, 1986, pp. 380–88. Zollitsch describes the apathetic disinterest in politics, the acceptance of the regime, "inner [psychological] emigration," and the occasional identification with the regime's successes to be hallmarks of the "integration" he discerns among Krupp workers during the Third Reich.

89. AGM DBAG Kissel IX, 2 Kissel to v. Stauss, Sept. 24, 1941, p. 2.

90. British Intelligence Objectives Sub-Committee, Report on Visit to Daimler-Benz A.G. at Stuttgart-Untertuerkheim PB 31248, pp. 5, 7–13.

91. Zentrale Stelle der Landesjustizverwaltungen, Ludwigsburg, "Betr: Erhardt (sic), Paul Georg." AGM DBAG Kissel VII, 7 contains a document regarding the design of a *Menschenvergasungsauto* by an engineer at the company, Paul G. Erhardt (sic), possibly for the euthanasia campaign of 1939–1942. The report contends that Erhardt was recommended for Hitler's praise after his special design work at the Mercedes factory. Its source apparently was the

former Daimler-Benz employee of German-Jewish descent, Joseph Ganz, who fled to Switzerland in 1936. "Erhardt" refers to Paul Georg *Ehrhardt*, who was an associate of the Daimler-Benz design engineer Gustav Roehr, but little is known about him. He was a Frankfurt engineer who worked at Untertuerkheim. It is known that Daimler-Benz coal-gas generating trucks were plagued by the defect of producing too much carbon monoxide gas, posing a threat to the life of those traveling inside. This was the way that the gas vans deployed in Poland and the Soviet Union actually functioned. It should also be noted that Daimler-Benz operated the biggest motor vehicle repair complex on the eastern front in Minsk, a city visited often by gassing vans. See Gerald Reitlinger, *The Final Solution. The Attempt to Exterminate the Jews of Europe* (London: Vallentine, Mitchell, 1953), pp. 243, 288. The gas vans were developed in the Technical Referat of the Reichsicherheitshauptamt. The work by Eugen Kogon, Hermann Langbein and Adalbert Rueckerl, *Nationalsozialistische Massentoetungen durch Giftgas* (Frankfurt/Main: Fischer, 1983), asserts that the Saurer firm produced gas vans. At this time there is no evidence in the available documents that Daimler-Benz ever actually produced such a vehicle.

92. On the committees and rings, see Dietrich Eichholtz, *Geschichte der deutschen Kriegswirtschaft 1939–1945*, vol. 2, Berlin: Akademie Verlag, 1985, pp. 49–50, 67–68, 105–06, 116, and Anhang 2; National Archives and Records Administration NNMR III a Box 1045 Manual for Economic Investigation of Daimler-Benz.

93. Max Domarus, *Hitler Reden und Proklamationen 1932–1945*, 2: 1823–24; AGM DBAG Kissel to Vomag, April 15, 1942; Kissel to Phaenomen-Werke, April 16, 1942; *Vorwaerts*, Dec. 31, 1946, p. 1. It is not possible to assess the extent to which Daimler-Benz used Jewish slaves from the Minsk ghetto in its Werlinwerke, but the fact is mentioned in evidence in the Zentrale Stelle, II 202 AR 1495/69 Betr. Heck (Anton o. Adolf).

94. National Archives Record Group 84 (Post Files), Zurich Confidential File, 800; Walter Laqueur and Richard Breitman, *Breaking the Silence* (New York: Touchstone, 1986), pp. 112–13. I would like to thank Richard Breitman for sharing his information with me on this point.

95. *Handbuch der deutschen Aktiengesellschaften, 1937*, Band 4 (Berlin: Hoppenstedt, 1937), p. 5217; Leistungsbericht, pp. 9, 12. Karl C. Mueller was born on May 25, 1886 in Heidenheim, studied at the Technische Hochschule in Stuttgart, and became director of the Daimler-Benz factory in Gaggenau in 1931. He joined the party on May 1, 1933 with membership number 2,632,681. He headed the Genshagen project and the later transfer of the complex to the Goldfisch underground facility in 1944–45. He could not rejoin the firm until 1947, and quickly rose to the leadership of the de-Nazified firm. In 1956, he received the Federal Republic's *Grosses Verdienstkreuz* for his "outstanding service in the development and completion of automobiles during almost three decades." Mueller, as Daimler-Benz asserted in his obituary in 1964, was a colleague "who remains inseparably bound up with the history of our house." The material on Mueller is from BDC Karl Christian Mueller; AGM DBAG Werksangehoerige and the *Stuttgarter Zeitung*, December 15, 1956.

96. British Intelligence Objectives Sub-Committee, Report on a visit to the Daimler-Benz A.G. at Stuttgart-Untertuerkheim, p. 14; Public Record Office London FO 935/113, p. 47.

97. *Leistungsbericht*, p. 16; National Archives and Record Administration NNMR III a Box 1045 Manual for Economic Investigation of Daimler-Benz, Genshagen, p. 2. The pressure to employ women at Genshagen, caused by the shortage of metalworkers was already strong in 1938. AGM DBAG Kissel VIII, 3, Mueller to Kissel, May 31, 1938, pp. 3, 16.

98. Office of Military Government United States Wuerttemberg/Baden Econ. Div. 12/24-1 Boxes 8–10. According to the U.S. report on the hundreds of machines which had been transported from Genshagen to the Goldfisch bunker complex in 1944 and 1945, most were drills, milling and grinding machines, built between 1937 and 1944, but mainly in the 1940s.

99. *Leistungsbericht*, p. 14.

100. *Ibid.*, p. 16.

101. On April 25, 1941, there were already 407 French POW's working at Genshagen, only "a small fraction" of whom were skilled workers. "The French are generally diligent and keep good order. A few contrary ones were immediately relieved by the *Kommandofuehrer* at our request." AGM DBAG Kissel XIII, 1 Mueller & Krumbiegel to Kissel, April 25, 1941.

102. Dietrich Eichholtz, *Geschichte der deutschen Kriegswirtschaft 1939–1945*, vol. 2, pp. 74, 77, 179–198; Ulrich Herbert, *Fremdarbeiter. Politik und Praxis des 'Auslaender- Einsatzes' in der Kriegswirtschaft des Dritten Reiches*, Bonn: Dietz, 1985, pp. 140–147; AGM DBAG DBAG and subdivisions. This statistical abstract gives the total of foreign workers in Genshagen as 6011.

103. Bundesarchiv Koblenz R 41 Reichsarbeitsministerium "Durchschnittliche Gefolgschaftsentwicklung," September 19, 1942; AGM DBAG statistics generated for the Gesellschaft fuer Unternehmensgeschichte, March 1986.

104. AGM DBAG Konrad Zapf, "Mercedes-Stern und Fremdarbeiter. Entwurf zu einer Disposition," Table C; Ulrich Herbert, "Der 'Auslaendereinsatz'. Fremdarbeiter und Kriegsgefangene in Deutschland 1939–1945 — ein Ueberblick," in *Herrenmenschen und Arbeitsvoelker. Auslaendische Arbeiter ind Deutsche 1939–1945* (Berlin: Rotbuch, 1986), p. 15.

105. Zentrale Stelle der Landesjustizverwaltungen. Verschiedenes 301 cq Bd. 176, NI-280 Anton Kaindl, Eidestaatliche Erklaerung, June 22, 1946, p. 5. The number of Sachsenhausen inmates for Daimler-Benz is given as 1,100 in *Damals in Sachsenhausen. Solidaritaet und Wilderstand im Konzentrationslager Sachsenhausen* (Berlin: VEB Deutscher Verlag der Wissenschaften, 1967), p. 58.

106. O.M.G.U.S. Econ. Div. Miscellaneous Records 149-1/3 Box 250 Office of the U.S. Chief of Counsel, U.S. Army, August 1, 1946. Wolf was born in Schwiebus on Sept. 25, 1888 and had the NSDAP membership number 4,576,092. Married, with two children, and a Lutheran, he had the titles Direktor, Geschaeftsfuehrer, and Wehrwirtschaftsfuehrer at Daimler-Benz/Genshagen. He was also a trustee of the R. Stock & Co., Berlin-Marienfelde. BDC Max Wolf; *Wer Leitet? Die Maenner der Wirtschaft und einschlaegigen Verwaltung* (Berlin:

Hoppenstedt, 1942), p. 1110. Despite Daimler-Benz's contention after the war that "the whole registry as well as all written documents were destroyed by the Occupation Troops" (DBAG report, August 30, 1947, p. 17, in O.M.G.U.S. Econ. Div. Record Branch 17/225-1 Box 503), an extensive collection of documents from Genshagen's chief, Mueller, can be found in London's Imperial War Museum, 2228/45. The name of the chairman of the board of trustees, Rummel, also appeared on the list of reputed war criminals.

107. On Ravensbrueck, a camp with over 42,000 women from 27 nations, see Sybil Milton, "Women and the Holocaust: The Case of German and German-Jewish Women," in Renate Bridenthal, et al., eds., *When Biology Became Destiny. Women in Weimar and Nazi Germany* (New York: Monthly Review, 1984), p. 307.

108. Raul Hilberg, *The Destruction of the European Jews* (New York: Holmes & Maier, 1985), pp. 934–35.

109. Wiener Library, Bestand P.III.h, No. 233, restricted. On the Manfred-Weiss concern in Hungary and its takeover by Himmler and the SS, see Speer, *Der Sklavenstaat*, Stuttgart, 1981, pp. 252–53.

110. NARA NNMR III a Box 1045 Manual for Economic Investigation of Daimler-Benz.

111. Wiener Library, Bestand P.IIIh, No. 233, p. 17.

112. *Ibid.*, p. 20. One still hears today what a defense of Krupp proclaimed almost 40 years ago: that German companies performed a humanitarian service for concentration camp prisoners by employing them at their factories, thus saving them from death in the camps. "For many prisoners, employment in private industry meant a lightening of their fate." Tilo von Wilmowsky, *Warum wurde Krupp verurteilt? Legende und Justizirrtum* (Stuttgart: Friedrich Vorwerk, 1950), p. 175. Given the circulation of prisoners through the German war economy and the frequent reports of the reshipment or *Abtransportierung* of inmates to other camps, it is doubtful that many were saved by the largesse of German companies. See also below, the shipment of Daimler-Benz's prisoners from Goldfisch.

113. Institut fuer Zeitgeschichte FA 146 Bl. 73–74 Romstedt (Daimler-Benz) to General (Waffen-SS) Gottlob Berger, November 16, 1943; Berger to SS-Gruppenfuehrer Breithaupt, December 7, 1943.

114. ZSL, NL Mannheim-Sandhofen IV 319 AR-Z 176/1969; NL Wesserling-Urbis 419 AR-Z 177/69; USA Ordner No. 15.

115. United States Strategic Bombing Survey, Aircraft Division Industry Report, Aircraft Division, January 1947, 2nd ed., pp. 28–29. During the transfer of another Mercedes facility, Daimler-Benz sought to take over a textile factory in Bruennlitz, provoking strife on which the SD later reported. *Meldungen aus dem Reich*, 15:5843.

116. Evidence regarding the fate of these inmates after their removal to concentration camps is not available. Imperial War Museum, London, 2228/45 K.C. Mueller to Krumbiegel, March 9, 1945. This extraordinary collection of Daimler-Benz directer Mueller's personal files affords a unique insight into the

utilization of foreign workers and camp slaves by a leading German firm. I would like to thank Joerg Mettke for informing me of the existence of this collection.

117. Czeslaw Madajczyk, *Die Okkupationspolitik Nazideutschlands in Polen 1939–1945* (Berlin: Akademie Verlag, 1987), pp. 439, 521; AGM DBAG Protokolle, Vorstandssitzungen 1941–1943, Protokoll der Vorstandssitzung, Oct. 23, 1941, p. 11.

118. Herbert, *Fremdarbeiter,* p. 180; Raul Hilberg, *Destruction of the European Jews,* p. 524.

119. AGM DBAG Vertriebsorganisation 175/24 Aktennotiz, July 20, 1942.

120. ZSL Reichshof (Flugmotorenwerk Daimler-Benz) 206 AR-Z 46/1962, G.A.Z. April 10, 1963, p. 3.

121. *Ibid.*, AGM DBAG Vertriebsorganisation 175/24 Reichshof to SS & Polizeifuehrer, Aug. 14, 1942; Martin Gilbert, *Endloesung. Die Vertreibung und Vernichtung der Juden. Ein Atlas,* Reinbek: Rowohlt, 1982, pp. 108, 112; Hilberg, *The Destruction,* pp. 491, 524, 537.

122. AGM DBAG Vertriebsorganisation 175/24 Baubeschreibung, Aug. 6, 1942.

123. *Das Diensttagebuch des deutschen Generalgouverneurs in Polen 1939–1945,* W. Praeg and W. Jacobmeyer, eds. (Stuttgart: Deutsche Verlags-Anstalt, 1975), pp. 516–17; ZSL, Reichshof (Flugmotorenwerk Daimler-Benz) 206 AR-Z 46/1962; Madajczyk, *Die Okkupationspolitik,* p. 260.

124. AGM DBAG Vertriebsorganisation 175/24 Aktennotiz, July 17, 1942. For the employment of Jews in productive departments, see Reichshof to Ruestungskommando Krakau, June 9, 1943.

125. BIOS, Report; AGM DBAG Kriegswerke 24 Debag-Ostwerke GmbH Reichshof, p. 3. About half the Germans may have been office workers. See *Das Diensttagebuch,* p. 727.

126. ZSL Tatort: Tyczyn, Jawornik-Polski und Rzeszow II 206 AR 63/70, (I.G.) 197–98.

127. The SS chief at the Daimler-Benz "ghetto," Oester, committed numerous atrocities at the factory and in the main ghetto in Reichshof. ZSL Judenghetto v. Reichshof (Rzeszow), Distr. Krakau II 206 AR-Z 214/77 -K-,7.

128. One man, described as a "department head," pursued a fleeing slave through a wheat field and struck him down. The Jew, Majbruch, was then tortured and executed in front of a group of Daimler-Benz's forced laborers. *Ibid,* 37. A survivor reported that the factory manager, Rahmig, turned in a Jew he saw outside of the main Reichshof ghetto—the man's father—to the SS chief Oester, who then summarily executed the "offender." ZSL Reichshof (Flugmotorenwerk Daimler-Benz) 206 AR-Z 46/1962, (J.R.), 211.

129. Gilbert, *Endloesung,* p. 136; AGM DBAG Vertriebsorganisation 175/24 Reichshof to Ruestungskommando Krakau, Nov. 18, 1942. The letter indicates that the Jewish workers were about to leave Reichshof. According to Gilbert, 2,000 Jews left the city on or about November 18, 1942, and were killed at Belzec. For Daimler-Benz's witnesses to the mass murders in front of the factory, see ZSL Polen 365a Akten Auerswald Bd. III, 18–20.

130. AGM DBAG Vertriebsorganisation 175/24 Reichshof to Ruestungskommando Krakau, June 9, 1943; Hilberg, *The Destruction*, pp. 539–40.

131. *Das Diensttagebuch*, p. 635 (General Max Schindler).

132. ZSL Reichshof (Flugmotorenwerk Daimler-Benz) 206 AR-Z 46/1962, Staatsanwaltschaft to ZSL, Dec. 12, 1976.

133. AGM DBAG Kriegswerke 24, p. 2. On the succession controversy in 1942, see below.

134. *Das Diensttagebuch*, p. 816; Piotr Matusak, *Ruch Operu w Przemysle Wojennym Okupanta Hitlerowskiego na ziemiach Polskich w Latach 1939–1945* (Warsaw: Wydawnictwo Ministerstwa Obrony Narodowej, 1983), pp. 320–21. I would like to thank the author and Piotr Madajczyk for their assistance with Polish.

135. Hilberg, *The Destruction*, pp. 482–83.

136. AGM DBAG Kriegswerke 24, p. 2; *Das Diensttagebuch*, p. 816. Frank regaled his Daimler-Benz hosts with a speech containing comments such as: "If I went to the *Fuehrer* and said to him: My *Fuehrer*, I report that I've once again killed 150,000 Poles, he would say: good *[schoen]* if it was necessary, but unfortunately the trains are standing still, the whole land is full of sabotage, every day another terrorist attack *[Attentat]* [is] carried out; that will not do. . . . We can no longer refuse to entertain a cooperation with the foreign peoples of Europe. Millions and millions from these foreign peoples have been sent to Germany to work. Here the GG marches at the fore, since it has already given up 2 million workers to the Reich." The speech is given in Stanislaw Piotrowski, *Hans Franks Tagebuch* (Warsaw: Polnischer Verlag der Wissenschaften, 1963), pp. 428–29.

137. HSG, O.M.G.U.S., "Report on the Investigation of the Deutsche Bank," Exhibits 114, 116.

138. AGM DBAG Kriegswerke 24, p. 3; *Das Diensttagebuch*, p. 892. In the wake of the evacuation, the SD arrested Romstedt, who was later released. The incident remains obscure. *Das Diensttagebuch*, p. 930.

139. AGM DBAG Kriegswerke 22 Bericht ueber die Demontage des Werkes Amerika (Mulde) der ehemaligen Daimler-Benz GmbH Kolmar/Elsass, p. 6.

140. *Ibid.*, ZSL, Lager Kamenz (NL Kamenz d. KL Gross-Rosen), Kamenz (Sachsen) 405 AR-Z 198/74. Investigators, who did not have access to the evidence presented here, were unable to fix precisely the identity of the company in Kamenz using the concentration camp inmates to build airplane motors and spare parts. They relied on a 1942 city telephone book which listed no armaments producers. No wonder: Daimler-Benz first moved to Kamenz at the end of 1944 and in early 1945. Interestingly, no survivor recalled ever seeing a company name during the short-lived operation, which lasted from January to March 1945.

141. AGM DBAG Kriegswerke 26 Flugmotorenwerke Ostmark GmbH Wien 1941–1944 Niederschrift ueber die 3. Beiratssitzung, Dec. 16, 1941, pp. 2, 3, 9, 15.

142. ADM DBAG Protokolle 31–43 Niederschrift ueber . . . die Praesidial-Sitzung (Daimler-Benz Motoren G.m.b.H.), Aug. 12, 1943, pp. 1–3.

143. *Aktenvermerk R.U. Ein Bericht ueber die Solidaritaet und den Widerstand im Konzentrationslager Mauthausen von 1938 bis 1945* (Berlin: Militaerverlag der DDR, 1979), pp. 65–66.

144. Gisela Rabitsch, "Das KL Mauthausen," in *Studien zur Geschichte der Konzentrationslager*, (Stuttgart: Deutsche Verlags-Anstalt, 1970), p. 77.

145. Hans Marsalek, *Die Geschichte des Konzentrationslagers Mauthausen. Dokumentation*, (Vienna: Oesterreichische Lagergemeinschaft Mauthausen, 1974), p. 64. At the beginning of 1944, 1,568 concentration camp prisoners and 592 POW's were employed at Ostmark. IWM, FD 422/140 Flugmotorenwerke Ostmark GmbH, Beiratsbericht fuer die Zeit vom 1.1.-31.3.1944, ergaenzende Angaben, B.

146. AGM DBAG Protokolle 31–43 Niederschrift ueber . . . die Praesidial-Sitzung (Daimler-Benz Motoren G.m.b.H.), Aug. 12, 1943, p. 3. See the extensive collection of copies of Flugmotorenwerke Ostmark documents in HSG.

147. United States Strategic Bombing Survey, Daimler-Benz AG, Untertuerkheim, Germany. Dates of Survey: 8 May–18 May 1945, pp. 1, 4, 6–7; British Intelligence Objectives Subcommittee, Report on visit to Daimler-Benz A.G. at Stuttgart-Untertuerkheim PB 31248, pp. 3, 4, 8.

148. AGM DBAG DBAG 31 Sonderbericht der Daimler-Benz Aktiengesellschaft Untertuerkheim 22 November 1945; USSBS, Daimler-Benz AG, Exhibits C1–C4.

149. *Ibid.*

150. AGM DBAG Kissel XIII, 2 DBAG to Arbeitsamt Stuttgart, June 17, 1941; DBAG to Kissel, Sept. 1, 1941.

151. AGM DBAG Kissel XIII, 2 Kissel to Griep, March 19, 1942; Kissel to Griep, April 14, 1942.

152. Herbert, *Fremdarbeiter*, p. 157.

153. AGM DBAG Kissel V, 21? to Kissel, Jan. 20, 1942, p. 1.

154. Tim Mason, "Women in Germany 1925–1940: Family, Welfare and Work (Conclusion)," *History Workshop*, (1976), 2: 22.

155. USSBS, Daimler-Benz AG, p. 9.

156. Bundesarchiv Koblenz R 41/228 Lahs to Milch, November 20, 1942. The USSBS figure seems high, but is buttressed with an impressive chart.

157. AGM DBAG Konrad Zampf, Mercedes-Stern und Fremdarbeiter 1941–1945. Entwurf zu einer Disposition. See exhibit N.

158. Hermann Bruder, ed., *Herzstueck im Schwabenland. Untertuerkheim und Rotenberg: Ein Heimatsbuch* (Stuttgart: Buergerverein, 1983), p. 571.

159. Bundesarchiv Koblenz NS 5 I vorl. 265 DAF Zentralbuero, Rundschreiben, Jan. 21, 1941; NSDAP Stellvertreter des Fuehrers, Stabsleiter, Rundschreiben, Dec. 7, 1940; Claudia Koonz, *Mothers in the Fatherland: Women, The Family, and Nazi Politics* (New York: St. Martin's, 1988), pp. 347–50.

160. Bettina Wenke, *Interviews mit Ueberlebenden. Verfolgung und Wilderstand in Suedwestdeutschland* (Stuttgart: Konrad Theiss, 1980), p. 117.

161. Michael Geyer, "The Nazi State Reconsidered," in Richard Bessel, ed., *Life in the Third Reich* (Oxford: Oxford University Press, 1987), pp. 61–62;

Detlev J.K. Peukert, *Inside Nazi Germany: Conformity, Opposition, and Racism in Everyday Life* (New Haven: Yale University Press, 1987), pp. 125–144.

162. USSBS, Daimler-Benz AG, p. 9a, Table 2.

163. *Ibid.*, p. 9b, Table 2, pp. 12–22, 31. The bombing contributed to a 2.5 month loss of productivity at DB in Stuttgart. Because of the widespread dispersal of Daimler-Benz facilities, there is no reason to doubt Abelhauser's conclusion that "the bombing campaign had only the smallest effect, even on the armaments industry." Werner Abelshauser, *Wirtschaftsgeschichte der Bundesrepublik Deutschland 1945–1980* (Frankfurt/Main: Suhrkamp, 1983), p. 21.

164. Rudolf Lusar, *Die deutschen Waffen und Geheimwaffen des zweiten Weltkriegs und ihre Weiterentwicklung,* 6th ed. (Munich: Lehmanns, 1971), p. 159; Karlheinz Kens & Heinz J. Nowarra, *Die deutschen Flugzeuge 1933–1945. Deutschlands Luftfahrt-Entwicklungen bis zum Ende des Zweiten Weltkrieges,* 4th ed. (Munich: Lehmanns, 1972), pp. 123–25, with drawings.

165. USSBS, Daimler-Benz AG, p. 30. The DB 603 L with double supercharger had been destined to become the most important German fighter engine in 1945.

166. AGM DBAG Kissel V, 19, esp. "Das koloniale Angebot"; *Anatomie des Krieges,* pp. 408–9; Radant, "Zu den Beziehungen," pp. 18–19.

167. Berlin Document Center, Sonderakte 3. Daimler-Benz, Bl. 33 Dickwach (DAF) to von Stauss, August 20, 1942.

168. Willi Boelcke, ed., *Deutschlands Ruestung im Zweiten Weltkrieg. Hitlers Konferenzen mit Albrecht Speer 1942–1945* (Frankfurt/Main: Athenaion, 1968), p. 430. Typical of the general praise for Haspel was one leading official's: "Haspel . . . outstanding organizer and business manager, motor specialist." HSG, Nachlass Saur, II. Die Dienstellen, Die Maenner und die Werke der deutschen Ruestung, p. 214.

169. BDC Sonderakte Daimler-Benz Bl.26 Werlin to Himmler, August 27, 1942.

170. Institut fuer Zeitgeschichte MA-144/4, August 8, 1942, for Goering's approval.

171. BDC Sonderakte Daimler-Benz Bl.31 Berger to Himmler, August 20, 1942.

172. BDC Sonderakte Daimler-Benz Bl.30 Himmler to Werlin, August 25, 1942

173. BDC Sonderakte Daimler-Benz Bl.18 Dickwach to Haspel, September 6, 1942.

174. BDC Sonderakte Daimler-Benz Bl.15 Dickwach to Jaezosch, September 18, 1942.

175. Vortrag von Direktor Dr. Haspel in Wirtschaftsausschuss, Oct. 15, 1945, p. 5. (Dr. Bauer's private collection).

176. BDC Sonderakte Daimler-Benz Bl.4 Himmler to Schwarz, January 22, 1945, indicates that someone had denounced Werlin. In addition, Himmler and Schwarz believed that the "Jewish" connections at Daimler-Benz were inhibiting the war effort. See also the bizarre letter in BDC Werlin, Himmler to Werlin,

August 9, 1944. Werlin had interceded with Himmler to request that the ballerina Friedericke Derra de Moroda—apparently a good friend—be made a German citizen. Himmler responded in a furious letter, noting her Greek, Slovak and Hungarian blood, the roles she had played in English dance circles before the war, and her alleged intention to dance on German stages once she received German citizenship. Himmler wrote that not only could he not grant Werlin's request, "but I must now order the imprisonment of the named women. I am unable to comprehend, how you as a member of the SS can exert yourself for this naturalization."

177. ZSL, USA Film 4 480–484 (Auschwitz, August 25, 1944), Film 4 Ordner No. 16 (Natzweiler, October 14, 1944). For Sachsenhausen and Ravensbrueck, see above.

178. Willi Boelcke, ed., *Deutschlands Ruestung im Zweiten Weltkrieg. Hitlers Konferenzen mit Albert Speer* (Frankfurt/Main: Athenaion, 1968), p. 430.

179. BDC Sonderakte Daimler-Benz Bl.11 Berger to Brandt, October 2, 1942.

180. Dietrich Eichholtz, *Geschichte der deutschen Kriegswirtschaft 1939–1946*, 2: 105–6.

181. This is based on a draft of Michael Fichter's article, "Der Krieg ist gemeinsam verloren—Das Tragen der Lasten ist aber nicht gemeinsam," (manuscript) in M. Broszat et al., eds., *Von Stalingrad zur Waehrungsreform*, and Geschaeftsberichte der Daimler-Benz Aktiengesellschaft Stuttgart (1945–1947), pp. 2–3.

182. O.M.G.U.S. Economics Division 17/225-1 Box 503 Report of the Daimler-Benz AG, Stuttgart-Untertuerkheim, August 30, 1947.

CONCLUSIONS

1. AGM DBAG Kissel XII, 9 Deutsche Betriebsfuehrer! Unser Dank ein freudiges "JA"!, April 4, 1938 (document reproduced in H. Pohl, et al., *Die Daimler-Benz AG in den Jahren 1933 bis 1945*, p. 227).

2. Quoted in Werner Reich, *Die Organisation der Produktion in der deutschen Automobilindustrie unter Beruecksichtigung neuzeitlicher Produktionsprobleme*, Dissertation/Berlin, 1923/24, p. 10.

3. H. L. Arnold & F. L. Faurote, *Ford Methods and the Ford Shops* (New York: Engineering Magazine Co., 1919), p. 41.

BIBLIOGRAPHY

I. ARCHIVAL SOURCES

1. AGM DBAG Archiv-Geschichte-Museum Daimler Benz Aktien-
   Gesellschaft, 7000 Stuttgart 60
   DMG Daimler-Motoren-Gesellschaft (246 files, untitled)
   DBAG Daimler-Benz Aktien-Gesellschaft (108 files, untitled)
   Ut Untertuerkheim
   Sifi Sindelfingen
   Marienfelde
   Protokolle
   Werksangehoerige
   VWMI
   Goldene Fahne
   Sindelfingen Huppenbauer
   Kriegswerke
   Bestand Kissel
2. Archiv der sozialen Demokratie, Friedrich-Ebert-Stiftung, 5300 Bonn 2
   Nachlass Keil
3. BDC Berlin Document Center, 1000 Berlin (West) 37
   W. Eckenberg
   A.F. Gedult v. Jungenfeld
   W.v. Hentig
   H.-J. Huschke
   W. Kissel

K.C. Mueller
F. Nallinger
M. Sailer
M. Wolf
Sonderakte 3. Daimler-Benz
4. BAK Bundesarchiv Koblenz
   R3 Reichsministerium fuer Ruestung und Kriegsproduktion
   R41 Reichsarbeitsministerium
   NS 4 Na Konzentrationslager (Natzweiler)
   NS 4 Ma Konzentrationslager (Mauthausen)
   NS 4 Anhang Konzentrationslager
   NS 5 Deutsche Arbeits-Front
5. HSG Hamburger Stiftung fuer Sozialgeschichte des 20. Jahrhunderts,
   2000 Hamburg 13
   Deutsche Arbeits-Front Arbeitswissenschaftliches Institut
   Flugmotorenwerke Ostmark (copies)
   Nachlass Saur (copy)
   O.M.G.U.S. Financial Investigations Section, "Report on the Investigation
   of the Deutsche Bank," with exhibits, November 1946
6. HStASt Hauptsstaatsarchiv Stuttgart, 7000 Stuttgart 1
   Quellen zur Geschichte der Arbeiterbewegung im Hauptstaatsarchiv
   Suttgart, Wilfred Braunn, ed.
   E 33 Koeniglicher Geheimer Rat III
      584: Fabrik und Gewerbe-Inspektion 1879–1905
   E 46 Ministerium der Auswaertigen Angelegenheiten III
      275: Kommission fuer die Arbeiterstatistik 1892–1905, 1913
      281: Beschaeftigung von Kindern u. jungen Arbeitern in gewerblichen
         Betrieben 1903–1919
      282: Gewerbeaufsichtsbeamte 1892–1919
      309: Vorschuesse u. Unfallenentschaedigungen . . . 1909–1921
      931: Unterfasz. 2. Fabrik-Arbeitswesen, Arbeiterfuersorge 1855–1912
      953: Unterfasz. 4. Arbeitervereine . . . 1863–1919
      1012: Arbeitsnachweis . . . 1893–1919
      1024: VWMI 1907
   E 74 Akten der Berliner Gesandtschaft. 2. Abt.
      170: Allgemeine Fragen ueber den Weltkrieg, Kriegsziele der
         Sozialdemokraten 1914–1917
      172: Arbeiter und Angestellte . . . 1914–1918
      217: Industrieorganisation 1919
      219: Soziale Reform 1919
      226: Vaterlaendischer Hilfsdienst 1914–1918
   E 130a Staatsministerium
      205: Sicherheitstruppen
      209–211: Innere Unruhen
      212–214: Generalstreik vom 26. Aug. bis 4. Sept. 1920

215–221: Innere Unruhen: Zeitungsausschnitten

355: Arbeits- und Sozialministerium 1919, 1923–1925

357: Lohn & Arbeitsverhaeltnisse, Tarifvertraege 1919–20

358: Koalitionsrecht . . . Streiks 1902–06, 1912, 1919–20

735: Staatsumwaelzung. Arbeiter-, Bauern- u. Soldatenraete 1918–20

957: Zentral-Arbeitsgemeinschaft der industriellen u. gewerblichen
    Arbeitgeber u. Arbeitnehmer Deutschlands 1919

958–959: Arbeitskammer (Arbeitsgerichte) 1908

1147–1150: Weltkrieg 1914–18. Kriegsbedingte Gesetze . . .

1154–1156: Weltkrieg 1914–18. Kriegsbedingte Gesetze . . .

1205–1206: Weltkrieg 1914–18. Vaterlaendischer Hilfsdienst

1251: Massnahmen zur Aufhebung der Kriegswirtschaft 1922–25

1458–1461: Politische Parteien, SPD

E 130b Staatsministerium

81: Anfragen, Antraege u. Petitionen im Landtag 1901–1918

83: Desgleichen

126: Ausuebung des Gnadenrechts

1040: Allgemeine Fragen, vor allem Ueberwachung von Auslaendern
    1919–1944

1078: Ausnahmezustand 1918–1924

1083: Massnahmen des Reiches u. der Laender aufgrund Artikel 48

1086: Untersuchungs- u. Schutzhaft 1915

1794: Eingaben einzelner Firmen u. Unternehmer in
    Betriebsangelegenheiten 1917–1943

1918: Vorlaeufiger Reichswirtschaftsrat . . . 1919–1934

1919: Mitglieder . . . 1920–1933

1952–1953: Kapp-Putsch

3517–3518

E 130 II Staatsministerium

496: Arbeiter u. Angestelltenausschuesse, Tarifvertaege, Betriebsraete
    1918–1920

537: Sozialistische Maifeiern 1919–1932

570: Weltkrieg 1917–1920

E 131 Pressestelle des Wuertt. Staatsministeriums

4–5: Pressekonferenzen 1919–20

107: Justizverwaltung. Politische Prozesse 1920–25

E 151a Ministerium des Innern V

829: Betriebsraetegesetz 1919–1922

E 151f II Wohnungswesen Ministerium des Innern V, Abteilung
    Wohnungs- und Siedlungswesen

94: Deutscher Verein "Arbeiterheim" 1911

J 150 Druck- und Flugschriften bis 1945

165: Innere Unruhen 1919–1923

7. HStASt M Hauptstaatsarchiv Stuttgart Militaerarchiv, 7000 Stuttgart 1

E 135 Revolutionsarchiv

M1/6 Wuertt. Kriegsministerium. Verwaltungsabteilung
73
837
920
1039
1176–79
1229
1262
1336
1414
1465–1493

M 1/9 Wuertt. Kriegsministerium. Abteilung fuer Waffen, Feldgeraet- und Kriegsamtsangelegenheiten
45
46
60
74
78
79
214
215
247
259
260
261
265
273
274
275
316a–c

M 1/11 Kriegsarchiv
938
977
1083
1109
1110–20

M 10 Militaerbevollmaechtiger in Berlin
22 Verschiedene Angelegenheiten 1914–1922

M 77/1 Stellvertretender Generalkommando XIII. (Wuertt.) A.K.
53
60
67
76
93
118

M 77/2 Denkschriften des Stellv. Generalkommando XIII. (Wuertt.) A.K.
  10
  85
M 340 Sicherheitstruppen
  8
M 660 Nachlass Ebbinghaus
M 660 Nachlass Hahn
M 744
E 361 Arbeitsministerium 1918–23
8. Institut fuer Zeitgeschichte, Muenchen
  Firmen II—Daimler-Benz
  Fa-146
  MA-144/4
  F-48
  NI
  NID
  NIK
9. NARA National Archives and Records Administration, Washington, D.C.
  NNMR 3a 1045 Genshagen, Box 61
  NNMR 3a 2748 Stuttgart, Boxes 152–154
  M 1013 Rolls 1, 7, 15
10. National Archives and Record Administration, Washington National
  Records Center, Suitland, Maryland
  Office of Military Government (United States), RG 260, Economics
  Division, Boxes 52, 54, 70, 132, 152, 250, 503
  Office of Military Government (United States), RG 260, Wuerttemberg-
  Baden Economics Division, Boxes 8, 9, 10, 12
11. StAL Staatsarchiv Ludwigsburg, Ludwigsburg
  E 326 Gewerbegericht Stuttgart 1911–1922
  E 392 Schlichtungsausschuss in Arbeits- u. Tarifangelegenheiten
  1919–1922
12. ZSL, Zentrale Stelle der Landesjustizverwaltungen, Ludwigsburg
  Betr. Erhardt, Paul Georg
  Betr. Heck (Anton o. Adolf) II 202 AR 1495/69
  Judenghetto von Reichshof (Rzeszow), Distr. Krakau II 206
  AR-Z 214/77 -K
  KL Natzweiler 419 AR-Z 33/61
  Minsk / Weissruthenian 202 AR 981/67
  NL Genshagen / KL Sachsenhausen 406 AR-Z 21/71
  NL Kamenz d. KL Gross-Rosen 405 AR-Z 198/1974
  NL Mannheim-Sandhofen d. KL Natzweiler IV 419 AR-Z 176/1969
  NL Schwechat / KL Mauthausen IV 419 AR 1797/69
  NL Wesserling-Urbis d. KL Natzweiler 419 AR-Z 177/69
  NL Wiener-Neustadt / KL Mauthausen IV 419 AR-Z 68/77
  Polen 365a Akten Auerswald Bd. III

Reichshof (Flugmotorenwerke Daimler-Benz) 206 AR-Z 46/1962
Tatort: Tyczyn, Jawornik-Polski und Rzeszow II 206 AR 63/70
USA Film 4 Ordner 15 & 16
Verschiedenes 301 aa 5 Band 81
Verschiedenes 301 cq Band 176

II. UNPUBLISHED SOURCES AND INTELLIGENCE REPORTS

British Intelligence Objectives Sub-Committee, "Report on Visit to Daimler-Benz A.G. at Stuttgart-Untertuerkheim."

Combined Intelligence Objectives Sub-Committee, "Daimler-Benz Plant at Wendlingen."

Combined Intelligence Objectives Sub-Committee, "Report on a Visit to Aero Engine Test Plant at Rothenbach."

United States Strategic Bombing Survey, Daimler-Benz Gaggenau Works, Gaggenau, Germany," second ed., January 1947.

United States Strategic Bombing Survey, "Daimler-Benz A.G. Mannheim, Germany," second ed., January 1947.

United States Strategic Bombing Survey, "Daimler-Benz AG, Untertuerkheim, Germany," second ed., January 1947.

United States Strategic Bombing Survey, "The Effects of Strategic Bombing on the German War Economy," October 31, 1945.

United States Strategic Bombing Survey, "German Motor Vehicles Industry Report," second ed., January 1947.

United States Strategic Bombing Survey, "Messerschmitt AG Augsburg, Germany, Overall Report," second ed., January 1947.

United States Strategic Bombing Survey, "Over-all Report (European War)," September 30, 1945.

United States Strategic Bombing Survey, "Summary Report (European War)," September 30, 1945.

III. PUBLISHED SOURCES

Anatomie des Krieges. Neue Dokumente ueber die Rolle des deutschen Monopolkapitals bei der Vorbereitung und Durchfuehrung des zweiten Weltkrieges. Eichholtz, Dietrich and Schumann, Wolfgang, eds. Berlin: VEB Deutscher Verlag der Wissenschaften, 1969.

Chronkik der Kgl. Haupt- und Residenzstadt 1903–1913. Stuttgart: Greiner & Pfeiffer (Kgl. Hofbuchdrucker), 1904–1914.

Die deutsche Nationalversammlung im Jahre 1919 in ihrer Arbeit fuer den Aufbau des neuen deutschen Volksstaates. Heilfron, Ed., ed. Berlin: Norddeutsche Buchdruckerei, n.d. Berlin, Joerg, ed. Koeln: Pahl-Rugenstein, 1979.

Deutschland-Bericht der Sopade (Sozialdemokratische Partei Deutschlands), 1934–1940. 7 volumes. Salzhausen: Verlag Petra Nettelbeck, 1980.

Das Diensttagebuch des deutschen Generalgouverners in Polen 1939–1945. Praeg, W. & Jacobmeyer, W., eds. Stuttgart: Deutsche Verlags-Anstalt, 1975.

Dokumente zur Geschichte der Arbeiterbewegung in Wuerttemberg und Baden 1848–1949. Scherer, Peter & Schaaf, Peter, eds. Stuttgart: Konrad Theiss, 1984.

Jahresberichte Gewerbe-Aufsichtsbeamten im Koenigreich Wuerttemberg, 1903–1913. Stuttgart, 1910–1914.

Jahresberichte der Gewerbebeaufsichtsbeamten und Bergbehoerden fuer das Jahr 1927. Berlin, 1928.

Krieg Revolution Republik. Eine Dokumentation. Cordes, Gunther, ed. Ulm: Vaas, 1978.

Meldungen aus dem Reich. Die geheimen Lageberichte des Sicherheitsdienstes der SS 1938–1945. Boberach, Heinz, ed. 17 vols. and Register. Herrsching: Pawlak, 1985.

Trials of War Criminals Before the Nuernberg Military Tribunals under Control Council Law No. 10, vols. 6 and 8. Washington: U.S. Government Printing Office, 1952.

IV. DAIMER & DAIMLER-BENZ: PUBLISHED & UNPUBLISHED MANUSCRIPTS (IN CHRONOLOGICAL ORDER OF COMPOSITION)

Zum 25jaehrigen Bestehen der Daimler-Motoren-Gesellschaft, 1915. 1915.

Werk Sindelfingen 1915–1935. Hans Sonntag, ed. 1939.

Gesamt-Leistungsbericht der Daimler-Benz Aktiengesellschaft. Aufgestellt im Arbeitsjahr 1940. 1940.

Leistungsbericht der Daimler-Benz Aktiengesellschaft. Aufgestellt im Arbeitsjahr 1940. Band 18, Ostwerk Koenigsberg. 1940.

Leistungsbericht der Daimler-Benz Aktiengesellschaft, Aufgestellt im Arbeitsjahr 1940. Band 19. Daimler-Benz Motoren GmbH. Genshagen (Kreis Teltow). 1940.

75 Jahre Motorisierung des Verkehrs, 1886–1961 Chronik Mercedes-Benz. Fahrzeug und Motoren. 1978.

Daimler-Benz Museum. Historische Datensammlung 1886–1980. 1981.

Das Werk Unterturerkheim. 1983.

100 Jahre Daimler-Benz. Das Unternehmen. Kruk, Max & Lingnau, Gerold. Mainz: Von Hase & Koehler, 1986.

100 Jahre Daimler-Benz. Die Technik. Barthel, Manfred & Lingnau, Gerold. Mainz: Von Hase & Koehler, 1986.

Die Daimler-Benz AG in den Jahren 1933 bis 1945. Eine Dokumentation. Pohl, Hans; Habeth, Stephanie & Brueninghaus, Beate. Wiesbaden: Steiner, 1986.

The Star and the Laurel. The Centennial History of Daimler, Mercedes and Benz. Kimes, Beverly Rae. produced *(sic)* by Lewine, Harris. Montvale, New Jersey: Mercedes-Benz of North America, 1986.

V. DEUTSCHER METALLARBEITER-VERBAND MATERIALS IN ZENTRALBIBLIOTHEK DER INDUSTRIEGEWERKSCHAFT METALL (IG METALL), FRANKFURT/MAIN

Die Arbeitsverhaeltnisse der Eisen-, Metall-, Modell-, Werkzeug-, Revolver,- und Automatendreher Deutschlands. Stuttgart: Schlicke, 1912.

Die Arbeitsverhaeltnisse in dem Wagenbau- und Karosseriebetrieben. Stuttgart: Schlicke, 1922.

Der Deutsche Metallarbeiter-Verband im Jahre . . . 1903–1926. Stuttgart: Schlicke, 1904–1927.

Geschaeftsberichte 1927.

Geschaeftsberichte 1928.

Jahr- und Handbuch fuer Verbandsmitglieder 1925. Stuttgat: Verlagsgesellschaft des Deutschen Metallarbeiter-Verbandes, 1926?

Protokoll der Konferenz des Reichsbeirats der Betriebsraete und Vertreter groesserer Konzerne der Metallindustrie. Abgehalten am 19. und 30. Dezember 1926 in Stuttgart.

Protokoll der Reichskonferenz der in der Autoindustrie Beschaeftigten. Abgehalten am 23. Feb. 1930 in Frankfurt/Main.

VI. NEWSPAPERS

Bosch-Zuender.
Daimler Werksnachrichten.
Daimler Werkzeitung.
Deutsche Metallarbeiter-Zeitung.
Schwaebische Tagwacht.
Schwaebischer Merkur.
Sozialdemokrat.
Voelkischer Beobachter.
Vorwaerts.

VII. BOOKS AND ARTICLES

Abraham, David. *The Collapse of the Weimar Republic. Political Economy and Crisis.* Princeton: Princeton University Press, 1981.

Achterberg, Erich and Maximilian Mueller-Jabusch. *Lebensbilder Deutscher Bankiers aus fuenf Jahrhunderten.* Frankfurt: Fritz Kapp, 1963.

Adelt, Richard. *Die Krise in der deutschen Personenautomobil-Industrie.* Dissertation/Munich, 1931.

Arnold, Horace Lucien and Fay Leone Faurote. *Ford Methods and the Ford Shops.* New York: Engineering Magazine Co., 1919.

Aroneanu, Eugene. *Konzentrationslager. Tatsachenbericht ueber die an Menschheit begangen Verbrechen. Dokument F 321 fuer den Internationalen Militaergerichtshof.* Baden-Baden: Arbeitsgemeinschaft Das Licht, 1946.

Bajohr, Stefan. *Die Haelfte der Fabrik. Geschichte der Frauenarbeit im Deutschland 1914–1945.* Marburg: Verlag Arbeiterbewegung und geschichtliche Wissenschaft, 1979.

Becker, Achim. *Absatzprobleme der deutschen PKW-Industrie 1925–1932.* Dissertation, Regensburg, 1979.

Bentley, J. and F. Porsche. *Ein Traum wird Wirklichkeit. Ein Auto macht Geschichte.* Duesseldorf: Econ, 1978.

Bernays, Marie. *Auslese und Anpassung der Arbeiterschaft der geschlossenen Grossindustrie dargestellt an den Verhaeltnissen der Gladbacher Spinnerei und Weberei A.G. zu Muenchen-Gladbach im Rheinland.* Leipzig: Duncker and Humblot, 1910.

Bieber, H.-J. *Gewerkschaften in Krieg und Revolution. Arbeiterbewegung, Industrie, Staat und Militaer in Deutschland 1914–1920.* 2 volumes. Hamburg: Christians, 1981.

Bieker, Bernhardt. *Fachrechnen fuer Former und Modellbauer.* Stuttgat: Klett, n.d.

Blaich, Fritz. "Die 'Fehlrationalisierung' in der deutschen Automobilindustrie 1924 bis 1929," *Tradition* (1973) 18: 18–34.

Blos, Wilhelm. *Von der Monarchie zum Volksstaat. Zur Geschichte der Revolution in Deutschland, insbesonders in Wuerttemberg.* Stuttgart: Berger, 1922/1923.

Boelcke, Willi. *Die deutsche Wirtschaft 1930–1945. Interna des Reichswirtschaftsministeriums.* Duesseldorf: Droste, 1983.

Boelcke, Willi, ed. *Deutschlands Ruestung im Zweiten Weltkrieg. Hitlers Konferenzen mit Albert Speer 1942–1945.* Frankfurt/Main: Athenaion, 1968.

Bohn, Willi. *"Hochverraeter!"* Frankfurt/Main: Roederberg, 1984.

Bohn, Willi. *Stuttgart: Geheim! Ein dokumentarischer Bericht.* Frankfurt/Main: Roederberg, 1969.

Brady, Robert A. *The Rationalization Movement in German Industry. A Study in the Evolution of Economic Planning.* New York: Howard Fertig, 1974.

Braverman, Harry. *Labor and Monopoly Capital. The Degradation of Work in the Twentieth Century.* New York: Monthly Review, 1974.

Bruder, Hermann, ed. *Herzstueck im Schwabenland. Unterteurkheim und Rotenberg. Ein Heimatbuch.* Stuttgart: Buergerverein Untertuerkheim, 1983.

Brune, Thomas, Silke Goettsch, Joerg Haspel and Ulrich Weitz. *Arbeiterbewegung — Arbeiterkultur. Stuttgart 1890–1933.* Stuttgart: Wuerttembergisches Landesmuseum, 1981.

Bruns, Hermann. *Die deutsche Automobil-Industrie mit besonderer Beruecksichtigung der Kleinauto-Industrie bei der Rationalisierung.* Hannover: Harbers, 1926.

Bry, Gerhard. *Wages in Germany 1871–1945.* Princeton: Princeton University Press, 1960.

Burawoy, Michael. *The Politics of Production. Factory Regimes Under Capitalism and Socialism.* London: Verso, 1985.

Carroll, Berenice A. *Design for Total War. Arms and Economics in the Third Reich.* The Hague: Mouton, 1968.

Christ-Gmelin, Maya. *Die wuerttembergische Sozialdemokratie 1890–1914.* Dissertation/Stuttgart, 1975.

Comite International de la Croix-Rouge, Internationaler Suchdienst. *Vorlaeufiges Verzeichnis der Konzentrationslager und deren Aussenkommandos sowie anderer Haftstaetten unter dem Reichsfuehrer-SS in Deutschland und deutsch besetzten Gebieten (1933–1945).* Arolsen, 1969.

Craven, Wesley Frank, James Lea Cate; and the Air Historical Group. *The Army Air Forces in World War II.* 7 vols. Chicago: University of Chicago Press, 1949.

Crew, David F. *Town in the Ruhr. A Social History of Bochum, 1860–1914.* New York: Columbia University Press, 1979.

Damals in Sachsenhausen. Solidaritaet und Widerstand im Konzentrationslager Sachsenhausen. Berlin: VEB Deutscher Verlag der Wissenschaften, 1967.

Daniel, Ute, "Fiktionen, Friktionen und Fakten—Frauenlohnarbeit im Ersten Weltkrieg." In Gunther Mai, ed. *Arbeiterschaft in Deutschland 1914–1918. Studien zu Arbeitskampf und Arbeitsmarkt im Ersten Weltkrieg.* Duesseldorf: Droste, 1986.

von Delbrueck, Clemens. *Die wirtschaftliche Mobilmachung in Deutschland 1914.* Joachim von Delbrueck ed. Munich: Verlag fuer Kulturpolitik, 1924.

Deist, Wilhelm, ed. *Militaer und Innenpolitik in Weltkrieg 1914–1918.* 2 vols. Duesseldorf: Droste Verlag, 1970.

Deutsch, Julius. *Auslese und Anpassung der Arbeiter in den oesterreichischen Siemens-Schuckert-Werken in Wien. Auslese und Anpassung der Arbeiterschaft in der Elektroindustrie, Buchdruckerei, Feinmechanik und Maschinenindustrie.* Leipzig: Duncker & Humblot, 1910.

Das Deutsche Fuehrerlexikon 1934/1935. Berlin: Verlagsanstalt Otto Stollberg, n.d.

Der Deutsche Imperialismus und der Zweite Weltkrieg. Beitraege zum Thema: "Die Vorbereitung des zweiten Weltkrieges durch den deutschen Imperialismus". Vol. 2. Berlin: Ruetten & Loening, 1961.

Didier, Friedrich. *Europa arbeitet in Deutschland. Sauckel mobilisiert die Leistungsreserven.* Berlin: Zentralverlag der NSDAP, Franz Eher Nachf., 1943.

Dienstaltersliste der Schutztaffel der NSDAP. Stand vom 1. Dezember 1938. Berlin: SS-Personalkanzlei, 1938.

von Ebbinghaus, Christof. *Die Memoiren des Generals von Ebbinghaus.* Stuttgart: Berger Lit. Buero, 1928.

Edwards, P.K. and Hugh Scullion. *The Social Organization of Industrial Conflict. Control and Resistance in the Workplace.* London: Blackwell, 1982.

Eichholtz, Dietrich. *Geschichte der Deutschen Kriegswirtschaft, 1939–1945.* Band I, 1939–1941. Berlin: Akademie, 1969. Band II, 1941–1943. Berlin: Akademie, 1985.

Eldridge, J.E.T., ed. *Max Weber: The Social Interpretation of Reality.* New York: Schocken, 1980.

Eley, Geoff. *From Unification to Nazism. Reinterpreting the German Past.* London: Allen & Unwin, 1986.

Enzensberger, Hans Magnus; Rainer Nitsche; Klaus Roehler; and Winfried

Schafhausen, eds. *Klassenbuch 2. Ein Lesebuch zu den Klassenkaempfen in Deutschland 1850–1919.* Darmstadt: Luchterhand, 1972.

Enzensberger, Hans Magnus: Rainer Nitsche, Klaus Roehler, and Winfried Schafhausen, eds. *Klassenbuch 3. Ein Lesebuch zu den Klassenkaempfen in Deutschland 1919–1971.* Darmstadt: Luchterhand, 1972.

Evans, Richard J., ed. *The German Working Class 1888–1933. The Politics of Everyday Life.* Totowa, N.J.: Barnes & Noble, 1982.

Evans, Richard J., ed. *Society and Politics in Wilhelmine Germany.* New York: Barnes & Noble, 1978.

Feldman, Gerald D. *Army, Industry, and Labor in Germany 1914–1918.* Princeton: Princeton University Press, 1966.

Feldman, Gerald D., Carl-Ludwig Holtfrerich, Gerhard A. Ritter, and Peter-Christian Witt, eds. *Die deutsche Inflation. Eine Zwischenbilanz.* Berlin: Walter de Gruyter, 1982.

Feldman, Gerlad D. "The Origins of the Stinnes-Legien Agreement: A Documentation." *Internationale wissenschaftliche Korrespondenz zur Geschichte der deutschen Arbeiterbewegung,* (1973) 19/20:45–104.

Feldman, Gerlad D. *Vom Weltkrieg zur Weltwirtschaftskrise. Studien zur deutschen Wirtschafts- und Sozialgeschichte 1914–1932.* Goettingen: Vandenhoeck & Ruprecht, 1984.

Feldman, Gerald D. "Wirtschafts- und sozialpolitische Probleme der Deutschen Demobilmachung 1918/19." In H. Mommsen, et al., eds. *Industrielles System und politische Entwicklung in der Weimarer Republik,* pp. 618–636. Dusseldorf: Droste, 1974.

Feldman, Gerald D. and Irmgard Steinisch. *Industrie und Gewerkschaften 1918–1924. Die ueberforderte Zentralgemeinschaft.* Stuttgart: Deutsche Verlags-Anstalt, 1985.

Ferencz, Benjamin B. *Less than Slaves. Jewish Forced Labor and the Quest for Compensation.* Cambridge: Harvard University Press, 1979.

Fichter, Michael. "Betriebsraete im Raum Stuttgart, 1945–1948." Unpublished manuscript, 1986.

Fischer, Albrecht. *Verband Wuerttembergischer Metallindustrieller e.V. 1897 bis 1934.* This book bears no publication data.

Fischer, Otto. *Die Lohnentwicklung in der Stuttgarter Metallindustrie von 1914–1920.* Dissertation/Frankfurt, 1921.

Flohr, Bernd. *Arbeiter nach Mass. Die Disziplinierung der Fabrikarbeiterschaft waehrend der Industrialisierung Deutschlands im Spiegel von Arbeitsordnungen.* Frankfurt/Main: Campus, 1981.

Franz-Willing, Georg. *Die Hitlerbewegung. Der Ursprung 1919–1922.* Berlin: Decker, 1962.

Friedenson, Patrick. "Herrschaft im Wirtschaftsunternehmen. Deutschland und Frankreich 1880–1914." In Juergen Kocka, ed. *Buergertum im 19. Jahrhundert: Deutschland im europaeischen Vergleich.* Bd. 2, pp. 65–91. Munich: Deutscher Taschenbuch Verlag, 1988.

50 Jahre Gartenstadt Luginsland. Festschrift zum 50jaehrigen Bestehen 1911 bis 1961. Stuttgart, 1961.

Gartenstadt Luginsland. Gemeinnuetzige Baugenossenschaft, e.G.m.b.H. Stuttgart-Untertuerkheim 1911–1936. Festschrift zum 25-jaehrigen Bestehen. Stuttgart: Schoellkopf, Pfund und Cie., 1936.

Geary, Dick. "Radicalism and the Worker: Metalworkers and Revolution 1914– 1923." In Richard J. Evans, ed. *Society and Politics in Imperial Germany.* New York: Barnes & Noble, 1978.

Geuter, Ulfried. "Das Institut fuer Arbeitspsychologie und Arbeitspaedagogik der Deutschen Arbeitsfront. Eine Forschungsnotiz," *1999*, 1/1987, pp. 87–95.

Geyer, Michael. "The Nazi State Reconsidered." In Richard Bessel, ed. *Life in the Third Reich.* Oxford: Oxford University Press, 1987.

Gilbert, Martin. *Endloesung. Die Vertreibung und Vernichtung der Juden. Ein Atlas.* Reinbek: Rowohlt, 1982.

Gillingham, John R. *Industry and Politics in the Third Reich. Ruhr Coal, Hilter and Europe.* Wiesbaden: Franz Steiner Verlag, 1985.

Glum, Friedrich. *Zwischen Wissenschaft, Wirtschaft und Politik. Erlebtes und Erdachtes in vier Reichen.* Bonn: H. Bouvier, 1964.

Gnant, H. *Der Bau- und Maschinenschlosser. Ein Buch fuer Bauschlosser, Maschinenschlosser, Anschlaeger, Schmiede, Mechaniker, Schweisser, Monteure, fuer Werkmeister, Betriebsleiter und namentlich solche, die es werden wollen.* Stuttgart: Dieck & Co., 1925.

Godfrey, John F. *Capitalism at War: Industrial Policy and Bureaucracy in France 1914–1918.* Leamington: Berg, 1987.

Gramsci, Antonio. *Selections from the Prison Notebooks.* New York: International, 1970.

Groh, Dieter. "Intensification of Work and Industrial Conflict in Germany, 1896–1914." *Politics and Society* (1978), 8: 349–397.

Groh, Dieter. *Negative Integration und revolutionaerer Attentismus.* Frankfurt/ Main: Ullstein, 1974.

Hammer, Marius. *Vergleichende Morphologie der Arbeit in der europaeischen Automobilindustrie: Die Entwicklung zur Automation.* Basel: Kylos & Tuebingen: J.C.B. Mohr (Paul Siebeck), 1959.

Handbuch der Deutschen Aktiengesellschaften 1937. Band 4. Berlin: Hoppenstedt, 1937.

Hanf, Reinhardt. *Im Spannungsfeld zwischen Technik und Markt. Zielkonflikte bei der Daimler-Motoren-Gesellschaft im ersten Dezennium ihres Bestehens.* Wiesbaden: Franz Steiner Verlag, 1980.

Hanf, Reinhardt. *Moeglichkeiten und Grenzen betrieblicher Lohn- und Gehaltspolitik 1933–1939.* Dissertation, Regensburg, 1975.

Hansen, Ernst Willi. *Reichswehr und Industrie. Ruestungswirtschaftliche Zusammenarbeit und wirtschaftliche Mobilmachungsvorbereiten 1923–1932.* Boppard/Rhein: Harald Boldt, 1978.

Haspel, Joerg, et. al., eds. *Arbeiter. Kultur und Lebensweise im Koenigreich Wuerttemberg.* Tuebingen: Ludwig-Uhland-Institut fuer empirische Kulturwissenschaft, 1979.

Hegele, Anton. *Die Drehbank.* Stuttgart: Franckh, 1921.

Hegele, Anton. *Die Fraesmaschine. Ihre Entwicklung, ihr Aufbau, ihre Werk-*

zeuge, ihre Einstellung und Bedienung. Stuttgart: Franckh's Technischer Verlag, 1924.

Heiss, Clemens. "Die Arbeitsteilung und die Beschaeftigung minderwertiger Arbeitskraefte in der modernen Grossindustrie," *Schmollers Jahrbuch fuer Gesetzgebung, Verwaltung und Volkswirtschaft im Deutschen Reich* (1913) 37(1).

Heiss, Clemens. "Die Entloehnungsmethoden in der deutschen Metallindustrie," *Schmollers Jahrbach fuer Gesetzgebung, Verwaltung und Volkswirtschaft im Deutschen Reich* (1913) 37 (3).

Hellpach, Willy & Richard Lang. *Gruppenfabrikation.* Berlin: Springer, 1922.

Hentschel, Volker. *Geschichte der deutschen Sozialpolitik 1880–1980.* Frankfurt/Main: Suhrkamp, 1983.

Herbert, Ulrich. "Der 'Auslaendereinsatz'. Fremdarbeiter und Kriegsgefangene in Deutschland 1939–1945 — ein Ueberblick," in *Herrenmensch und Arbeitsvoelker. Auslaendische Arbeiter und Deutsche 1939–1945.* Berlin: Rotbuch, 1986.

Herbert, Ulrich. *Fremdarbeiter, Politik und Praxis des "Auslaender-Einsatzes" in der Kriegswirtschaft des Dritten Reiches.* Bonn: Dietz, 1985.

Hilbert, Raul. *Die Vernichtung der Europaeischen Juden. Die Gesamtgeschichte des Holocaust.* Berlin: Olle & Wolter, 1982.

Hinrichs, Peter. *Um die Seele des Arbeiters. Arbeitspsychologie, Industrie- und Betriebssoziologie in Deutschland.* Cologne: Pahl-Rugenstein, 1981.

Hinton, James. *The First Shop Stewards' Movement.* London: Allen & Unwin, 1973.

Hobsbawm, Eric J. *Labouring Men. Studies in the History of Labour.* London: Weidenfeld & Nicolson, 1964.

Hoffmann, Rudolf. *Daimler-Benz Aktiengesellschaft Stuttgart-Untertuerkheim.* Berlin: Organisation Verlagsgesellschaft, 1930.

Hofmann, Hans Hubert, ed. *Bankherren und Bankiers. Buedinger Vortraege 1976.* Limburg: C.A. Starke, 1978.

Homburg, Heidrun. "Anfaenge des Taylorsystems in Deutschland vor dem Ersten Weltkrieg." *Geschichte und Gesellschaft* (1978) 4:170–194.

Homze, Edward L. *Foreign Labor in Nazi Germany.* Princeton: Princeton University Press, 1967.

International Labour Office. *The Exploitation of Foreign Labour by Germany.* Montreal: ILO, 1945.

Jacobi, Willi. *Die Massnahmen zur Foerderung des Automobilabsatzes in Deutschland und die bilanzmaessige Auswirkung der Absatzsteigerung.* Dissertation, Frankfurt/Main, 1936.

James, Harold. *The German Slump. Politics and Economics 1924–1936.* Oxford: Clarendon Press, 1986.

Keil, Wilhelm. *Erlebnisse eines Sozialdemokraten.* 2 vols. Stuttgart: Deutsche-Verlagsanstalt, 1947/48.

Kens, Karlheinz and Heinz J. Nowarra. *Die deutschen Flugzeuge 1933–1945. Deutschlands Luftfahrt-Entwicklungen bis zum Ende des Zweiten Weltkrieges.* 4th ed. Munich: J.F. Lehmanns, 1972.

Kern, Horst and Michael Schumann. *Industriearbeit und Arbeiterbewusstsein.*

Eine empirische Untersuchung ueber den Einfluss der aktuellen technischen Entwicklung auf die industrielle Arbeit und das Arbeiterbewusstein. 2 volumes. Frankfurt: Europaeische Verlags-Anstalt, 1970.

Kielmansegg, Peter Graf. *Deutschland und der Erste Weltkrieg.* Stuttgart: Klett-Cotta, 1980.

Kirchberg, Peter. *Entwicklungstendenzen der deutschen Kraftfahrzeugindustrie 1929–1939.* Dissertation/Dresden, 1964.

Klapper, Edmund. *Die Entstehung der deutschen Automobil-Industrie.* Berlin: Boll und Pickardt, 1910.

Klein, B.H. *Germany's Economic Preparations for War.* Cambridge: Harvard University Press, 1959.

Klemm, Friedrich. *Die Hauptprobleme der Entwicklung der deutschen Automobilindustrie in der Nachkriegszeit und der Wettbewerb dieser Industrie mit dem Ausland, insbesondere mit den Vereinigten Staaten von Nordamerika.* Dissertation/Marburg, 1929.

Kling, Gertrud. *Die Novemberrevolution 1918 und der Kampf um die Verteidigung der Demokratie im Fruehjahr 1919 in Wuerttemberg.* Dissertation/Halle/Saale, 1967.

Kluge, Ulrich. *Die deutsche Revolution 1918/1919.* Frankfurt/Main: Suhrkamp, 1985.

Kocka, Juergen. *Die Angestellte in der deutschen Geschichte 1850–1980. Vom Privatbeamten zum angestellten Arbeitnehmer.* Goettingen: Sammlung Vandenhoeck, 1981.

Kocka, Juergen. *Klassengesellschaft im Krieg.* Goettingen: Vandenhoeck & Ruprecht, 1978.

Kocka, Juergen. *Lohnarbeit und Klassenbildung.* Bonn: Dietz, 1983.

von Koehler, Ludwig. *Zur Geschichte der Revolution in Wuerttemberg. Ein Bericht.* Stuttgart: Kohlhammer Verlag, 1930.

Kogon, Eugen et al. *Nationalsozialistische Massentoetungen durch Giftgas.* Frankfurt: S. Fischer, 1983.

Kolb, E. and K. Schoenhoven, eds. *Regionale und lokale Raeteorganisationen in Wuerttemberg 1918/1919.* Duesseldorf: Troste, 1976.

Koopmann, Klaus. *Gewerkschaftliche Vertrauensleute. Darstellung und kritische Analyse ihrer Entwicklung und Bedeutung von den Anfaengen bis zur Gegenwart unter besonderer Beruecksichtigung des Deutschen Metallarbeiter-Verbandes (DMV) und der Industriegewerkschaft Metall (IG Metall).* 2 vols. Muenchen: Minerva-Publikation, 1979.

Krausnick, Helmut, "Judenverfolgung." In M. Broszat, et al., eds. *Konzentrationslager Kommissarbefehl Judenverfolgung.* Olten: Walter-Verlag, 1965.

Kuczynski, Juergen. *Die Geschichte der Lage der Arbeiter unter dem Kapitalismus.* Berlin: Akademie, 1964.

Kuehnrich, Heinz. *Der KZ-Staat. Die faschistischen Konzentrationslager 1933–1945.* Berlin: Dietz, 1980.

Kugler, Anita. *Arbeitsorganisation und Produktionstechnologie der Adam Opel Werke (von 1900 bis 1929).* Berlin: Wissenschaftszentrum, 1985.

Kugler, Anita. "Von der Werkstatt zum Fliessband. Etappen der fruehen Automobilproduktion in Deutschland," *Geschichte und Gesellschaft* (1987) 13:304–339.

Lande, Dora. *Arbeits- und Lohnverhaeltnisse in der Berliner Maschinenindustrie zu Beginn des 20. Jahrhunderts.* Leipzig: Duncker & Humblot, 1910.

Landes, David. *The Unbound Prometheus. Technological Change and Industrial Development in Western Europe from 1750 to the Present.* Cambridge: Cambridge University Press, 1969.

Laubscher, Gerhard. *Die Opposition im Allgemeinen Deutschen Gewerkschaftsbund (ADGB) 1918–1923.* Frankfurt: Haag & Herchen, 1979.

Laux, James M. *In First Gear. The French Automobile Industry to 1914.* Liverpool: Liverpool University Press, 1976.

Lidtke, Vernon L. *The Alternative Culture: Socialist Labor in Imperial Germany.* New York: Oxford University Press, 1985.

Lucas, Erhard. *Zwei Formen von Radikalismus in der deutschen Arbeiterbewegung.* Frankfurt/Main: Roter Stern, 1976.

Luczak, Czeslaw. "Mobilisierung und Ausnutzung der polnischen Arbeitskraft fuer den Krieg," *Studia Historiae Oeconomicae* (1970), 5:303–313.

Ludwig Loewe & Co. Actiengesellschaft Berlin 1869/1929 [herausgegeben zum sechzigjaehrigen Jubilaeum der Firma von der Gesellschaft fuer elektrische Unternehmungen.] Berlin: Ludw. Loewe & Co. AG, 1930.

Ludwig, Heinz. "Die Arbeitsloesigkeit in der deutschen Automobilindustrie" in *Die Arbeitslosigkeit der Gegenwart.* Zweiter Teil. Saitzew, Manuel, ed. Schriften des Vereins fuer Sozialpolitik, 185/II. Munich: Duncker & Humblot, 1932.

Ludwig, Karl-Heinz. *Technik und Ingenieure im Dritten Reich.* Duesseldorf: Droste, 1974

Lueders, Marie-Elisabeth. "Die Entwicklung der gewerblichen Frauenarbeit im Krieg," *Schmollers Jahrbuch fuer Gesetzgebung, Verwaltung, und Volkswirtschaft im Deutschen Reiche,* pp. 241–67; 569–93. Munich: Duncker & Humblot, 1920.

Lusar, Rudolf. *Die deutschen Waffen und Geheimwaffen des Zweiten Weltkrieges und ihre Weiterentwicklung.* 4th ed. Munich: J.F. Lehmanns, 1962.

Madajczyk, Czeslaw. *Die Okkupationspolitik Nazideutschlands in Polen 1939–1945.* Berlin: Akademie, 1987.

Maeckbach, Frank and Otto Kienzle, eds. *Fliessarbeit. Beitraege zu Ihrer Einfuehrung.* Berlin: VDI Verlag, 1926.

Mai, Gunther, ed. *Arbeiterschaft in Deutschland 1914–1918. Studien zu Arbeitskampf und Arbeitsmarkt im Ersten Weltkrieg.* Duesseldorf: Droste, 1986.

Mai, Gunther. *Kriegswirtschaft und Arbeiterbewegung in Wuerttemberg 1914–1918.* Stuttgart: Klett-Cotta, 1983.

Mai, Gunther. "Die Nationalsozialistische Betriebszellen-Organisation. Zum Verhaeltnis von Arbeiterschaft und Nationalsozialismus." *Vierteljahrshefte fuer Zeitgeschichte,* 31(4): 573–613.

Mai, Gunther. "Die Sozialstruktur der Wuerrtembergischen Arbeiter- und Bauernraete 1918/1919." *Internationale wissenschaftliche Korrespondenz zur Geschichte der deutschen Arbeiterbewegung* (1979) 3: 377–407.

Maier, Charles. "Between Taylorism and Technocracy. European Ideologies and the Vision of Industrial Productivity in the 1920's." *Journal of Contemporary History* (1970) 2:27–61.

Maier, Charles. *Recasting Bourgeois Europe. Stabilization in France, Germany, and Italy in the Decade after World War I.* Princeton: Princeton University Press, 1975.

Marsalek, Hans. *Die Geschichte des Konzentrationslagers Mauthausen. Dokumentation.* Vienna: Oesterreichische Lagergemeinschaft Mauthausen, 1974.

Marx, Karl. *Capital.* Volume I. New York: International, 1967.

Mason, Tim. *Arbeiterklasse und Volksgemeinschaft. Dokumente und Materialien zur deutschen Arbeiterpolitik 1936–1939.* Opladen: Westdeutscher Verlag, 1975.

Mason, Tim. "Labour in the Third Reich 1933–1939." *Past & Present* (April 1966) No. 33: 112–141.

Mason, Tim. *Sozialpolitik im dritten Reich.* Opladen: Westdeutscher Verlag, 1977.

Mason, Tim. "Zur Entstehung des Gesetzes zur Ordnung der nationaler Arbeit, vom 20. Januar 1934: Ein Versuch ueber das Verhaeltnis 'archaischer' und 'moderner' Momente in der neuesten deutschen Geschichte," in Mommsen. Hans, et al., eds., *Industrielles System und politische Entwicklung in der Weimarer Republik.* Duesseldorf: Droste Verlag, 1974.

Matthias, Erich and Hermann Weber. *Widerstand gegen den Nationalsozialismus in Mannheim.* Mannheim: Quadrant, 1984.

Mauersberg, Hans. *Deutsche Industrien in Zeitgeschehen eines Jahrhunderts. Eine historische Modelluntersuchung zum Entwicklungsprozess deutscher Unternehmen von ihren Anfaengen bis zum Stand von 1960.* Stuttgart: Gustav Fischer Verlag, 1966.

Megerle, Klaus. *Wuerttemberg im Industrialisierungsprozess Deutschlands. Ein Beitrag zur regionalen Differenzierung der Industrialisierung.* Stuttgart: Klett-Cotta, 1982.

Meibes, Otto. *Die deutsche Automobilindustrie.* Berlin: Markwart-Verlag, 1928.

Meidlein, Hans. *Der Akkordlohn in der grossindustriellen Maschinenindustrie.* Dissertation/Erlangen, 1914.

Meissner, Erwin; Friedrich Rothhaupt; & Hans Schenkel. *Technologie des Maschinenbaus.* 7th edition. Berlin: VEB Verlag Technik, 1973.

Militaergeschichtliches Forschungsamt, ed. *Handbuch zur deutschen Militaergeschichte 1648–1939.* Vol. 3. Munich: Bernard & Graefe, 1979.

Militaergeschichtliches Forschungsamt, ed. *Militaerluftfahrt bis zum Beginn des Weltkrieges 1914.* Vol. I. Frankfurt/Main: Mittler & Sohn, 1965.

Milward, Alan S. *Die deutsche Kriegswirtschaft 1939–1945.* Stuttgart: Deutsche Verlags-Anstalt, 1966.

Mommertz, Karl Heinz. *Bohren, Drehen und Fraesen. Geschichte der Werkzeugmaschinen.* Reinbek: Rowohlt, 1981.

Mommsen, W.J. & Husung, H., eds. *Auf dem Wege zum Massengewerkschaft.* Stuttgart: Klett-Cotta, 1984.

Mooser, Josef. *Arbeiterleben in Deutschland 1900–1970.* Frankfurt/Main: Suhrkamp, 1984.

Mueller, Roland. *Stuttgart zur Zeit des Nationalsozialismus. Lokalgeschichte und nationalsozialistische Herrschaftssystem.* Dissertation/Stuttgart, 1987.

Mulert, Juergen. "Erfolgsbeteiligung und Vermoegensbildung der Arbeitnehmer bei der Firma Rober Bosch zwischen 1886 und 1945." *Zeitschrift fuer Unternehmungsgeschichte* (1985) 9:1–29.

Nachtmann, Walter. "Robert Bosch. Grossindustrieller und Weltbuerger." In Michael Bosch and Wolfgang Niess, eds. *Der Widerstand im deutschen Suedwesten 1933–1945*, pp. 217–25. Stuttgart: Kohlhammer, 1984.

Neebe, Reinhard. *Grossindustrie, Staat und NSDAP 1930–1933. Paul Silverberg und der Reichsverband der Deutschen Industrie in der Krise der Weimarer Republik.* Goettingen: Vandenhoeck & Ruprecht, 1981.

Neebe, Reinhard. "Unternehmerverbaende und Gewerkschaften in den Jahren der Grossen Krise 1929–1933," *Geschichte und Gesellschaft* (1983) 9:302–330.

Nettl, J.P. "The German Social Democratic Party 1890–1914 as a Political Model." *Past & Present* (1965) vol. 30.

Neuschl, Sylvia. *Geschichte der USPD in Wuerttemberg oder ueber die Moeglichkeit einig zu bleiben.* Esslingen: Marzahn, 1983.

Nevins, Allan. *Ford: The Times, the Man, the Company.* New York: Scribners, 1954.

Nolan, Mary. "Economic Crisis, State Policy, and Working-Class Formation in Germany, 1870–1900." in Ira Katznelson and Aristide R. Zollberg, eds. *Working-Class Formation. Nineteenth-Century Patterns in Western Europe and the United States.* Princeton: Princeton University Press, 1986.

Nolan, Mary. *Social Democracy and Society: Working Class Radicalism in Duesseldorf, 1890–1920.* Cambridge: Cambridge University Press, 1982.

Oberschall, Anthony. *Empirical Social Research in Germany 1848–1914.* Paris & The Hauge: Mouton & Co., 1965.

von Oertzen, Peter. *Betriebsraete in der Novemberrevolution. Eine politikwissenschaftliche Untersuchung ueber Ideengehalt und Struktur der betrieblichen und wirtschaftlichen Arbeiterraete in der deutschen Revolution 1918/19.* Duesseldorf: Droste, 1963.

Office of Military Government for Germany (O.M.G.U.S.), United States Finance Division—Financial Investigation Section. *Ermittlungen gegen die Deutsche Bank 1946/1947.* Noerdlingen: Franz Greno, 1985.

Opel, Fritz. *Der Deutsche Metallarbeiter-Verband waehrend des ersten Weltkrieges und der Revolution.* Hannover: Norddeutsche Verlagsanstalt O. Goedel, 1957.

Oswald, Werner. *Mercedes-Benz Personenwagen 1886–1984.* Stuttgart: Motorbuch, 1985.

Osswald, Richard. *Lebendige Arbeitswelt. Die Sozialgeschichte der Daimler-Benz AG von 1945 bis 1985.* Stuttgart: Deutsche Verlags-Anstalt, 1986.

Overy, Richard J. *Goering, The "Iron Man."* London: Routledge & Kegan Paul, 1984.

Pasternak, Marion, ed. *Fachkunde Giessereitechnik.* Leipzig: Deutscher Verlag fuer Grundstoffindustrie, 1984.

Petzina, Dieter. *Autarkiepolitik im Dritten Reich. Der nationalsozialistische Vierjahresplan.* Stuttgart: Deutsche Verlags-Anstalt, 1968.

Pfahlmann, Hans. *Fremdarbeiter und Kriegsgefangene in der deutschen Kriegswirtschaft 1939–1945.* Darmstadt: Wehr und Wissen, 1968.

Potthoff, Heinrich. *Gewerkschaften und Politik zwischen Revolution und Inflation.* Duesseldorf: Droste, 1979.

Prachtl, Guido. *Von der Reihenfertigung zur Fliessarbeit insbesondere im deutschen Automobilbau aus dem Gebiete der neuzeitlichen Betriebstechnik und Fabrikorganisation.* Berlin: VDI, 1926.

Prinz, Detlef and Manfred Rexin. *Beispiele fuer aufrechten Gang. Willi Bleicher und Helmut Simon. Im Geiste Carl von Ossietzkys.* Frankfurt/Main: Europaeische Verlagsanstalt, 1979.

Projekt Zeitgeschichte Landeshauptstadt Stuttgart. *Stuttgart im Dritten Reich. Anpassung Widerstand Verfolgung. Die Jahre von 1933 bis 1939.* Stuttgart, 1984.

Projektgruppe "Fremde Arbeiter" am Ludwig-Uhland-Institut fuer empirische Kulturwissenschaft Universitaet Tuebingen, *Fremde Arbeiter in Tuebingen 1939–1945.* Tuebingen: Tuebinger Verein fuer Volkskunde, 1985.

Pross, Helge. *Manager und Aktionaere in Deutschland. Untersuchungen zum Verhaeltnis von Eigentum und Verfuegungsmacht.* Frankfurt: Europaeische Verlagsanstalt, 1965.

Rabitsch, Gisela. "Das KL Mauthausen." Institut fuer Zeitgeschichte. *Studien zur Geschichte der Konzentrationslager.* Stuttgart: Deutsche Verlags-Anstalt, 1970, pp. 50–92.

Radant, Hans. "Zu den Beziehungen zwischen dem Konzern der Deutschen Bank und dem Staatsapparat bei der Vorbereitung und Durchfuehrung des Zweiten Weltkrieges." *Der deutsche Imperialismus.* Band 2. Berlin: Ruetten & Loening, 1961.

Reichshandbuch der deutschen Gesellschaft. Das Handbuch der Persoenlichkeiten in Wort und Bild. Berlin: Deutscher Wirtschaftsverlag, 1931.

Reif, Heinz. " 'Ein seltener Kreis von Freunden.' Arbeitsprozesse und Arbeitserfahrung bei Krupp 1840–1914." In Klaus Tenfelde, ed. *Arbeit und Arbeitserfahrung in der Geschichte.* Goettingen: Vandenhoeck, 1986.

Ritter, Gerhard. "Workers' Culture in Imperial Germany: Problems and Points of Departure for Research." *Journal of Contemporary History* (April 1978), pp. 165–190.

Rosenberg, Arthur. *Die Entstehung der deutschen Republik 1871–1918.* Berlin: Rowohlt, 1930.

Roth, Guenther. *The Social Democrats in Imperial Germany. A Study in Working-Class Isolation and National Integration.* Totowa, N.J.: Bedminster, 1963.

Roth, Karl Heinz. *Die andere Arbeiterbewegung.* Munich: Trikont, 1974.

Roth, Karl Heinz. "Der Weg zum Guten Stern des Dritten Reichs: Schlaglichter auf die Geschichte der Daimler-Benz AG und ihrer Vorlaeufer (1890–1945)." In *Das Daimler-Benz Buch. Ein Ruestungskonzern im "Tausendjaehrigen Reich."* Noerdlingen: Greno, 1987, pp. 27–389.

Rueck, Fritz. *Schriften zur deutschen Novemberrevolution 1918.* Cologne: Rode-Stankowski, 1978.

Ruerup, R. "Demokratische Revolution und 'dritter Weg'. Die deutsche Revolution 1918/19 in der neueren wissenschaftlichen Diskussion," *Geschichte und Gesellschaft* (1983): 278–301.

Rupieper, Hermann-Josef. *Arbeiter und Angestellte im Zeitalter der Industrialisierung. Eine sozialgeschichtliche Studie am Beispiel der Maschinenfabriken Augsburg und Nuernberg (MAN) 1837–1914.* Frankfurt/Main: Campus, 1982.

Ruppert, Wolfgang, ed. *Die Arbeiter. Lebensformen, Alltag und Kultur von der Fruehindustrialisierung bis zum "Wirtschaftswunder."* Munich: Beck, 1986.

Ruppert, Wolfgang. *Geschichte von Arbeit und Industrialisierung in Deutschland.* Munich: C.H. Beck, 1983.

Sachse, Carola, Tilla Siegel, Hassa Spode, and Wolfgang Spohn. *Angst, Belohnung, Zucht und Ordnung. Herrschaftsmechanismen im Nationalsozialismus.* Opladen: Westdeutscher Verlag, 1982.

Salm, Fritz. *In Schatten des Henkers. Widerstand in Mannheim gegen Faschismus and Krieg.* Frankfurt/Main: Roederer, 1979.

Saul, Klaus. *Staat, Industrie, Arbeiterbewegung im Kaiserreich. Zur Innen- und Aussenpolitik des Wilhelminischen Deutschland 1903–1914.* Duesseldorf: Bertelsmann Universitaetsverlag, 1974.

Schaefer, Hermann. *Regionale Wirtschaftspolitik in der Kriegswirtschaft. Staat, Industrie und Verbaende waehrend des Ersten Weltkrieges in Baden.* Stuttgart: Kohlhammer, 1983.

Schaetzle, Julius. *Stationen zur Hoelle. Konzentrationslager in Baden und Wuerttemberg 1933–1945.* Frankfurt/Main: Roederberg, 1980.

Scheck, Manfred. *Zwischen Weltkrieg und Revolution. Zur Geschichte der Arbeiterbewegung in Wuerttemberg 1914–1920.* Cologne: Boehlau, 1981.

Scheel, Hans. *Die Schmiedearbeiten. Technik, Formgebung und Anwendung.* Stuttgart: Hoffmann, 1954.

Schelkle, F. and P. Greiner. *Formen Schmelzen Giessen.* Stuttgart: Holland & Josenhans Verlag, 1958.

Schiffmann, Dieter. *Von der Revolution zum Neunstundentag. Arbeit und Konflikt bei BASF 1918–1924.* Frankfurt/Main: Campus, 1983.

Schmaedeke, Juergen and Peter Steinbach. *Der Widerstand gegen den Nationalsozialismus. Die deutsche Gesellschaft und Widerstand gegen Hitler.* 2nd ed. Munich: Piper, 1986.

Schmidt, Ernst Wilhelm. *Maenner der Deutschen Bank und der Disconto-Gesellschaft.* Duesseldorf: Deutsche Bank, 1957.

Schmidt, Karl. *Die deutsche Automobil-Industrie und ihre Leistungsfaehigkeit auf dem Weltmarkt.* Dissertation/Giessen, 1927.

Schmiede, Rudi and Edwin Schudlich. *Die Entwicklung der Leistungsentlohnung in Deutschland. Eine historisch-theoretische Untersuchung zum Verhaeltnis von Lohn und Leistung unter kapitalistischen Produktionsbedingungen.* Frankfurt/Main: Aspekte, 1976.

Schnabel, Thomas, ed. *Die Machtergreifung in Suedwestdeutschland. Das Ende der Weimarer Republik in Baden und Wuerttemberg 1928–1933.* Stuttgart: Kohlhammer, 1982.

Schneider, Hans. *Die Entwicklung der deutschen Automobilindustrie nach dem Kriege.* Dissertation Frankfurt/Main, 1929.

Schneider, Michael. "Der Kampf um die Arbeitsverkuerzung von der Industrialisierung bis zur Gegenwart." *Gewerkschaftliche Monatshefte* (1984) 2:77–89.

Schneider, Michael. *Streit um Arbeitszeit. Geschichte des Kampfes um Arbeitsverkuerzung in Deutschland.* Cologne: Bund Verlag, 1984.

Schomerus, Heilweg. *Die Arbeiter der Maschinenfabrik Esslingen.* Stuttgart: Klett-Cotta, 1977.

Schorske, Carl E. *German Social Democracy 1905–1917: The Development of the Great Schism.* New York: Harper & Row, 1972.

Schrag, Hans. *Die deutsche Automobilindustrie unter dem Einfluss des neuen deutschen Automobilzolls.* Dissertation/Stuttgart, 1929.

Schroeder, Wilhelm Heinz. *Arbeitergeschichte und Arbeiterbewegung. Industriearbeit und Organisationsverhalten im 19. und fruehen 20. Jahrhundert.* Frankfurt/Main: Campus, 1978.

Schumann, Fritz. *Die Arbeiter der Daimler-Motoren-Gesellschaft.* Leipzig: Duncker & Humblot, 1911.

Schumann, Hans-Gerd. *Nationalsozialismus und Gewerkschaftsbewegung. Die Vernichtung der deutschen Gewerkschaften und der Ausbau der "Deutschen Arbeitsfront."* Hannover: Norddeutsche Verlags-Anstalt O. Goedel, 1958.

Schweitzer, Arthur. *Big Business in the Third Reich.* Bloomington: Indiana University Press, 1964.

Seeber, Eva. *Zwangsarbeiter in der faschistischen Kriegswirtschaft. Die Deportation und Ausbeutung polnischer Buerger unter besonderer Beruecksichtigung der Lage der Arbeiter aus dem sogenannten Generalgouvernement (1939–1945).* Berlin: VEB Deutscher Verlag der Wissenschaften, 1964.

von Seherr-Thoss, H.C. Graf. *Die deutsche Automobilindustrie. Eine Dokumentation von 1886 bis heute.* Stuttgart: Deutsche Verlags-Anstalt, 1974.

Seidel, Anneliese. *Frauenarbeit im Ersten Weltkrieg als Problem der staatlichen Sozialpolitik.* Frankfurt/Main: Bayers, 1979.

Seidenzahl, Fritz. *100 Jahre Deutsche Bank 1870–1970.* Frankfurt/Main: Deutsche Bank, 1970.

700-Jahre-Feier der Grossen Kreisstadt Sindelfingen. Sindelfingen: Roehm, 1964.

Siebetz, Paul. *Karl Benz. Ein Pionier der Verkehrsmotorisierung.* Munich: Lehmanns, 1943.

Siegel, Tilla. "Wage Policy in Nazi Germany." *Politics and Society* (1985) 1:1–51.

Speer, Albert. *Erinnerungen.* Berlin: Propylaeen Verlag, 1969.

Spur, Guenter. *Handbuch der Fertigungstechnik. Band I Urformen.* Muenchen: Carl Hanser Verlag, 1981.

Starcke, Gerhard. *NSBO und Deutsche Arbeitsfront*. Berlin: Reimar Hobbing, 1934.

Stern, Fritz, ed. *Geschichte und Geschichtsschreibung. Moeglichkeiten Aufgaben Methoden. Texte von Voltaire bis zur Gegenwart*. Muenchen: Piper, 1966.

Steudel, Hanns. *Geschichtliche Entwicklung der Maschinenindustrie in Wuerttemberg bis zum Weltkrieg*. Dissertation/Tuebingen, 1923.

Stollberg, Gunnar. *Die Rationalisierungsdebatte 1908–1933. Freie Gewerkschaften zwischen Mitwirkung und Gegenwehr*. Frankfurt: Campus, 1981.

Stolle, Uta. *Arbeiterpolitik im Betrieb. Frauen und Maenner, Reformisten und Radikale, Fach- und Massenarbeiter bei BASF, Bosch und in Solingen (1900–1933)*. Frankfurt/Main: Campus, 1980.

Taylor, Frederick W. *The Principles of Scientific Management*. New York: Norton, 1967.

Tenfelde, Klaus, ed. *Arbeit und Arbeitserfahrung in der Geschichte*. Goettingen: Vandenhoeck & Ruprecht, 1986.

Tenfelde, Klaus and Heinrich Volkmann, eds. *Streik. Zur Geschichte des Arbeitskampfes in Deutschland waehrend der Industrialisierung*. Munich: Beck, 1981.

Teuteberg, Hans-Juergen. *Geschichte der industriellen Mitbestimmung in Deutschland. Ursprung und Entwicklung ihrer Verlaeufer im Denken und in der Wirklichkeit des 19. Jahrhunderts*. Tuebingen: J.C.B. Mohr, 1961.

Thomas, Georg. *Geschichte der deutschen Wehr- und Ruestungswirtschaft (1918–1943/45)*. Boppard: Harald Boldt, 1966.

Tilly, Charles, Louise, and Richard. *The Rebellious Century 1830–1930*. Cambridge: Harvard University Press, 1975.

Tobin, Elizabeth. "War and the Working Class: The Case of Duesseldorf 1914–1918." *Central European History* (Sept./Dec. 1985) 18(3–4): 257–298.

Turner, Henry Ashby. *German Big Business and the Rise of Hitler*. New York: Oxford University Press, 1985.

Untertuerkheimer Heimatbuch. Stuttgart: Druck der Buchdruckerei der Union Deutsche Verlagsgesellschaft, 1935.

Verhandlungen des Vereins fuer Sozialpolitik in Nuernberg 1911. Schriften des Vereins fuer Sozialpolitik. Vol. 138. Leipzig: Duncker, 1912.

Vetterli, Rudolf. *Industriearbeit, Arbeiterbewusstsein und gewerkschaftliche Organisation*. Goettingen: Vandenhoeck und Ruprecht, 1978.

Voelker, Karl-Heinz. *Die deutsche Luftwaffe 1933–1939. Aufbau, Fuehrung und Ruestung der Luftwaffe sowie die Entwicklung der deutschen Luftkriegstheorie*. Stuttgart: Deutsche Verlags-Anstalt, 1967.

Vorlaender, Herwart, ed. *Nationalsozialistische Konzentrationslager im Dienst der totalen Kriegsfuehrung. Sieben wuerttembergische Aussenkommandos des Konzentrationslagers Natzweiler/Elsass*. Stuttgart: W. Kohlhammer, 1978.

Walcher, Jakob. *Ford oder Marx. Die praktische Loesung der sozialen Frage*. Berlin: Neuer Deutscher Verlag, 1925.

Weber, Max. *Gesammelte Aufsaetze zur Soziadologie und Sozialpolitik*. Tuebingen: J.C.B. Mohr, 1924.

Weisert, Hermann. *Geschichte der Stadt Sindelfingen von den Anfaengen bis heute*. Sindelfingen: Roehm, 1975.

Wengenroth, Ulrich. "Technisierung, Rationalisierung und Gewerkschaftsbewegung." *Neue Politische Literatur*, (1984) 29(2):236–246.

Wenke, Bettina. *Interviews mit Ueberlebenden. Verfolgung und Widerstand in Suedwestdeutschland*. Stuttgart: Konrad Theiss, 1980.

Wer Leitet? Die Maenner der Wirtschaft und der einschlaegigen Verwaltung einschliesslich Adressbuch der Direktoren und Aufsichtsraete 1941/42. Berlin: Hoppenstedt, 1942.

Werner, Wolfgang Franz. *"Bleib uebrig." Deutsche Arbeiter in der nationalsozialistischen Kriegswirtschaft*. Duesseldorf: Schwann, 1983.

Wette, Wolfram. "Reichstag und 'Kriegsgewinnlerei' (1916–1918). Die Anfaenge parlamentarischer Ruestungskontrolle in Deutschland." *Militaergeschichtliche Mitteilungen*, 36, 2/1984, pp. 31–56.

Wickham, James. " 'Social Fascism' and the Division of the Working Class Movement: Workers and Political Parties in the Frankfurt Area, 1929–1930." *Capital and Class* (1977) pp. 1–34.

Wicki, Hans. *Das Koenigreich Wuerttemberg im ersten Weltkrieg. Seine wirtschaftliche, soziale, politische und kulturelle Lage*. Bern: Peter Lang, 1984.

Die Wiege des Automobils. Internationale Industrie-Bibliothek, Vol. 38. Berlin: Max Schroeder, n.d.

von Wilmowsky, Tilo Frhr. *Warum wurde Krupp verurteilt? Legende und Justizirrtum*. 2nd ed. Stuttgart: Vorwerk, 1950.

Winkler, Heinrich August. *Der Schein der Normalitaet. Arbeiter und Arbeiterbewegung in der Weimarer Republik 1924 bis 1930*. Bonn: Dietz, 1988.

Winkler, Heinrich August. *Von der Revolution zur Stabilisierung. Arbeiter und Arbeiterbewegung in der Weimarer Republik 1918 bis 1924*. Bonn: Dietz, 1984.

Winkler, Heinrich August. *Der Weg in die Katastrophe. Arbeiter und Arbeiterbewegung in der Weimarer Republik 1930 bis 1933*. Bonn: Dietz, 1987.

Wohlfeil, Rainer and Hans Dollinger. *Die deutsche Reichswehr. Bilder Dokumente Texte. Zur Geschichte des Hunderttausend-Mann-Heeres 1919–1933*. Frankfurt/Main: Bernard & Graefe, 1972.

Yano, Hisashi. *Huettenarbeiter im dritten Reich. Die Betriebsverhaeltnisse und soziale Lage bei der Gutehoffnungshuette Aktienverein und der Friedrich Krupp A.G. 1936–1939*. Wiesbaden: Franz Steiner Verlag, 1986.

Zollitsch, Wolfgang. *Integration oder Isolation? Die Arbeiterschaft von Grossbetrieben zwischen Weltwirtschaftskrise und Nationalsozialismus (1928–1936)*. Dissertation/Freiburg, 1986.

Zunkel, Friedrich. *Industrie und Staatssozialismus. Der Kampf um die Wirtschaftsordnung in Deutschland 1914–18*. Duesseldorf: Droste, 1974.

INDEX